CURIOUS

English WORDS

AND *phrases*

D0682461

ALSO BY MAX CRYER

The Godzone Dictionary

Love Me Tender

Who Said That First?

Preposterous Proverbs

CURIOUS

English WORDS
AND *phrases*

THE TRUTH behind the *expressions* we use

MAX CRYER

First published 2012

Exisle Publishing Limited,
P.O. Box 60-490, Titirangi, Auckland 0642, New Zealand.
'Moonrising', Narone Creek Road, Wollombi, NSW 2325, Australia.
www.exislepublishing.com

National Library of New Zealand Cataloguing-in-Publication Data

Cryer, Max.
Curious English words and phrases / Max Cryer.
Includes bibliographical references.
ISBN 978-1-921966-01-9
1. English language—Etymology. 2. English language
—Terms and phrases. 3. English language—Idioms. I. Title.
422—dc 23

10 9 8 7 6 5 4 3 2 1

Text design and production by IslandBridge
Cover design by Dexter Fry
Printed in Singapore by KHL Printing Co Pte Ltd
This book uses paper sourced under ISO 14001 guidelines
from well-managed forests and other controlled sources.

Acknowledgements

The author thanks Graeme and Valerie Fisher, Robbie Ancell, Geoffrey Pooch, Graeme Hill, Emma Sloman, Paul Barrett and Ian Watt for their assistance in the preparation of this book.

For more information about this book, visit:

www.curiousenglishwordsandphrases.com

Introduction

It is possible (if admittedly fanciful) to envisage the English language as being like a vast and ancient city – magnificent and full of interest, but at the same time shambolic. It has been subject to suburban sprawl, has constantly added new edifices, upgraded heritage precincts in some quarters, demolished them in others, and has complex roading systems freely negotiable only by those who have long lived in that area.

And the 'city' has wrenched benefits from other civilisations by shamelessly raping, pillaging and outright thieving from them – words, images, expressions and proverbs. No other language has been safe from the grasp of this great conurbation known as English: Sanskrit, Hindustani, Arabic, Turkish, Russian, Japanese can be found in its small winding alleys besides, on the main streets, the more expected Latin, Dutch, German, French, Spanish, Swedish and Russian ('more expected' because Britain is only 35 kilometres from the Continent at the closest point).

Noel Coward's character Countess Mitzi is an aristocrat with a complex ancestry. She sings:

> And if I'm not
> A polyglot –
> I'd like to know who is!

Like her, our language is something of a polyglot – it is an entity made up from many different tongues. And there are many people who want to know the which, the where and the why of it. I hope to provide at least some of the answers.

Max Cryer

@ symbol

A

Many people can recognise and give the name for a question mark, an ampersand, a hash sign, an asterisk, a colon, a chevron, a slash. But the @ or 'squiggly at' is not so easy to pin down.

Italian academics claim that the symbol has been around since at least the 1500s. In those days it had a strong position in commerce, because grains and liquids were transported in jars which held a strictly measured amount. The jars were called amphorae, so the single letter 'a' signified goods to the weight or volume of one amphora jar, and the a was written with an Italian flourish.

The sign settled to mean 'at the price of' and was used that way in Europe for centuries, e.g. 3 metres of lace @ 500 lire per metre.

The @ sign took a while to get onto typewriter keyboards, but it was there by 1880 and by the 1960s it began to be carried over to computers. In 1972 the symbol was chosen to be the separator in email addresses and it has been so successful that even languages like Tamil and Japanese and Arabic have taken it on board even though they don't use Latin alphabet letters.

But it still isn't clear-cut what to call it. Most languages have their own version: the Germans call it 'spider monkey', the Danes, Norwegians and Swedes alternate between calling it 'pig's tail' or 'elephant's trunk'. The Finns call it a 'cat's tail' and in Hungary it's a 'worm'. In Israel it's called 'strudel', the French, Italians and Koreans call it a 'snail' and in the Czech Republic it's a word meaning 'rolled-up herring'. The Greeks call it 'little duck' and the Russians call it 'little dog'.

Initially, electronic messages could only be sent between users of the same computer network. American technologist Ray Tomlinson devised a way of sending messages to users of other computers – but needed an 'address' which was neither a recognisable letter nor a number. He examined a keyboard, and settled on the @ symbol to separate the name of the user from the domain identity. He sent the first message, in what is now known as email, in 1972 – and the @ symbol took on a whole new life.

There are no rules about its name. English has turned out to be the most colourless – no elephants or rolled herrings or curly-tailed monkeys. In English it is just called 'commercial at', or 'curly at.'

Action figures

'Action figures' is a name used to market dolls for boys.

AD/BC

There is no clear answer to this. The only clue is that in the English language, Latin and Greek expressions occur frequently (like *Anno Domini* and *kilometre*) and are sometimes mixed up with English-based expressions.

The expression *Anno Domini* dates from the days of Dionysius Exiguus, who in the sixth century more or less invented the basis of our current calendar. He got it about four years wrong, but it's understandable that Jesus was commemorated with a Latin phrase, *Anno Domini*, because it was the Roman emperor who asked for the job to be done.

The idea of referring to years before Jesus was born is much more recent. The first generally known reference to a scale of time before Jesus didn't surface until the seventeenth century, and didn't become common until the eighteenth century. And here's the rub: whereas AD seemed to stick in Latin, other languages made up their own versions of the time before Jesus. Germans refer to it as *VC* (*vor Christus*) and the French call it *AvJC* (*avant* Jesus Christ), while English speakers use BC – Before Christ.

And since there are other major religions which don't attribute the same significance to Jesus, outside Christian circles you'll come across CE – Common Era, and BCE – Before Common Era.

Adult and adultery

Adult and adultery have two slightly different paths of development: adult is from the Latin meaning a grown-up person, but adultery is believed to come from another Latin origin, *alter*, meaning 'to debase or render impure'. When that word went into French as *avouter* it developed the meaning 'to stain or defile'.

10

Avouter drifted into English as 'adultery' and by the time Shakespeare used the word, it carried the French sense of a blot, a stain, or something extra which is not pure, as adulterate still does – 'milk adulterated with water'.

Eventually adultery came to mean anything spurious or counterfeit, including sex between a married person and a partner other than the legal spouse. Now its use seems to be confined to that sense only.

Aerobics

Exercising to music (which is basically what aerobics describes) has been going on for centuries. The activity now called aerobics is the descendant of what used to be called PT (physical training) or sometimes PE (physical exercise). Once upon a time it was called eurhythmics. However, although the activity itself was not dissimilar, that name seems to have been discarded because it had an overly feminine image (and eurhythmics somehow doesn't sound as if the participants enjoyed endorphin highs).

The word aerobics was first published in 1968 in a book by Kenneth Cooper, a former military flight surgeon, who 'created' the fitness regime – and the name to go with it. The word is made up from the Greek *aer* meaning air, plus Greek *bios*, meaning life. Together they give the clue to what makes aerobics slightly different from all the other exercise forms – the process aims to increase oxygen in the blood. The routines are not static: you have to keep moving (and to be fashionable, give out falsetto yips as well).

The associated terms jazzergetics, stretchomatics and limbercize, all mean much the same.

Afghan hounds, rugs, biscuits

These are examples of toponymy – the naming of things after places. Bikinis, denim, currants, tangerines, mayonnaise, camembert, tweed, jodhpurs, muslin, dollars and spaghetti bolognaise are all named after places (note, however, that turkeys don't come from Turkey and guinea pigs don't come from Guinea).

Afghan hounds actually originated in Egypt several thousand years BC, but spread to India and Afghanistan where they became

A renowned as strong, fast, agile hunting dogs, favoured by shepherds and excellent as watchdogs. For centuries the particular breed within Afghanistan was kept pure and no dogs were sold for export, but the breed gradually filtered to the outside world in the early 1900s – and became known as Afghan hounds.

Shawls and rugs called 'afghans' have been woven in Asia for centuries. The word 'shawl' comes from the Iranian language, but for many years the most desirable shawls were made in Kashmir in India. By the eighteenth century, styles and techniques were being copied and shawls called Kashmiri (or 'cashmere' – another toponym) may actually have been made somewhere else.

During the nineteenth century hundreds of shawls and rugs were being brought into Britain and by 1833 the term 'afghan' was being used to describe a lightweight shawl for the shoulders – though it may not have come from Afghanistan, just from somewhere in Asia. By 1877 larger items described as knee-rugs were in use and these too were called afghans. The most recent development in this fashion is a rug-like shawl called a pashmina (*pashm* is the Iranian word for wool). They are normally woven from goat's wool, but the shawls themselves are often made in Nepal. So we can say only that afghan shawls and afghan knee-rugs sometimes came from Afghanistan, but were more likely to have been made in the Afghan style (just as rugs advertised as 'Persian' may have been woven in Pakistan, but in a Persian style). Toponymy can sometimes be vague.

The term 'afghan biscuits' defies explanation. They appear to be known only within Australasia, and only a vague and seemingly unsubstantiated theory has been put forward about their name: that they somehow honoured the Afghani camel drivers working in Australia in the late 1860s (whose presence was responsible for the name The Ghan, the train that carries supplies to Alice Springs).

An afghan biscuit has a thickish chocolate-flavoured biscuit base onto which a rich dark chocolate icing is swirled, with a half walnut kernel placed in the middle of the icing. The theory – and it is only a theory – associating the biscuits with the camel drivers is that the chocolate base is the darkly tanned Afghani, the dark chocolate icing is his darker hair, and the walnut kernel represents his turban! But food expert Alan Davidson in his 1037-page *Oxford Companion to Food* says quite straightforwardly that the biscuits known as afghans 'have no obvious connection with Afghanistan'.

Pragmatists suggest that afghan biscuits are called that simply because they are dark.

Airport, aerodrome, airfield, airstrip

In some ways they're all the same: places at which aircraft land and take off. But in other ways they're slightly different.

Words sometimes change meaning over the years, and are subject to fashion. One example of the latter is airport and aerodrome. In the days when ports were only for ships, the word aerodrome was the usual term for a central place serviced by air traffic. But a slight change in emphasis took place and in general the current usage is:

- **Airport**   a take-off and landing area for civil and commercial aviation with surfaced runways and passenger facilities.

- **Aerodrome**   a take-off and landing area, usually for private planes and in general smaller than an airport.

- **Airfield**   a take-off and landing area, which usually has some permanent buildings, and is often used to describe centres for military air traffic.

- **Airstrip**   a cleared area for take-off and landing which may be temporary and does not have considerable passenger facilities.

Alas and alack

The two words have different ancestry. 'Alas' is the older: it started to be used in English in the thirteenth century and was taken from the Old French *ha-las*, meaning 'Oh wretched!' Two hundred years later, the word 'alack' arose in English. It actually means what it says – ah-plus-lack, an exclamation of loss/lack.

At some point in history, the image of one was strengthened by coupling it with the other. Alas and alack translates into modern English as: Oh wretched, oh lost.

Alimony

Although the word is familiar, it isn't a legal term in every country. In some places it is called 'spousal maintenance' – which means the same thing (often shorthanded to just 'maintenance'). Alimony is derived from Latin *alere*, to nourish, then *alimonia*, sustenance. The same word occurs in 'alimentary canal' – the passage for food and sustenance. So when someone is awarded alimony, they're actually being awarded sustenance, since they are no longer with the spouse who (theoretically) used to provide that.

Alleluia

Alleluia is a Hebrew word, or rather words, combined to form an instruction. The main portion of the word is part of the Hebrew verb 'to praise'. The part we hear is the second person plural imperative form of the verb – 'you shall praise' – plus a symbolic word for God at the end, a shortened form of Jehovah. So the word means 'Now everyone must praise Jehovah'. God, that is: Jesus was still a long way in the future when the word alleluia first came into use.

All my eye and Betty Martin

It means: 'I don't believe it – it's nonsense.' This used to be considered a bastardisation of the Italian prayer *An mihi beate martine*, addressed to the patron saint of beggars, but there is no such prayer, so that explanation was abandoned.

The more likely background is that for years the expression 'my eye' meant much the same as 'my foot': that's rubbish, tell me another, you're pulling my leg . . .

There's also a theory that at one time there was a London actress called Betty Martin who was well known for her outspokenness and directness, and that somehow adding her name to the expression doubled it and made it stronger – my eye, and Betty Martin. But in some parts of England they say 'all my eye and Peggy Martin' so that further confuses an issue that was already murky. Knowing what it means and how it's used are not quite the same as knowing exactly where it came from.

All of a hoo

It usually means that a person is discomforted but unable to pinpoint the exact area of discomfort. There is quite a collection of such sayings – feeling 'any old how', or just 'all anyhow', or 'all of a tiswas' or 'all of a doodah'. Those last two do have fairly recent origins. Tiswas developed from 'tizzy' as airmen's slang for 'over-excited'. Doodah, too, was a flying term, referring to someone becoming nervous in mid-air.

Within the same family of expressions is 'out of sorts', the usual explanation for which is that it arose among old-time printers when 'sorts' was the name given to particular pieces of type. If a printer had used up all the pieces of that type, he was out of sorts and naturally became a bit grumpy and distracted as a result.

'All of a hoo' originated in Somerset dialect among tailors as 'all of a huh' – meaning clumsy and unworkmanlike. By 1820 it had developed into 'all of a hoo' as a non-specific, semi-nonsense phrase indicating that things are haphazard, chaotic and disorganised. The person saying it (or about whom it is said) is not at their best but can't give a specific reason.

All over bar the shouting

The expression means that eventual success is certain. The only theory is that it arose as a result of boxing matches where it became quite clear, long before the finish, that one opponent was going to win. But the winner is not the winner until the referee makes a formal declaration and, when he does do that, there will be shouting and noise from the crowd. So over time, if it was abundantly clear what the final decision was going to be, people came to say that it was all over – except the shouting.

From boxing this expression has spread to almost any situation where there is some sort of a battle going on, from the FIFA World Cup to a general election, and you feel confident enough to predict the result.

All's fair in love and war

This was first seen in print in 1578, in a book called *Euphues* by British poet John Lyly. His original wording was: 'The rules of fair play do not apply in love and war.'

Over the following centuries the aphorism narrowed down to the form as we now know it. (It's also worth making the distinction between 'euphu-ism' – an elaborate and artificial prose style, and 'euphem-ism' – a delicate way of presenting that which may otherwise give offence.)

Alpha state

According to the *The Penguin Dictionary of Psychology*, the alpha state is the state of consciousness when the electrical activity of the brain sinks to between eight and 12 waves per second. Thus it is a condition of deep relaxation.

When the brain is relaxed in its alpha state, it's the time for intuition, healing, and emotions that defy scientific analysis.

There are various circumstances under which one can enter the alpha state: by being absolutely relaxed; the repetition of mantras; the use of hypnosis or self-hypnosis; the calm feeling associated with yoga; certain types of music that fit the natural rhythm of the heartbeat; and some stages of being actually asleep.

The beta state is a different situation, when the brain's activity changes to a rhythm between 17 and 25 hertz, which is a sign that the brain is involved in analysis.

Alzheimer's disease

It is named after Dr Alois Alzheimer, the man who identified and researched the condition. He was born in Germany and became a professor of psychiatry and neurology in Poland. In 1907 he clarified that in some people, apart from the general slowing down of old age, an actual disease can affect the efficiency of the brain cells. The particular condition has been named after him, as Alzheimer's disease, or Alzheimer's syndrome.

Amazon: river and woman

The word Amazon has come to refer to a tribe or race of warrior women in ancient times, though it has never been clear where they lived. Various accounts have them in Arica, or Asia, sometimes Europe, or the Ukraine and even Iran.

Amazons have a very firmly fixed image in legend and fiction. Shakespeare's *Midsummer Night's Dream*, for instance, is about an Amazon called Hippolyta and her marriage to a Duke of Athens. But sometimes they pop up in history. There are accounts of Alexander the Great enjoying thirteen nights of love with an Amazon princess in around 300 BC, and he was of course a real person. So although it is impossible to establish if there ever really were Amazons, their image in our minds is fairly firm.

They were said to be bossy, warlike, live entirely without men (except for capturing prisoners to use now and then for procreative purposes), to destroy male babies, and to remove one breast from each girl so that when grown, she could use a shield and spear without hindrance.

There are several differing explanations for the name Amazon, but the most widely credited is that it arose from the Greek word *mazo* (breast) with the prefix *a* (meaning 'without').

But does the South American river called the Amazon have anything to do with warrior women? Well, yes and no. There are two available explanations for the name of the river. One is that the word *amas-sunu* means 'big wave' in the local Tepi-Guarani language. But the explanation most commonly advanced is that early Spanish explorers believed that the native women of the Tepua tribe fought alongside their men. Hence the explorers gained an impression that tribes of all-women warriors lived in South America, and the area where they were supposedly seen became referred to as Amazonia – and the shortened version attached itself to the river.

But the explorers may have been mistaken: the men of the Tepua tribe customarily had long hair, and explorers not used to such a custom could have been confused about gender. Perhaps the native word for 'big wave' is a more secure basis.

A American spelling

The first spelling book dictionary specifically for America was published in 1783, followed by a dictionary in 1803 and then a larger dictionary in 1828. The lexicographer in all three cases was Noah Webster. Webster was a journalist, an author of textbooks, a teacher, philosopher, essayist, an orator, a public figure and political commentator. In addition, he was two other things: a passionate American patriot and a self-appointed reformer of spelling.

When he started to compile the basis of his dictionary, he made a conscious decision – he reasoned that it must be demonstrated that Americans had developed a different dialect from the British. There were languages widely used in America which weren't prominent in Britain, such as Spanish, Yiddish, African languages and those of the Native Americans (known then as 'Red Indians').

So Webster deliberately set out to rationalise what he saw as the American language – and when compiling his dictionary, made a decision to modify and often simplify the spelling of many words, into a new 'American' style. He often streamlined existing English spellings (e.g. 'theater' and 'center') and discarded unnecessary bits such as the final two letters of catalogue. The -our ending often became -or (e.g. 'honor', 'flavor'). He also included new local vocabulary (skunk, chowder, fiesta, gumbo, etc.) for which there was no established British spelling.

Not all of his offerings worked. He tried to replace 'tongue' with 'tung', but that fell by the wayside. And although color and favor dropped the -our, 'glamour' didn't and never has. Thus it can be seen that much of so-called American spelling was inaugurated by Noah Webster, and grew from there.

Note, however, that the growth of American language is a much more complex subject than mere spelling. Oscar Wilde showed awareness of it in *The Canterville Ghost* (1888), where a character is described as 'an excellent example of how we really have everything in common with America nowadays, except of course, language.'

America's Cup

The cup was originally called the Hundred Guineas Cup and was first competed for in 1851 when the winning schooner was called *America*. In time, by popular usage, it was referred to as the America's Cup, with an apostrophe designating that it belonged to the boat called *America*. And, according to *The Encyclopaedia Britannica*, that's how the name has stayed.

(The) Andrew

See **Royal Navy**

Angostura bitters

This is a concoction made with the dried root of the gentian plant to which various vegetable juices and spices are added. The result is an intriguing bitter mixture intended to be added to cocktails and also to soups, salad dressings, gravies and even some desserts. The particular Angostura mixture was invented in 1824 by a German doctor living in Venezuela, and intended as a possible relief for patients in pain, or those who suffered with sea-sickness. But its recognition as a savoury additive to food and drink grew, and the mixture was first exported from Venezuela in 1830. By 1850 the demand was international.

There is a South American tree called the angostura which has a bitter bark, but the makers of Angostura bitters (J. Siegert & Sons of Trinidad) are adamant that the still-secret formula of the bitters does not contain this bark – and that the mixture is named after the city of Angostura where the mixture originated. (It is slightly confusing that the tree is also named after the city – and that the tree is still around, but the city isn't. In 1846 the city of Angostura had its name changed to Ciudad Bolivar.)

Arctic and Antarctic

We'll start with Arctic: from *arctos*, the Greek for 'bear'. The constellation of stars known to the Greeks as the Great Bear is to the extreme North – thus we have a combination of *arctos* for bear,

A

plus Greek *ikos* meaning 'pertaining to': pertaining to the bear. This became attached to the area believed to be underneath the relevant group of stars, hence the extreme North.

Anti is Greek for 'opposite'. So Anti-arctos means 'opposite the bear': Antarctic.

Argentina or the Argentine?

This in part reflects the old problem of words from one language being pronounced differently in another language. In its own language, the country is called *Republica Argentina*. When referred to in English (at least up until the Second World War), the final 'a' was often dropped, an 'e' put in its place, and 'the' put in front – the Argentine.

There can also be a small problem in describing the people who live there. *The Encyclopaedia of Peoples of the World* explains that a man living there is called an Argentino and a woman is an Argentina (like Filipinos and Filipinas). In plural, the people call themselves Argentine. But *The Encyclopaedia Britannica* confidently calls them Argentinians.

So, two authorities differ. Neither seems to be wrong.

Armageddon and apocalypse

In formal terms these two are slightly different, although both words are sometimes used rather loosely to describe the end of the world as we know it.

Armageddon is a real place in Israel, mentioned several times in the Bible, and known now as Megiddo. It is believed to be the place where the last armed conflict in human history will occur on the Day of Judgement. In the English language, the name Megiddo is still usually said as Armageddon and its meaning has broadened in use to mean the scene of a large-scale decisive conflict, and sometimes the battle itself.

Apocalypse is also biblical and strictly means the vision of a prophecy, especially a violent or climactic event. That strict meaning is now extended to refer to the actual disastrous events themselves.

In contemporary times, dictionaries acknowledge the change in use, and Armageddon and apocalypse are now used almost inter-changeably, to refer to a cataclysmic event.

Ashet

Ashet is an adaptation of the French word *assiette*, which has several meanings, most of them to do with being a base or foundation; the word can be used to mean one course of a meal, or a platter on which a large amount of food can be placed.

English, particularly Scottish English, modified the word to ashet. It usually refers to the big plate for holding meat, often with grooves along the bottom into which the juices drip. Like everything else, food is subject to changes in fashion, and it's not all that common now to serve huge amounts of meat from a big ceramic platter. But if this does happen, the plate can correctly be referred to as an ashet.

Asymmetrical warfare

This incorporates the word asymmetric in its sense of being unequal or unbalanced. Asymmetrical warfare is a term that has been used by the military for some time. In the past it referred to a situation where a small group with ardent beliefs attempted to attack or terrorise a much larger group, such as terrorists pitting themselves against an organised nation state.

These days the term is being used with a slightly different con-notation. Asymmetrical war seems sometimes to describe a state of conflict, though not one between two nation states. Asymmetrical war can mean a conflict in which no country has actually made a formal declaration of war against another country.

At the drop of a hat

The expression dates back to early America when boxing and wrestling matches occurred and races were run without modern formalities or equipment. The beginning of a fight was signalled by someone throwing down or dropping a hat (it's mentioned in Mark Twain's *Life on the Mississippi*), and also waving a hat downwards was a common signal for starting a race. Nowadays the phrase indicates that something happens abruptly, without delay or any fuss.

At this point in time

Apparently the expression started quite legitimately. When astronauts are communicating they have to give precise and exact information about their location and they specify the various measurements by distinguishing the difference between a location in space or in time. So, saying 'at this point in time' has a perfectly reasonable technical ancestry.

But the expression caught on among people who were attracted to word grandeur, and during the 1970s they developed the habit of saying 'at this point in time', or 'at this particular point in time', when they simply meant 'now'.

In strict etymological terms this is called orotundity, meaning bombastic and elaborate speech, from the Latin for 'with rounded mouth', as employed by those who like to use five or six words where one would do.

Au pair

The practice of having a young woman in the house to help look after the children and yet to be more or less equal with the family and not treated as an employee appears to have originated in Germany. The Germans called such a girl the 'house daughter'.

The English language used a French term to describe exactly the same situation: in French, the term *au pair* means on an equal footing. The word *pair* in French is the origin of our English word peer, as in peer group or peer pressure, to describe people of equal status.

The term has been around in English for a long time, but it was first recorded in a dictionary with this meaning in 1928. Nowadays the term is often extended to 'au pair girl', and sometimes used as a verb – to au pair.

Australasia

This word has its origins in French. *Australasie* dates back to 1794 and apparently referred to Australia and Asia. Over time the meaning was modified to mean Australia and all its neighbouring islands.

When New Zealand established an identity of its own, the word had another slight refinement of meaning: namely the nations of Australia and New Zealand, plus both countries' outlying islands.

The term was used frequently throughout the nineteenth century, at which time the district of New Zealand was included for the purposes of the Anglican church within the diocese of Australasia. And for a time the colony of New Zealand was actually administered from New South Wales.

There was a belief that Australians favoured the word because it discreetly dominated New Zealand. But conversely, a feeling also grew that the word Australasia was used by New Zealanders to link themselves with a more powerful neighbour.

From 1960 onwards the use of the word in either of the countries it supposedly (jointly) describes has markedly diminished.

Australian Constitution

The Australian Constitution, established in 1901, states: 'The Commonwealth means the Commonwealth of Australia. The States shall mean such of the colonies of New South Wales, New Zealand, Queensland, Tasmania, Victoria, Western Australia, South Australia, including the Northern Territory of Australia as for the time being are parts of the Commonwealth and such colonies or territories as may be admitted into or established by the Commonwealth as States.'

So what is actually being said, in paraphrase, is that New Zealand may be admitted – it if wants. The constitution doesn't list it as already being a state and it never has. And the sentence remains exactly the same in the current constitution – so the gate is still open.

Automobile

Automobile is a combination of Greek *auto* meaning self, and Latin *mobile*, meaning to move. The car as we know it is actually a German invention, and the German language quite commonly used the word *Auto-mobil* to describe cars, and still does. Americans also quite commonly use the word, perhaps having picked it up straight from the German usage.

A

Autumn or fall?

The word 'fall' is used in the United States, referring to the fact that before winter sets in the leaves fall off deciduous trees, leaving the landscape stark. It is an abbreviation of the term 'fall of the leaf', which was commonly used in England up to and during the sixteenth century. Emigrants took that term with them to America, where it narrowed down to just 'fall'. But during the same period, the word gradually fell out of use in Britain, to be replaced by the more formal 'autumn'.

Avocado

Apart from a partial similarity of shape, the avocado has nothing to do with pears. It is from the laurel family and is native to the Andean region of South America, which is where the name comes from.

When explorers first noticed the avocado trees, with their blackish hanging fruit, they asked the natives what they were called and the locals told them their name for the fruit was *ahuacatl*, which is more or less what the rest of the world now calls them.

What the explorers didn't realise at the time was what *ahuacatl* actually means: it is a South American native word for testicles, which the locals thought the avocados resembled. So every time you ask for avocados in the vegetable section, you're actually asking for 'testicles'. It's a clear case of getting away with saying something fairly indelicate as long as you say it in another language.

Axe (musical)

In general this means the particular instrument a musician plays and carries around. The term axe is believed to have originated in reference to the saxophone – partly because the shape is remotely like an axe, and partly because the two words axe and sax have a similar sound. The use has broadened into referring to other non-symphonic instruments, particularly among rock musicians and their guitars.

Bachelor's degree

B

Bachelor is an ancient word, arising centuries ago from the Greek *bacca laureus*, referring to the berries of the laurel tree (which were made into wreaths worn on the heads of poets). The term has always been connected with a junior position in various hierarchies. Medieval young men who travelled in the service of a knight were known as bachelors and they aspired to become knights themselves. Their position survives today in one of the lower orders of knighthood – Knight Bachelor. In the days of the powerful guilds or early trade unions, a bachelor was a yeoman member of a trade guild.

Gradually the word drifted into two separate strands of popular meaning:

1. A man who wasn't married, thus somehow suggesting he was like the knight's assistant and the junior yeoman – a person who was unfinished, not fully qualified in life.

2. A university qualification called a bachelor's degree, which again was rather junior on the hierarchy scale, indicating the beginning of the climb towards higher academic levels.

All this development and usage took place over hundreds of years, and the terms bachelor and master were well established as names of university degrees before women ever entered the system. By the time they did so, there was a word for a woman who wasn't married – spinster – but quite understandably women didn't want to be identified as Spinsters of Arts or Spinsters of Science. So the word bachelor remains as a degree title but, in that particular context, without any connotation of gender.

Back of beyond/beyond the black stump

The term 'back of beyond' was in use in Britain by 1816, when it is mentioned in Sir Walter Scott's *Antiquarian* referring to a place of exile by the sea 'at the back of beyond'. Later, both Kipling and Tolkien also used the expression.

But its use in Australia may have come about by a slightly different path. On 5 September 1826, Governor Darling specified a Government Order by which settlers were permitted to select land within certain prescribed limits. The Nineteen Counties of New South Wales were defined as the Limits of Location beyond which settlement was prohibited. This Government Order was expanded on 14 October 1829 and land outside the prescribed limits was considered to be waste land (though that very land later became Victoria and Queensland!).

The ruling's concept of 'beyond' caught on, and was joined by another descriptive factor. One of the boundaries outlined in the Nineteen Counties specification was near an area known as Black Stump Run. It was so called because of an existing rural custom of giving directions by naming natural features such as a rock, a river, an outstanding tree – or a large and noticeable burnt-out stump.

From the original Government statement, two common sayings grew. 'Beyond' and 'back of beyond' came to mean places especially distant from those who called them that – thus joining other Australian terms for distant places: 'the never-never' ; 'the Outback'; 'back of nowhere'; 'back of Bourke'; or simply 'the backblocks'.

So, too, 'beyond the black stump' came into common use and eventually widened into a metaphor that can be applied to anything or anywhere the speaker considers distant from familiar surroundings – or familiar thought. The reverse, 'this side of the black stump', indicates that the region being mentioned is within familiar territory.

Bags that

In late Middle English the word 'bag' first became used as a verb: 'to bag game', meaning to shoot game and put it into a bag. During the nineteenth century the verb grew another meaning: to reserve, to claim, especially on the grounds of being the first. It also developed a peculiar ending. Instead of 'I bag this', meaning 'I declare that this is going in my bag', the saying became 'I bags this' or, in reverse for something you don't want: 'I bags not.'

Bald as a badger

Badgers aren't bald; they live mainly underground and are very hairy. The perception that they might be bald is related to an old-fashioned men's accessory called a shaving brush. Time was when legions of men foamed up their faces with wetted soap and special brushes with long, soft bristles. The brush industry was inclined to be discreet about exactly where the soft shaving brush bristles came from, but there was a widespread belief that the longest, softest hairs available came from around a badger's bum.

So the belief arose that all the badgers in Britain must have had their bums plucked, hence the saying arose, 'bare as a badger's bum'. Thousands of men had shaving brushes, but badgers are rarely seen – bald-bummed or otherwise.

So the expression remained unproven, but stayed current. Over years 'bum' was dropped, and the line became shortened to just 'bald as a badger'.

(It's similarly irrational to say 'bald as a coot' because a coot isn't bald either – it's a bird but, with a band of smooth white feathers across the top of its head, from a distance looks as if it might be. An Australian version – 'bald as a bandicoot' – is just a semantic novelty, since it gives the pleasure of alliteration, but bandicoots aren't bald either. Better to say 'bald as a billiard ball'.)

Balderdash

The word balderdash is a bit mysterious, but it is associated with drink. The actual origin of the word itself is unknown, but in the sixteenth century the word was used to describe frothy liquid, and then it came to mean a mixture of liquids – leftovers, slops, often liquids that shouldn't be mixed and couldn't be drunk. So by the late seventeenth century people had extended the use of the word to mean not just messy liquid, but anything useless, nonsensical, trash.

Bali Ha'i

The idyllic place is first mentioned in James Michener's 1947 book *Tales of the South Pacific*. The stories take place in the Solomon Islands in the Western Pacific. There is no place in the Solomons actually called Bali Ha'i, but the locals point to a remote spot called Bala'la'e as the place name that reputedly inspired Michener.

The name might have appealed to him – but that wasn't the actual place Michener had in mind. Many years later, in 1970, Michener wrote a piece in the *Philadelphia Sunday Bulletin*. He revealed that no real Bali Ha'i existed anywhere. But the fictional image of it had grown from contact with a 'steaming, savage island called Aoba', in what is now Vanuatu (the island of Aoba is now called Ambae). Michener explained that as a writer, he had taken 'the privilege of dressing them up a little ... creating an island of loveliness and imagination named Bali Ha'i'.

In 1949 the Rodgers and Hammerstein musical theatre version, *South Pacific*, moved the entire story from Micronesia much further east into more picturesque Polynesia. By the time the movie was made in 1958 the entire setting of Michener's original stories was a distant memory. Filmed sequences supposedly taking place in Bali Ha'i were actually filmed on Santa Monica Boulevard in Los Angeles.

Several places in the Pacific claim to be the real or original Bali Ha'i, but, alas, there's no such place and, if there were, it would be in Vanuatu.

Balmoral

'Bal' is the contemporary English spelling of an Old Gaelic word *bala*, which means 'place of' or settlement, as in Balmacewan – the place where the Macewans live.

But this doesn't indicate that Balmoral means place of the morals – moral in Old Gaelic has the meaning of 'big and stately', 'the gentry', so the name Balmoral carries the connotation of place of the gentry.

Bamboozled

This word, which means to confuse, cheat, or mislead, goes way back to ancient Greece, where *bombux* was the word for silkworm. From that developed the French word *bombace* and eventually the English 'bombast', describing a kind of light fabric. Because it was mainly for padding, it was not considered valuable, and so the practice arose of using the word bombast to refer to high-sounding, inflated speech – words that were only padding.

Somewhere round about 1700, the word bombast developed into 'bumbazzle', meaning to play tricks with words and to confuse people with elaborate speech. This in turn became 'bamboozle'.

Bandicooting

An Australian expression, referring to the bandicoot (bandicoot is a corruption of a Telugu word from India, meaning 'pig rat'). It causes mayhem in gardens by burrowing and eating tuberous vegetables such as potatoes, leaving only the tops showing above.

In 1898 George Dunderdale wrote in *The Book of the Bush*: 'You bandicooted my potatoes last night, and you've left the marks of your dirty feet on the ground.' And *The Joseph Furphy Poems* (1916) included:

> You may forgo your stylish duds
> And trade away your pin and studs
> To live on bandicooted spuds
> But you must never whine.

Since about 1920 the term 'bandicooting' has sometimes been used in Australia to mean 'above ground' stealing, especially when it is not immediately obvious.

Bar

The word itself dates back to the obscure ancient Latin *barra*, which appears to mean 'rod' – and through the centuries came to mean something long and narrow made from a firm substance. In English this came to refer to a lengthy wooden structure at which people could stand (though even a chocolate bar is part of the same etymological equation).

The term 'bar' with the general meaning of 'an area where alcoholic drinks are served' came into print in 1592. At the time there was a practice of lowering and bolting an actual iron bar to keep the stock safe at night. In later centuries the meaning broadened away from the wooden strip and the metal bar that protected its stock, and began to include the whole room in which the bar area was situated.

Then the application widened even further to include any smallish establishment where one commodity was available – a coffee bar, a shoe bar, a salad bar etc.

Similarly, in old courtrooms there were two actual bars or rails: one separated the Judge's bench from the rest of the room; the other bar shut off the area for lawyers engaged in trials. Persons who were permitted to appear as counsel before the court were therefore separated from more junior lawyers by an actual bar, and by the 1600s these lawyers became known as barristers because when they spoke in court they were literally 'called to the bar', which was seen as a privilege.

Barking dogs

Cockney rhyming slang habitually drops off the word that actually rhymes and uses only the preceding word. So Barnet fair (hair) becomes Barnet; loaf of bread (head) becomes loaf; and daisy roots (boots) are daisies. In this tradition, feet are sometimes called 'plates of meat', and sometimes 'dogs' meat'. And dogs' meat is, of course, shortened to dogs.

So if feet are quite commonly referred to as dogs, it's a natural development that when they're worn out and tired, the dogs are in distress – they're barking. More seriously, if your feet are sore and in pain, then your dogs are biting.

Bash

Bash is believed to come from a combination of bang and smash. Around 1930 the word began to be used to describe the loud and cheerful playing of dance music, and the noise of a party going with it. Eventually another meaning arose – to attempt something, as in 'have a bash at it'.

Bastard

The word is believed to have arisen from the old Latin word *bastum* meaning saddle.

In ancient times there developed a French expression *fils de bast*, meaning 'child of the saddle', which referred to a child born of an unmarried mother whose father had been a travelling herder, shepherd or muleteer. He had probably used his saddle as a pillow, and then afterwards slung it back on his mule and ridden away.

Two things happened to the French expression. The association between transient saddles and children with transient fathers gradually extended to be used about any child born out of wedlock, and the French was modified into the English version, bastard – a child born from a saddle rather than a marriage bed.

Bated breath

It's all in the spelling. Bated breath has nothing to do with fish bait and it mustn't be spelt that way. It's short for the word 'abated', which means made less, smaller in amount.

You hear it nowadays mainly in the contexts of weather or law: a storm has abated, or a court order has abated something, meaning that it's been removed, suppressed or annulled. But you don't hear the word much anywhere else, except in 'bated breath', which has dropped the 'a', but is the same word. The breath is being held tight and not allowed to expand.

Batman

It has nothing to do with bats. The word comes from an Old French word which itself comes from the Latin *bastum* meaning saddle – the same word which is ancestor to 'bastard'.

In early times, the batman was the soldier in charge of the packhorse carrying the officer's luggage. Eventually packhorses weren't used so much in the military and it is believed that, during the First World War, non-regular officers used the term quite erroneously to describe an officer's servant and the usage stuck.

Bearded like the pard

The origin is Shakespeare, from the famous 'Seven Ages of Man' speech in *As You Like It*: 'Then a soldier, bearded like the pard, Jealous in honour, sudden and quick in quarrel ...'

Pard means a panther or leopard, but 'bearded like' isn't quite so straightforward. In earlier times 'beard' didn't always mean the bit under the chin – it sometimes meant hair on the face generally. In Burke's *History of England* (1757), he writes, 'Britons shaved the beard on the chin, but that on the upper lip was suffered to remain.' So when Shakespeare said 'bearded like the pard', he could have meant great bristling moustaches, like the whiskers on a leopard.

There is also another possibility. Another meaning of 'to beard' survives into modern English as 'to face fearlessly', 'to beard someone in their den'. So because Shakespeare was describing a soldier, when he wrote that line he might have meant as fierce as a leopard when it is confronted.

Either way, whether the man looks like a leopard, or is as formidable as an angered leopard, the image is one of bravery and courage.

Beat about the bush

This term originated with beaters who travelled with game hunters and literally beat the bushes in order to flush out birds or other wildlife. If a person spent too much time beating a bush in a roundabout way, the prize game being looked for might get away and be shot by some other hunter. So the term came to mean travelling a long way round, and from there it has extended to refer to long-winded speech about something that could be revealed quite briefly.

Beeline

Bees leave their hives to go out looking for nectar and they can travel long distances from home. Considering the size of a bee in relation to the distance it can travel and how huge the landscape must seem to it, it is impressive that after a day's work the bee knows exactly in which direction home is, and can fly there in a direct line without distraction. Hence 'making a beeline'.

Beer and skittles

Skittles is an ancient game, the ancestor of today's indoor or ninepin bowling. Traditionally it was accompanied by light-hearted activity

– and drinking, usually of port. Charles Dickens mentions it in *The Pickwick Papers*, which was serialised in 1836.

But the alcohol seemed to go downmarket in the next few years, and the expression in print had changed the drink from port to beer by the time George Du Maurier wrote the novel *Trilby* in 1894. In that book you'll find the expression as we know it today – 'Life isn't all beer and skittles'.

Bee's knees

This nonsense phrase has no particular origin; it comes into the same category as 'cat's pyjamas'. It means 'the acme of perfection' and, according to Eric Partridge, has been in use since about 1930.

Begonia

Like many botanical names, it commemorates a person – a French government officer sent on a naval mission to Santo Domingo in 1681. He brought back to Europe the first plant of the species that was later named after him. His name was Michel Bégon.

Begs the question

This is very often misused – often by people who are trying to sound better educated than they actually are. The expression dates back to the Latin *petitio principii*, where someone stacks the cards in an argument by assuming something that hasn't been proven before the argument begins. Begging the question is an attempt to provide an answer which incorporates material that the responder assumes is correct, and thus presents an answer that the questioner assumes is valid.

For example: 'Does God exist?' Answer: 'The Bible is divinely inspired, so what the Bible says must be true, and the Bible says that God exists. Therefore, God does exist.' That answer begs the question: it uses the phrase 'divinely inspired' as part of its explanation, thus making the assumption that there is a divinity.

Misuse of the phrase can happen in the following manner, exemplified by a fictional news item: 'The government has announced that all schools are going to be supplied with completely new computer equipment during the first half of 2014. This begs the question of where the money is going to be found. '

This use is absolutely incorrect. The government's announcement simply raises the question of where the money is to come from. It does not beg the question at all.

Behind the eight ball

This refers to someone being in a potentially losing position. The expression comes from a pool game, where the black ball is numbered eight. If your move is positioned behind the eight ball, then you have a major problem. Being behind the eight ball is like being on the back foot.

Better and best

In English, adjectives and adverbs come in three degrees of comparison: positive, comparative and superlative. For example, one thing is good (positive), another thing is better (comparative) than the first one, and a third thing is the best (superlative) of all three. If there are only two, you can't have a best, only the better.

Over the years there have been various glitches about this. For instance, the saying 'Put your best foot forward' should really be 'Put your better foot forward' because we have only two feet, not three. When some media outlets forbade the use of superlatives in advertising, the marketers invented descriptions that avoided the forbidden: soap powder washed 'whiter than white' (because they weren't allowed to say whitest) and peas were 'fresher than fresh'.

Better the devil you know than the devil you don't know

The ancestor of the expression appears to be the words of the Dutch scholar Desiderius Erasmus, in 1539: 'An euyl thynge knowen is best.' Later in the sixteenth century the phrase had become: 'You had better keep those whom you know, though with some faults, than take those whom you know not, perchance with more faults.'

At some point over the next 300 years the concept of bad things or evil was replaced with the word devil, and by 1857 Anthony

Trollope in *Barchester Towers* used exactly the version we've become more familiar with: 'Better the devil you know than the devil you don't know'.

Beyond the pale

In this expression the 'pale' means the bounds of propriety or good taste or good sense, and its origin lay in a specific place. In this context, the word pale comes from the Latin word *palus*, meaning a wooden stake, which survives in modern English as a fence paling.

During the fourteenth century, the part of Ireland under English rule was marked out with a boundary of wooden stakes, and the boundary line was known as the English Pale. If Englishmen crossed over that line into Irish territory, they were leaving behind all the familiarities and niceties of English custom and rule – they were beyond the pale.

This meaning became rather exaggerated, implying that you were leaving security and safety and going into the unknown. Gradually the expression settled down to mean outside the bounds of normality. By 1654 it had become a general expression. An archbishop of the Church of England wrote, 'No salvation to be expected outside the pale of the church.'

Big Apple

New York City has been compared to a big apple tree since 1909 when Edward Sanford Martin commented on the proportion of the Midwest's wealth which New York attracted, making the city like a great tree whose roots extended far and wide, but failing to provide any benefit to the source of its nourishment. In informal speech the image of the city as a big apple crept into use among out-of-town jazz musicians and stable hands as a synonym for work in New York being the 'big time'.

John J. Fitzgerald was a sports journalist on the *New York Morning Telegraph*, and having heard the term 'big apple' among stable hands as far away as New Orleans, he used the expression as the title of his column in 1924. The nickname caught on very quickly, and by 1971 had become the official advertising slogan for New York City.

Big Ben

Big Ben is not really the name of the famous clock in the British Houses of Parliament; it is the name of the bell inside that sounds the hours – and just the hours.

The bell of Big Ben has been ringing since 1859. It strikes 156 times a day. There are four other bells; they strike the 'chimes', so in total there are 960 strikes a day. Strictly speaking, Big Ben does not strike chimes at all, just the hours, but over the years the meaning of the name has widened so that Big Ben is now generally used for the whole clock, all the bells and even the tower.

The bell is named after Lord Benjamin Llanover, who was Minister of Works in Britain when the House of Parliament clock had its bell cast to chime the hour. It was a very big bell, and Lord Benjamin Llanover was a big man, so the bell became known as Big Ben.

Big Ben is set to ring on the note E natural, the same as the big bell at St Peter's in Rome (which can be a worry to people producing the opera Tosca, where that very deep E note is not always easy to achieve).

The tune of the chimes that come before the hour originated from Cambridge, where a new clock was installed in 1793 and the Reverend Joseph Jowett was asked to compose a chime. He is believed to have been helped by one of his students, and between them they came up with the distinctive 'Cambridge chime', which was based on a fragment from Handel's Messiah: 'I Know that My Redeemer Liveth'. That chime was copied for the bells of the London clock and is now better known as the Westminster chime. A version of it is often found in domestic grandfather clocks.

Big girl's blouse

This is usually said to a man, and tells him that he's weak, indecisive, shy and – here's the operative word – soft. It is heard occasionally on *Coronation Street* because it's set in the area the expression comes from, the North of England.

The verb 'to blouse' something has been in use for some time in certain circumstances, and simply means to fill with air. This is because, traditionally, a woman's blouse is made of soft fabric, and although it is filled with a woman, there is a certain amount of air in there as well. And if the blouse is too big for the girl wearing it, then of course there is more air in it than girl.

In the world of machismo – the Mexican word for strong maleness – men are not supposed to be soft creatures. The sensitive new-age guy may be gentle and considerate and caring, but there is still a very strong image that a real man is tough and hard. That image has not changed at all – if anything, it has intensified.

So to call a man a blouse, or a girl's blouse, implies that he is malleable, gentle, floppy, and that can be amplified by adding 'big'. (Note that it's the blouse that is big, not the girl, and therefore the blouse is even floppier.)

Big kahuna

The word *kahuna* is native Hawaiian and has been used there for centuries. The easiest way to translate it is to say that it's Hawaiian for wizard – not in the Harry Potter sense of pointy hats and magic spells, but more like a sage or counsellor – an expert with particular powers in the field of nature science. It is similar to our use of the Hindi word guru – a spiritual leader and guide.

In recent decades kahuna has drifted into occasional use in English, sometimes in doubtful taste, because the word's real meaning has connotations that don't quite fit into contemporary English. It is distinctly disrespectful to translate the big kahuna as the big cheese, though this occasionally happens.

Bigot

The word is French in origin and its origin was racist. 'Bigot' was said by the ancient French with contemptuous reference to the Normans because they had different ways of doing things, particularly in the area of religion. From that early connotation of religious hypocrisy, by the time the word drifted into English (sounding a bit like 'by God') it had come to describe someone who stubbornly believes that their own views are the only ones possible, and that everyone else is wrong.

Bimbo

Bimbo is an Italian word – an affectionate abbreviation for *bambino*, meaning a little boy. There used to be a song about it: 'Bimbo, bimbo, where ya' gonna go-e-o . . . goin' down the road to see a little girleo.'

By some strange misunderstanding, and in spite of the popularity of the song, in English the word bimbo began being used to describe a girl or young woman – ignoring the fact that in Italian when a word ends in 'o' it is masculine – a little girl is called a *bambina*, or *bimba*.

After bimbo had settled into English in its new and curious feminine guise, someone invented a matching word to describe an attractive young man – a 'himbo'. But they needn't have bothered, since that's what bimbo really meant all along.

Bird brain

The expression is believed to derive from the assumption that, because birds' heads in general seem very small in proportion to their bodies, their brains must be very small too. It isn't necessarily true, but bird brain also has a pleasing alliteration, so because of those two factors it's often used to mean someone dizzy or with a small attention span.

Birdcage Walk, London

Unlike many strange names in England, this one means exactly what it says. The street has been called that for over 300 years, and it's believed to have come about because one of the early English kings established aviaries of exotic birds there. Most of the creatures died in London's winters, but the name remains.

Bitch

The word bitch, meaning a female dog, was derived originally from a Scandinavian word, and has been in English for 1000 years. Since 1400 it gained a secondary application, meaning a derogatory word for some women – mainly those whose moral standards were questionable in terms of the time.

38

Another layer of meaning, developed much later – in the 1800s
– applied to women who were malicious or treacherous, and that
eventually broadened to cover a much wider field: the weather, the
government, the law, a car that won't start – all can be a 'bitch'.

During its passage through history, 'bitch' was sometimes used
as a derogatory term referring to either women or men. Robert
Louis Stevenson used the word to describe a man (in a letter to
W.E. Henley, 1882), as did James Joyce (*Portrait of the Artist as a
Young Man*, 1916), and Kipling used it metaphorically in *Traffics &
Discoveries*: '... cheated by your bitch of a country ...'. Shakespeare
used it to refer to a woman, and that's how it is most often heard
in contemporary times. (For the origin of 'son of a bitch', look no
further than that same Bard, in *King Lear* (1605): 'One that ... art
nothing but the composition of a knave, beggar, coward, pandar,
and the son and heir of a mongrel bitch.')

Black affronted

In Scotland one of the many subtle shades of meaning for the word
'black' is 'extreme', as in, for instance, black shame or black disgrace.
Thus to be black affronted means to be highly insulted and very
embarrassed.

Black dog

Mention of a black dog as a demonic hellhound or even the devil
himself in disguise is a frequent and powerful image in folklore over
many centuries. The black dog brought fear to the superstitious and
some kind of mysterious link to worlds other than the one we live in.
Roman poet Horace in around 25 BC referred to the belief that even
seeing a black dog (especially one with pups) was an unlucky omen.
And by AD 856 a French reference made the connection between
black hounds and Hell.

Gradually a connection grew between the image of the evil hound,
and the human condition of melancholy or depression. In England
in 1783, Samuel Johnson was referring to his periods of melancholy
as a 'black dog'. Depression as a 'black dog on one's back' also occurs
in the writings of Sir Walter Scott (1826) and Robert Louis Stevenson

(1882), and the image of a black dog as demonic and terrifying is the title character in Conan Doyle's *Hound of the Baskervilles* (1902).

In more recent times the image of the 'black dog of depression' became associated with Sir Winston Churchill, but the term was widely used for many centuries before him.

Blighty

Blighty comes from an Urdu word *b'layti*, meaning a foreign place. Military men who'd served in India picked up the word and during the First World War it came to mean England. It was also heard in the expression 'a blighty' – meaning a wound that would ensure a soldier got sent home to England.

Blimey

It's a shortened version of an oath meant to express surprise or disbelief. The original full version is 'God blind me', as in, 'I'm so surprised at what you've just said that it's as if God suddenly struck me blind.'

Over the years it was modified to Gor blimey (Gor being an abbreviation for God), and sometimes Cor blimey. This was still further abbreviated to just blimey, or Cor.

On *Coronation Street* Hilda Ogden once memorably looked up at an enormous oil painting of a huge battle scene and said: 'Cor, must 'ave 'ad a lot of numbers.'

Bling

The term began as a nonsense phrase used by American gangsta rap and hip-hop performers in the 1990s, originally referring to money and believed to be based on the ringing sound of a phone – a sound which could mean a paid job might be offered.

By 1999 it had made a slight shift to mean jewellery, and was immortalised by a New Orleans rock group called Cash Money Millionaires and their soloist 'B.G.' with a recording called 'Bling Bling' – which featured extravagant watches, pendants, cars and the occasional silver candelabra. The term moved into mainstream use very quickly, usually as a put-down description referring to jewellery of an extravagant (and probably fake) kind. An American lottery firm trade-marked the phrase, with the intention of marketing lotto-type games with that as a title.

The term has undergone a subtle shift so that now, besides jewellery, it can also be applied to other fashion accoutrements – anything that can be described as 'showy style' or 'over the top'. And the term has been reduced to the single 'bling'.

Two sideline developments have been that when the Queen, for instance, or other leading celebrities appear in what are obviously real diamonds and pearls, this is acknowledged to be 'good bling'. And in contrast, some marketplaces have embraced the early 'fake' connotation and offer watches that are cheerfully acknowledged as 'bling Rolex'.

Blocking the scene/setting the scene

Both terms are used in the theatre, occasionally interchangeably, but 'block' is the word usually used when a director is just starting to plan out exactly where everyone will stand and where they will move to.

There are over 40 different meanings for the word block, and this one appears to have evolved from the practice many directors have of starting from a drawing of the stage, onto which they pencil the divisions of the acting areas or blocks. When the actors eventually assemble, the director can then start moving them around to make interesting groupings, or to ensure that a certain character is prominent at an important moment, and often to keep the stage picture changing so that actors aren't standing in the same places for too long. They're being moved from block to block. Once the movements and groupings have been finalised, the word 'blocking' usually ceases to be used and the meetings then become rehearsals.

The expression 'setting the scene' can sometimes mean something similar, as in setting the table or the fire, where you arrange certain things in a way that will use them effectively. But in theatre that expression usually has a slightly different connotation: you arrange certain incidents and props and lighting in order to highlight some-thing – often something which is about to happen. It's almost as if you should say setting up a scene, because it's leading to something else.

Blog

It is a contraction of 'web log', which means a diary – of a certain kind. Unlike a traditional diary – usually regarded as for private consumption (except perhaps after death) – a blog is intended to be read by anyone who wants to, on the Internet. Blogs are frequently updated, and usually written by one person, who is a non-professional writer.

Bloody

For many years it was believed that the word 'bloody' was a contraction of a Christian oath referring to the Virgin Mary – 'by our lady'. But in recent times this has been cast into serious doubt by scholars who believe that the term bloody as an intensifier began from meaning exactly what it says – causing blood to flow, or being covered in blood. In this context it was used as a description of cruelty as early as the year 970 about Pope Otto II, and again regarding Queen Mary Tudor in the 1550s for killing Protestants, and the Duke of Cumberland who, in the 1750s, was known as the Bloody Butcher for killing Highlanders.

These people, and places like the Bloody Tower where two princes were supposedly murdered in 1597, and events like the Bloody Assizes in the 1600s and Bloody Sunday in 1887, were all connected with actual blood. The general image of blood being connected with unpleasant situations gradually guided use of the word into situations where a lurid intensifier was wanted. 'Bloody' this and 'bloody' that – even when no actual blood was involved.

The word is an interesting example of the shifts that take place as some words move from unacceptability to acceptability – and vice versa. Until 1940, 'bloody' was regarded as serious swearing.

When Mrs Patrick Campbell said it on stage in the first English performance of Bernard Shaw's *Pygmalion* in 1914 there was an absolute sensation. The sensation continued for many years wherever the play was presented. Often the word 'pygmalion' was used in conversation and in print when the word 'bloody' was actually meant.

Forty-two years later, the play was made into the musical *My Fair Lady*. By 1956 the word 'bloody' had become so commonplace that the writers had to think up something completely different to startle the audience as well as the other characters around the protagonist.

Bluebird of happiness

This concept was invented by the writer Count Maurice Maeterlinck, who in 1908 wrote a play about a boy and a girl who were seeking a visionary bluebird which represented happiness (birds that are a beautiful blue do exist, but they're far from common).

In 1934 Sandor Harmati, Edward Heyman and Harry Parr Davies composed the song 'Bluebird of Happiness'. The famous tenor Jan Peerce sang it in 1936 and his subsequent recording of the song probably did more than anything else to make the concept of a bluebird of happiness very famous indeed.

In 1940 Maeterlinck's original play was made into a movie, *The Blue Bird*, starring Shirley Temple. The film was remade, under the same title, starring Elizabeth Taylor, Jane Fonda and Ava Gardner. Curiously, though, Peerce's recording seemed to affect more people than the screen versions of the story.

Blue blood

Aristocrats don't actually have this, but the expression originated in Spain as *sangre azul*, which means exactly that – blue blood. In centuries past, some areas of Spain were home to many people of Arabic or Moroccan descent, and racial mixtures produced families whose skin was darker than that of people of pure Spanish blood. Along with that, there was reluctance on the part of rich people, especially indolent rich people, to expose themselves to the harsh summer sun. Spain is very hot in summer and those who had to work outdoors to keep themselves fed and housed grew very swarthy.

On many people, the blood vessels show a bluish colour through the skin. But if the person has dark skin, or if they've been working outdoors, their skin colour precludes that blueness showing. Hence, only those people rich enough not to have to work in the sun, and of an ancestry that excluded anyone from North Africa, had blood vessels that showed as blue. So the description blue blood arose in Europe to describe people of unmixed European ancestry, but now we use the expression to mean those of aristocratic descent.

Blue chips

In the gambling industry blue chips have the highest value. This has become a descriptive term for non-gambling entities which are considered reliable and valuable, such as a blue-chip company or blue-chip shares.

Blue-eyed boy

This expression was based on the belief that a person with genuinely blue eyes was fairly uncommon and usually attractive. So the person with blue eyes was often favoured by authorities. For much the same reason, a similar cachet attached to a 'white-haired boy'.

Blue (for a boy)

For many centuries – and for obvious reasons – the colour blue has been linked with the sky, and therefore heaven. This gave the colour a connotation of superiority. Some cultures regarded male babies as more important than females, so the colour blue was associated with boy babies because it was a colour for superior people (meaning males!). On the other hand, because warmth and gentleness seemed to be associated with pink, girl babies tended to be represented by that colour.

Blue moon

Some people think that under very special conditions – when there's forest-fire dust high in the air, or clouds of ice crystals, or after the eruption of Krakatoa – the moon takes on a blue colour. Even if this is true (and many doubt it), the occasions on which it happens must be very rare. Hence the saying 'once in a blue moon'.

A view has also been put forward that when two full moons occur in a calendar month, the second of those is called a blue moon. But that isn't very unusual at all: it happens about every three years.

The first known mention of a blue moon can be found in the year 1528, but in a sardonic way, referring to something that's never going to happen. The implication is that a blue moon is a ridiculous impossibility. And that seems to be the most likely explanation for the way the phrase is used nowadays. It's rather like mentioning the twelfth of never.

Blue movies

Blue may be the colour of heaven and of superiority, but it's also the colour of dirty jokes and pornographic movies.

Associating the colour blue with sexual activity comes from several sources. There was a Chinese custom of painting the outside of brothels a bright blue, and the association of that colour carried over into Western culture to describe sex movies and jokes. But there's also the Christian image which associates the devil with burning brimstone (see also **The blues**), another word for sulphur, which burns with a blue flame. Hence in some circumstances the colour blue is associated with being bad.

There's also a third contributing factor. For many generations, sub-editors in newspapers used blue pencils to make text corrections or to cut out material – either because it exceeded the space available or because it could be seen as offensive. Hence the term 'blue-pencil' began to mean 'eliminate'. And the term also led to an association with jokes or remarks which weren't suitable for publication, and were therefore 'blue' jokes.

(To scream) blue murder

The expression arises from a double corruption. It began as a French expression, *mort Dieu*, the death of God, which was an exclamation of horror and shock, not necessarily involving a murder. Gradually the French corrupted that into a slang version, *mort bleu*, which became abbreviated to *morbleu*. By the time the phrase crept into English the progression from *mort Dieu* to *mort bleu* to *morbleu*, plus the way the English heard it, finally arrived at 'blue murder'.

Blue (nickname)

There is something of a mystery about why red-haired men might be called 'Blue'. The connection has been in use in Australia since the 1890s. Only one explanation seems to be on offer and although it doesn't have a solid provenance, it can appear to make fragile sense if connected with a vague belief about red-headed people.

'A blue' is believed to have originated as a reference to being in trouble with the law because summonses to court were issued on blue paper. Henry Lawson's Jack Cornstalk (1895) 'gets on the spree and into a row, and so into trouble that merits the serving on his person of what he calls "a blue piece of paper".' Because red-haired men were believed to be hot-tempered, it was also believed that they often had problems and fights – resulting in a blue court summons.

So if that explanation of the nickname is correct, then red-haired men have been stuck with a connection not all of them deserve!

Blueprint

This photographic process, invented in 1842, reproduced draughtsmen's and engineers' plans as white lines on a dark blue background. The meaning has extended to refer to a plan or project, or a copy – not necessarily on paper – that other people can follow.

Blue ribbon

This goes back to the concept of the colour blue representing superiority. The Knights of the Garter, the highest British order of publicly recognised achievement, began in 1348. Their insignia is a blue velvet band and a blue velvet cloak. The theme is often echoed in public competitions, where the blue ribbon indicates the best level, the highest attainment, Number One.

(The) blues

The image of the devil was associated with the blue flame of brimstone/sulphur. There is also a connection with describing unhappy people, who during the eighteenth century were said to be having the blue devils. They were depressed and dejected, so the devil must be getting at them with his blue fire. Gradually the term became simply 'the blues'. (A fanciful variation occurred in Truman Capote's *Breakfast at Tiffany's* where Holly Golightly suffered occasional 'mean reds'.)

'The blues' is also a term used for a type of music. Originally it was American music expressing the unhappiness of black people in the southern states. The music uses flattened notes on the third, the fifth or the seventh of the scale, which gives a sound falling between major and minor pitch. To ears accustomed to the diatonic scale, this sounds sad and carries a distinct connotation of melancholy.

Bluestocking

The term itself dates back to the fifteenth century, when intellectuals used to meet in Venice and deliberately wore blue-coloured stockings. The idea later surfaced in Paris in the 1500s, and women were prominent within that group.

By the eighteenth century a similar set-up had started in England, where a women-only group met for discussion – and this was thought to be a little unusual. But those groups continued into the nineteenth century, and at times the women would invite eminent men such as Horace Walpole and Charles Dickens to special meetings. One man declined because he didn't think he was appropriately dressed and was told to just come as he was – which he did, wearing ordinary blue-grey daytime stockings.

So for various reasons the term 'bluestocking' has been associated with intellectual thinkers for 500 years.

The word has a negativity about it that may in part be explained by the fact that for many years men were very reluctant to concede that women might be clever. So it was used fairly dismissively about women with active intellects, some of whom actually did wear blue stockings, with the connotation that they were probably plain and dull. However, it must be remembered that blue has some significance as a colour of supremacy.

See also **Blue**.

BMW

The letters stand for *Bayerische Motoren Werke* (Bavarian Motor Factory). In 1916 two aircraft manufacturers in the Bavarian area of Germany merged to become BMW. Their work was halted when the 1919 Treaty of Versailles forbade further manufacture of aircraft in Germany, so BMW moved on to motor cycles and railway parts. The company's first car was manufactured in 1928.

Bobby dazzler

Bobby dazzler is a British expression, but there never was an actual person of that name. The word 'dazzle' came into English in the 1400s from an old Scandinavian word meaning to confuse, bewilder and confound. A fragment of this meaning remains – if you get hit over the head you are 'dazed'.

But a secondary meaning also developed: dazzled, which referred to something that bewildered only the eyes (the words have the same ancestor, but their meanings are slightly different – if you're dazzled by a bright light, it's not necessarily the same as being dazed). By 1800, the word dazzled had shifted to include things that weren't actually bright lights, but filled your eyesight only metaphorically. So anything or anyone who was particularly attractive was a dazzler.

The word 'bobby' is an odd one. Used in the north of England in the eighteenth century, it had a connotation of being in good health and good humour. Later on it developed an image of being small and neat, as in bobby calf, bobby socks, bobby pin.

But in the 1800s when bobby was combined with dazzler, it became an intensifier. Anyone who was in sparkling good health and good humour, and was good-looking, was a bobby dazzler. The term also extended to apply even to inanimate things. For example, a bobby dazzler was also a particularly good marble!

Bob's your uncle

The expression is British and has been in use since the 1880s. There's only one explanation for the possible origin of the phrase. In 1886, the Prime Minister of Britain, Robert Cecil, appointed Arthur Balfour as President of the Local Government Board and then later as Secretary for Scotland with a seat in the Cabinet. The following year he was given the highly prestigious post of Chief Secretary of Ireland.

Arthur Balfour was Robert Cecil's nephew, so it is believed the phrase may have grown from the gossip that said when you had an influential Uncle Bob, things would go well for you.

Bodum

Not to be confused with Bodrum, a port in Southern Turkey, Bodum is the trade name for a range of kitchen cookware manufactured in Denmark by the Bodum family. The main characteristic of their range is the use of a heavy heatproof glass – most frequently seen in various kinds of coffee-making equipment, utensils and on-element glass saucepans.

In the same way that trade names like vaseline and ping pong have moved into general use, the name bodum is sometimes heard as shorthand when giving a recipe or discussing a kitchen activity, especially making coffee: 'After adding very hot water to the coffee in the bodum, leave it standing for four minutes.'

Bogan

This is one of those mysterious words. An exact definition is difficult because the word is extremely subjective. Anyone who says it will know what they mean by it, as will the people to whom they say it. But another group will have a slightly different understanding.

In general terms, bogan is a contemptuous description applied to someone perceived as socially uncouth with a misguided fashion sense. The term is usually used in a downward direction on the socio-economic scale. It's remotely possible that an unkempt tramp could refer to someone on the rich list or the best-dressed list as a bogan, but it wouldn't really work.

Bogan sounds similar to the word 'vogan'; the latter were the despised race of people in the radio series and 1979 novel *The Hitch-hiker's Guide to the Galaxy*. (Vogans were known for their officious, bureaucratic and rude behaviour – and as creators of the third-worst poetry in the galaxy. If you transgressed their rules they punished you by reading passages of their poetry to you.) But in fact there is no known connection between vogans and bogans. It also sounds like 'bogon', which is an esoteric computer word and has no connection.

The word Bogan originated in Australia and its public use began in the 1980s. It does exist in a real placename, the Bogan River in New South Wales – Banjo Paterson mentioned it in *The City of Dreadful Thirst* (1899) as a 'Bogan shower – meaning three raindrops and some dust'. But it's not regarded as a source of the term.

Whether or not it has any connection with the Bogan River, the word grew to become a pejorative term for people whose clothes didn't please you – in much the same way as other negative terms like nerd, dork, yobbo and geek. There are various other words which can substitute for bogan: booners, boons, kevans, bevans – and, in some places, westies.

The big boost for the word bogan came in 1988 when a TV character called Kylie Mole performed weekly monologues that put several terms into the vernacular, such as spack and bogan. Mary-Anne Fahey, who wrote and performed the Kylie Mole scripts, said in various interviews that she caught the flavour of her monologues by listening to her 13-year-old daughter and her friends. So we might safely presume that bogan had been in use for a while before Kylie Mole made it commonplace in 1988.

Kylie Mole also clarified to whom the term could be applied, which turned out to be quite simple. Bogan described anyone she simply didn't like or didn't approve of; even something as minor as their socks could earn her stern criticism. Those criteria still apply, which is why the word is difficult to define – but useful.

Bogey (golf)

It's a variation on an old Scottish word *bogle*, meaning ghost or goblin – and a 'bogeyman' was the devil. The lyrics of a British song in the late 1900s included the lines 'Hush, hush, hush, here comes the bogeyman ... he'll catch you if you can'.

In 1890 there was a move among golfers to standardise the number of shots at each hole that a good golfer should take. This was to be called the 'ground score'. Gradually, golfers attempting to match this ground score – the ideal number of strokes to reach a hole – began to feel as if they were playing against the devil, otherwise known as the bogey.

Golfers with military leanings felt they could do better than playing against just an ordinary bogey, so in 1892 gave this mystic figure the honorary title of Colonel. Hence the figure of Colonel Bogey (who in 1913 became the focus of a popular march composed by the son of a Cockney coal merchant).

A subtle adjustment occurred with bogey, which used to be the ideal number of strokes – the par – but gradually had an extra stoke added, so a bogey is now one over par. Over time, par became the ideal in the eyes of professional golfers, and bogey was used more by recreational golfers.

Boggles

Usually preceded by 'the mind' – meaning that you have become confused, surprised, or unable to work through a complex set of information. The expression dates back to the early 1500s, but has changed its meaning somewhat since then.

Boggle is thought to have come from a Scottish word, *bogill*, meaning 'goblin' and thus closely related to 'bogey' and the 'bogeyman'. So when a person was said to be boggled, it meant they were frightened, startled or alarmed. Over time the meaning adjusted and mellowed slightly; it still indicates that someone's mind is in an alarmed state, but puzzled, confused or amazed, rather than frightened.

Bohemian

Bohemia was a country, and for hundreds of years it was believed that gypsy people were based there. So the word Bohemian began to take on the connotation of people living casually and unconventionally.

Many art students in Paris did live like that, even when they weren't from Bohemia, and the word bohemian, meaning unconventional and arty, gradually came into common use. In 1848 Thackeray used the word in *Vanity Fair* to describe Becky Sharp's parents – 'wild, roving and Bohemian'.

But something else happened in 1848 – writer Henri Murger wrote his novel *Scenes of a Bohemian Life* about French art students living in an unconventional way. That book was the basis of an opera, Puccini's *La Bohème*, which became very famous indeed, and ever since the word bohemian has meant an arty kind of life. In the meantime, the country that was Bohemia had become part of Czechoslovakia.

Bohunk

This old-fashioned politically incorrect term was used to mean someone from Eastern Europe: it blends Bo(hemian) with Hunk-(arian). There's an old American song, 'Bohunkus', about a farmer with a clumsy son. The term isn't heard much nowadays.

Boncer

This comes from an old British dialect word *boncer* or *bouncer*, meaning a big marble (shortened in British slang to 'bonce', meaning the head). Because the marble was big, and therefore rather splendid in comparison with other marbles, the word bouncer, or boncer, came to be used to mean things that were splendid or superior.

Then along came the word 'bonanza', from a different source: the Latin *bonus*, meaning good. Bonanza grew in use in America, originally applied to a mine, rich in ore, which made its owner wealthy. And a kind of melding took place so that 'boncer' (with a 'c') gradually became 'bonzer', meaning great, outstanding, sudden and unexpected riches.

So you have bouncer, boncer, bonsa, bonza and bonzer, all of which are variations on the same thing and all mean the same thing: splendid.

Katherine Mansfield used the word – she wrote about a fine house with a boncer garden, and you'll find it with two spellings: one edition has boncer and another has bonzer.

Bookbinder soup

The name conjures up images of thick white paste, possibly made from a lot of potatoes or, even worse, a sticky brown mixture made from boiled horses' hooves – like the glue associated with bookbinding.

But no, it's an American recipe, named after the Bookbinder family who ran some well-known restaurants. They made a characteristic soup that is in fact red, because it's based on a tomato broth in which pieces of red snapper are cooked. It could be classified as chowder, and sometimes includes clams.

A bowl of Bookbinder soup is very rich, and it isn't cheap. It is usually served as part of a seafood meal, and would be followed by smoked salmon or crab cakes.

(To) boot

We use it only when we're saying two things about a situation, for example, 'he is very handsome, and clever, to boot'. To boot is an Old English expression meaning 'in addition to' or 'as well', from an ancient word *boot*, meaning to compensate or counter-balance two pieces of information that aren't connected with each other.

Bosh

The word comes from Turkey. In Arabic *mâ-fîsh* means 'there's no such thing' and this is often shortened to *mûsh*. Turks somehow changed the 'm' into a 'b', and by the time the word appeared in English (1834) it had become 'bosh', meaning nonsense, useless, there's no such thing.

Boston marriage

The phrase is heard only occasionally, usually in the United States. It means that two women are living together, independently of any financial support from a man. This can sometimes be a lesbian relationship, but not necessarily. When the expression was current, it was not uncommon for single women from the academic professions to share housing, and being university or school teachers, or writers or artists, they could of course make a living without there being any husband in the equation.

If they continued to live together after retirement, the arrangement was sometimes referred to as a Boston marriage, whether they were sexual partners or not. A Boston marriage could simply be an arrangement of convenience and companionship between women who had like interests and didn't get on each other's nerves.

The expression arose in the United States after the publication of Henry James's novel *The Bostonians* in 1886. This book featured two strong-minded women of lively intellect who shared each other's lives – at least to a certain extent.

The phrase found renewed usage recently after David Mamet wrote a new play called *A Boston Marriage*, which concerned two outspoken women.

Bottoms up

It is believed to have originated at sea (as hundreds of commonly used words and expressions have done) and simply means raising your glass, then tipping it and emptying it into your mouth so that the bottom of the glass is pointing upwards!

Bought/brought

The distinction is very simple. Bought means to have paid money – to have purchased. Brought means to have caused movement from a distant place, to the place where you are.

Fund-raising fairs are often called bring and buys. The apparent confusion could possibly be allayed if they were called Brought and Boughts.

Bounder

Like cad, bounder means someone capable of ungentlemanly behaviour, but its ancestry is a bit different. Originally it simply meant an animal that leaps about a lot.

Social conventions have always been very strongly held in British life, and anyone who broke The Rules was bound to get themselves talked about. People who did break the rules, usually men, were seen as having 'bounded over' the conventions or bounded away from normal behaviour.

During the nineteenth century this term took hold but, curiously, it was more or less confined to men in the higher reaches of society and usually said only about well-dressed men who normally kept elegant company, but tended to be offensive, vulgar and irrepressible, particularly about women.

Box of birds

One etymologist describes this as a 'pleasing alliteration', rather like the similar phrase 'fighting fit' – which is actually what it originally meant. The phrase means that the speaker is feeling bright and breezy – even 'chirpy' – and has been in use since about 1940. It is thought to have originated with the Anzac troops in the Second World War.

(The) boy stood on the burning deck

The line has proved more enduring than the poem from which it comes. Felicia Hemans was a prolific and eminent poet during the early 1800s, a friend of Wordsworth and Sir Walter Scott. Times change, and since her death in 1835 the profile of Mrs Hemans has been considerably lower than before – almost invisible. Nowadays 99 per cent of her output is totally forgotten – except that she did create one line which every person in the English-speaking world knows.

It comes from a poem called 'Casabianca' published in 1826, which commemorates an incident that supposedly happened during the 1798 Battle of the Nile. Legend maintains that when one ship was in flames the youthful son of the ship's commander remained at his post on the ship and died when the flames caused the magazine to explode.

The poem 'Casabianca' is 40 lines long, 38 of which are not easily summoned to mind. But the opening two lines still crop up: 'The boy stood on the burning deck/Whence all but he had fled …'

Brand spanking new

Two different expressions have merged here. 'Brand' in this case means the metal symbol, hot from the forge, which is used to burn a mark into cattle and other animals or articles. When a thing has just been branded, the mark is clearly visible, not overgrown or weathered, so it is brand new. Shakespeare used a version of the expression when he called something 'fire new'.

'Spanking' is a dialect word from the seventeenth century which meant fit and lively, exceptionally showy and striking; it was often used to describe a dashing horse that moved briskly. The two expressions gradually merged, and the impact was doubled.

Brass monkeys and balls

The rack of brass or bronze on which a ship's cannon balls sat was known as a brass monkey. Some people are convinced that because iron freezes at a different temperature from the brass or bronze housing, the balls, when frozen, no longer fitted their indentations, and rolled off all over the deck. Thus, freezing weather did cause the balls to fall off the brass monkey.

Other people steeped in marine tradition feel strongly that in low temperatures the balls became frozen but stayed where they were – they were frozen on the brass monkey, so saying the balls froze off is a semantic mis-statement.

Yet another explanation is that ice surrounding the balls pushed them a little apart and slightly out of kilter with their indentations. When warmer winds meant that the ice melted, and no longer held them, the balls would respond by falling about.

So it's something of a paradox; marine lore seems to indicate that cold weather can freeze the balls on or off a brass monkey – but either way it is an amusing way of referring to freezing weather, and is here to stay.

(Parted) brass rags

It means an unpleasant separation, and is thought to have originated among sailors, who kept a particular pile of old rags just for cleaning brass – because such cloths became dirty and smelly and weren't used to clean anything else. Thus, if the phrase 'brass rags' describes something unpleasant and disagreeable, 'parted brass rags' means a separation that is acrimonious.

Bread buttered on the right side

It means being alert to one's own interests, knowing what to do in order to gain an advantage for yourself. The expression came into common use as a quote from Sir Walter Scott's novel *The Bride of Lammermoor* (1819) where one character, speaking of another, says, 'No man knows so well on which side his bread is buttered.'

Break a leg

This way of wishing good luck in the theatre before going onto the stage is an old custom that has nothing to do with the famous actress Sarah Bernhardt, who for part of her career actually did have a wooden leg.

There are two aspects to the probable origin of this theatre expression. First, for many centuries people have believed that you might be able to avert an unexpected unpleasant event if you pretend to foresee it as a facetious wish. It still happens in ordinary life when you hear someone say, 'I don't want it to rain today – so I'll take an umbrella with me.' The premise is that if you don't take an umbrella it will rain, and if you do take an umbrella, it won't.

In line with that old superstition, there was an old Yiddish expression originating in Germany – *Hals und Beinbruch* – that, although it means 'neck and leg both broken', was actually said to people to wish them luck.

There's no proof that the theatre tradition did uplift the old Yiddish or German phrase, but it is widely believed that one is a condensed version of the other. If you say 'break a leg' to someone who's about to go out on the stage and give a performance, what you're really saying is, 'I hope things go well for you and you don't have any accidents that could jeopardise the performance.'

Bric-a-brac

Miscellaneous small objects, from French *bric* meaning 'a piece, an undefined thing'. When it came into English the word was repeated with a different central vowel – 'brac' – to add a certain rhythm, a pleasing alliteration.

The same thing happened with the Old English word 'nac', meaning small objects, trinkets, trifles; the word gradually acquired a 'k' at the beginning, and again moved into pleasing alliteration by doubling itself then changing the vowel in the second part, becoming 'knick-knack'.

See also **Tranklements**.

Brown study

It has very little to do with the colour brown. Being in a brown study means that you're concentrating entirely on what's going on inside your head so you don't notice the passing of time or anything else happening in the real world. Your eyes are open, but you're not really seeing.

The origin of the expression is French. When people were lost in concentration it was usually thought that they were feeling sad, so it was referred to as *sombre rêverie* – sad thoughts. In French the word *brun*, meaning brown, also can mean gloomy, as does the word *sombre*. Some confusion arose when *sombre rêverie* drifted into English. The *sombre* became muddled with the *brun*, and it's been called a brown study since 1800.

Buckley's chance means no chance

Two influences seem to have combined to form this concept. William Buckley was transported from Britain to Australia as a prisoner for 'receiving a bolt of cloth knowing it to be stolen', and was in an Australian jail. In 1803 he escaped and headed for distant bush territory, relentlessly pursued by the law. His chances of survival were considered in popular assessment to be forlorn, if not hopeless.

At a later time (starting in 1851) a large department store in Melbourne was called Buckley and Nunn, and established an upmarket reputation which caused it to become a household name. By then it was known that Buckley had survived – and had published an account of his life as an escaped convict later pardoned, who became a tourist guide to Aboriginal areas.

It is believed that the earlier consideration of Buckley's unenviable position when he was an escapee living in the bush, gradually melded with a pun on the department store's name of Buckley and Nunn. The result: that 'Buckley's chance' was the same as none at all.

W. H. Ogilvie's *Fair Girls and Gray Horses* (1898) reports that they 'didn't have a Buckley's show to take the boasters down'.

Buckshee

It has come to mean 'free', but it didn't actually start out that way. Buckshee comes originally from a Persian word meaning 'gift' and the word travelled through Hindi and Urdu into Hindustani as *backsheesh*, which beggars in the street called out, asking for a handout, a gift.

The word drifted into use among English people in India, but it received its main boost into English during the First World War when the military used it freely. Instead of meaning just 'gift', it developed the meaning of being something free, that didn't have to be paid for. After the war, the meaning of being free remained.

Bulldozer

The machine we now call a bulldozer was developed between 1904 and 1922. But the word 'bulldozer' has a rather muddled origin. The generally approved version of how the machine arrived at that name is that the process began some time before the machine.

In America during the late 1800s the word 'bull' tended to become an intensifier and was put in front of words to emphasise that something big was being talked about. This particularly applied to medicines and strong drink and punishment – so that a big portion of something was called a 'bull' dose.

This extended to other things, and by the 1880s the term had developed into 'bulldoze' and was being used to describe intimidating behaviour, or getting things done in a blunt rather than subtle manner – anything that got in the way was levelled. A certain big pistol was known as a bulldozer. So there was an established idea that the term bulldoze implied big.

People in a less academic and more rural context always knew that strong bulls push their rivals aside during the mating season, so the term bulldozer became attached to the new machine we are now familiar with, because it too was big and strong. Gradually that rural use took over and the big machine became virtually the only thing known as a bulldozer.

Bum

The human posterior has been called a bum for more than six centuries and the reason why is lost in time. One school of thought is that it might be a sort of visual version of onomatopoeia, in that the shape of the word itself seems very appropriate – a short, plump, round word. Another possibility is that 'bum' is an abbreviated form of 'bottom'.

The origin of the American term, meaning 'tramp' or 'hobo', is a lot clearer. It's believed to be derived from the German word *bummler*, meaning useless or idle. So in English, a bum was originally a dawdler or loafer, and the term developed from there, at least in American English, to mean a person who is so idle they don't have a job, and from there to meaning someone who roams around without the stability of a home or employment.

There's also a slight influence springing from the concept of someone who is idle and sits on their bum a lot.

Bum's rush

This term dates to approximately 1920 and originally meant forcible ejection. Some believe it simply indicates that when a person is thrown out of somewhere, the onlookers see only the rejected one's bum rapidly leaving the premises. But a parallel belief is that when someone disreputable, such as a bum, staggered in somewhere, badly dressed and probably a bit smelly, they were sent packing. Hence anybody else given the runaround or asked to leave in a hurry was being treated as if they were a bum – getting the bum's rush.

Bum steer, bum rap

These also appear to come from North America, where 'bum' had gained a flavour of disapproval as a description of a dawdler, a useless person. As the word bum had a connotation of being bad, so bad advice or bad treatment could be implied by using the word at the beginning of an expression. We even say something is bum when it won't work properly.

Bunny

Bun is a very old British dialect word meaning a little round cake. Sometime in the sixteenth century it began to be used to refer to rabbits and squirrels, possibly because they were small and warm and roundish. By the seventeenth century the squirrels had drifted out of the picture and bunny remained an affectionate term for rabbits.

Burley/berley

Spelling is varied: 'burley' or 'berley' or 'berlie'. The word has been in use since 1855 (in *Our Antipodes*, by G.C. Munday) but its origin is not at all clear. It seems to have been connected with an earlier use of the same word when referring to nonsense or rubbish. But it also seems strongly connected to the expression 'to give it a burl', which itself may be derived from 'whirl'. A fanciful connection can be made with the notion of seasick fishermen vomiting over the side of a boat – sometimes described as 'giving a burl' – and the vomit attracting fish.

Bus boy

In the United States this describes the person in a restaurant who clears away the dishes and cutlery after they have been used. The term comes from Latin. A large horse-drawn conveyance, which held a lot of people, developed during the nineteenth century. The French called this a *voiture omnibus*, a French-plus-Latin combination meaning a vehicle that was for everyone – 'omnibus' meaning everyone, everywhere. This was the beginning of urban mass transport.

In time, and especially in Britain, the *voiture* was dropped, and the large vehicles became simply an omnibus, which became a common word to describe large-scale transport for people all going in the same direction. It became shortened to today's 'bus'.

The same meaning of omnibus – everyone, all people – also drifted into the American restaurant trade and by 1888 there is evidence that it was being used to describe assistants who did everything in a restaurant that the waiters didn't do, including the clearing of tables. In big restaurants, waiters usually have responsibility for an area or a number of tables, but an omnibus boy or girl, in the original Latin meaning of the word, can go everywhere to everyone, wherever there's a need to take away dirty cups, plates or cutlery.

The term 'bus boy' first appeared in print in 1913 and has been very common in the United States ever since – referring to a lowly restaurant assistant who isn't a waiter, and doesn't serve.

Butcher's hook

This was originally Cockney rhyming slang – butcher's hook rhymes with 'look', so 'to take a butcher's hook' means to take a look – and in the usual way with rhyming slang the second word is dropped, so it becomes 'take a butcher's'.

Australia and New Zealand have developed a secondary rhyming slang where butcher's hook rhymes with crook – in the sense of angry, disagreeable. So in Australia and New Zealand, 'going butcher's hook', or just 'going butcher's', means going crook.

Buttons (right and left)

There are several different versions of the reason for this, but this is the usually accepted one: Buttons originated in the thirteenth century. In the fifteenth century men, particularly in battle, dressed themselves, so their buttons were on the right because most men were right-handed.

Whereas women who could afford them, had servants (and because, in those times, buttons were very decorative and expensive, most women who had buttons also had maids.) So customarily, buttons on women's clothes were the mirror image of men's so that a right-handed maid could face the woman and button her clothes more easily.

Tailors caught on to this and made it normal practice to put men's buttons on their right, and women's on their left.

BVD underwear

BVD were the initials of an American firm, Bradley, Vorhees & Day, which made underwear in the first part of the twentieth century. The name was too long to say all the time, so the firm was referred to by its initials, BVD. In time the men's underwear they manufactured was also called BVDs, and the term is still used in the United States.

By and large

The term has a nautical origin and dates from at least 1670. To sail 'by and large' is to sail close to the wind and slightly off it, thus making it easier for the helmsman to steer and less likely for the vessel's course to be upset. In other words, it means to keep a ship on course so that it is sailing a good speed even though the direction of the wind is changing. The expression now means 'generally speaking', which is very roughly equivalent.

Cack-handed

For some time, 'cack' has been a fairly common vernacular term for excrement – something which is usually messy. People who are clumsy often find it difficult to be tidy, so the expression cack-handed really arose to describe anyone who had a clumsy, untidy way of doing things. It was not very complimentary and not very formal.

One source refers to the expression coming into wide use among the armed forces with a slightly different slant. Servicemen in some Asian areas discovered that toilet paper was unknown there, and consequently there was a customary division of duties between the left and the right hand: the right hand was always used for handling food, and the left hand was designated to do what toilet paper does in other cultures.

The servicemen who came across that interesting fact may have already been familiar with the term cack-handed, meaning just clumsy, and some bright spark extended it: in some areas the left hand was the 'cack' hand, so left-handed people were cack-handers – although left-handed people are not necessarily clumsy at all.

Cad

Cad is an abbreviation of 'caddie' or 'caddy', derived from the French word *cadet*. It's believed that this word was introduced to Britain by Mary Queen of Scots – she lived many years in France, and was a keen golfer. But one way or another, the word *cadet* slowly changed to caddie, which had several meanings: a caddie was not only someone who carried the clubs during a golf game, but the word was also used to describe an errand boy, and someone who hitched rides on carriages without paying.

Gradually the word divided into two. Caddie remained fixed to golfing duties and was quite respectable, but the shorter version 'cad' carried with it the connotation of people jumping onto the backs of carriages and hitching a ride without paying, so it was applied to bad boys and vulgar men, capable of ungentlemanly behaviour. Bounder is a similar term.

Caddy

The Malayan word *kati* is a unit of weight, just over half a kilogram – roughly a pound – so a pound of tea was a kati and somehow that became the name of the box or tin it was kept in.

Cajun

The provinces of Canada located on the Atlantic Ocean were collectively known as Acadia (note: not Arcadia). Settlers there had strong links with France and spoke French. After Canada came under the rule of Britain, many Acadians refused to swear allegiance to the king, and from 1750 onwards started to emigrate to the United States, seeking a new life around the Mississippi in Louisiana.

When asked who they were, the Acadians' French accent caused some confusion: the reply sounded like 'Ah-kay-jun'. From this the word 'cajun' developed, pertaining to these people, their language, their music and, most famously, their food.

Calibre

Describing someone as being 'of the highest calibre' and the measuring term applied to firearms are versions of the same word. The English words 'calibre' and 'calliper' and 'calibrate' are all descended from an ancient Arabic word *qalib*, which meant 'shoe last'. That word gradually underwent both a form of corruption and a corruption of sense. From being just the last of a shoe, it came to mean 'a mould' and it developed a subsidiary meaning of referring to a person's quality, character, and social standing – hence the expression 'of the highest calibre'.

Later, when gun manufacture became common, the word calibre underwent a corruption of sense, and became the word used to describe the internal diameter of a firearm or the diameter of a shell or bullet. But its meaning of quality of character remains quite valid.

Calling bird

In the song 'Twelve days of Christmas' to say 'calling' bird is a mistake. The song was first published in 1780 and in those days it said 'colly' birds. The word colly means something related to coal, therefore blackened by coal dust (colly survives in collier and colliery). So a colly bird was a bird which looked as if it were covered in coal dust. In other words, a blackbird.

Sometime in the following 200 years, people forgot that name for blackbirds, so colly didn't make any sense. So printers started putting in 'calling' bird, though that doesn't make any sense either.

Cancer/crab

The disease we call cancer was known well over 2000 years ago, and it was named by Hippocrates, often called the father of medicine. He used the ancient Greek word for crab – *karkinos* – but not because of how the disease felt to the sufferer.

The cancers Hippocrates was able to identify were malignant tumours which had horrible veins stretching out from them, so he called them *karkinos* because they looked like a crab. The Greek word was modified by the Latin language into the word cancer, and has remained that way ever since.

There is an echo of the Greek *karkinos* in the word 'canker', which is still used but seems to be applied more to animals and plants than to humans.

Then there is the sign of the zodiac known as Cancer, which doesn't actually look much like a crab. It's called that because of an ancient legend that Hercules was bitten by a crab while he was fighting the beast Hydra, and Hercules crushed the crab. So one of Hercules' enemies, Hera, rewarded the creature for having tackled Hercules by giving it a place in the heavens – and the constellation of stars with that name travels backwards and sideways, like a crab.

In recent times there has been some resistance to the name Cancer being applied to a zodiac sign, and there is a move in the United States to replace it with the name Moon Child.

Candy

The word is very old – its ancestor lies in the Dravidian languages (75 related languages spoken by over 200 million people in India,

Pakistan, Nepal, Bangladesh, Iran, Singapore and Malaysia). From there it came through Arabic as *qand* – which referred to cane.

At about the same time, Arabic was borrowing from Persian and Sanskrit the word *shakar*, which eventually became 'sugar' in English. As far back as the year 900, Arab nations were making sugar into sweetmeats, and because sugar came from canes, by association the words *shakar* and *qandah* came to be associated with cooked sugar. When the term drifted into other languages it was usually double-barrelled – sugar candy. In English, eventually everybody knew that sugar candy was made from sugar, so that word was dropped and we were left with just candy, meaning cooked sugar.

The word is used mainly in America, less so elsewhere except for specific confections such as candied fruit – but even that is often referred to as crystallised.

Can of worms

To 'open a can of worms' is a comparatively recent expression, first noticed in Canada during the 1950s. The imagery is fairly straightforward. The concept refers to a fisher's little pot of bait – which with its lid on might look neat and harmless. But if you take the lid off, there are worms and maggots inside – not an attractive sight.

By the 1970s the term was in general use in the United States, and then around the English-speaking world. It generally signifies the revealing of unpleasantness or difficulties that were previously concealed, and may have been better left alone. Some people see in the expression a link to the ancient legend of Pandora – she who opened a box which let out all the evils the world now knows. The perceived similarity is that worms and maggots tend to crawl out of their bait tin once it is opened, and are difficult to put back inside.

Canola oil

A plant crop whose seeds are widely used for the extraction of oil is called 'rape'. In this context the name is related to the Latin *rapum* – turnip. The change of name resulted from the Canadian producers of cooking oil deciding to rename the product because 'rape oil' had an unattractive connotation. So, can (for Canada) combined with *ola* (oil) to make a new word.

The same thing happened with tamarillo, which used to be called tree tomato but has nothing to do with tomatoes. Its new name is a made-up word from New Zealand, starting with tomato – changed to 'tama' to give a Maori feel to the word – and adding 'illo' to suggest that it is small. The new name has been universally accepted.

Kiwifruit, too was deliberately renamed; it used to be called Chinese gooseberry, and it does come from China but isn't a gooseberry. In Chinese the fruit's name means 'monkey peach' but in English it was re-named kiwifruit in 1959.

(Can't have your) cake and eat it too

In this context, the word 'have' means 'keep' – to simultaneously eat your cake but also keep it – which isn't normally possible.

The saying has been in use since the sixteenth century but its first known appearance (in John Heywood's *Proverbs,* 1546) was the other way round: 'Both eat your cake and have your cake.' The expression was used of people who, for example, behaved with religious purity one day a week, and then were ruthless landlords and business sharks on the other days. They were serving God and Commerce – two opposing advantageous things going on at the same time. The phrase was almost one of envy.

Over time, two things happened: first, the saying somehow became reversed and, second, it changed into the negative. So instead of saying, 'Eat your cake and have it,' which was a statement of envy and disapproval, the expression developed into, 'You can't have your cake and eat it,' which is an admonition.

Car

There are four words associated with transport vehicles that sound similar: chariot, cart, car and carriage. Chariot, cart and car are closely related; they've come into English through Old French in the two forms *carre* and *carete*, originating from the Latin *carrus*, which was a kind of wagon. It's not quite right to say that car is short for cart; they are related, but one is not intended to be a shortened version of the other. Carriage also comes from Old French, but from the word *carier*, to carry, so its ancestry is marginally different.

Carboy

Carboys, the big, beautiful coloured glass jars once found in chemists' shops, have nothing to do with cars or with boys. The word originated in Persia (now Iran): *qaraba* simply meant a big jar, especially one that could hold acid and corrosive liquids – and glass will resist most of those. The Persian word was adopted into the English language during the 1700s and is still there, though very few chemists seem to have carboys now.

Carol

Carol comes from an Old French word which actually meant 'singing and dancing while standing in a circle', so early Christmas carols were much more lively and rambunctious than we think of them now.

Nowadays, the word carol is used very loosely to describe songs which actually fall into three separate divisions:

1. genuine old Christmas carols such as 'God Rest ye Merry, Gentlemen' and 'Oh, Come all ye Faithful'

2. Christmas hymns, which are rather less lively

3. songs that are somehow about Christmas but don't actually mention Jesus, such as 'Santa Claus is Coming to Town' or 'Rudolph the Red-Nosed Reindeer'. These are not carols, but Christmas songs.

Carte blanche

In simple terms, it is French for white paper or blank sheet and when used in a military context referred to situations of unconditional surrender. When a foe was clearly defeated, he was required to put his signature on a blank piece of paper, knowing he would therefore have to agree to whatever terms the victors filled in at their leisure.

In English, it was first seen in print in 1707.

Nowadays the expression is used in a figurative sense only,

meaning that a person with a job to do or a project in hand has no restrictions and no budget limit.

Cat has got their tongue

There are about eight different 'explanations' for how this phrase came about – most of them speculation. The following story is the one that has gained the most attention:

In ancient centuries there was a custom among Oriental potentates to punish a thief by cutting his hand off, and punish a liar by cutting his tongue out. In both cases the severed body parts were actually given to the ruler's cats so, in some cases, the cat really did have someone's tongue – and that person wasn't able to speak.

Catch a break

In an American context, 'break' is often a shortened form of break-through. You'll hear it as 'a lucky break' or just 'a break', meaning an unexpected advantage, while 'a bad break' is an unforeseen stroke of bad luck. To give someone a break is to allow them an opportunity, and 'catch a break' could be explained as seizing a chance that's fleetingly available.

The popularity of surfing during the 1960s brought all kinds of surfing terms into wide public use – 'catch a break' was one. Surf language also includes beach breaks, reef breaks and shore breaks. Surfers use it about very precisely defined moments, but in general use it signifies the taking of an opportunity.

Catchword

Back in the days of handwritten manuscripts, a catchword was the separate word written right at the bottom of a page, after the main text finished. This let you know what the first word was going to be on the next page when you turned over. You could catch the word on the hoof, so to speak, and not lose the flow of the word order while you were turning the page. Gradually the catchword shifted to the top of the page and can be seen in dictionaries as a guide to which spellings appear on the page beneath.

In time, catchword came also to mean a few other things, such as the last word of an actor's speech, which the next actor would pick up on, to deliver his lines. It was like a cue.

Then catchword came to be used for any word that caught attention. The term is widely used in advertising and politics when public attention is attracted with a word, or group of words known as a catchphrase.

(Let the) cat out of the bag

For years this expression has meant to reveal a secret, or put about damaging information that was supposed to be confidential. There are two schools of thought about its origin. Some scholars say it is directly related to the pig in the poke or pouch-bag (see also **Pig in a poke**) – if the buyer demanded that the vendor actually show him the squealing animal within the poke, then he'd see a cat; a secret would be revealed, and the cat would be out of the bag.

But there is also a parallel explanation arising from the old-time shipboard practice of punishing sailors with an evil whip known as a cat-o'-nine-tails. When a sailor was summoned for some mis-demeanour, and he saw that the cat had been removed from the pouch it was kept in and was ready for use, then the cat was out of the bag and he knew something unpleasant was about to happen.

Cats have nine lives

It's a myth, of course: cats don't have nine lives. But they're particu-larly good at surviving disasters with the one life they do have. Cats are small, lightweight, fast and flexible and have excellent balance. Everybody has always known that cats can survive falls that other animals can't, and they can escape very quickly from risky situations. This somehow engendered the idea that cats have more chances at life than other creatures.

Ancient Egyptians revered cats, not only because they regarded them as having god-like qualities, but also because they were pract-ical beasts and killed rats. And the Egyptians noticed cats' ability to survive falls and accidents. Thus they reasoned the animal had more lives than the usual one.

Ancient Egyptians were also keen on numerology and the number three had significance for them, as it still does to many cultures. Anything three times three was especially significant, so it was honouring the cats to declare that they possessed three times three lives – nine. This belief inevitably drifted out from Egypt – it was mentioned in Arabic and Indian fables in the eighth century – and eventually reached the English language.

Ancient Egyptians weren't the only people to find significance in certain numbers. Even in modern times, the figure nine is ubiquitous: nine holes of golf, a cat-o'-nine-tails, ninepins for bowling, Deep Space Nine, nine months of pregnancy, Cloud Nine, the whole nine yards (see also **Dressed to the nines**). So it's not surprising that the concept of nine lives has a ring to it.

Besides the athleticism of cats, and the various resonances of the figure nine, the belief that cats had nine lives got tangled up with the medieval European belief in witches, so that the myth grew that witch-women could change themselves into cats a total of nine times. That superstition faded away, but the belief in the cat's nine lives remained. It found its way into print in a book called *Beware the Cat* written by William Baldwin in 1553 and it's mentioned in *Romeo and Juliet* in 1596. From then on the myth of cats having nine lives has remained in the English language.

Catwalk

Obviously there's a connection between a cat's ability to walk along a narrow strip with no side support, and fashion models parading on a raised ramp with no rail. The word isn't new. It has been in use since at least the middle of the nineteenth century, or possibly earlier, when parts of sailing ships were known as catwalks and building sites used the term for high, narrow communication bridges.

The phrase started to move into more common use around 1910–20 in relation to dirigible aircraft. A horizontal ladder-type structure on which the crew could move inside the aircraft from one part to another was called a catwalk. Later the term moved to other aircraft and was used in the Second World War to describe the long plank that stretched between the cockpit and the tail inside bomber aircraft.

All these applications were sometimes called cat's walk rather than catwalk, but the 's' was gone by the time the term started being used in theatre and fashion shows, from about 1950 onwards. During the 1960s the terms ramp and walkway were still being used to describe the long narrow platform on which fashion models walked, but by the 1970s catwalk seemed to have become the universal term.

Census

The practice of taking a census, which records the numbers making up the population and also their ages, sex, financial situation and so on, dates back to ancient Rome, and the name comes from the Roman word *censere*, meaning 'to assess'. A census is not only a counting, it is an assessment.

Chairman

The 'man' in chairman is from the Latin *manus*, which specifically means 'hand' but carries the strong connotation of power. We hear the basic Latin word for hand in several surviving languages: Italian and Spanish *mano*, French *main*.

In English, *manus* survives in words like manual. But the connotation of hand meaning power also survives in such words as manager (which has nothing to do with being a man, but means the power of administering) and emancipate (which means to give power). We hear the connotation of the hand having power in such expressions as 'the hand of God'.

By coincidence, the English word 'man', meaning male, looks the same as the Latin derivation 'man', meaning hand or power of the hand. So 'chairman' refers to the power of the person holding a superior office in an organisation; it doesn't really mean the person is male. The word has been in use since 1654.

There is no real need for words like chairwoman or chairperson; chairman would do. But it must be acknowledged there has been confusion for some time, and the word chairwoman has also been used for some years. When discussion was widespread about whether 'chairman' or 'foreman' cast a connotation of maleness on an administrative post, one Judge in a publicised trial solved the matter neatly by addressing the jury spokesperson as Madam Foreman, which sounded absolutely right.

Charwoman/cup of char

There is no relationship between the 'char' in these two terms; they come from entirely different ancestries. A very Old English word *cerr*, meant small amounts of work, developed into two modern words – 'chore', which is usually a domestic job, and 'char' which means much the same thing and is associated with a woman doing domestic jobs. But 'char' when it means tea is Chinese – *ch'a* – and was simply absorbed into English more or less intact.

There's a third player in the field – 'char' meaning to burn and blacken. This has no relation to the others; it's a shortened form of 'charcoal'.

Chatham House Rules

A building in London called Chatham House is the base for the Royal Institute of International Affairs. Confidential matters discussed within the building have given rise to the phrase Chatham House Rules. This is a restriction placed on information discussed there: when you're told something under Chatham House Rules you can use the information but you must cover your tracks and not attribute a view or any information to any particular person.

Another version is sometimes said of a meeting held somewhere else, but 'under Chatham House rules', meaning that information discussed at the meeting stays in the room (even though it's not at Chatham House) and the details must not be discussed outside.

Cheapskate

It hasn't anything to do with actual skating. But there is argument about how 'cheapskate' came to be. One school of thought says it is related to the Scottish and English dialect word *blatherskite*, meaning a boastful person (often shortened to skite). But there's also an old word 'skate' meaning a worn-out horse. Therefore a cheapskate was a horse which didn't cost much but also wasn't much use. This has

74

developed into meaning a stingy person who orders a job which is done for a low cost, but shoddily.

Chestnuts

The nuts originated in Asia and were cultivated and grown by ancient Greeks. One region of Greece the trees grew freely in was the state of Thessaly – a place called Kastania, known for its prolific crops of chestnuts. It is believed to have been named after the Greek word for chestnuts (which is, of course, *Kastania*).

Later the Romans were also partial to the nuts, and the Latin version of the Greek town's name was Castanea, which became the official Latin name for the chestnut tree (and still is). When the nuts came to England they were referred to in English as castanea nuts, which was corrupted to chesten nuts, then narrowed down further to chestnuts.

But another legacy of the town's name in English is castanets. Their Spanish name *castañuelas* relates to their being similar in colour to, and shaped like, big shiny chestnuts.

Chip off the old block

The concept dates back to 270 BC, when Theocritus wrote of 'a chip off the old flint', meaning one who reproduces a parent's characteristics (usually the father's).

By the 1600s the image had moved from flint to wood. The phrase can be found in a 1626 play called *Dick of Devonshire*: 'Your father used to come home to my mother, and why not I be a chippe of the same blocke, out of which you two were cutte?'

Chip on the shoulder

It means to have a grievance, to bear a grudge, to be convinced that you're somehow disadvantaged and that things are deliberately set against you.

The concept relates back to an ancient practice in Britain's Royal Navy dockyards whereby shipwrights took home any chips resulting from the day's work. But exploitation was suspected – that some perfectly good timber was being cut up to masquerade as 'chips' that the men took home. A ruling in 1756 stipulated that men might take home only enough chips to form a bundle carried on their shoulder. This was met with resentment.

Much later, the expression as we now know it took form in America. In 1830, a Long Island newspaper described a schoolyard practice whereby an aggressive boy would place a piece of wood on one shoulder and dare someone else to knock it away. This was the equivalent of throwing down the gauntlet. It is believed that aggressive American boys had learnt of the practice from aggressive frontier men. He who knocked the chip off did so at his peril. So having a chip on your shoulder meant you were belligerent and always ready for a fight.

There's an alternative belief about the expression: that it comes from the days of saw-pits, when logs were sawn by hand. One person sawed from a top position on the log and the other was placed underneath. The man sawing in the lower position would be showered with chips from the upper sawyer, which was annoying and uncomfortable. Complaining about this led to his irritation being described as resulting from a chip on his shoulder.

(Musicians') chops

In this context, 'chops' is a down-to-earth replacement for *embouchure*, which is the formal word meaning the position and control of the muscles around the lips and mouth, crucial for playing brass and wind instruments. This has given rise to the myth that women enjoy being kissed by brass instrument players because they're notably powerful in the lips!

Gradually chops, meaning the mouth and lips in particular, has moved to a wider area so musicians now use it to indicate musical skill in general.

Chutney/relish

There is not much difference between the two. 'Relish' was originally a French word, used by the English since 1530 to describe special enjoyment, usually something that was available occasionally as a treat and might not last long, just as nowadays you can relish swiming in summer. By the late 1600s, 'relish' had also come to mean something special and tasty added to the dinner table – again, a little treat.

Later, when the British started travelling to India a lot, they brought back jars of spicy mixtures known by the Hindi word *chutni*. This was always chopped-up sweet fruit treated with acids, sour herbs and hot flavourings. Mango chutney was the big one, and still is. Gradually, the new-fangled *chutni* became the attractive thing added to the dinner table, rather than the relish. And the two words became more or less interchangeable.

There are some people who insist that there is a difference, that real chutneys are made with a fruit as the main ingredient, whereas relishes are made with vegetables, but food experts concede that there really isn't any difference.

Clean as a whistle

It is generally believed that this has been an example of one word being corrupted into another. In strict literal terms, the expression no longer makes sense because a whistle might not be clean – it could be full of someone else's cold germs. But, whether it's clean or not, a whistle is always clear, and that's the reason for the saying.

When the expression came into use – at least as early as the 1800s – it was 'as clear as a whistle', because although a whistle is small, its tone can usually be heard across a great distance. No matter how noisy an environment, you can usually identify the sound of a whistle and you're not likely to mistake it for anything else.

So, for example, in the 1800s if the roof fell off a derelict building and no remnant was left, you would say it fell off clear as a whistle. Totally, utterly, completely.

But over the decades, 'clear' became corrupted to 'clean' and the expression moved with it so people started to associate cleanliness with whistles: 'she scrubbed the floor as clean as a whistle', which doesn't really make sense. It would have made marginally better sense if the words had stayed as they were before: 'she scrubbed the floor as clear as a whistle'; that is, totally clean, no marks visible.

Cleave

The word has two distinct and opposing meanings. To cut something in half is to cleave it, possibly with a cleaver. Yet if you adhere to a form of thinking or religion, or a particular relationship, it will be said that you are cleaving to it – sticking to your belief through thick and thin. It is as bizarre as 'flammable' and 'inflammable', which look like opposites but in fact mean the same thing.

Cloud nine

It's a genuine meteorological term! In 1803 a British scientist called Luke Howard was studying the differences between clouds, and he formed some classifications that became the basis of what was called a Cloud Atlas, which eventually came to be published in 1896.

The development of aviation during the First World War increased interest in and emphasis on cloud formation, and an updated atlas was published in 1932. After the Second World War, a major update was published in 1956. This described ten identifiable types of cloud divided into 14 subspecies, based on factors such as their transparency, their geometrical arrangement and their height above the earth. Their depth is also taken into account – the distance from the base of the cloud to its top.

Within the cloud species category, Number Nine is classified as a cumulo-nimbus cloud, which is slightly unusual because it is the only cloud within the classification which can have a base almost right down on the earth's surface. But the top of that kind of cloud is the highest that standard meteorological cloud measurements go – about 18,000 metres (approx. 60,000 feet).

So cloud nine does exist, and can be very high indeed. When a person is very happy, they feel in an elevated state; hence the expression 'being on cloud nine'.

Clowder

This word is not often heard, but it is the internationally recognised term used to describe a gathering of cats. This is a rare occurrence; a herd of cows, a flock of sheep, or a flight of birds are commonplace phenomena, but cats don't normally gather in large groups.

The background to 'clowder' is very strange. It developed from two ancient words, 'clot' and 'clod', which were more or less interchangeable and both meant a shapeless lump. Descendants of the two words are still around. Clot came to mean a shapeless lump which had gathered in liquid, like milk or blood. Clod refers to a shapeless lump of something solid, like soil.

But clod was also sometimes said as 'clodder', and it gradually developed an extra connotation: it was used to describe a shapeless disorganised mass or group that was accompanied by pandemonium and even noise.

By the late nineteenth century four distinctly different words had settled down:

1. **clot**   a shapeless lump, usually associated with liquid

2. **clod**   another shapeless lump, usually solid

3. **clutter**   a disorganised collection of generally stationary objects

4. **clowder**   an untidy assembly of objects which moved around and possibly even made a noise.

Thus, clowder is the perfect word to describe an assembly of cats.

Coarse fishing

The term originated in Britain, where 'game' fish (salmon and trout) could be fished in waters to which the gentry had access. All the other people were confined to fishing in fresh water for other species.

International fishing contests have developed into being a very big deal, and the rules governing them are precise. But to describe fishing in more general and conversational terms: 'fly fishing' (obviously) uses flies; 'lure' fishing uses spinners and lures; and 'coarse' fishing uses bait, and is in fresh water – lakes, ponds and rivers.

Cockles of your heart

The medieval Latin name for the heart gave us the word 'cockles' to describe its inner structure – although it's been translated two different ways. In 1669 the English physician and physiologist Richard

Lower wrote *Tractatus de Corde* (Treatise on the Heart) in which he referred to the ventricles of the heart as *cochlea cordis* where *cochlea* was interpreted to mean 'shell shaped', and the casual version of that word – cockle – seeped into English.

But the Latin *cochlea* could also refer to the shape of a snail, and is still used as the name for the inner ear. So whichever interpretation of *cochlea* has given us cockle, in either case the heart is being compared to a mollusc.

Cocky, cocksure, cockeyed

A number of words and expressions are connected to birds – and 'cocky' and 'cocksure' are part of the family of rooster expressions. Cocky and cocksure are believed to be shortened versions of 'cock of the walk': proud and self-confident and perhaps even a bit cheeky because of it, exactly like a stroppy rooster. This image of the cock rooster looking you in the eye and standing tall also carries an echo of the 'cocked hat' and a gun being 'cocked' – both refer to something being turned up, and a confident rooster certainly stands up.

The odd one out is 'cockeyed'. This means off-balance, out of kilter, and is believed to be a survival of a very old use of the word cock, meaning 'fight', as related to the once-popular sport of cock-fighting. 'Cock' plus 'eye' meant one eye fighting with the other.

Codger

Codger normally describes a slightly eccentric old person and is faintly affectionate. It becomes a criticism only when it has a couple of adjectives in front of it – for example, a mean old codger, a drunken old codger.

The origin of the word dates back to the 1400s when Britain had a good many travelling salesmen, attending village fairs and also going door to door. They were known as 'cadgers' and had a slightly disreputable air. Over the space of 200 years, 'cadger' developed into two different words. One of those came to mean a person who borrowed stuff all the time, or was always looking to use someone else's advantage. That meaning remains today.

But cadger also slowly developed into codger, meaning an old person who was a little contemptible. Gradually the contempt died away from the word, and from the 1800s onwards calling someone a codger ceased to be a put-down. It simply means that they're old, and possibly a wee bit eccentric.

Codswallop

There's no definite scholastic proof about the origin of the word codswallop, but the generally accepted version is as follows.

Besides the usual meanings of 'wallop', in nineteenth-century Britain the word was also used as a slang term meaning beer. Round about 1875 a man called Hiram Codd took out a patent for a kind of bottle that could hold bubbles inside because it contained a marble that 'stoppered' it. The bottles were used for selling mineral water, which was fizzy. The people who associated bubbles and fizz with beer, which was alcoholic, started to refer to Mr Codd's fizzy drinks as 'Codd's-wallop' because it wasn't.

This gradually narrowed to 'codswallop' – and extended its meaning to anything somewhat deceptive or not delivering what it promised, and eventually it came to mean anything that wasn't true or was just nonsense, a waste of time.

Cohort

Cohort is a word which has developed from a military term in Latin. *Cohors* was a unit of infantry in an ancient Roman legion. Probably because the men all fought in a united cause, the English version (with a 't') developed, meaning a group with the same purpose or having a common factor.

Cold shoulder

The expression was first seen in print in 1816 in Sir Walter Scott's novel *The Antiquary* when a countess turns her back dismissively on someone (Scott himself explained the meaning as 'cold and reserved'). Thus the expression appears to have begun as literal – showing disdain by actual body language. In later years it has extended to a figurative sense – to ignore, to be unwelcoming, to treat with hauteur.

A secondary explanation is sometimes offered. In medieval times, when house guests were staying, new meats were cooked for them every day and served hot. If the guests stayed too many days and became a nuisance, then the host would stop cooking new meals and would serve them the previous day's meat – often a shoulder of mutton – now cold and considered inferior. So the overstaying guests would get the message.

Collateral damage

This began as a euphemistic description of the number of civilians actually killed in a military attack. Instead of saying 'Hundreds of civilians were killed', the report referred only to 'collateral damage'.

Besides dead bodies, the expression can now include upheavals of other kinds caused by an attack.

College

In strict dictionary terms, 'college' describes an institute of higher learning, for instance a constituent part of a larger university. But, over time, the meaning of words can move into different contexts, and the word college is often used to describe secondary schools. It may be some form of snobbery to make things sound better than they are, but there's no law against it.

A 'college' can be an ordinary secondary school (either state or private), a top-level university (Magdalen College, Oxford; Kings College, Cambridge; the twelve Colleges of Yale), organisations granting approval in a specific activity (Trinity College of Music; Occupational Therapy College; Royal College of Heraldry), or commercial organisations for trade training (College of Chiropractic; International Travel Training College; Hairdressing College).

These days the word college is used anywhere, anytime, to name any institution where people assemble in order to learn.

Collywobbles

The word has been around for nearly 200 years and most sources, including the *Oxford Dictionary*, relate it to colic, which is a painful condition named originally from the word colon. The strong suggestion is made that the word collywobbles is actually an evolved combination of the word colic, meaning trouble in the stomach, with wobbles, meaning general disorientation. So it's not just a painful stomach, like colic, but a general feeling of unease, usually nervousness, or diarrhoea.

Columbia

A country, a university, a film studio, the district co-extensive with Washington – most of the places and institutions named Columbia are named after Christopher Columbus. There was a Saint Columba in Ireland in 597 and an Italian theatre character called Colomba or Columbine, but neither of those made the same impact on the world as Christopher did. He is the reason why we have so many Columbias. From 1738 the name 'Columbia' was sometimes used as a fanciful name for the whole of America.

Conchologist

The Latin for spiral-shaped or snail-like is *cochlea*, which itself is connected to the Greek word *konkhe*. English words are derived from each, all connected with a curved shape. From *konkhe* comes conch, a spiral mollusc (and also a style of domed roof). People who collect shells of all kinds, not just conch shells, are known as conchologists.

From *cochlea* we get the naturally curled or twisted part of the human inner ear, and sometimes a winding staircase. But the word can also refer to a gentle curved shape, not necessarily spiral. So cochleariform means 'spoon-shaped'. And a cochlear is the spoon from which consecrated elements are administered in some Christian services, Cochlearia is a kind of grass with spoon-shaped leaves, and cochlearius is a heron with a spoon-shaped beak. All have a connection with a gently curving shape.

And so, over time, the name cochlearist has become attached to someone who collects spoons.

Contumely

Contumely is a noun meaning 'lies or invective'. Normally English words ending -ly are adverbs – they add to the meaning of a verb, e.g. she walked slowly, he ate ravenously. But this word is derived from the Latin noun *contumelia*, which itself is related to the Latin *tumere*, to swell (as in tumescence). *Contumelia* in Latin means insulting language, scornful rudeness, disgrace and ignominy – and is a noun. This gravitated into English with its final 'ia' changed into a 'y', so it looks the same as English adverbs, but isn't one.

The word isn't heard much today, but survives in one famous context – the 'to be or not to be' speech of Shakespeare's Hamlet:

> For who would bear the whips and scorns of time,
> The oppressor's wrong, the proud man's contumely,
> The pangs of disprized love, the law's delay …

Cool

This used to have one meaning: 'a temperature which is not quite cold', but has since become one of the most difficult words to elucidate. Its many (new) meanings are usually quite clear to the person using it and those hearing it, but it's hard to pin down what might be called a dictionary definition. In some paradoxical way 'cool' has replaced the former use of 'hot', meaning 'interesting and currently very fashionable'.

Apart from its early straightforward reference to temperature, the creeping in of cool meaning 'imperturbable' was pinned down as early as 1732 by British poet John Gay in 'New Songs on New Similes' and the proliferation of meanings began from there and continued through the following centuries.

When the term travelled to the United States it found popularity there – Scott Fitzgerald used it in *The Great Gatsby* (1925) and from the 1930s it became familiar as a term of praise among jazz musicians and fans for new and pleasing jazz styles. From then on a bewildering variety of applications has grown. As synonyms for 'cool' a selection includes: discreet, excellent, audacious, sophist-icated, assured, controlled, cautious, unruffled, confident, wonderful, aloof, pleasant, shrewd, laid-back, stylish, tranquil, disengaged, postponed, ended, uninvolved, desirable, agreed …

These have bred many subsidiary expressions – a 'cool million' originally indicated that the person dealing with that amount of money was stoic and not showing naïve excitement. But in general 'cool' simply designates something, anything, of which the speaker approves.

Of course cool can also still mean slightly chilly, but using it with that meaning is hardly cool.

Cop

Some policemen did wear copper badges and copper buttons, but the word 'cop' has nothing to do with that; it's much older than the badges. And there is a vaguely held belief that cop is an acronym for Constable on Patrol – but that's an old wives' tale as well.

Cop was actually a verb in English before it became used as a noun. The verb 'to cop' has been used in English since 1700, meaning 'to catch' or 'lay hold of'. Its ultimate ancestor is Latin: *capere*, to seize (which also survives in the word 'capture'). It seems that the term 'to cop' was first used not about policemen but quite the opposite. It referred to thieves and low-lifes, so that someone stealing from the public was called a 'copper' because he was seizing and laying hold of property.

But in the middle of the 1800s the term shifted to describe the situation where policemen were apprehending criminals – they were seizing them and laying hold of them, so they were copping them. This verb form shifted the action so that the law enforcement officer doing the seizing and holding became a copper or a cop.

Cordon bleu

In medieval France, high-ranking knights wore medallions of rank hanging on blue silk ribbons. When they met, they wore their medals on the blue ribbon and they were fed magnificent meals. Gradually the name of the ribbon on which the medal hung shifted to describe the splendour of the cooking.

Corn syrup

Corn contains no syrup (unlike, say, maple) but its kernels do contain starch, which is turned into cornflour. From this subsidiary product, corn syrup is made by chemically processing the cornflour with acid, which manipulates the cornflour's starch components into three kinds of sugar: glucose, dextrose and maltose. The result is a clear, intensely sweet syrup which can be described as 'natural', but only just. (Golden syrup is entirely different; it's extracted from sugar cane and is totally natural.)

Corporal (rank)

Two influences combined to form this word. It dates back to Italian armies of the 1400s when an important tactical formation was the *squadra* or square, headed by a veteran soldier known as the *capo de squadra*, the 'head of the square'. Gradually this term was shortened to *caporale* and it came to mean the leader of a small body of soldiers.

The term was picked up by the French and was influenced by the Latin *corpus*, meaning 'body'. The term settled into being corporal. By the 1700s the word had come into English and has been there ever since, its Italian origins and Latin influence long forgotten.

Cos lettuce

The ancient Arabic word for what we call lettuce was *xus*, and one particular kind of this vegetable appeared to proliferate on the Greek island of Kos. From this later influence, or possibly from both, the name Kos settled into use. It is also sometimes called 'romaine' lettuce, the French version of its name in Italy where it is known as Roman lettuce.

Cotton on

It means to understand an idea that's being presented, or to like someone and become friendly with them. The saying is believed to have originated in cotton mills, where tiny bits of thread or cloth were inclined to stick all over whatever you were wearing and were a nuisance to pluck off. So 'cotton on' gradually acquired the sense of adhering to something or someone. Eventually, when someone grasped the basis of an idea they were being told, it was as if the idea had stuck, and was being understood. So, they had cottoned on.

Couch potato

When television became popular, Americans created a slang term for it: the boob tube. This term was never used in Britain, where boob tube meant a tight knitted top (Americans prefer not to be reminded that television was a British invention). People in America who watched a lot of television became 'boob tubers'.

In 1976 American illustrator Robert Armstrong published an iconic cartoon showing a well-known tuber – a potato – lying indolently on a couch watching a television set. Robert Armstrong registered the name Couch Potato as a trademark for his lounging potato to appear on T-shirts and in several books: *The Couch Potato Handbook*, *The Couch Potato Guide to Life* (by Dr Spudd) and *The Couch Potato Cookbook*. The term rapidly became a standard description for someone watching too much TV.

Country mile

A 'country mile' is often used as a metaphor for something very lengthy and far-reaching. The term arose as a matter of perception. A mile in the country and one in the city are exactly the same, but in times when rural roads were winding, less well-formed than urban routes, and more sparsely housed, to urban folk travelling a mile in the country seemed longer than it was.

The concept is mentioned in Frederick de Kruger's poem 'The Villager's Tale' in 1829:

> The travelling stage had set me down
> Within a mile of yon church-town;
> 'Twas long indeed, a country mile.

Coward

The word seems as if it might be related to 'cow-herd' but it isn't. Coward is derived from an Old French word *cuard*, which was borrowed even further back from the Latin *cauda*, meaning tail. The word coward is generally used about someone scared of danger or pain or difficulty, and it is thought that the Latin word for tail was applied because such a person is like a dog with its tail between its legs.

Cowlicks

On people, a cowlick is a tuft of hair that appears to grow in a different direction from the hair around it, thus bearing a resemblance to the same phenomenon frequently seen on cow hides. Although it is something of a misnomer (cowlicks can occur on cows in places they couldn't possibly lick), the term was familiar to Italians before it came into English in 1598 when Richard Haydocke translated an Italian book about painting, and included the line 'The lockes of plaine feakes of haire called cow-lickes are made, turning upwards' (*feake* is an old word for 'wipe').

Creek

This comes from an ancient Dutch word, *kreke*, but the meaning has changed somewhat. The Dutch word and its relative in Scandinavia, *kriki*, both mean an inlet or a bay, and that's what the word originally meant in English.

The word travelled to America with the early British settlers and they began to use it to mean a small river or stream. There are still places where the word creek occurs as the name of a little bay or inlet. But in general early settlers in Australia and New Zealand used the word to mean a stream or small river.

Cricket

The English language has two crickets and it used to have three. First, there is the insect, a cricket, whose name comes from an ancient French word meaning 'to creak' and a slightly more modern Dutch word, *krekel*. Both are imitative of the noise a cricket makes.

Then there is the game of cricket, and its name is also French, from the word *criquet*, meaning a post or wicket.

Third, over 300 years ago, another version of 'cricket' in English meant a three-legged stool. Scholars seem to agree that the game of cricket is not named after the stool or the insect, but after the French posts.

Crikey

Crikey is recognised in English as a euphemism for Christ and the word has been well established for a long time. Incidentally, Christ is not an English word and Christ is not Jesus' second name and never was. It is Greek for 'the anointed one'. Greek translators put it next to the name Jesus to indicate status, in the same way that a British title or the position of mayor or prime minister has an honorific indicating status.

Crook

Sometimes you will hear 'crook' indicating that a person or a thing is sick or somehow disabled; to 'go crook' means to get angry; and a criminal is frequently referred to as a 'crook'. In its original application, a crook means a curved shepherd's stick. The connection between the shepherd's stick and the three subsidiary meanings mentioned above is that they all relate in some way to being bent out of line.

A person whose morals do not abide by the norm and who commits deliberate crime, or a person who is suffering a curve away from their normal good health, or from their usual calm disposition – all could be seen to compare to a shepherd's crook.

Croquet/crochet

There is a link between crochet and croquet, but it's complex. There are two different things going on here: the origin of the game, and the origin of the name.

The game we call croquet had its origins in an Italian game, *palla maglio*, meaning to hit a ball with a mallet. From that Italian term came two English expressions: first, 'pell mell' meaning to rush about and, second, because the game *palla maglio* was often played in a certain London street, that street became known as the Mall, a long avenue. From that came the modern word 'mall', usually meaning a collection of shops where you walk and there's no traffic.

In the meantime, the actual game of *palla maglio* took on a new name, based on the French word for hook, *crotchet*. In modern English, the French word has two descendants. Crochet is a kind of embroidery done with a hook. And the game formerly known as *palla maglio* slowly came to be called croquet because, apparently, the very early versions of the game did have a hooked mallet for hitting the ball.

Crow's feet

This somewhat unwelcome reference to the sign of ageing has been so described for nearly 500 years. In his 1591 play *Sapho and Phao* author John Lyly refers to the effects of time upon women in these terms: 'The crowe shall set his foote in their eye and the blacke oxe tread on their foote.' (A black ox is an ancient symbol of approaching death).

In later centuries those people on whose eyes the crow has set his foot preferred an alternative image: laughter lines.

Curate's egg

The curate's egg, which was good only in parts, dates back to a famous 1895 cartoon by George Du Maurier in the magazine *Punch*. The cartoon, titled 'True Humility', showed a bishop and his curate eating breakfast, and the bishop exclaims, 'I'm afraid you have a bad egg.' The curate was replying bravely, 'Oh no, my lord, parts of it are excellent.'

This latter clause has been contracted over the years into the vernacular 'good in parts'. The original cartoon still survives.

Curtain raiser

The origins of the term lie in the French theatre, where before the main show started, a little event took place in front of the curtain – a *lever de rideau*. Now the expression is applied to anything preliminary to a bigger happening, whether there's a curtain or not – and it is frequently used in a sporting context.

(Turned to) custard

When something goes wrong and everything turns into a disaster. Custard by its very nature is formless, shapeless and difficult to control. Much as we enjoy it, it's a bit of a mess. Thus its connection with a misfortune: pouring rain on an outdoor wedding; a mismanaged firm going bankrupt; a political argument with no clear resolution.

Cut above

One of the meanings of 'cut' is a grade, or quality. So if a person or a thing or an event is a cut above, it is of a higher quality than something else.

(Took off like a) cut cat

There are at least 12 different meanings for the word 'cut', and one of these is to be drunk, but another is to move fast, as in 'he cut down a side street'. This latter meaning is believed to be the origin of the fast-moving cat, particularly as a subsidiary use of 'cut' can mean 'castrated' – to which any self-respecting tomcat takes objection. Even if unable to escape during the operation, he will get away as quickly as possible afterwards.

D-Day

Famously, D-Day was 6 June 1944, the date of the Normandy landings in World War Two. The 'D' is often explained as just an abbreviation of day, a sort of alliteration, but in 1964 General Eisenhower was asked for an explanation and Brigadier General Robert Schultz replied on Eisenhower's behalf: 'Be advised that any amphibious operation has a "departed date" and therefore the shortened term D-Day is used.' Thus, D simply stood for 'Departed'. Since the Second World War, the meaning of the expression has broadened to signify a specific date for a planned event, or a deadline.

(A bit of a) dag

Dag has two separate derivations. In English, for over 300 years, the word 'dag' has meant a loose, hanging bit of something, and it was even used to describe a skirt or jacket with a pointy hem, for instance sleeves with a dag edge. (There's a possible relationship with the word 'tag', which also meant a small strip of something – for example, a price tag.) When the word dag was first used to mean the lump of rubbish hanging off the back of a sheep it was called a dag-lock, and in time that was shortened to just dag.

Dag, meaning hard case, a lively fellow, is a different thing altogether, but also about 300 years old. Some people think it is a relative of the word 'wag', but scholars reveal that, in the seventeenth century, an artful or impudent fellow was called a 'degen', which is a kind of sword. So if you said the word about a person it meant he was a knowing blade, or was willing to be daring. Degen eventually became contracted to dag.

Rattle your dags, meaning to move fast, probably derives quite simply from sheep running – when they do, their dags rattle.

(Get your) dander up

The expression is usually believed to be of mid-nineteenth century American origin. At that time many immigrants to the United States were Dutch or German. The German word for thunder is *Donner* and the Dutch word is *donder*, so etymologists think it arose as a misuse by other Americans when they heard such settlers using *donder*, in particular, to mean anger.

So eventually the word crept into a phrase, the rest of which was in English, and people got their 'dander' up.

Dashboard

The word is over 100 years old and dates back to the days of carriages when there was an upright board near the front to prevent water and mud splashing onto the driver and passengers. A similar protection board, with the same name, was also used on boats.

When cars and aircraft were invented, they were fairly open and also needed a protection sheet, which was called the dashboard. Over the years vehicles became more enclosed and their dials and instruments, logically enough, were situated on a panel in front of the driver.

Days of the week

In English, the seven days of our week come variously from ancient Latin, ancient German and ancient Scandinavian. They just grew that way.

Monday is named after the moon. Tuesday comes from the word Tiu, the Norse word for one of the gods of war. He was a relative of Odin, another god of war, who was sometimes called Woden, thus giving us Wednesday. So Tuesday and Wednesday are both named after gods of war.

Thursday is pretty noisy too; it's named after Thor, the Norse god of thunder. Venus was the goddess of love (you'll find her in the French name for this day – *vendredi*) but the Scandinavian version of Venus was a lady called Freya; the English language adopted the Scandinavian name rather than the Roman one, and so Freya became Friday. Saturn was the Roman god of seeds and the harvest, who unfortunately ate nearly all his own children, but Saturday is named after him nevertheless.

Everybody needs light and heat, so Sunday is named to commemorate the sun, source of both.

Dead certainty/dead giveaway

'Dead' doesn't just describe the absence of life. It has a secondary meaning: completely and thoroughly – as in dead drunk, dead beat, dead against, dead heat, dead accurate, dead certainty, dead right, dead broke, dead tired, dead stupid, and so on. In that context the word dead becomes an intensifier – that is, making whatever it's describing more intense.

Dead reckoning

The term dates from the 1600s and refers to a way of piloting in contrast to navigating by visible landmarks. Admiral Smyth's *Sailors' Word Book* defines dead reckoning as: 'The estimation of the ship's place without any observation of the heavenly bodies. It is discovered from the distance she has run by the log, and the courses steered by the compass, rectifying these data by the usual allowance for current, leeway etc.'

A similar use in aviation describes navigation solely by reference to compass readings and time elapsed. There is a belief that the term 'dead' reckoning is inaccurate and the system should be called 'ded' reckoning (from 'deduced' reckoning), but which term is historically correct has never been established, and both versions are used.

Deal to/deal with

At some time in the past, the verb 'to deal' meant only giving out cards. But now 'deal to' instead of 'deal with' seems to be a new use of words, because 'deal to' doesn't mean giving out cards, and it doesn't mean the same as 'deal with'.

The latter means to treat a particular subject ('this book deals with . . .'), or to be active and to cope ('to deal with a difficult situation'). But to deal to someone has come to mean to effect retribution, or take punitive action against them.

Deciles

A decile is a method of placing things in order or rank, from one to ten. In theory it could be used to describe anything, such as one of those talent quests where people hold up a card with a number to evaluate the performance. Or when someone says, 'On a scale of one to ten, how did you enjoy the party?'

It is sometimes used as a way of describing the financial position of the district in which a school is situated, one being at the lowest socio-economic level, and ten at the highest.

This ranking has absolutely nothing to do with the quality of the school, the integrity of its principal, the expertise of its staff or the potential success of its pupils. It describes only the district surrounding the school, based on a study of the census information about that district, and the level of wealth of its population.

Decimate

The correct and original meaning was that, of a group or assembly, one tenth was destroyed. But gradually the word has tended to become confused with 'devastated' and is frequently used to indicate general destruction, so when you hear that a cyclone has decimated farmers' crops, it is not intended to mean that the cyclone mowed down just one plant in every ten (which is what decimate actually means). It's intended to mean that a large number of plants was destroyed.

Dekko

In the context of 'Have a dekko at this', meaning to take a look. It's an Indian word from the Hindi language. The verb *dekhna* means 'to see'. From that, *dekh* means 'look', and *dekho* means 'take a look at …' Military personnel who'd served in countries where Hindi was spoken brought the term into English.

Desert, dessert

- o Desert   a region almost devoid of vegetation, especially because of low rainfall (from the Latin *deserere*, to abandon).

- o Desert   to leave without intending to return, to abscond responsibility (also from Latin *deserere*, to abandon).

- o Desert   a reward or punishment which has been earned (from the Old French *deservir*, to be worthy of).

D

○ **Dessert**   the sweet course of a meal, usually at the end (from French *des* + *servir*, to clear a table).

Diaper

The word can be claimed by babies and also by mathematicians. The English word diaper comes from the ancient Greek *aspros* meaning white, which gives *dia-aspros* – pure whiteness. During the fifteenth century the word was used to describe a type of white fabric characterised by being woven in a diamond pattern, with a little woven insignia inside each shape. Some 200 years later, in the seventeenth century, the term diaper began to move away from describing the fabric towards being applied to the geometric design on the fabric. The term's use then broadened to describe any geometric shapes that were repeated to fit into a prescribed space.

In the United States the word diaper is widely used to mean a baby's nappy, and is sometimes shortened to 'didy' (it's a great demonstration of faith that Americans call a baby's nappy by a name which means white).

Clearly, then, diaper means two quite different things. Diaper meaning a nappy is descended from the name of the centuries-old white cloth weave. And the cloth with its repeated pattern gave its name to a geometric design based on a repeated pattern.

Dilemma

Dilemma is a word used in the study of formal rhetoric, where it has a specific meaning, namely a form of argument wherein a choice between two or more alternatives is possible, but the alternatives are equally unfavourable.

But there is a human failing, found particularly in the media, called Making Things Sound Grander Than They Are, and so dictionaries nowadays will note that the word dilemma is often used to describe a position of doubt or perplexity, a difficult situation.

So we have to accept that dilemma has undergone an expansion of meaning and can now be used to apply to any sort of a problem, without there necessarily being two equally undesirable results.

Dis/dis

This is sometimes the answer to a crossword clue. *Dis* is from Latin and it comes sometimes with a capital letter, and sometimes without.

With a small 'd' in Latin it means 'apart' and has come into English meaning separated or reversed, as in disappear, disconnect and disembodied.

But when *Dis* has a capital letter in Latin it means the Roman god of the underworld, or the underworld itself. In Roman mythology the god is called either Dis or Pluto. In Greek mythology the underworld is called Hades.

Discombobulated

Discombobulated means disturbed, upset or disconnected, and versions of the word have been around since the 1830s. One of its earlier relatives was 'discombobricate'. It has been used to describe one aspect of politicians campaigning: getting on and off a bus for speeches and photo opportunities without being sure what town they're in or what day it is, makes candidates feel discombobulated.

The *Oxford Dictionary* suggests that it is a deliberately doctored version of the older word 'discomposed', which has the right meaning, but rather a Jane Austen sound to it. Discombobulate has the advantage of sounding novel and slightly more technological.

Disgruntled

You can dismantle something and be disgruntled, but you don't often hear mention of anything mantled, or anyone being gruntled (this is a linguistic peculiarity sometimes described as 'a lost positive'). It's true that 'dis' means reversed, as in disgrace or disestablish, but it can also be just an additive to an existing word – there doesn't have to be an opposing prefix available to negate the 'dis'.

There is a word 'mantled'. You don't see it often, but it does exist. If someone is mantled, they are wrapped in a cloak, covered, complete. If dismantled, they are uncovered and pulled apart.

Disgruntled isn't quite the same. Gruntled comes from the Old English word *grunnettan*, which indicated a short, snuffling noise, rather like the snort of a pig. Pigs make this snuffling sort of noise when they're happy, so the word disgruntled developed the opposite meaning, calling to mind the noise pigs make when they're not happy.

Dish, dishy

The word dish is partly an interesting example of meaning reversal. Expressions sometimes do this: what used to be praised as hot, is now praised by calling it cool; bimbo actually means boy, but it used to mean girl; chuffed, which means pleased and lively, once meant sour and morose; bully once meant a fine fellow, a friend – but morphed into meaning a cruel persecutor.

When Shakespeare used the word 'dish' about a woman, he used the full expression: dish-clout (rag), and he applied it to an ugly woman. But a change came during the twentieth century and by the 1930s the meaning had reversed; dish and dishy were commonly used by men to describe an attractive woman. The first known publication of the expression was in 1936.

In more recent years the term 'dish' has begun to be considered politically incorrect when referring to women, but it is now considered completely acceptable for women to say it about men.

Dissing

This is a shortened version of 'showing disrespect'. The term arose from hip-hop language, which is heavily influenced by Black-American vernacular.

Distaff side

In contemporary times distaff is a perfectly respectable word meaning female. It isn't offensive and it isn't a put-down; it's simply a way of designating ancestry through the female line – the distaff side – or mentioning the proportion of women employed on a project – the distaff numbers.

The term relates to spinning. The distaff is a staff around which flax fibre is placed, and the flax drawn from it is spun into thread. Historically this was always done by women and the word distaff came to mean women in general. So descent from the distaff side came to mean 'through the female line'. (Another spinning term developed to describe unmarried women who, with no husband to support them, made a living at their spinning wheels was spinsters.)

In genealogy, the male version of the distaff side of a family is correctly called the spear side, because only men carried spears. In contemporary times, neither term is relevant; few women spin and fewer men carry spears.

But it remains an historic way of referring to either gender without offence.

'Distance lends enchantment'

Many people believe this was written by William Wordsworth, but no, the poet was Thomas Campbell (1777–1844) in 'Pleasures of Hope', written in 1820:

> 'Tis distance lends enchantment to the view,
> And robes the mountain in its azure hue.

See also **Few and far between**.

Diva/divo

Diva comes ultimately from the Latin *divinus* meaning godly or divine; it is the feminine form of the word (like *bambina*). A goddess, a diva, has two essential requirements: she must seem to be elevated from ordinary mortals, and she must have a following – there's no point in being a goddess if nobody takes any notice of you.

In earlier centuries, women opera singers were the megastars of their time. Dame Nellie Melba and Jenny Lind, for instance, were mega-mega-stars. Of course in the time before microphones and sound reproduction, female opera singers were the only type of star there could be because they were the only ones you could hear. And gradually they began to be referred to as divas – elevated beyond the norm, and with huge numbers of fans.

The practice of referring to the really famous women of opera as divas remained in place until electricity changed everything. In the late 1920s when the microphone came into use, radio followed, a recording industry, and then sound movies and eventually television, CDs, Walkmans, iPods – and gradually it became possible for charismatic women with smaller voices also to become elevated beyond the norm. So, very tentatively at first, the word diva was occasionally also used for the new kind of star – the star reliant on electricity. The word diva is still most effective when used about famous women singers, though occasionally you hear the description used of a prominent woman who is not a singer.

In mythology there were plenty of male gods, so linguistically divo would be a masculine god, or later a masculine opera star. Curiously however, the word is seldom if ever heard in its male version despite there having been many famous male singers, with microphone and without: Caruso, Gigli, Sinatra, Crosby, Pavarotti, Elvis and so on.

It's the same with the other theatre expression: prima donna or first lady – you never hear primo uomo for a leading man. And the female ballerina will be partnered by a ballerino – but few people ever say so.

The use of the term diva is so old that it is actually part of the historic relationship between male and female. In the days when goddesses were genuinely worshipped, the social position of women in general was fairly suffocated. So, among women at least, there was a greater attraction in paying attention to female goddesses than to male ones, partly because these were feminine figures with charisma and power, and that didn't occur much in real life.

The same applied to the famous women singers: they had marvellous voices, their performances transcended the male/female power imbalance, they evoked huge admiration – and yet they were real. And throughout the ages the most famous opera stars and ballet dancers have overwhelmingly been women – there have been only a handful of famous men.

Dobbin

The word 'dobbin' is very old, a child's version of Robin, which itself is a form of Robert. The dobbin version has been in use, attached to horses, since the sixteenth century. It was used to describe the wickerwork horse shape worn by people at carnivals – a 'dobby horse'. Sometimes it was a fairly primitive wooden bar with a horse's head and tail, which children pretended to ride.

(Dobby horse eventually became 'hobby horse' and developed a new shade of meaning – namely, that when a person is rattling happily on about some topic that interests them, you say they're on their hobby horse because they think that what they're saying is of interest to everyone, when really it isn't.)

During the nineteenth century, the dobbin word had a big boost. And a slight change came about regarding the kind of horses to which the word was applied. This change came, as language expressions sometimes do, from a work of fiction, William Makepeace Thackeray's *Vanity Fair*, which began to appear in serial form in January 1847. That book has a character called William Dobbin who is a figure of patience and long suffering, and the book became so well known that the existing horse word Dobbin drifted towards horses of a similar ilk: patient, amiable, slow-moving and kind-natured.

Doctorate

The word 'doctor' arises from an ancient French word meaning 'to teach'. Obviously the person who taught something had to have detailed knowledge of the subject being taught, so gradually the word doctor came to be used to describe someone with great knowledge. By the thirteenth century there was a firm connotation that someone called a doctor was very learned and so the word became attached to the highest degree in the university system, and it still is.

As a side issue, because people with medical knowledge and expertise were the ones the public had most contact with, the custom developed of calling these people doctor whether they held a doctorate or not. This practice remains current, and the title doctor is used variously among dentists, vets, opticians and general practitioners of medicine.

Qualifying for a doctorate can happen in various ways, according to different universities' rules. One kind is awarded on the evidence of examination and practicalities such as clinical work in the medical area. A doctorate of philosophy is sometimes slightly different because it is usually awarded on the result of a thesis (a formal and systematic examination of a key area within the subject being studied). A thesis is seen to be an intellectual exercise rather than a hands-on practical demonstration of knowledge and, because philosophy means 'the love of learning', that degree is referred to as a doctorate of philosophy 'in' whatever the subject is. The graduate has demonstrated a love of learning – and intellectual fitness.

Doff

Ancient Assyria (from Egypt to Iran) required all military captives to strip nude in order to demonstrate subjugation, and the ancient Greeks required all new servants to strip from the waist up. Gradually there evolved the idea of taking off an article of clothing to demonstrate respect. Ancient Romans took their sandals off before approaching a holy shrine, and taking shoes off to demonstrate respect still survives in several cultures today.

In Europe, by the time of the Middle Ages, inferior social status was shown by the person of lower rank taking off their hat when a person of superior rank was present. This action said, in effect, 'I am your servant'. The custom survives in the Christian church where men are expected to take their hats off because they are in the presence of a greater power.

Outside the church, taking hats right off continued as an acknowledgement to a person of superior rank. This dwindled eventually into simply touching the hat.

Doff = do + off (and the opposite is don = do + on). The 'do' has the same meaning as in: do out, do down, do in, do over, do up, do without.

Dog

Various dog expressions, such as 'mongrel' or 'cur', have been used for centuries to downgrade men. By 1700 the word 'dog' was being attached to expressions which meant low-rated things – 'a dog's breakfast', 'dog Latin'.

But there's a contradiction, because about 300 years ago the word dog was also used to mean a rakish, lively man – usually with an adjective, as in 'lucky dog', 'jovial dog', 'sly old dog'.

The word was also widely used in the United States to describe something poor or mediocre, for example, 'I made a financial investment which turned out to be a dog.' Since about 1930 that meaning has extended to include certain women. *Webster's American Dictionary* says a dog is a woman inferior in looks or character.

Dogfight

Dogs when they fight each other specialise in close combat. In the First World War when air combat involved planes fighting each other at close quarters, this quickly became known as a dogfight, and the term seemed to stick.

(In the) doghouse

The saying can be dated back to *Peter Pan*, a play by Sir James Barrie, which opened in London in 1904. In the story, the Darling children were looked after by a motherly dog named Nana, to whom Mr Darling was not always kind. When the children disappeared (on a trip to Neverland), Mr Darling was so contrite that, to atone for his earlier ill temper, he moved into Nana's kennel and remained there in disgrace until the children came back.

The story of the play and all its characters became very famous, reappearing in later books, as pantomimes, a Broadway musical and a movie. And anyone in disgrace was said to be – like Mr Darling – 'in the doghouse'.

Dogsbody

The word is believed to originate in the navy (as many colourful expressions do). If you take a lot of dried peas and boil them up in a cloth for several hours you get a pease pudding, a messy kind of lump which at one time was often served in the navy. It was very nutritious but the men said it looked like the cooked body of a dog.

By the early twentieth century, this pudding word had become a pejorative term for a lowly person, a drudge who carries out menial tasks for others. Lawrence of Arabia used the term – 'I'll get used to being a dogsbody' – in 1922.

Doh, re, mi

Guido d'Arrezzo was an eleventh-century Italian monk who is credited with organising the writing of musical notation into the ancestor of the system we use today. He originated names for the notes of the scale, based on the first words in each line of the Latin hymn *Ut queant laxis*:

> *Ut queant laxis*
> *Resonare fibris*
> *Mira gestorum*
> *Famuli tuorum*
> *Solve poluti*
> *Labii reatum*
> *Sancte Ioannes*

In those days Ut was the first note and Si the seventh – S-I being the initial letters of *Sancte Ioannes* – Latin for St John. At a later time Italy changed the Ut into Do (as the first syllable of Dominus – Italians prefer a syllable ending in an open vowel) and in the nineteenth century an English musician replaced Si with Ti, so that each scale note had a different alphabet letter representing it: doh; re; mi; fa; so; la; ti; doh.

Dollar ($)

The word dollar has its origins in Bohemia (now the Czech Republic), from a place called Joachimstaler (St Joachim's valley) where there were silver mines and coins were minted. Eventually the *taler* became 'dollar' in English.

There are various beliefs about the origin of the dollar sign. It may relate to a very old Spanish sign for pesos, which is believed to be a symbolic depiction of the pillars of Hercules with a scroll wrapped around them. But that scroll could also have been a distorted figure eight, because that coin was worth one-eighth of a Spanish real –

hence the expression 'pieces of eight', meaning gold coins of smallish denomination.

As usual, there is some confusion about how the sign became established in the United States and how it changed. The word was first used there in 1683, and Thomas Jefferson wrote a memo with the dollar sign in it in 1784 – he gave it two vertical strokes, which was the norm at that time.

Later there were many Americans who liked those two vertical strokes to be joined up like a letter 'U' – when you put that over the 'S' shape, to an imaginative person it says US. The two vertical lines remained for some time, but custom and usage gradually reduced them to just one. Both versions of the sign are acceptable, but the double line is now perceived as historic.

Done in his dough

This is said when someone being referred to is in financial difficulty. Done is the past tense of do, and one of its meanings is to indicate something is finished – the cake is done, the gardening is done, the job has been done. The expression 'done in' generally means physically exhausted; after a sports match or a tiring day a person says, 'I'm done in' to mean that they're tired out and can't do anything more. If a person's money has run out, is exhausted, finished, then it, too, is done in.

A passion for abbreviation often causes the 'in' to be left out, so you'll hear, 'He's done his dough,' meaning (perhaps) that he won a big lottery and developed a lavish lifestyle, and now he's spent all the money; or that he put money into an Internet business scheme and lost the lot.

Sometimes the expression doesn't mean totally broke, but just that the specific money referred to has been lost and never regained.

Donkey deep

Although they are smallish creatures, male donkeys in particular are not small in all their components. And as someone once explained with supreme diplomacy, male donkeys are 'enthusiastic and skilful opponents of birth control'. It would seem therefore that whatever other derivations the phrase 'donkey deep' has according to etymologists, male donkeys with only one thing in mind can display a distinct potency that gives the expression a particularly physical connotation.

Dope

Dope comes from the Dutch word *doop*, meaning sauce (from *dopen*, to dip). It drifted into English and was used to mean the liquid applied to fabric on early aeroplanes. But, as some people know, when opium has been prepared, it also starts out as a thick sticky liquid, and this rather treacly commodity began to be referred to as dope because it was not unlike the goo used on aircraft fabrics.

This secondary meaning gradually came to be used to refer to any form of narcotic, whether it was stimulating or stupefying, and whether it was liquid, powder, solid or even smoke. From there came the word 'dopey' to describe a person influenced by drugs and, eventually, a person acting sluggishly as if he or she were influenced by drugs (one wonders if Walt Disney knew the history of that word).

And because the dope used on aeroplane fabrics was also an additive, the silicon chip industry uses the word when it deliberately adds any kind of impurity to a computer chip to make it act a certain way.

Dopey, dozy, dippy, drippy

The words are not connected. Dopey does come from dope, but dozy obviously comes from doze, and therefore has a different origin, although it does also mean sleepy and slow.

Dippy and drippy both seem to have the same ancestor in the Old English *dyppan*, meaning 'to let down into a liquid briefly'. It is sometimes used to describe a person, presumably to mean that they haven't been properly immersed in something (like good sense), and intelligence comes off them only in small drips.

So there you have dopey, dozy, dippy and drippy – a good name for a pop group perhaps?

Doryphore

This ancient Greek word meaning 'spear carrier' was attached by an entomologist to a beetle he'd discovered, which presumably looked as if it were carrying a spear. And then, by a process of evolution, it has become a word you can say about nasty critics – possibly because they carry a spear and are always ready to strike at public performers.

Draw a line in the sand

A line drawn in the sand is totally unstable – any reference to sand immediately indicates something that shifts. But curiously, the expression is frequently heard in a sense indicating firm action, a final decision, which seems rather to mistake the solidity of anything made with sand. A line in the sand sounds silly if you're wanting to sound decisive, but recently it has been used in that sense.

It seems to be an example of one expression becoming confused with another. Scholars and etymologists believe it to have arisen from confusion with another expression: 'to draw the line'.

The expression 'to draw the line' wasn't sighted until 1793. The image was of a boundary which was quite firm: either the new-fangled game of tennis, where lines were drawn inside which the game took place, or a plough-line in farmland to demonstrate a farmer's territory. Either way, the meaning has always been quite clear: a limit has been defined and a perimeter of acceptability has been laid down.

There's also a similar American expression – 'to draw a line in the dirt', which denotes a boundary. In a children's playground a bossy child will draw a line and say, 'You're not allowed over that line.'

Around 1970 these various meanings appeared to blur in the United States, especially among politicians (who often appear to prefer six words where three would do).

They began to say 'drawing a line in the sand' when they actually wanted to indicate the creating of a firm limit. People who say they're in the know report that when the first President Bush spoke of a line in the sand when referring to Saddam Hussein, he intended to say 'draw a line in the dirt' but changed the words because of the vast areas of desert in the territory to which he was referring.

To be safe, best forget sand if a statement is intended to sound firm. There are less confusing expressions, like 'engraved on tablets of stone' or 'set in concrete'.

Drawing room

The word dates from a time when, among the moneyed classes, women were expected to be separated from men at certain times of the social day, especially after dinner. So the men would stay at the table drinking port, and the women would withdraw – to the withdrawing room. In time, for convenience, the word became shorter, just as omnibus became bus and taxi cabriolet became taxi or cab.

So the withdrawing room eventually was called just the drawing room, and although the notion of women withdrawing to it quietly faded from custom, the room itself retained a certain image of proper behaviour. Then it became known as the sitting room, before it relaxed a bit further and is now often called the lounge or living room.

Dressed to the nines

Some think it refers to members of the 99th Regiment of Foot, who were notable for their splendid uniforms. Others think it refers to a scale of values where ten is the top so nine means you've dressed with considerable effort.

But the main opinion is that the expression is much older than that. In olden times the word 'eye' was singular, as it is now, but the plural used to be 'eyne' (not eyes), and it is believed that dressed to the nines was once 'dressed to the eyne' – making yourself look as good as possible, wearing everything, pleasing for other people to see.

Drizzle

Drizzle means light rain falling in small drops, specifically drops that are less than half a millimetre in diameter. Given the viscosity of oil at room temperature, 'drizzling' oil onto a salad seems highly improbable. What is actually happening is that the olive oil is being dribbled – because 'dribble' means flowing in an unbroken thin stream.

Television cooks resist the word dribble because it has other connotations, and they've simply taken up saying drizzle because it sounds cute. So the short answer is that when they say drizzle, they mean dribble. If the fluid is pumped in fine drops out of a machine, then it is neither a dribble nor a drizzle, but a spray.

But usage often dictates language growth, and I suspect that soon we will find that dictionaries say drizzle means light rain in very small drops, or to moisten food with an unbroken stream poured from above by the method formerly known as dribbling.

(Out for a) duck

Cricket usually has a visual scoreboard, and if a player leaves the field having made no runs, a great big zero stands next to his or her name on the board. A practice arose many years ago of referring to this zero – because of its shape – as a duck's egg, and this has shortened to just a duck. So if he or she was out for a duck, it means there was no score.

There is a similar development with the tennis score called 'love', which also signifies zero. Tennis originated in France, and when the player scored zero and that appeared on the board, the French thought exactly the same as the English – that it looked like an egg. So the French said a person's score was *l'œuf* (an egg). English people began to say it too but got it slightly wrong: *l'œuf* became pronounced as 'love' and for the last 250 years, that's the word the English language has used for a zero score in tennis.

Duck shove

Ducks do shove each other out of the way of course, but this use of the term involving humans originated in Melbourne, when taxi drivers there (of 'wagonette cabs') jumped the queue for customers, not putting their taxis at the end of the line as they came in. The other drivers called them duck-shovers – first reported in 1870 –

D

because, by not taking their proper place, they were not playing fair and were avoiding a long wait.

Duffer

It's a fairly common word, meaning a person who is foolish, clumsy, or simple, but the origin isn't simple at all. Duffer appears to be a combination of several old British words – possibly influenced by one Norse word. The old Scottish *duffer*, meaning a dull or stupid person, was related to another word with a rather indelicate sound, *dowfart*, which also meant a slow-witted person. At the same time a thieves' term for cheating someone, making something old look new, or making fake money, was 'to duff'. Just over the sea, the Norse word *daufr* meant 'deaf' – but carried an unfortunate connotation of being slow on the uptake.

Put all that together and 'duffer' seems to be the result. Combinations of influences like that are not uncommon with language development. But there is no connection between a duffer and a duffel coat, which is named after the town of Duffel in Belgium.

Dunderhead

The Dutch word for thunder is *donder,* and this joined up with the English word 'head' to form the combination dunderhead, a person whose head gives out a lot of noise but not necessarily a lot of sense.

Dutch

There are many English expressions containing the word 'Dutch'. English, meaning English as spoken in Britain, is alarmingly non-PC about its references to foreigners (just watch *The Benny Hill Show* or *Fawlty Towers*).

These days the term 'Dutch treat' (meaning that the people involved pay for themselves) has quite a pleasant resonance, just as the relationship between the Dutch and the English is now pleasant. But things were not always that way, and the term 'Dutch treat' is a relic of a time when relations between Britain and the Netherlands were at a very low point. In the seventeenth century both nations were powerful seekers of global empires, and were intense rivals.

From this rivalry there arose nearly 30 sayings invented by the English as a put-down of the Dutch. 'Dutch treat' was based on the English observation that Dutch were well-organised financially and not given to reckless extravagance, qualities seen now as virtues, but interpreted then as meanness.

Hence the invented scenario in which a Dutchman invited you to a meal or a drink, but you ended up paying for yourself. The saying remains, but instead of being a put-down is now seen as a social custom which is far from miserly, but quite graceful and sensible.

Some anti-Dutch sayings have disappeared: Dutch act (suicide); Dutch dumplings (buttocks); Dutch doggery (grog shop); Dutch feast (meaning a meal where the host gets drunk before the guests do); and Dutch nightingale (a frog). Others have survived: 'Dutch courage', meaning false bravery bolstered by alcohol (the Dutch were perceived to be too fond of the bottle, which simply isn't true); 'Dutch auction', which is an auction that goes more or less backwards; and 'double Dutch', meaning any language which English speakers don't understand.

Duvet

There's a difference between how it has come to be used in English, and what it actually means. *Duvet* is French for down – the fluffy type, from birds. So we call the whole thing a duvet, assuming it is filled with down and soft feathers. The French call the same thing a *coquette*, and there are other English names: an eiderdown, a continental quilt, a comforter, a puff.

The Australian trade name for a similar soft-filled cover is doona, a variation on the Scandinavian word *dyne*, which also means down.

Dyscalculia

This is a genuine but seldom-heard word, meaning difficulty in understanding even the simplest of mathematics. It is the partner word to dyslexia, a disorder that causes grave difficulty in relating to written words. Both incorporate the prefix 'dys', which indicates a difficulty or abnormality in the subject-word that follows.

Dysfunctional

The prefix 'dys', which crops up occasionally in English, is Greek and means bad, difficult, abnormal or faulty. Originally it was used in various medical terms in English, to indicate that whatever followed it was not in good working order. So dysentery is a malfunction of the enteric or intestine system, dyslexia is the inability to recognise whole words, and dyspepsia is an upset stomach and digestion.

Gradually the prefix crept into more general use. There is also a move towards spelling 'dys' as 'dis', because people somehow prefer to avoid the 'y'. But doing this could muddy the meanings, because where 'dys' indicates that something bad is afoot, 'dis' indicates an opposite condition (like/dislike, agree/disagree).

So at the moment if you spell it dys-functional, you mean things are going badly but are still lumping along, but if you spell it dis-functional you mean that things have stopped working altogether.

Dystopia

Back in 1516, Sir Thomas More dreamed up an image of a perfect society, living in a place he called Utopia (from the Greek for 'no place'). Over 300 years later, British philosopher John Stuart Mill launched his own cynical variant – Dystopia. Like Thomas More's Utopia, this was an imaginary place, but a stark and unpleasant counter-image to a perfect society ('dys' meaning faulty and bad).

The word is usually used now to refer to a fictional situation where social trends being practised in the present have gone very sour. The theme frequently occurs in contemporary science fiction.

Eagle (golf)

Two golfing terms are connected to birds. Because birds fly so expertly and silently, the American expression 'birdie' was applied to anything that appeared to be excellent. So in golf, a birdie was reaching the hole in one stroke under par (the notional ideal). From that developed an 'eagle', a grander version of birdie, meaning two strokes under par.

Earth

Among the beliefs of the ancients there was a concept of four localities: the one where we currently live, as separate from both wherever we were before we came here to this place, and wherever we go when we die. And then there is the sea, where we can't live.

Of those four areas, the Old High German word *Erda* had the meaning of 'the material of the ground on which we walk'. This went into Anglo-Saxon and eventually English as *eard*. From around 1000 AD the word eard developed in English as (1) earth, the soil (exactly as the old German meant); and (2) the name for the entire place in and on which we live, land and sea. Thus, the Earth.

Eavesdropping

The little piece of roof that hangs over and beyond the outside walls is the eave. People used to believe that if you wanted to hear private conversations going on inside a house, then you should stand hard against the wall, as close as possible to the eaves because sounds would echo just there. So you could stand around underneath the eaves and if anybody saw you, you could pretend you were just dropping in to visit.

Modern building materials and high-rise housing have made such clandestine activity impossible, but when someone is listening when they shouldn't be, it's still called eavesdropping.

Egg on

It's an example of usage contraction, like 'giving me gyp', which started out as 'giving me gee-up' (as in kick-starting, an irritation that starts something going). Originally this expression was to 'edge' someone on; instead of leaving them comfortably in the middle, to get them moving and push them over the edge of their comfort zone. Over time, edge turned into egg.

Egg on your face

It means to come out of an experience badly, and to look foolish, usually because you have brought humiliation upon yourself through some massive lack of judgement.

It's not a very old expression. A hint of it was seen in print in America in 1902 – about wild dogs that, besides bothering stock, were also referred to as egg-sucking. As 'egg on your face', it was first seen in print in 1941 in America, then came to light in the 1970s and was swept into worldwide use by Sir Freddie Laker, who was widely quoted as using it when he was in dispute with British Airways about running Concorde at a profit. This often happens, where an existing expression becomes famous overnight.

A wise cook sounded a caution about microwave cooking involving eggs – always prick the yolk before putting an egg into a microwave. If you forget to do this, you will only ever forget once.

'Elementary my dear Watson'

This phrase does not appear in any of the Sherlock Holmes books written by Sir Arthur Conan Doyle. Holmes sometimes said, 'Elementary', and he also sometimes said, 'My dear Watson', but never the two together. The two were amalgamated by screen writers Basil Dean and Garrett Fort for the 1929 movie *The Return of Sherlock Holmes* – several years after Conan Doyle had stopped writing Holmes stories. But everyone who saw the movie believed they were hearing a genuine Conan Doyle line.

Elephant and Castle

This district in London has been the subject of several legends. The most popular is that the district's name originated from the inability of Cockney Londoners to pronounce the title of the king's wife, Eleanor of Castile, who was a Spanish princess and therefore correctly called Infanta de Castille. But the king was Edward I in the thirteenth century, so it's difficult to verify.

Another story focuses on the fact that for many years trained elephants have carried a little box on their backs called a howdah, in which nobles sat, or sometimes soldiers armed for battle. This was referred to as 'the castle on the elephant', and since British pubs frequently have fanciful names and signs, could possibly have been the origin of the sign outside the pub in Newington Butts which is the source of the legend and contributed to the district itself being called by the same name.

End of your tether

The image is strictly from the animal kingdom. A tether is the rope or chain used to confine an animal to a certain area. This can become extremely frustrating for the animal. Therefore when someone is in a situation that is causing similar tension and is straining their endurance, they say they are at the end of their tether.

England and Europe

This juxtaposition is completely invalid: England is a part of Europe. Occasionally you hear comment and see travel brochures describing them as two separate things, but this is nonsense. Geographically, Europe is a mass of land and islands, each with a connection to the others through race, language, history and culture. Saying England and Europe is like saying Hawaii and the United States, Australia and Tasmania, or New Zealand and Stewart Island. More accurate terminology is 'England and continental Europe'.

Some people are vague about distinctions, and will talk about going to England to see the Edinburgh Festival, or going to England to visit their relatives in Cardiff. When referring to anywhere in England, Scotland, Wales or Northern Ireland, it's safer to say Britain.

Errant/error

It's largely a matter of connotation. King Arthur's knights were referred to as 'errant' when in general they seemed to be involved in praiseworthy projects. Whereas 'error' usually means a mistake – and it could be serious.

The words err, errant and error all come from the same ancestor, the Latin *errare*, meaning to wander or stray. And in contemporary English (rather than King Arthur's) their exact meanings do not differ much from one another.

Error and to err describe a departure from what was meant to happen, or what would have been sensible, and instead causing something different to happen. Often this means someone has made a mistake, been incorrect or strayed from accepted standards. This can be seen as a somewhat negative thing.

But virtually the same word, errant, is often perceived as describing a noble calling, though such a view isn't strictly accurate. King Arthur's knights were 'errant' because they were wandering around in search of noble deeds to perform, which was a departure from their contemporaries' normal pursuits.

Etcetera

Definitely not 'eckcetera'. The phrase is Latin for 'and the other things' and it must be pronounced 'et-cetera'. Scrambling the letters and putting the 'c' before the 't' just doesn't make sense (similarly, it's vulnerable, not 'vunlerable').

Ethereal

Ethereal means delicate and almost as light as air. It comes from the Greek *aitherios*, which means to burn. It is related to the ether – the spaces high in the atmosphere where it's as if all content is burnt and empty and there's just floating nothingness.

The same word was used in connection with a chemical compound called ethoxy-ethane, which is an anaesthetic known as ether, presumably because if the anaesthetic is applied to you, it's as if you're floating in the upper reaches of the atmosphere. The Melbourne Cup winner in 2001 had the name Ethereal, which seemed entirely suitable for one who gave the impression of lightness as well as speed.

Ethicals

Ethics is the branch of knowledge which deals with human duty and moral principles. When abiding by those principles a person is said to be an ethical person. But the noun ethicals is a different word. It is a medicine or drug not advertised to the general public because it is only available on a doctor's prescription.

That situation is becoming confused by media advertising of certain prescription-only drugs to the public, who are exhorted to ask their doctor for them. Many people think this inappropriate and undermines a doctor's experience and decisions; in other words, they believe it is not ethical to advertise ethicals.

Ethnic cleansing

This is a particularly euphemistic expression, meaning racially based murder. Because it deliberately contains the word 'cleansing' there seems to be something pure and attractive about the activity, but it actually means genocide.

Eudaemonism

The people who understand this word are likely to be associated with a philosophical concept which has quite a substantial following. But the straightforward definition is a bit confusing: 'the normative centrality of living well.'

This philosophy was first proposed by Aristotle and given the name eudaemonism, which in Greek means 'aided by a good genius'. Those who promote eudaemonism believe that the chief good which can exist within people is a state of happiness. In other words, eudaemonism is a system of ethics which evaluates actions in terms of their capacity to produce happiness, or it means flourishing by nurturing the feeling of well-being. (Note, however, that you must not make yourself happy by creating circumstances which make someone else unhappy – that is not part of the deal.)

Noel Coward's Mrs Wentworth Brewster may well have been a eudaemonist. Each evening, 'beaming with goodwill, she'd just slip into something loose – and totter down the hill' to the bar on the Piccola Marina.

Evil eye/roving eye

A roving eye usually describes a person who has a lively interest in successive members of the opposite sex. The evil eye is rather more ominous. For many centuries there was a strong belief that certain powerful people possessed an evil eye that could kill with a glance, blight crops, cause impotence or be responsible for such disabilities as blindness or deformity. One mythical Celtic king in Ireland had the gift so powerfully that when his eyelid was lifted in death, those who saw the dead eye died.

It was sometimes creatures who had the power, as in the legends of the Gorgon, or the basilisk (a kind of serpent). Some people think that peacock feathers contain a depiction of the evil eye, and won't have them in the house.

Executioner/executor

Nearly all words relating to 'execute' and its derivatives come from the Latin *sequi*, to follow. *Sequi* is the grandfather of whole pages of English words like sequel, sequence, persecute, pursue, consecutive, consequence and execute. All of these have something to do with following, or following through, or proceeding to completion.

In that context, execute means to follow a plan and carry out a project. In order to administer the project and make sure it is carried out, there is an executive. To take a person's life to its conclusion and carry out the law in doing so, might involve an executioner. And to carry out the wishes contained in a person's will there is likely to be an executor. They are all following a situation to its conclusion.

Expiry and expiration

The verb 'expire' means to cease, to end, to come to a finish or to breathe out. The noun 'expiration' means the state of having done these things. Credit card transactions sometimes ask for the 'expiration' date, which sounds as if the credit card is breathing out. Asking for the expiration date of a credit card isn't exactly wrong, it's just being orotund and clumsy. An expiry date would do, but to some businesses that doesn't sound grand enough.

Faggot

Faggot comes from the Greek *phakelos* meaning a bundle, and when the word came into English it retained that meaning – a bundle of sticks gathered out in the wild, or perhaps stored in the household as firewood.

But there was a side issue. Religious heretics, witches and people perceived to have social or sexual aberrations were often burned on a bonfire. The blaze would normally be built from a pile of faggots, so the word faggot developed a connotation of being connected with heresy.

A bundle of twigs isn't an attractive-looking object and it can be a burden to carry, so the term crept into being a term of abuse, especially of a crabby wife. On *Till Death Us Do Part* Alf Garnett used to call his spouse 'you old faggot'.

The word also crops up in at least three other areas. Faggots are a kind of rissole made from minced liver and breadcrumbs and although it's not entirely clear why they're called that, it may be because the various ingredients are usually bundled up inside a wrapping of animal stomach.

Then, dating from about 1916, criminal slang in the United States started to include the term faggot meaning a homosexual man. The word gradually went into more or less general slang use. The explanation for this usage lies with the punishment of those outside the norm, which included homosexuals.

And third, a kind of embroidery is called a faggot because originally faggoting was gathering threads into bunches that resembled little bundles of twigs. The name later developed to describe other kinds of stitches.

When the word faggot went into wide use in the United States in the mid-twentieth century, it was often abbreviated to fag, which brought up another complication.

The American abbreviation fag, short for faggot and meaning homosexual, has nothing to do with either of the British words fag, meaning a cigarette; or fag, meaning the junior boy who does errands for a senior boy in a school. Both those British words are derived from 'flag', meaning tired and drooping. The schoolboy has his normal work plus errands for the senior, so he is overworked and flagged (or fagged). And a cigarette hanging from someone's lips can look droopy and tired, so it too became a fag.

The German word for bassoon is *Fagott*. This elegant instrument is usually made from beautiful sycamore wood but, to some unkind person in Germany centuries ago, it looked like a bundle of sticks.

Failsafe/foolproof

Failsafe means something which may have a malfunction, but only temporarily, and then is able to return to a stable condition. In other words, if it fails, it fails in a safe way. When you mean something that won't go wrong at all, that's foolproof.

Famous for fifteen minutes

The line has been misquoted many times. The original statement was written by Andy Warhol in the catalogue for an exhibition of his works in Stockholm in 1968. He wrote: 'In the future, everyone will be world famous for fifteen minutes.'

Fay nits

This is a very old expression, now seldom if ever heard. The word 'fain' is an old way of saying 'willing', and is heard in such archaic structures as 'She fain would be dead', meaning she'd prefer to be dead, or is willing to die.

Fay nits was an expression that grew from this. Originally, an argument could be brought to an end by saying 'Fain I am to call a truce', meaning 'I'm willing to cease hostilities'. 'Fain I' was corrupted into fay nits, with crossed fingers as some extra sort of submission symbol, and that was the sign for a truce or some kind of withdrawal. Paradoxically, the expression also occasionally meant the opposite and became a statement of opposition or irony: 'Fay nits' (I'm willing to believe you, but I don't really).

Fellow/fellow

Over the centuries this word has been used with various shades of meaning. In the fifteenth century the word 'Fellow' described a senior member of an academic foundation, or a privileged member of a learned society – and it still does mean both of those things. But over time the word's social status drifted downwards, so that it began to be used meaning just a companion, a bloke, someone you shared something with, sometimes even a servant.

Currently, most of those meanings are still in use: an eminent medical man may be a Fellow of the Royal College of Surgeons (with a capital F), but the person sitting next to you in the bus is just a fellow traveller.

Few and far between

This phrase originates from a poem by the Scottish poet Thomas Campbell, who wrote:

What though my winged hours of bliss have been,
Like angel-visits, few and far between?

He wrote the lines about 1840 and since then 'few and far between' has cropped up many times – often in weather reports about intermittent showers.

ff

The system of lower-case letters and upper-case letters to which we have become accustomed wasn't always like that. There was a time when the use of capital letters wasn't consistent, and the way of showing the beginning of a word or a name was simply to write the initial letter twice. Hence surnames like ffoulkes or ffrench. Families with such names are proud of them, since they denote an unusual level of antiquity.

It must be remembered however, that if a name begins with a doubled initial letter, they must both be lower-case. To write Ffoulkes or Ffrench is inappropriate and inaccurate. The double 'ff' is there instead of a single upper-case 'F' and is not an alternative.

(Don't care a) fig

Prior to the sixteenth and seventeenth centuries, real figs were not commonplace in England, but if you stuck your thumb between the next two fingers and pointed at someone, this was called a *fico* – the Italian word for fig. The gesture and the word (in Italian) had a sexual connotation, but instead of indicating pleasure, it signified contempt.

Gradually the expression came to be applied more generally, not just to specific people. In Shakespeare's *Merry Wives of Windsor* the character of Pistol says 'a *fico* for the phrase'. In English, the Italian word was eventually replaced by 'fig', but the meaning retained its overtones of being small in value. Anything 'not worth a fig' was hardly worth even making a contemptuous hand gesture.

Fido

Although you don't often hear Fido as a name for someone's actual dog, the word does seem to mean all dogs or any dog. This came about as an early example of celebrity endorsement because Abraham Lincoln had a dog he decided to call Fido. Even in the days before mass media, television and women's magazine covers, people were still keen to know all about famous people – and in America there's nobody more famous than the President.

In 1863 most of the population knew that their President's dog was called Fido, so the name rapidly went into general use, even internationally, to indicate not just his dog, but any dog. Abraham Lincoln's choice of Fido for his dog's name was perfectly logical – *fido* is the Latin for 'faithful'.

Filipinos

Early in the sixteenth century Portuguese navigator Ferdinand Magellan first saw the country we now know as the Philippines. The date he sighted the islands was 17 December, which Catholics identify as the feast of Saint Lazarus, so Magellan named the country as Saint Lazarus.

Some years later, in 1543, it was renamed after the future king of Spain, Philip II, then only 16. It was spelt with an 'F', as the

King's name in Spanish was Felipe. When the country was referred to by English-speaking people, they spelt it with 'Ph', reflecting the English spelling of Philip.

But when writing in English about the inhabitants, we seem to have retained some tribute to the Spanish king's spelling and we refer to them as Filipinos or Filipinas (though the occasional reference to Phillipinos does creep in).

(In) fine fettle

Fetel is a very Old English word for girdle or belt, so when you were dressed and then held together with a good belt or fetel, you were 'in fine fetel' (with one 't'), which later became fettle.

From there, the word developed an association with tidying up other things – such as cleaning off stray fragments and flecks that adhered to anything which had been cast in iron or moulded in china or porcelain. When the process is finished, the piece is looking 'in fine fettle'. The piece has been fettled, and is 'wearing its best belt'.

Fettle is not to be confused with 'fetlock', which is derived from the German *vizzeloch* meaning that part of a horse's leg.

Finicky

This is a close relative of the word 'fine', in its sense of being excellent, well organised. From fine there developed the word 'finical', which we don't hear now. Finical meant concentrating rather too much on detail, and becoming excessively particular. By the 1800s finical had become the more slangy finicky, meaning fussy, paying attention to trivia.

(Of the) first water

In classifying diamonds, the quality of the stone is described as its 'water' – based on its clarity. Diamonds sometimes have visible imperfections, which either can or can't be disguised by cutting, but if a stone is totally clear and transparent with no coloration, as is pure water – then it is a stone of the finest kind, and is referred to as 'of the first water'.

Less transparency in other diamonds, according to the amount thereof, causes them to be graded 'second' or 'third' water.

Originally intended only for diamonds, then term 'first water' has moved into use to describe other gems – and sometimes an idea or concept, or even an outstanding person.

Diamond comes from the old Greek word *adamas*, meaning invincible, hard. It came into English through a Latin adaptation and was corrupted into the English word diamond. But the Greek meaning still occurs in 'adamant' – unyielding.

Fishwife

This dates from distant times when the word *wif* simply meant woman. In British coastal towns the men went out and caught fish and the women sold it, often in the open air. This was extremely competitive and the women selling fish were known for a strident style of voice and a fierce flow of invective, sometimes against each other. This element of scolding and using a rather coarse vocal style eventually broadened its application and is sometimes applied to women whose use of voice is less than attractive. (Critics said it about Elizabeth Taylor after her movie *Cleopatra*.)

Fit as a fiddle

The word 'fit' hasn't always meant active. In the seventeenth century it meant finely built and suitable for its purpose. This could well be said of a beautifully made violin, and often was – sometimes also 'fine as a fiddle'. By the nineteenth century, 'fit' was beginning to gain a sense of also being physically efficient, and came to be applied to the men who wielded the fiddles.

In an earlier era, long before electricity, a solo fiddler was frequently the only provider of music in the street, and at a banquet or a party, fiddlers provided the music to eat by and, above all, for dancing. This required energy; a fiddler had to be fit. So being as fit (well-made) as a fiddle and being fit (physically) as a fiddler started to slide together. People like alliteration, so either phrase is pleasant to say. People like abbreviation too, so the phrase settled into 'fit as a fiddle'.

In both its forms the saying has been around a long time. Sherlock Holmes says it. And in the previous century the Fezziwigs' party in Charles Dickens' *A Christmas Carol* has an excellent depiction of a busy solo fiddler who was certainly fit.

Fit the bill

This term is believed to be a variation on 'fill the bill', meaning to fulfil the necessary requirements and come up to the required standard.

'Fill the bill' has been in use since 1861 and could refer to any written document, especially an invoice or catalogue, where the goods being delivered or paid for matched the document listing their despatch. Over time, 'fill' changed to 'fit the bill', which had a particular connection with theatre. An actor could be selected for a play because he fitted the bill; that is, he had the right experience, look and skills to play a particular role.

But a further endearing legend survives, referring to the size of lettering used for a performer's name on the 'bill' or poster. If the printing type was all laid out and then suddenly one actor had to drop out, the new actor who replaced him should ideally have exactly the same number of letters in his name, so that the type took up the same space – and filled, or fitted, the bill.

Either way, to 'fit the bill' or 'fill' it mean the same thing: to be suitable, right for the purpose.

Flannel

Flannel is a pleasantly soft and warm fabric, but the word has gained an extra pejorative meaning of useless talk and evasive words. A place in Egypt called Fustat specialised in making a fabric of cotton mixed with some flax. The fabric, known as 'fustian' after its place of origin, was used very widely. But although it looked quite good, its reputation gradually withered because it was without substance. People used the fabric's name, fustian, to describe anything pompous or worthless, anything that looked or sounded more important than it actually was.

Fustian began to fade from use, and flannel came into favour.

Flannel is made from wool and is thus a better fabric than fustian. Although flannel is bulky, it folds easily and can be used for padding. Gradually, flannel replaced fustian and as the fabric changed, so did the words. Instead of using the word fustian to mean pompous and empty, people rather unfairly used the word flannel instead to mean talk with very lightweight meaning, just filling in a space, like folded flannel being used for padding.

Flat stick

'Flat stick' means travelling as fast as possible or making the maximum effort. Expressions closely related to this are 'flat tack', 'flat out' and 'flat to the boards'. There are 38 separate meanings of the word 'flat', and one of those is 'level, not displaying any angle'. The consensus is that the expressions involving 'flat' and going fast, originated from the fact that the accelerator of a car is normally set at an angle, but when it is pushed hard, it is flat and parallel to the floor of the vehicle.

But there is a similar use in horse-riding, referring to the whip used by riders. Presumably when the whip is upright it isn't being used, but if it is in the horizontal (or flat) position, then generally the horse is being spurred to go faster.

Flautist/flutist

There are many discrepancies of language in the field of music, particularly with words of foreign origin being used alongside English words. One of those discrepancies concerns the flute. Most players of instruments are described simply by modifying the name of the instrument – a clarinet is played by a clarinetist, a violin by a violinist, a bassoon by a bassoonist. The flute, which is an Anglicised word, somehow escaped the system, and the person who played it was called a flautist, which is a version of the Italian word *flautista*.

Musicians in the United States began to grumble that it was ridiculous to single out one instrument and refer to its player by a foreign word. So began the new practice of calling a flute player a flutist.

Floccinaucinihilipilification

The word dates from the 1700s when a collection of Latin words (*flocci-nauci-nihil-pili*) was gathered together to mean 'the habit of estimating almost everything as worthless'. In current times the word is seldom if ever used (although perhaps it could be said to describe tabloid-style journalism). It is sometimes said that its 29 letters make it the longest word in the English language, which certainly pips the childhood favourite, antidisestablishmentarianism, which has 28. Note, however, that a lung disease associated with inhaling fine dust particles has 45 letters.

Flunky

It usually means a servant or attendant of some kind and is used disparagingly to describe an equerry or assistant attached to a very important person. Those people attendant to VIPs were once called 'flankers', standing on the VIP's left and right flanks, and usually dressed in a uniform (livery) that designated the master's rank.

About 200 years ago the word 'flanker' evolved into 'flunky' to mean anyone in livery, a servant. The word flunky was first noticed in common usage in the Navy, where it meant a wardroom attendant. From its use in the Navy there evolved a more general meaning for flunky, of someone rather parasitic and toadying, a person of low rank who was associated with people of high rank, but in a menial capacity.

There's another similar word, to flunk, meaning to fail. It is related to 'flunky' because they are both derived from the ancient word *flangir* – 'the side of something, to turn or bend'. So someone who has flunked an exam has 'turned away' from a successful result, and a flunky is someone 'at the side' of another person.

Other relatives of the same ancient word are 'flank' and 'flinch'.

Fly in the ointment

The phrase is a slight variation on an image found in the Bible, in Ecclesiastes 10:1 – 'Dead flies cause the ointment of the apothecary to send forth a stinking savour.'

Follow the van

The song was composed by Fred Leigh (who also wrote 'There was I, waiting at the church', and 'Always the blushing bridesmaid') and his 'Follow the van' song was made famous by Marie Lloyd around 1900. It begins 'We had to move away, cause the rent we couldn't pay, the moving van came round just after dark ...' They are doing a moonlight flit, with everything they own packed into a van (which would probably have been a horse-drawn vehicle with a covered-in back section). The husband rides up front and the wife is told to walk behind, carrying their pet bird in its cage.

Hence the chorus: 'My old man said "Follow the van ..."' (often mistakenly sung as 'follow the band').

Foolscap

Because foolscap paper is quite big and you can make a dunce's hat out of it, many people assume that's how the paper got its name. But in fact it's all to do with one of the most successful paper manufacturers in sixteenth-century Britain, a Mr Spielman.

Because *Spielmann* is German for a showy person, a clown, Mr Spielman used a picture of a jester in a cap as the watermark on his paper. That image became so associated in people's minds with the size of this paper that they eventually referred to it as foolscap.

There is an alternative version which maintains that Oliver Cromwell, in dealing with official papers of the realm, took the royal crown off the letterhead and replaced it with a jester, but that one doesn't seem to be proven.

Foreign muck

The phrase may have been popularised by the television character Alf Garnett, but it was certainly not a new concept; people are often suspicious of unfamiliar foods and have been for a long time. Such an attitude can be traced to AD 100 when the ancient Roman writer Juvenal expressed dislike of everyone and everything outside his own immediate circle.

The fictional Alf Garnett was played by British actor Warren Mitchell in the TV show *Till Death Us Do Part*, first seen in 1965. It became immensely popular for many years and imitation versions were made in Holland and Germany, and eventually the United States in 1971. The American version was called *All in the Family* and the central character was Archie Bunker.

Alf Garnett specialised in shock-value put-down phrases. He referred to dark-skinned people as coons, called his wife a silly old moo and his son-in-law a randy scouse git. Most of these expressions were clever adaptations by the scriptwriter of existing phrases.

In Garnett's view, foreign muck included avocados, lemon grass, tandoori chicken, lasagne, sushi and aubergines. People who lived in England as long ago as the 1920s report that although the phrase 'foreign muck' was well within the common vernacular, it was a shock to hear Warren Mitchell announcing it loudly on television the moment anyone mentioned pasta or pizza.

So we can conclude that the attitude towards foreign muck had existed for over 2000 years but that scriptwriters for the fictional character of Alf Garnett certainly made the expression popular.

Fourth estate

At least until the 1700s, within Britain the ruling power was perceived as belonging to three groups: the Lords Spiritual (meaning the Christian clergy): the Lords Temporal (the nobility); and the House of Commons, representing the ordinary people. Those levels of power were each called an 'estate'; hence there were three estates at the ruling level.

In 1787 under a new dispensation, newspaper reporters were allowed into the British Parliament to write about what they saw and heard. The first known use of the term 'fourth estate', referring to these reporters, was from Lord Macaulay, who wrote in 1828: 'The gallery where the reporters sit has become a fourth estate in the realm.'

Somewhat later, the author Thomas Carlyle claimed that the term originated with politician Edmund Burke in 1787, but there is no report at all of his saying it, and Carlyle wasn't born until eight years later and couldn't have heard it. So the credit must go to Lord Macaulay.

Originally the term was applied only to print journalists, because that's all there was. The gradual growth of other forms of communication (radio, satellites, telephone, television and the Internet) eventually gave rise to what is known as the media, and the term 'fourth estate' has come to include them all.

Franchise

Besides franchise meaning 'the right to vote in elections', the word also occurs in connection with shops and other businesses which carry a famous name but are locally owned.

'Franchise' comes from the same word as France, which used to be called Gaul, but was taken over by the Franks, and their name became attached to the new country. Franks meant 'free men', so France meant 'free country'. Thus franchise means to be given the freedom to do something (vote in elections, sell a particular kind of vacuum cleaner or hamburger, and so on).

Free, gratis and for nothing

In formal terms, this could be described as: a deliberate tautology, involving a mildly comic assumption of syntactical sophistication on the part of those who hear it, with the intention of emphasising and intensifying the meaning of a basically simple and rhythmically pleasing statement.

The expression isn't modern; it's in Frank Smedley's book *Frank Farleigh* (1850) and in the *Melbourne Herald Standard* in 1895.

Friend of Dorothy

The usual explanation for this expression is that in 1900 Frank Baum wrote a book called *The Wonderful Wizard of Oz*. It was made into a film, *The Wizard of Oz*, in 1939 starring Judy Garland in the role of the young girl Dorothy who has some eccentric misfit friends – a scarecrow, a tin man and a cowardly lion.

Garland became very famous and she had many personal problems, all of which the public got to hear about, and in her concerts she displayed an extraordinary vulnerability which appealed to the public in general and to gay people in particular. Without knowing

Judy Garland personally, somehow their liking for her was described as being a 'friend of Dorothy's', which carried a connotation of being a slightly offbeat character. And eventually the phrase 'friend of Dorothy's' narrowed down to mean gay people who admired Judy Garland and then, long after she was gone, just gay people.

Frog-marched

This refers to a prisoner or person being apprehended who is recalcitrant, unwilling, and determined not to be moved. In extreme cases, this person is knocked to the ground and four people pick him up, one at each limb. Thus he is carried face-down and spread out, which is the same kind of position as a frog in mid-jump.

Over the years the meaning of the term has shifted somewhat; it still means someone being taken where they do not want to go, but usually now with arms pinned behind them.

Frogs' sound

Aristophanes famous play *The Frogs* was written 400 years BC. The play was written in Greek so there are slight differences in the translations into English letters and sounds of what Aristophanes thought the Greek frogs were saying. One translation has the frogs saying Ak-ak-ax, Co-ax-co-ax, but in another translation from the Greek the frogs say Brek-ek-brek-ek – Co-ax-coax, and yet another version has them saying Cax-ee-cax-ee. Those are 'translations' of what Aristophanes heard Greek frogs say.

But other people hear something quite different. Most Americans hear frogs as saying Ribbit-ribbit and occasionally someone thinks they are hearing Knee-deep, knee-deep. In Finland the frogs say Kwak-kwak and the Italians hear Cra-cra. Japanese frogs seem to say G'ar-g'ar Garow garow, but frog listeners in the Southern Hemisphere hear Herbert-herbert.

There are two factors are work here: as with most animals, there is a variation in how people hear their cries or calls, depending on what language the listener is accustomed to hearing; and frogs' sounds do differ, depending on the locality and the breed.

From the bottom of my heart

The meaning is: with sincere and deep feeling. There is a school of thought that strongly felt emotions are centred on the area of the chest, and another school of thought that says this is rubbish and the heart is just a clever life-sustaining pump. Those latter folk maintain that we only think about the heart in connection with emotion because a million songs and poems and stories have perpetuated a romantic notion that the heart is the seat of all emotion.

That 'seat of the emotions' concept is so inescapable that it has grown some side effects, and this is one. Because if you think of the heart as the seat of all emotion or at least as the register of all emotion, then it's going only a small step further to imagine the heart as being like a container which fills up with feeling. 'From the bottom of my heart' somehow indicates that the heart is absolutely full (not just partly filled) with love, gratitude, grief or whatever.

Funk/funky

Funk has two meanings. In Britain the word has been used since the eighteenth century to mean 'scared', 'shrinking from'. But it has developed another shade of meaning in the United States – a strong smell. And since the late 1950s, this term has been used to describe a certain type of music; it's funky, meaning earthy and rough.

After that, Americans widened the term to include people, clothes and furnishings, and eventually it has come to mean fashionable and a bit cheeky.

G-string

A G-string is worn very low on the torso, and the lowest string on a violin is G. That's one possible explanation. But most scholars think it is a Native American word. When Europeans first met the people they called them Red Indians, and the men wore a little loin cloth known in their native language as a *gee*.

There is also some vague belief that because of what a G-string usually covers, the G stands for genital.

Galleyed

Galley is a term of the old printing trade, referring to the tray which held the metal type. But galley was also once a kind of ship propelled by oars, and working those oars was very hard, so a person who was galleyed – a galley slave – was overworked, a drudge.

In more recent times the word galley is used only to describe the ship's kitchen, which may be hot and crowded, so being on duty there is also liable to make a person overworked.

But there is also an old dialect word *gally*, meaning to frighten, or to vex. So sometimes galleyed can also mean uncertain, wavering, or fatigued with worry.

Game's not worth the candle

This saying comes from France and it began with people gathering to play cards. Sometimes the money being played for was less than the price of the candles required to light the room; hence the game was not worth the candles. The expression moved into the theatre, which was also illuminated by candles, so a put-down of the play was to say that the value of the candles was higher than the value of the play (or any performance).

Eventually usage of the expression expanded to become a put-down for anything.

Gamut and gambit

On the very old musical scale, 'gamut' was the lowest note, usually the low G on the bottom line of the stave. Its meaning widened to refer to the whole musical scale, and has now extended to mean the whole range of anything, usually emotions.

But 'gambit' is different – it comes from the Italian *gambetto*, meaning to trip up. The term is often used in chess. A gambit is a manoeuvre intended to gain some advantage, and it has come to mean the proposing of a certain point of view, a way of persuading people to think something is advantageous.

Gandy dancers

The term became associated with maintenance people on early American railways. As well as checking bolts and tracks, workers attended to balancing the crushed rock underneath the sleepers when the vibration from a passing train rendered it uneven. Why they were called 'gandy dancers' is not clear. A large engineering firm in Chicago called the Gandy Manufacturing Company made many of the parts used in trains, and the firm's name may have been combined with a reference to the characteristic dance-like movements workers made with their long levers when aligning the tracks. But there is no absolute certainty about the term's origin.

Garibaldi biscuits

Garibaldi biscuits do have a connection with Giuseppe Garibaldi, known as the unifier of Italy. This process included storming the island of Sicily. After Garibaldi's triumphant entry into Palermo, he took a liking to a pastry shop called Antica Focacceria San Francesco, which made a special kind of bun filled with cooked beef spleen. (Spleen is often eaten. It features frequently in Jewish cooking with the name milts.) The same shop is still there in Palermo, and still serves these spleen-filled buns, and other focaccia filled with boiled bull's lungs.

This delicacy was not to everyone's taste, but the idea grew that Garibaldi liked munchies with a dark-coloured textured middle.

This image somehow transferred Garibaldi's name to biscuits with dark-coloured currants, raisins and figs in the middle (such biscuits are also found in Palermo). They're roughly similar to what are sometimes called 'fly cemeteries'.

Gauntlet

This is one of those awkward situations where the English language has acquired two words that seem exactly the same but actually have separate meanings and differing origins.

'Throw down the gauntlet' derives from a Germanic word *gant*, meaning glove. This gives us gauntlet, meaning a leather glove with armouring. So throwing down the gauntlet was an old form of offering a challenge.

Then we have gauntlet number two, as in 'running the gauntlet', which is entirely different. This comes from the Swedish word *gantlope*, meaning a passage between soldiers. There was an old military punishment where a solider had to run the *gantlope* – he ran between two lines of soldiers armed with ropes to whip him. Hence the modern meaning – to be attacked from all sides.

Geezer

One school of thought sources this from an old dialect word, *guiser*, meaning an actor, a strolling player, which connects it with 'guise', meaning appearance or clothes (and by extension, 'dis-guise'). Somehow, *guiser* came to be applied to an old man or old woman.

What may be a better theory refers to the Duke of Wellington's troops fighting in France, about 1811. They came into contact with Basques, who use the word *giza* to mean an ordinary man, a bloke. The military men used the word and it gradually came to mean the same thing in English.

And then, for some unknown reason, it tended to drift towards denoting an ordinary man who was getting on in years. Geezer has been in use in English since the mid-nineteenth century, so the dates match up.

(By) George

There have been six Kings of England called George, but the saying 'By George' refers to the saint, not to any of the kings.

There is very little definite information about St George. He is believed to have been born in Israel and joined the Roman army based in Turkey. Everything else supposedly 'known' about George is mythical or legendary.

Many years after his death, the story grew that after he became a respected officer in the army, the Roman emperor suddenly announced that Christianity was not acceptable among his troops. George, who was Christian, refused to recant, was tortured and lacerated with swords but still refused, and was executed in Izmir in Turkey in the year 303 on 23 April (by the modern calendar).

The main legend concerns George travelling in Libya, where he learned that the town of Sylene was regularly being attacked by a dragon. The dragon required two sheep a day to be appeased, and every now and then demanded a human sacrifice.

At the time of George's arrival, the sacrifice was to be a princess. George announced to the townspeople that if they would become Christians, he would fight and vanquish the dragon and save the princess. The townspeople agreed, and so it came to pass that he killed the dragon. The entire town converted to Christianity, and George possibly married the princess.

Did it happen? Nobody knows, but it seems unlikely since dragons don't exist – though, to be fair, one version of the story says it was a crocodile. Many fanciful poems, paintings and statues have depicted versions of this story, and it is from these that we get our impressions of George rather than from historical facts.

That story about his being a dragon-slayer did not emerge until hundreds of years after George's death. Nevertheless, he gained a huge reputation as a brave fighter and leader.

St George is the patron saint of Portugal, Germany, Aragon, Genoa and Venice. And in spite of his being an Israeli, during the 1300s King Edward III adopted Saint George as the patron saint of England and patron saint of the Order of the Garter. He was associated with the red cross on a white background, which became part of the Union flag of Great Britain.

St George became a figure who was called on in times of need, particularly in times of battle, to assist English soldiers. Originally the soldiers would simply call out 'St George!' – presumably to attract his attention. It's mentioned in Shakespeare's *King Henry V*: 'Cry God for Harry, England, and St George.'

In non-military use, the term evolved into 'by George' simply as an epithet of intensity.

By George is short for 'by St George', and is probably also used as a replacement or avoidance word for God (as in 'by God'). The epithet 'by George' is first recorded in English in 1598.

One small mystery: just as many things about saints aren't logical, it is not entirely clear why St George is the saint who is invoked against the problem of syphilis.

Get knotted

This admonition is intended to thwart someone, to dismiss them, and seems to have originated in the armed services early in the twentieth century.

'Get knotted' is actually a variation on 'get knackered', knackers being a slang word meaning testicles. Therefore getting knackered has a connotation of being castrated, which is definitely a condition of being thwarted and dismissed.

Getting knackered was considered such a severe fate that the word took on a connotation of being ruined or even killed. The word is still used to describe the place where horses are sent to be killed, a knacker's yard. The association with decrepit horses is twofold, since being knackered or castrated was equivalent to being killed, but knacker was also an ancient term for a saddle.

Although the above version is the accepted history of 'get knotted', there are one or two less scholarly interpretations of an anatomical nature which may be best left unexplored.

Gets my goat

Dating from 1911, this is a very American expression but it matches up with a French expression, *prendre la chèvre*, to 'take the goat'. Unfortunately three different explanations have come forward for how the term arose:

1. Goats were a mainstay of European village life, and if someone stole a poor man's goat, then he became angry.

2. A goat was often put into a stable as a companion for a horse. If the goat was stolen before a big race, the horse would become upset, and lose its competitive edge.

3. Goat is short for goatee, as in beard, so if you got someone by the goatee, you would certainly annoy them.

(Acting the) giddy goat

For many centuries the image of a goat has been associated with sin and even the devil, but the connection with acting stupidly is not clear. One theory about the term's origin is that it is a way of hauling someone back onto the straight and narrow when they're misbehaving. But goats do act quite skittishly sometimes and get a mad look in their eyes, so it might mean exactly what it says.

Gig (horse-drawn)

The small horse-drawn carriage known as a gig gained its name as a development from an earlier use of the word 'gig' to refer to a spinning top. And that word came into English from a Scandinavian word giga, which meant 'whirling'. The link between a whirling top and a small carriage was that the horse-drawn gig was very light in weight and, although not spinning, was at least able to move freely and rapidly.

Gig (music)

'Gig' has been in use by musicians since at least 1905, meaning a music performance job. It was commonly used to mean just one night, but has gradually extended so that it can now mean a booking lasting several weeks.

There are two theories about its origin. Ever since the 1700s, the word gig or jig has been used to signify a party or a spree. And because jazz by its very nature often arose from people making music together, often quite festively, the party connotation of a gig spread over into a new connotation of job – when musicians weren't playing together just for fun, but were actually being paid.

Then there is the second theory: that classical musicians often refer to a job as an engagement, which could be a violin concerto, a chamber music recital or a full symphony concert. Jazz and pop musicians found this term rather grand, and began to make fun of it by using it themselves, especially when referring to jobs in murky night clubs and venues of a dubious nature. Eventually their joking use of 'engagement' became shortened to just 'gig', which means exactly the same: a paid musical performance.

Gilt off the gingerbread

Once upon a time in certain circles, gold was applied to gingerbread. Not the moist cake nowadays often called 'gingerbread' – but on its origin, which wasn't 'bread' at all. The word ginger comes originally from the Sanskrit language, meaning 'horn-shaped' and reflecting the way the ginger root looked when it was harvested.

For several hundred years ginger was used only as medicine; until about the thirteenth century nobody ever thought of combining it with sugar as a confection (rather like cocoa, which in our culture is mostly combined with sugar and thought of as a confection, but in South America has a life in main course meals, as in rabbit with chocolate sauce).

But when ginger met up with sugar, it began to feature in British culture as a sweetmeat, baked into a solid block with breadcrumbs, flour, honey and spices and known as gingerbras, a version of the Latin name for the spice – *Zingebar*. This firm block was quite often pressed into animal-shaped moulds, or into a flat slice on which someone's portrait was painted. It was made into biblical scenes and even into miniature houses and castles, and all these were often brushed with egg white stuck with gold-leaf, thus genuinely putting gilt on the gingerbread.

In earlier centuries, the hard blocks of sweetened gingerbras occupied much the same social position as a box of chocolates does now. As a special festive thing, the gilding remained for many centuries – it's mentioned in *Mary Poppins* (1934) – but something quite major was happening underneath the gilding.

The hard block of confectionery gradually became lighter with more flour and fewer breadcrumbs, and then eggs and butter began to move in and the name changed from gingerbras to gingerbread.

For many centuries ginger was an expensive delicacy, available only to the wealthy. But sometimes even in the grandest of houses, a batch would be baked which wasn't quite first class. So decorating it and putting gilding on it could cover a multitude of sins. A concept arose that once you nibbled the gilding off the gingerbread, the true quality of what lay underneath would be revealed; if the gilding turned out to be the main attraction, and only a very thin superficial part of the indifferent whole beneath – the illusion was spoiled.

A maritime application also exists; the elaborate carving at the stem and stern of some sailing vessels was often decorated and gilded, and was known to seamen as gingerbread – and any accidental damage to the decoration was called 'taking the gilt off the gingerbread'.

Gingerbread assisted in the development of a famous sport. When Queen Elizabeth I first encountered gingerbread she liked it very much; she frequently had gingerbread men made, then painted in the likeness of visiting VIPs. Her supplies of ginger and other condiments came from Lawrence Sheriffe, a spice importer who died a wealthy man in 1657. He left a handsome legacy to provide for establishing a school in his home town, Rugby.

The adverb 'gingerly', meaning with reluctance and caution, has nothing to do with ginger; it is believed to be derived from the Latin *genitus*, meaning well-born, and has progressed to mean wary and tentative.

Give up the ghost

Many cultures subscribe to the concept that there are two parts to a human being: the physical body; and the life force that inhabits the body and makes it into a complete person. The expression 'give up the ghost' derives from the Jewish idea of people having an immaterial ingredient as well as their physical body. You'll find it in Chapter 11 of the Book of Job, which is where a translation problem starts. The King James translation uses the word 'ghost' to mean the non-material part of a person's life force, and uses the same word to mean the active essence of God.

Over time the word ghost gradually took on a secondary and quite different connotation, and in later centuries it came to be used in English for two things: (1) the spiritual, immaterial part of a living person; and (2) the soul of a dead person which manifested itself to the living world, and was nebulous because it had no physical body.

So there can be confusion with the phrase 'give up the ghost', which in Job 11:20 appears as: 'But the eyes of the wicked shall fail, and they shall not escape, and their hope shall be as the giving up of the ghost.' Here it means 'to die' in the sense of surrendering the spirit without which the physical body cannot continue living.

Although the two connotations of ghost have some similarity, they are confusing. Because of this deviation, some more modern translations of the Bible use the word 'spirit' both in the Book of Job and in the Book of John, where 'ghost' also occurs. And some branches of the Christian church deliberately use the word spirit and avoid ghost.

Giving me gyp

This has nothing to do with gypsies. It is an example of verbal contraction, like 'goodbye' (God be with you). Originally, when something was irritating a person, they made reference to a horse, saying about whatever was irritating them: 'It's giving me gee-up', as in jerking a horse into action. Over the years the gee-up has simply shortened to gyp, but the meaning has stayed the same: a probably unpleasant sensation which has the effect of stimulating something.

Gloop

The word does exist. The three words 'goop', 'glop' and 'gloop' have become fairly interchangeable; they all refer to sticky, gluey things. They are all versions of gloop, which is a word first noticed in a 1944 comic about a dopey character called Sloop the Gloop. Twenty years later Roald Dahl wrote *Charlie and the Chocolate Factory*, which had a very greedy character called Augustus Gloop.

The book became a movie called *Willy Wonka and the Chocolate Factory* (1971) in which Augustus Gloop was the subject of a song sung to him by the Oompa Loompas, called 'the Gloop song'. And after they'd sung 'the Gloop song', the Oompa Loompas turned Augustus Gloop into fudge.

Gloop is used as a name for a nourishing food, made of milk and mayonnaise with gelatine, golden syrup, yoghurt and egg, for sick kittens and puppies.

Gobbledegook

This is confusing, dense and possibly meaningless writing or speech. The word originated in America during the Second World War and was first seen in the *New York Times* in 1944. It was coined by a lawyer called Maury Maverick. He, incidentally, was the grandson of Sam Maverick, whose careless ways with cattle led to the term 'maverick' being used to describe cattle with no branding on them who roamed into other ranchers' herds.

His grandson Maury Maverick was serving in the US House of Representatives during the Second World War, and was placed in charge of overseeing factory production for the war effort. He grew to dislike the bureaucratic jargon and double-talk he encountered among politicians, and to describe this he invented the word 'gobbledegook'. He explained that he based the word on the behaviour of turkeys back in Texas, because turkeys were always 'gobble-de-gobbling and strutting with ludicrous pomposity. At the end of this gobble there was a sort of gook.'

Mr Maverick went on to issue a memorable edict stating that 'Anyone using the words "activation" or "implementation" will be shot.' From then on nobody did use those words, but the word gobbledegook remained.

Gobsmacked

Gob is an ancient word meaning 'mouth' in North-West England. The combination of gob with smacked, meaning absolutely astonished, was commonly used in Liverpool.

But it didn't leap into national or international use until 1991, as the direct result of one incident. A member of the British Labour Party made a particular comment about the government's health service, and when this remark was reported to Chris Patten, the chairman of the Conservative Party, he said he was gobsmacked. This announcement made huge headlines, and overnight gobsmacked became common parlance, first throughout Britain and then further afield. So although he didn't originate it, the honour of popularising the word goes directly to Chris Patten in 1991.

God stiffen the crows

For centuries, young children (and others) in Britain were employed as bird scarers, especially of crows. They used whatever means were available to frighten crows away from young crops growing in the fields.

In 1922, British MP Sir George Edwards published his auto-biography, *From Crow Scaring to Westminster*. Sir George told of his rural childhood during the late 1800s when, like many of the local children, he was sent out to the fields to throw stones and scare the crows away from crops. This was common practice in country areas, and young George was paid sixpence (five cents) a day for crow scaring.

So although 'stone the crows' originally meant exactly what it says, the story doesn't end there. The comedian Tony Hancock seemed to pick up part of the rural expression, and was fond of saying 'stone me' – as if he were a crow – as an expression of surprise or disbelief.

In parallel, and just as historic as Sir George Edwards' childhood memories of throwing stones at crows, was the Old English expression

'God stiffen it', meaning to destroy something or render it useless. A variation of this was 'stiffen the sinews', meaning to summon courage, as Shakespeare's Henry V instructs his troops: 'imitate the action of the tiger; Stiffen the sinews, summon up the blood ...' (1598).

In time these expressions reached Australia, and gradually two developments took place. The crows were re-introduced to Tony Hancock's abbreviation but its essence was retained, so 'stone the crows' remained an exclamation of surprise. And the crows were occasionally grafted onto the old expression about sinews being stiffened, resulting in the variation 'stiffen the crows' (and sometimes, in Australia, 'stone the crows and stiffen the lizards'.

The earlier 'stoning' and 'stiffening' had lost touch with their original image of either scaring or being brave, and had become images of surprise and/or exasperation.

Going like the clappers

The word 'clappers' is usually connected with noise: striking your hands together to make a sound of approval; or whirling round a toy which makes a wooden version of the same sound.

But 'clapper' is also an old slang word for tongue – either a real person's tongue, or that dangling bit inside a bell which makes the actual ding-dong. Hence, 'going like the clappers' means something is being compared to going as fast as many tongues all gossiping together.

Going on the ran-tan

The name and what it stands for date back to a very old British custom. Years ago, if a person was alleged to be a wife-beater, villagers would gather outside the house and beat pots and pans and kettles and buckets, making a terrible noise as they marched round and round the property – hence the onomatopoeic 'ran-tan'. This was repeated for three nights.

In time, the custom transferred to other misdemeanours; one recorded case concerned a woman who made unkind gossipy remarks about another woman, so all the victim's friends gathered and ran-tanned her house, resulting in 23 arrests.

The last known ran-tan of this specific folk-custom kind occurred in 1930, but the word has remained, associated with a noisy progress to somewhere, and it has become strongly connected with jollity, drinking and celebration rather than criticism and condemnation.

See also **Tin-canning**.

Gold–digger

> Sure they don't sow potatoes, nor barley, nor wheat,
> But there's gangs of them digging for gold in the street.

'The Mountains of Mourne', from which these lines come, was composed by Percy French who died in 1920. This was slightly earlier than the expression a 'gold-digger', meaning a person who befriends the rich in the hope of enjoying the fruits of their wealth. That is believed to have originated in the United States a few years later, around 1925.

So although the song and the expression did arise within a short time of each other, one speaks of digging gold literally, and the other of digging gold metaphorically. And we have to remember that expressions about digging for gold aren't found only in that Irish song: it was a common description of people who actually did dig during gold rushes.

Golden boy

The term refers to a young man of outstanding promise who is expected to do well in life. Shakespeare used a very similar term in *Cymbeline* (c. 1609): 'Golden lads and girls all must/As chimney sweepers come to dust.' The expression was possibly already known to him when he penned those words, and it's more than likely that the phrase 'golden lads' slowly changed to golden boys or boy.

The phrase assumed a new meaning in 1919 when a striking statue was erected in Manitoba, Canada. It was of an athletic young man, gilded, and known as the Golden Boy.

But the event that really nailed it into the wider public's mind was when the famous American playwright Clifford Odets' play *Golden Boy* was staged in 1937. The drama concerned a young Italian-

American who was a gifted amateur violinist. He realised he could never fulfil the family's ambition that he become a star fiddler, and he determined to achieve the same success and fame as a boxer.

It was filmed in 1939 with William Holden, and in 1964 the play was made into a stage musical with the story changed to that of a young black man, starring Sammy Davis Jr. For those people who'd never heard the expression before, it must have become familiar after a famous play, movie and musical.

There are many ancient references to 'gold' and 'golden': the Greek legends about the golden ass and the golden fleece; the golden apple of the judgement of Paris; the golden calf in the Bible; and the golden horde of Mongol Tartars.

In modern times we often hear of a 'golden handshake', an expression dating from 1964 meaning a considerable payment made to an employee whose service is prematurely terminated. This generated 'golden hello', which is bonus money promised to someone if they will leave one organisation and join another, and 'golden handcuffs', money paid to keep someone in their job when they've been made another offer.

Some of those expressions concern money, but some of them don't involve money at all: 'golden oldie', for instance, doesn't mean a rich old person; and 'golden boy' doesn't necessarily mean a rich boy. The expression is focused more on someone being special or much loved by family and friends; whether famous or not, he is as precious as gold would be.

Goliard

Not a word you hear every day, but it does exist. It was more common in the thirteenth and fourteenth centuries, and described educated jesters who could make up satirical verses in Latin, on the spot. They were roving scholars renowned for their riotous behaviour.

Gondwanaland

In the 1920s German meteorologist and geophysicist Alfred Wegener believed all the present continents derived from one large supercontinent comprising all the Earth's land mass. He called his continent Pangea, and believed that when the mass broke up over 100 million years ago, it formed a northern supercontinent called Laurasia and a southern supercontinent called Gondwanaland. Those two continents subsequently broke to form the land masses we recognise today.

The name Gondwanaland appears to come from a region in central India called Gondwana, where three million people known as the Gondi still live.

Gone for a Burton

There are two brand names which might be the source of this expression: Burton's beer and Burton's menswear. Etymologist Eric Partridge believes it was an RAF euphemism from around 1939, saying that someone had gone for a glass of Burton's ale when actually he was missing after an air raid – and presumed dead. The Burton's brewery's big advertising campaign of the time showed a huge crowd of people with one blank person-shaped hole in the middle – he'd 'gone for a Burton', and that is thought to be the origin of the pilots' expression.

But also the RAF wireless officers' training school in Blackpool was in a Burton's clothing store, and those who failed their tests were said to have gone for a Burton.

Another possible explanation is that a bomb dump which exploded near Burton-on-Trent may have generated the phrase. But really, nobody is sure.

Gone to pot

This can be said unkindly about someone who has put on weight, but its original meaning covers a number of other factors. For once, the origin of the expression is absolutely literally what it says – the pot referred to is a big cooking pot.

Since the 1500s the expression 'all to pot' has signified that something or someone has become devalued, isn't functioning properly, is less effective than it or they used to be, has deteriorated and in general gone downhill. The saying arose through the domestic practice of carefully collecting up the leftover cooked meat served at

G

the table. The leftovers were chopped into pieces and went, literally, into a pot, where they became stew, which was rather looked down on as inferior to a haunch of venison or breast of goose.

So, from meat, the connotation of the expression moved outward to include just about anything that had become a lower grade than it had started out, and 'all to pot' developed into 'gone to pot'.

Gone to the dogs

This expression appears to have been subject to several influences over the centuries. It dates from a time in history when social organisation wasn't the same as now, and when dogs weren't common as domestic companions. In many urban environments dogs led vagabond lives and were considered to be dirty and rather dangerous. So the idea of leaving an ordered, comfortable life and becoming reduced in standards was seen as someone's life descending to the level at which most dogs lived.

A version was seen in print during the 1500s in the phrase 'Bequeath him to the dogs', indicating that the person they were talking about wasn't much good for anything.

Reinforcing this attitude in parallel were the country households where dogs did in fact play a valuable role in rural activities. But often the gentry or whatever household owned them fed the dogs only scraps of food which had been discarded or disdained by people. This was thrown to the dogs, so again you get this downgrading. The expression turns up in 1775, in the play *Germanicus*, where prostitutes 'like Jezebel of old, will go to the dogs'. Thomas Hardy also uses the expression, and Charles Dickens in *Nicholas Nickleby*: a character gives it a faintly comic spin, saying someone has gone to 'the bow-wows'.

And there is also a third stage. Mankind (more so than womankind) loves to bet on things, especially things that run fast – the great joy of it being that one of those always finishes before the others do. Horses are the most obvious, but keeping and training a horse needs space, time and money.

So at a lower economic level, the racing of dogs became an established activity. But this too developed an unfortunate con-

notation because it involved betting, time away from home, and an
occasional complaint about the dogs themselves. There were those
who disapproved of going down the road to see dogs racing, and so a
further connotation attached to a very old expression – 'going to the
dogs' now suggested unconstrained spending of money necessary to
a working-class home. You'll find it mentioned in comic style in one
of A.P. Herbert's quirky verses: 'Don't let's go to the dogs tonight – for
Mother will be there.'

Over five centuries the image of 'going to the dogs' has accumulated
various influences which add up to its signifying that things are
perceived to be heading very much downhill.

Gone west

The sun rises in the east, moves across the sky, and every day in
recorded history has set in the west. So when a thing has followed
the sun, gone away, become ineffective, disappeared down the drain,
gone with the wind, performed a fade-out, it has gone west.

Gone with the wind

English poet Ernest Dowson, who died in 1900, was responsible for
what has become a very famous phrase in our language. Dowson is
not exactly a shining light among memorable poets, but his 1896
poem with the rather forbidding title 'Non Sum Qualis Eram Bonae
Sub Regno Cynarae', was about the break-up of a romance with a
woman called Cynara.

The poem may have languished unseen except for one notable
occurrence – American author Margaret Mitchell read it in 1937
and was intrigued with just one line: 'I have forgot much Cynara!
Gone with the wind!' She used that as the title for the novel she was
writing, which sold 30 million copies.

Ernest Dowson also penned another phrase that was later to
become very famous: 'The days of wine and roses ...'

Google

The Google Internet search engine was invented by Larry Page and
Sergey Brin in 1998. The name was chosen because it evoked the

similar word 'googol', which is a real word – a mathematical term denoting a figure followed by 100 zeros. This 100-zero association evoked an image of the Google search engine sweeping through hundreds of thousands of search options. (It is also believed that Page and Brine had in mind to tease the CEO of competitor Yahoo, whose name was Koogle.)

The Google search engine has no known connection with the other similar word 'googly', which is a cricketing term describing an off-break bowled with a leg-break action.

(For) good

Like many words in English, 'good' has more than one meaning. Obviously its usual meanings are commendable, desirable, praiseworthy. Back in the 1500s the original full saying was 'for good and all' and in that context 'good' and 'all' were both functioning as reinforcers and intensifiers – meaning for ever, completely and finally. It is now rare to hear the full phrase 'good and all', but the abbreviated version fulfils the same purpose – to intensify a statement.

Gordon Bennett

The name Gordon Bennett is often said as an expletive in times of shock or stress. There are some people who believe that Gordon Bennett is a mangled way of saying 'God and St Bennett', but the overwhelming belief is that the origin of the term is built on the amazement that grew about the exploits of a real person, born in the United States in 1841, called James Gordon Bennett – a man about whom stories have gathered, some true, some doubtful.

Gordon Bennett caused a major scandal in New York in 1877 when, at a very grand party, he got drunk and mistook the fireplace in the main lounge for a lavatory. Then because of what he'd done in the fireplace he had to fight a duel, after which he escaped to Europe.

Bennett then founded the Paris edition of the *New York Herald*, which eventually made money, and lived an extravagant life. He had an enormous yacht with its own Turkish bath and 24-hour masseur.

There was also a padded cell to house a cow who provided fresh milk at sea. In restaurants, he would eat up large, then simply offer the proprietor a handful of banknotes saying, 'Take what you think is right.'

He liked mutton chops for lunch and because a certain restaurant in Monte Carlo served them, he went there frequently. One day there were other people sitting at the table he liked for himself and, in a pique, he told the owner he would buy the restaurant on the spot. He did and, after lunch, gave the restaurant to the waiter who'd served him – his name was Ciro, and eventually Mr Ciro's three restaurants were among the best-known in the world.

Bennett's impetuous spending continued throughout his life and he became very famous. A street in Paris is named after him – Avenue Gordon-Bennett.

By the time he died in 1918, people were saying his name as an expression of wonderment or extravagant disaster. They may have wanted to say 'Oh God', but in those days any blasphemous expression was socially unacceptable, and the name of Gordon Bennett sounded close enough to the real thing. And it had the added frisson of actually being the name of someone synonymous with outrage and shock.

Gormless

This is a very old word in English, though it actually comes from the Norse language in Scandinavia, where in ancient times the word *gaumr* meant 'heed', as in 'paying close attention'.

Gaumr travelled into Old English and by the eighteenth century was being used only in the negative – gaumless, meaning failure to pay attention, being dull and stupid. The spelling gradually changed to gormless, but it has always stayed negative. You seldom hear of anyone being gorm-ful.

Some people use gorm in the positive, e.g. 'He never gormed me,' or, 'We take no gorm of him,' both demonstrating the exact meaning of gorm, which is 'heed'.

Gotten

This word isn't American – its origins are in British English as the past participle of 'to get'. The word must have travelled to America in the 1600s and remains in use there, but curiously has virtually disappeared in its place of origin, Britain.

As a past participle 'gotten' is now regarded as a totally American expression, though remnants of it are found in English words such as forgotten, begotten and ill-gotten, all of which are related to the old fifteenth-century 'gotten'.

When British actress Vivien Leigh was playing a classic English-woman in a movie, she became ill and was replaced by British-born Elizabeth Taylor. But by then Taylor had lived in the United States for many years, and sharp-eared critics were nettled that in one scene the director hadn't noticed that Miss Taylor inadvertently said 'gotten', which an Englishwoman would never have done.

Graffiti/graffito

It's not uncommon for a word from one language to be corrupted when it crosses a border into another language. For instance, media is plural, but is often used to refer to just one thing – television, for instance – as 'the media', which correctly should be 'the medium'.

Strictly speaking, a single drawing on a wall could be called a graffito and several offerings would be needed to constitute graffiti. But English-speaking people seem more comfortable using the term graffiti for every wall decoration, however many of them there are. The *Collins English Dictionary* acknowledges that graffiti can now be regarded as singular – when speaking in English.

(With a) grain of salt

This saying has survived intact from ancient Latin *cum grano salis* (with a grain of salt). Quite simply it meant that some foods were more palatable after the addition of a little salt (not unlike the notion that a spoonful of sugar helps the medicine go down). The phrase, which has been used in English since the 1600s, has come to mean that when there may be some truth in what you're being told despite your reservations, if you took some salt with it that might make the proposition easier to swallow and believe.

Gramophone

The various appliances and devices that now reproduce sounds are in fact gramophones, but are called something else. It all began in 1873 when sound was first captured on wax and could be played back on a machine that turned the little grooves back into music or voice. As the invention developed, it became known as a graphophone, a phonograph, a victrola or a gramophone – from the Greek for 'sound captured and written' onto a recording. This last term became the most familiar and, in 1909, 'gramophone' was ruled to be in the public domain.

Many improvements have taken place in the twentieth and twenty-first centuries – the invention of the flat disc, the addition of electricity, extending the playing time, adding stereophonic sound, digital recording and devising compact discs, Walkmans and iPods. New names took over, such as record player, stereo, even music centre. But the essential purpose of the first invention remained exactly the same: reproducing the captured sound. So at a pinch, according to the original meaning of the word, they are all gramophones – but the word simply went out of fashion.

See also **Walkman**.

Grandfather clock

Big, tall clocks with pendulums are correctly called long-case clocks – always were and still are. But in 1876 a man called Henry Clay Work visited a small hotel in England and learned about its clock – which had stopped on the day the hotel owner died – and would never go again. Henry Work went back to the US and wrote a song about a fictional grandfather to whom a similar thing happened.

Within a very short time the song 'My Grandfather's Clock' became known round the world, and the title phrase underwent a mysterious shift. Quite quickly the apostrophe was dropped, and instead of the clock belonging to the grandfather, as in the song title, the word grandfather was used to describe the clock itself – a grandfather clock.

The term is now fairly universal and has widened to include slightly smaller long-case clocks, which are known as grandmother clocks.

Grandmother/great-aunt

This is mysterious. It would appear that for many centuries the prefix 'grand' was most commonly used to describe the generation beyond one's parents – as in grandmother, grand-aunt, grand-uncle.

Grandmother and grandfather had many shortened versions – grandmama, grandpa, granny, gran, grandma, granddad – but those are all changing: the 'd's are slowly being eliminated, and you'll hear and see granpa and granma.

The prefix 'grand' remains for one's parents' parents, but in the late nineteenth century or somewhere in the early twentieth, the prefix 'grand' was moved away from parents' aunts and uncles, who became great-aunts and great-uncles – and nobody seems to know why.

(Doesn't let the) grass grow under his feet

It refers to an energetic person who does not allow things around him or her to drift or grow fallow. The expression first appeared in print in the 1500s and has turned up in English in various forms. In the 1500s it used to be 'no grass grows on his heel' or 'no grass grows under his heel', among other variations.

A century later the grass growing under the heel had developed into the version we're familiar with today. It can also be found in an old book about the history of four-footed beasts, published in 1607, which talks about hares: 'The hare leaps and lets no grass grow under his feet.'

Gravy train

This expression does have a connection with a real train – but not one which carries actual gravy. 'Gravy' is one of the many slang terms for money that come in and out of fashion: spondulicks, bikkies, the tin, the readies, folding stuff, and so on. In American slang during the 1920s the word 'gravy' had a run of popularity, based on the idea that meat was daily sustenance, and gravy was a pleasing addition.

When railway workers looked at their work roster and discovered that they were scheduled for a short-haul trip that was not a huge effort but paid the same as the difficult long-haul duties, they described that day's service as being on the gravy train – a day's work that wasn't too long or too hard. Gradually the expression became more generally applied and now means a sinecure, a situation where personal rewards come easily in return for very little effort.

'Green Grow the Rushes–O'

Some people ardently believe this song has religious significance, but little concrete evidence exists about exactly what significance, and there are many differing interpretations of the song. The most recognisable version ('one is one, and ever more shall be so') wasn't published until 1893, when it was called an 'English country song' and little is known about it.

The song is certainly full of biblical and astronomical imagery, but time and usage have made some of the lines unintelligible. Diligent speculators say that the 'nine bright shiners' are the nine planets, but some really convoluted reasoning is required for the 'April rainers', the 'six proud walkers' and quite a lot of the rest.

There is a plagiarised pagan version you sometimes hear about the triple goddess, the silvery wheel and the nine-foot circle, but that doesn't help much.

We need to be careful when saying what these old songs 'mean', because the words get corrupted over with use over time (see **Calling bird** for a discussion of 'The Twelve Days of Christmas'). This appears to be the case with 'Green Grow the Rushes-O'. The twelve apostles and the Ten Commandments and the four gospel makers could be seen as obvious, but the lily-white boys and the symbols at your door are not. Whichever interpretation people were told first is the one they tend to believe.

Just for the record, here is one interpretation that combines those symbols which appear to be widely accepted, with some of the beliefs held about the remainder. The result is a weird mixture of

G

G Jewish and Christian imagery and astronomical features. There is no scholastic authority to back up any of these:

- Twelve for the twelve apostles

- Eleven for the eleven who went to heaven (minus Judas)

- Ten for the Ten Commandments

- Nine for the nine bright shiners (could possibly be a set of bell rings)

- Eight for the April rainers (this might be a reference to the constellation of Hyades, which has eight stars and was sometimes known as the rainy Hyades because of rains coming in April. Or it could be Gabriel and the Archangels)

- Seven for the seven stars in the sky (perhaps Ursa Major)

- Six for the six proud walkers (could be a corruption of waters, thus referring to the pots used by Jesus at Cana when he turned water into wine)

- Five for the symbols at your door (this could refer to the books of Moses, or it may be a reference to the Jewish mezzuza, which all Jewish houses have on their doorpost to show that this is a house watched over by God, though it normally contains more than five prayer verses)

- Four for the gospel makers (Matthew, Mark, Luke, John)

- Three for the rivals (possibly the Father, the Son and the Holy Ghost, though the word 'rivals' doesn't fit their spiritual significance at all and may be a corruption of another word)

- Two for the lily-white boys (may represent Jesus and John the Baptist, though it's rather odd they should be clothed all in green. Or it may be a reference to the constellation of Gemini the twins, green being a reference to the coming of spring)

- One is one and all alone (the Jewish Jehovah, the Almighty God).

The Journal of American Folklore says that the entire song arises from the Hebrew chant of the 12 numbers, a form of which is found in the Passover service that Jews have observed annually for several thousand years. That Hebrew chant, which is called 'Who knows one', has references to the five books of the Torah, the seven days of the week, the patriarchs, the matriarchs, the Tablets of the Law and other strictly Jewish imagery. The much later development of Christianity appears to have resulted in a mixing of some Christian imagery with the ancient Jewish imagery.

Besides the original Hebrew chant, there was a German version of the 'Rushes' song in the 1500s and a Latin version in the 1600s. The English-language version seems to have picked up bits from all the previous versions.

But people can sing the song, enjoy it, put scholarship aside and stay with the interpretation they're happy with. Nobody else's view is any more certain than your own.

Green room

Before the invention of efficient night lighting, theatres presented performances only in daylight. Candles could be used for smallish performances and then eventually illumination by gas lighting became common. Also on record is that at least one nineteenth-century theatre used lighting provided by whale blubber.

Solo performers were highlighted on-stage by a rudimentary spot-light that burned lime (calcium hydroxide) at extreme heat and gave out a hard, white light; hence the expression 'in the limelight'.

Gas lighting and limelight are very glaring when they shine in your eyes for a long period, so the custom arose that the actors' waiting room or lounge backstage be painted a restful, cooling green. (There is a theory that the colour green is placid, and also that green is the colour the human eye needs least of in order to see efficiently.)

For many years the green room was actually green; the term has appeared in print since 1834. Modern lighting is not as harsh, but theatres and television studios still have off-stage waiting rooms called green rooms, whatever colour they may be painted.

Grip (film)

The term originates in the United States where the film industry as we know it first flourished, using a lot of people with backgrounds in theatre. The scene-shifters in theatre were called 'grips' because they physically gripped the scenery and moved it around, creating the environment in which the drama was to take place.

On film sets, there was seldom the same necessity to shift scenery around to a timetable, but the same term came to refer to someone who did a similar job: he or she was in charge of adjustments to the set, placement of props, building platforms for important features or perhaps for the camera itself. If the camera is to move, the grip will lay the tracks the camera will roll on, and get them absolutely exact. If a scene needs to be shot from slightly higher than the existing tripod, the grip is responsible for locating a bigger tripod.

The grip has become more or less one of the cameraman's extended hands, which is a distinct responsibility. In spite of the odd-sounding name, the grip is a crucial person in the making of a film. The cameraman doesn't usually leave the camera but when he looks through the viewfinder and the scene doesn't appear exactly as he wants it, he will ask the grip to adjust it. If the film involves large numbers of people and sets, there will be a key grip who supervises the other grips.

Ground Zero

This term used to relate to either (a) the exact area where a bomb hit the earth, or (b) the point of detonation of a fixed device. But the term has undergone a change. No bomb was dropped on the New York World Trade Centre towers on 11 September 2001, but the damage to them and to the ground around them was as if a bomb had dropped. So you'll hear 'ground zero' being used now to designate the area damaged because of an attack of some kind.

Guinea pigs

They are not pigs but rodents, properly called *Cavia porcellus*. The porcellus bit suggests that they do have a pig-like qualities: they're short-legged and stout and make little grunting noises. Their common name is a complete mistake – guinea fowl do come from Guinea, on the coast of Africa, but guinea pigs don't.

The family of animals called Cavia actually originates in South America, and the little animals were introduced into Europe soon after Europeans learned that America existed. The most generally accepted explanation for the guinea part of their name, is that, during the 1600s, British sailors brought them into Britain and sold them for a guinea (£1 plus 1 shilling).

For many years guinea pigs were used in laboratory experiments because they're small, easy to handle, easy to feed and they breed quickly.

Since the 1920s their name gradually became associated with anything or anyone who was the subject of an experiment. But the first widely publicised use of the expression came during the Second World War when pioneering New Zealand plastic surgeon Sir Archibald MacIndoe did miraculous restorative work on badly burnt fighter pilots in particular. Many of his patients belonged to an organisation set up for their welfare after terrible operations: it was called the Guinea Pig Club because some of MacIndoe's work was seen as breaking new ground.

From then on the term became widely used to describe anyone who was in a new situation, even if it wasn't exactly experimental.

Gun

Within the culture of the American gangland, people were assigned various roles: the car man organised getaways, the banker looked after the money, and the gunman had the job of resolving a situation, if necessary by shooting. 'Gunman' eventually became shortened to just gun, and that word became shorthand for an effective person who didn't mess around but got things done. Now it seems to mean: the best.

Gurn

It means a grotesque face, deliberately pulled to look bizarre and awful. The word has been in use for many centuries in northern England and Scottish dialect, and is thought to be a variation on 'grin'. On festival days in some places, 'gurning' contests are held to see who can pull the ugliest face – sometimes when framed by a horse collar. The town of Egremont in Cumbria has a gurning contest, which has been held annually since 1267.

Guru

The word comes from the ancient Indian language Sanskrit: *guruh*, meaning 'weighty' in the sense of authoritative. The word is used in the Hindu religion to signify an elder or teacher, and is used in English to mean anyone looked up to as a source of wisdom.

Guts for garters

The meaning is fairly clear: to put it politely, you have reached a fair level of annoyance with someone, and you propose to wrench out their innards and use them tied around your legs to keep your socks up.

The expression isn't polite and never has been. It has been in use in English since the sixteenth century. The first time it appeared in print was in 1598 in a rather grand play called *The Scottish History of James the Fourth* written by Robert Greene who, according to contemporary critics, was a man who knew a lot about low life.

So it wasn't exactly a surprise to the critics when, in that play, one of the nobles at the court of King James said to another, 'I'll make garters of thy guts.' Slightly modified, the expression has stayed in the language ever since.

It did go into obscurity for some time, and was known during the nineteenth and early twentieth centuries as being peculiar to the slang of racecourses. But then it surfaced into what might be called common parlance and although, with the invention of stretch-knit fabrics, garters have become almost obsolete, you still hear people say, 'I'll have your guts for garters.'

Guy Fawkes Day

Little is ever said about Mr Fawkes himself, but his most famous adventure has been celebrated enthusiastically on 5 November each year for many decades (albeit often misnamed as Guy Fox Day).

Popular though the celebration is, there is some vagueness about exactly what is being celebrated.

During the reign of Henry VIII and through until Elizabeth I's time, there was a great deal of religious terrorism in Europe; Christians killed hundreds and hundreds of other Christians for not believing exactly the same things.

Elizabeth I accepted Protestantism and the Church of England, and so did her successor James I. The remaining Catholics in England weren't happy; they thought the reigning monarch should be Catholic, so they set out to kill King James, who wasn't Catholic and wasn't well disposed towards those who were.

Guido Fawkes was a Catholic who had left England for Spain because of the Protestant king's oppressive policies. But a rebel Catholic group asked him to come back and instigate the blowing-up of Parliament Buildings in November 1605, with the intention of killing the king and all the Protestant members of parliament. Fawkes never accomplished what he intended to – he was captured and hanged (not burned), and his plot was foiled.

Now, centuries later, legions of people throughout the world celebrate 5 November with bonfires, effigies and references to Guy Fawkes – though exactly why is a puzzle. Is the celebration a show of support for Fawkes, jubilation that he failed, or just an excuse for a good party?

Ha-ha

A 'ha-ha' is a deep ditch dug around the perimeters of a stately home's grounds, rather like a miniature moat. It prevents livestock from straying into the grounds, but allows uninterrupted views of the surrounding landscape. There is one at Glyndebourne Opera House, which stops the cows in the next field from walking among the picnicking opera patrons.

The origin of the name is odd. It comes from the French Ah-ah – an exclamation of surprise, and was first published in the English version by English architect John James, who in 1712 wrote of 'a large and deep ditch at the foot lined on both sides to sustain the earth, which surprises the eye upon coming near it, and makes one laugh, Ha! Ha! from where it takes its name'.

Hails from

There was an ancient nautical practice of attracting or hailing a passing ship to ascertain its port of origin or departure. From that, 'hailing' as connected to a point of origin came to refer to people, even when not at sea.

Hair of the dog which bit them

This expression is based on fact. In times gone by people who had suffered a dog bite actually did capture the dog, pluck some of its hairs, and put them into a poultice to cure the wound. By the middle of the 1500s this concept was manifested in the belief that you could cure a hangover by having another drink first thing next morning.

Both practices spring from the belief that like cures like, similar to the basis of homeopathy, which is still widely used.

Hale fellow, well met

The greeting 'hail' comes from the Old Norman word *hale* meaning 'complete and all in working order' – thus healthy and strong. It survives in the modern English 'hale and hearty', and the word 'whole'.

Hale became an exclamation of welcome, an expression of the

hope that the person you meet up with is in good health; there's an echo of it in the modern 'Hi' (short for 'How are you?'). It also survived as part of the old word *wassail*, which is really two words – *wes hal* ('be healthy'). It was used as an exclamation before having a drink of liquor, especially among friends and with a feeling of good fellowship.

So if you go back to the original, 'hale fellow, well met', it actually meant: 'I'm pleased to see you and I hope you are in good health.' (Note that this expression is not correctly spelt 'Hail fellow ...')

Hamburger

The word 'hamburger' has nothing to do with ham; hamburgers get their name from the German city of Hamburg, which means 'fortified city on an inlet' and was founded in the year 811.

But what we call hamburgers don't actually come from Hamburg. Because Hamburg is a port, sailors were frequent visitors and there developed a kind of meat known as 'Hamburg steak'. It was basically what we would call 'corned beef' minced and mixed with onions and breadcrumbs, then pressed into a slab. One writer described it as having 'an emphasis more on durability than taste'.

German sailors travelled all over the world, and by the early 1800s, eating stands on the streets of New York were attracting the custom of German immigrants and visiting sailors by offering 'steak cooked in the Hamburg style'. This gradually moved away from being salted corned beef into low-grade ordinary beef, chopped up. The word 'hamburger' came to mean this chopped meat – what we would call 'mince'. The first menu to show mince being available described as 'hamburger' was in 1826, and this description remains – in America minced meat is still often referred to as 'hamburger'.

The street vendors reasoned that if a lump of this minced hamburger meat was put between two halves of a bun, then people could eat it while they were walking, and by 1900 early versions of what we now called a 'hamburger' were being sold. Their popularity took off, and it would not be possible to estimate the number of them made and sold since 1900. Often their name is reduced to just 'burger', and

163

– although hamburger means beef mince, not ham – we have seen the development of turkey-burgers, pork-burgers, venison-burgers, lamb-burgers, bacon-burgers, fish-burgers, ostrich-burgers, buffalo-burgers and vege-burgers – a long way from the city of Hamburg, where it all began.

Hangar

The word has been in use much longer than aircraft have. By the mid-nineteenth century, 'hangar' in English meant a large building with open spaces inside it, used for housing carriages. Hangar is a modified version of an old French term meaning an enclosed space or large shed. When it moved into English, the last three letters were lost, and the initial silent French 'h' was pronounced, so the word became hangar and that's how it has stayed.

William Thackeray used the word in his novel *The History of Henry Esmond*, published in 1852. Early zeppelins were sometimes kept hanging in a large building, but the word hangar pre-dates that. After doing duty describing housing for carriages, the word became a convenient name for the large buildings where aircraft are put at rest.

Hanky–panky

The origin (of the word, not the activity) lies in Latin, but there are several degrees of separation. If the Roman Catholic Mass is said in Latin, the consecration section contains the words *Hoc est Corpus* ('This is the body'). When old-time magicians wanted to pronounce a so-called magic spell before they carried off a conjuring trick, they often recited a 'spell' in fake Latin, which included a phony version of *hoc est corpus*, 'reconstructed' as hocus pocus and intended to sound as if it were bringing about magic. It wasn't, of course, so hocus pocus came to signify trickery and something that seems like magic but is actually false.

The term hocus pocus remains in English and its meaning hasn't changed. But from this magicians' fake Latin 'spell', it has developed into two other words. One is 'hoax', which means a joke based on something false. The other is the term 'hanky-panky'.

So the original Latin gave rise to a joke version, which engendered another joke version. Hanky-panky includes the hocus pocus meaning of trickery of some kind, but has developed its own reference – to surreptitious sexual activity.

Happy as a sandboy

This has nothing to do with beaches and summer. It originates from English pubs and houses which, in earlier centuries, often had slabs of stone for flooring in the kitchen and living areas. It was quite common practice to scrub a stone floor thoroughly and then sprinkle clean sand over it. The sand, and anything that spilled on it, could be swept out each day. But the sand didn't come from beaches – it came from ground-down blocks of sandstone, and was delivered to houses in bags carried by donkeys driven by young lads.

Housewives in those days had a fairly grim time. Every day they swept the dirty sand off the floor, scrubbed the stones and waited for the sandboy to bring a new bag. The traditional belief is that these women envied the sand-delivery lads their apparently free and cheerful life. Hence the expression grew: 'happy as a sandboy'.

The stone floors and the delivering of sand are now long gone but the expression has remained, and it might be that, over the years, this old phrase has come to fit an entirely new context: sunshine, sandcastles and swimsuits.

Happy Birthday

The song was written by two school-teaching sisters in Kentucky, Patty and Mildred Hill. They intended it to be a song for starting the day in the schoolroom, and it was called 'Good Morning to All'. That was published, including the tune, in 1893.

But in 1924 a pirate publisher printed it and without permission altered the words, from 'Good Morning' to 'Happy Birthday'. This was a huge success and the song was sung all over the place and republished several times, until the third Hill sister, tired of her two sisters' song being exploited, sued.

She won the case, and the court declared in 1935 that the tune of 'Happy Birthday' was owned by the Hill sisters, and every time it is used commercially, a royalty payment must be made to the Hill estate, right up until the year 2030.

(hash)

The little 'noughts and crosses' sign on the computer keyboard and the phone button is customarily called hash. Much the same thing is made when artists fill in an area by drawing vertical lines and then put horizontal lines over them; this is called hatching, or cross-hatch. They are actually all the same word, just said differently. Both are derived from the French word *hacher*, meaning to chop up, and in their English version, they both mean exactly that.

'Hatch' means to change a space with crossed lines so that it finishes up with a lot of squares – the space has been broken up. And 'hash' is to cut into pieces, as in hash brown potatoes, or making a hash of something, meaning you have broken something from the form it should have had.

There is no known reason that the keyboard and the phone dial key are pronounced differently from the artist's cross-hatching, since they manifest the same concept – a little drawing of a space which has been broken up, or cross-hatched. (The same applies to hash browns: the potatoes were grated – their shape broken up – before being fried.)

Hatch (chickens)

This is an entirely different word from 'hash' or the artist's 'cross-hatching'. English has borrowed three separate words with three separate meanings, but unfortunately they've all finished up being pronounced much the same.

'Cross-hatch' (as in drawing noughts and crosses) and 'hash' (as in the phone button and the potatoes) both come from the French *hacher*, to break up.

Then there's 'hatch', meaning a sort of opening, like a serving hatch, or as in 'down the hatch'. That comes from an old Dutch word *hek*, meaning gate.

And when chickens hatch, yes, they do break up the shell, but they're not doing it in French. This 'hatch' comes from an old German word *hecken*, which is to do with birds mating and breeding, and as a result of their mating, we speak of the new breed which the mating has given rise to: a hatch of chickens, or chickens hatching.

It's also that same word we use when speaking of people hatching a plot, because they cluster together (like birds mating!), out of which some event occurs (like a bird being hatched).

Hat-trick

It was an old custom of cricket players that if a bowler bowled out three opponents successively, he was entitled to buy a new hat at the club's expense. The expression has come to mean anything successful which is repeated three times.

Have the pip

There is a poultry disease which causes the birds to pine and wilt away. Its name comes from the Latin *pituita*, which means phlegm, and in English it's known simply as 'the pip'. In past decades, when more people kept poultry, the pip was a fairly recognisable word. If a person was out of sorts or in some way abnormal, they too were said to have the pip. Gradually the meaning drifted to mean sulky or bad-tempered, but its actual origin is a droopy, sick hen.

(The expression might cause confusion in the United States where 'the pip' tends to mean 'the best', and the seeds inside a fruit are called the 'pits'.)

Haywire

Two influences caused the evolution of the term 'haywire', meaning that things have got out of control. The image began referring to actual wire holding a hay bale tightly together. This wire came in coils, which sometimes sprang apart so that the wire went twisting and turning all over the place and was very difficult to control. In addition, farmers were known occasionally to use the leftover pieces of wire to do rudimentary mending jobs on broken machinery.

Hence there arose the term 'haywire' to mean anything that was either out of control and in a mess, or something slightly shambolic, makeshift and poorly organised.

(Lavatories as the) heads

Sailing ships had their own version of sanitary facilities. From early times the short horizontal beams on either side of a ship's bow (for hauling up or lowering the anchor) had borne a carving of a cat, and were called catheads. Since they were suspended directly over water, the catheads provided support for direct discharge plus a convenient natural wave-flushing system. So arose the expression 'going to the heads'.

Officers sometimes had use of a chamber pot or oak bucket, but the crew were expected to attend to their needs on the leeward side (pronounced loo'd, and believed by some to be the origin of the word 'loo').

The heads were in the front region of the ship rather than its rear because the ideal motive force for a sailing ship was a following wind. This meant that waste discharged at the bow was blown away from the ship. Hanging over the stern to 'discharge' would have affected everybody downwind in the main body of the ship.

Long after sailing ships were a thing of the past, seamen continued to refer to a boat's toilet as the heads and the expression is sometimes heard on dry land. But the original is plural – referring to the 'head' apparently identifies the speaker as a landlubber.

Head sherang

Head sherang, the boss, is from an Urdu word *serang*, meaning the principal authority, a commander, especially of a ship. The word has somehow floated into English, and is used to mean the absolute boss – the chief executive officer or the managing director.

It can be pronounced serang but is often said as sherang, and usually has the word 'head' added, which is unnecessary since the serang is the head person; doubling that makes a tautology (like saying 'rich millionaire').

Heads up

The meaning of the expression is fairly clear: notification of something to be aware of; advice that something is about to happen that needs your attention. Sometimes it's a warning or an indication of a possible impending event which might involve negative consequences.

The basic idea is as old as evolution, because it carries the image of grazing animals which become aware of a distant threat. They hear/smell/sense an enemy, their heads come up and they're poised for flight.

The expression is often heard in a sports context, and now crops up in digital formats, including information being projected onto an aircraft pilot's windscreen, and inside the visor of a racing-car driver's helmet.

But the expression's origin predates technology by many centuries; the image of being alert or 'heads up' can be found in one of the oldest Jewish references of all, the Bible. In the Book of Judges, Chapter 7, the Lord tells Gideon to take the people to the water. Those who drink with their heads down like a dog will be set aside, but those who take the water to their mouths while their heads are up and their eyes watchful will be given authority.

Heavens to Murgatroyd!

The name Murgatroyd has a wonderfully Gothic sound. Sir William Gilbert deliberately used it that way in the 1887 Gilbert and Sullivan operetta *Ruddigore* in which the ghost of Sir Rupert Murgatroyd is prominent.

Decades later, in 1961, an American cartoon television series featured Snagglepuss the Cat. Whenever Snagglepuss got into a fix, which was often, he yelled out, 'Heavens to Murgatroyd! – exit stage left.' This rapidly became a children's catch-cry across the United States, and is still occasionally heard now as an exclamation of great surprise.

Hell for leather

Top speed and especially reckless – the term's origin is surprisingly literal. In the days of horse transport, insisting on high speeds was hard on both the beast and the equipment: the saddles, bridles and so on. In other words, continued high speeds were hell for the leather.

The expression has been in use since at least 1889, when Rudyard Kipling used it in *The Story of the Gadsbys*, where a character says, 'Take the note and ride hell for leather.' There is also the slight possibility that hell for leather is an ages-old corruption of 'all-a-lather', describing an overexerted horse.

(Note that Kipling's Gadsbys bear no relation to Scott Fitzgerald's Gatsbys.)

Hemmed in

'Hem' did not always mean the sewn edge of fabric. It comes from an old Belgian word *hemme* meaning an enclosed piece of land. When that word came into English it was slightly modified into hem and retained a similar meaning – an enclosure with an edge or border. Gradually this meaning shifted to refer to just the edge, rather than what it was enclosing. And since edges of garments are seldom left raw, but turned up and stitched into place, the word 'hem' began to be applied to this border.

But when a person is said to be 'hemmed in' there is a leap backwards in language history because they're really using the old meaning of land being enclosed. It fits quite well with the modern meaning in that a garment usually has a hem right around its perimeter, but that hem carries no connotation of restricting the garment. Whereas in olden times, being beyond the hemme or inside the hemme meant being restricted – you were probably on someone else's property and out of bounds.

Herb

The English language has thousands of words borrowed from other languages and many of these are French. French people do not pronounce the letter 'h' at the beginning of a word, and it has been a linguistic custom in English for many centuries to follow this pronunciation, as in honour or heirloom.

'Herb' is an odd one. It was borrowed into English from French (originally from Latin) and most English-speaking people have not followed the rule about dropping the initial 'h'. But, curiously,

Americans have followed the old rule and customarily drop the 'h' at the beginning of herb, as if it were still a French word.

To add one inconsistency to another, if an American man is called Herbert, Americans do pronounce the first letter.

Herbs and spices

How do you tell the difference? This is a bit like trying to decide if a tomato is a vegetable or a fruit. Tomatoes are fruit because they have seeds – as does a pumpkin, which seems rather unlikely to be perceived as a fruit. (But sake is not a wine; it is made from grain so is properly a beer.)

In this case, herbs are everything green and all the rest are spices (seeds, stalks, bark, leaves, stamens).

Hermetically sealed

The art of sealing foods without air was known many centuries ago and the process was eventually named after the Greek god of science, Hermes, who was said to be able magically to seal a box so that it could never again be opened.

In parallel, there once were monks called Hermetics, who were philosophers and followers of occult scientific writings attributed to an ancient mystic called Hermes Trismegistus. There was a connotation of secrecy about Greek gods such as Hermes, and also about the philosophic mystics who used the Hermes name; the monks, like the air-tight seal, were totally protected and free from outside influences, and both were known by a name derived from the god Hermes.

Hermit

The English word hermit arises originally from the Greek word *eremia*, meaning a desert. That became *eremos*, meaning lonely, then *eremites*, who lived in a desert. From there it was only a short step to the English hermit – a person living alone and without contact.

Hey baba rhubarb

This is a product of the jazz era, when the word 'bop' was invented to describe a new kind of music that was fast and rhythmic with complex harmonies and slang lyrics. Bop engendered several variations, such as re-bop, presumably meaning 'do the bop again', and then someone put 'Hey' at the beginning, as a sort of attention-getting exclamation.

Thus, the phrase originally was sung as 'hey, bop a-re-bop', somehow through usage ending up as 'hey baba rhubarb', which is even more meaningless than the original.

Hiccup/hiccough

They are exactly the same. The word arose as an imitation of the sound you make during a respiratory spasm. Several languages have similar sounding words for the same phenomenon. English has three: the earliest version in the mid 1500s was 'hicket', which within a century had become 'hiccup'. There was some confusion between respiratory sounds, so sometimes 'hiccup' became 'hiccough'. The original hicket has long vanished – the other two survive and neither is incorrect, but hiccup is by far the more commonly used.

Hick

A distinctly rural person as seen by an urban dweller (who in their turn the hick may dismiss as a 'slicker' or 'yuppie'). 'Hick' came into use several centuries ago as a diminutive of Richard. This was in parallel to the fact that Richard has also long been the name of princes; there had been three kings of England with that name before the 1500s.

Richard is Germanic, combining the two words *ric* (powerful) and *hard* (brave), so is an ideal name for a prince or king.

But after King Richard III in 1485, the name Richard drifted into 'country' use and gained a parallel image as suitable for bumpkins. So much so that its childish diminutive, Hick, came to mean a bumpkin. Yet the full name Richard retained its brave and courtly image even as its diminutive came to mean a yokel – and the abbreviation moved from Hick to Dick.

Hick is now heard largely in the US, where it has become an adjective as well as a noun, giving us combinations such as 'hick town'. In 1933 American journalist Robert Quillen defined this as: 'A hick town is one where there is no place to go where you shouldn't be.'

High cockalorum

The term arose in the eighteenth century, based on the high-strutting self-importance of a rooster. Its base word 'cock', as in rooster, had the Latin intensifier *orum* added, meaning the rooster of all roosters. Sometimes it was written as 'high cockalorence'. It has come to mean a bossy superior person whose importance may be only in their own estimation.

Some scholars also point to an old-time game actually called Cockalorum, which was a bit like leap-frog where the person who could jump the highest was cockalorum, the rooster of roosters.

High jinks

The word jinks originally meant a kind of game. In Sir Walter Scott's novel *Guy Mannering*, set in the late 1700s, the characters play this game of 'high jinks'. By throwing dice, one person becomes 'it', and that person for a period of time has to move into the character of somebody fictitious and act as that person.

Among people of the time this was considered terribly funny; thus, 'high jinks' has taken on the meaning of lively good times. (Jinks is related to other English words: jig, jigsaw, jiggle and jog. They're all connected with movement; in the case of jigsaw, putting together pieces which initially don't seem to belong.)

Hijack

This describes the theft of goods when in transit, and its exact origin is buried within the American underworld. One widely accepted theory is that a gunman's usual command to his intended victim was, 'Stick 'em up high, Jack', which became contracted to hijack.

There is also a suggestion that 'hijack' is a corruption of the French *échaquer* – a word used in pre-revolution France. Related to *éjecter*, from the Latin *eicere*, this was the word describing the attacks made by peasants on nobles in their carriages, 'ejecting' them, then forcing the 'ejecting' of valuables from them. Mispronunciation in English, minus the evocative sound the word has in French, may have resulted in 'hijack' – whose meaning it much resembles.

In recent years its use has also been extended. From meaning to steal from a vehicle travelling somewhere, it can now mean stealing the vehicle itself, or stealing control of it (as in aeroplanes). It is also now possible to hijack something ephemeral: the market, or publicity, or someone else's idea. Or you can hijack a person – someone who is valuable to one organisation can be hijacked away by a rival firm.

His nibs

The origin of the expression goes back to the eighteenth century when the word knob was used to mean a person's head, and was also slang to indicate the man in charge – the head man, the knob.

The 'k' was slowly dropped, but the slang meaning stayed the same. By the nineteenth century the term had crept into university colleges but had changed spelling again, and a superior person was colloquially referred to as 'his nabs'.

Sometime early in the twentieth century the vowel changed again, and instead of bossy or superior people being nobs or nabs, they became nibs. Hence His Nibs as a sort of joke title, echoing a real title like His Worship or His Lordship, but usually for people whose demeanour or position was rather grand without their having a real title at all.

Hobson's choice

Thomas Hobson was a real person in sixteenth and seventeenth-century Britain. He operated a carrying and horse-hiring business in Cambridge, and he had plenty of horses. But Mr Hobson was very careful about the well-being of his horses, and very strict about letting each one out only in the order of their having rested. He always kept the ones who'd been properly rested near the door.

So when you went to his stables, no matter how many horses it seemed there were to choose from, you had to hire the one nearest the door. You really had no choice at all, and that's what the saying means. Hobson died in 1631 and the saying has been around ever since.

Hoik and oik

There are three 'h' words describing coughs: a 'hack' is a short dry rasping sound; a 'hawk' is a rather more moist and prolonged affair, often with a resulting delivery; a 'hoik' is similar – an energetic cough always followed by a significant spit. Hoik is thought to be a variation on hawk, both influenced by hike, which means to lift up and carry. So a moist cough was originally called a hawk and that became a hoik sometime in the nineteenth century.

There is a connection with an 'oik' – a yahoo. A custom developed among British schoolboys of pulling a face and spitting when hearing the name of a rival school, or when a person they didn't approve of was mentioned (exactly like Madame Fanny in 'Allo 'Allo! whenever anyone mentioned Germans). By then an unpleasant cough-and-spit was being called a hoik, so it gradually developed that the person being spat about, whose name was mentioned, was referred to as an oik.

The word oik came to be a term referring to someone generally regarded as a yokel, an uncouth nuisance the speaker held in contempt.

Hoi polloi

This is Greek for 'the masses, the many' and is taken to mean the general public. The phrase has been commonly used in English since at least the 1600s. There has been no attempt to anglicise it; the Greek is still used.

But strangely, it has somehow developed a very inaccurate resonance. There is sometimes a vague idea nowadays that 'hoi polloi' means the upper or ruling classes, the management. Nothing could be further from the truth. The confusion seems to arise from a perceived similarity between hoi polloi and hoity toity, although the two have almost entirely opposite meanings. Hoity toity is a seventeenth-century expression which began as highty-tighty. It originally meant being riotous or giddy before it moved into meaning superior and stuck-up.

Nor does hoi polloi mean 'the rabble, the mob'. The Latin phrase *mobile vulgus*, meaning the ordinary people has, in English, been shortened to 'the mob' and gained the meaning of a riotous and disorderly group, which has a rather different connotation again. Hoi polloi refers to ordinary folk.

By the way, there's no need to say *the* hoi polloi – hoi means 'the'.

Hold your tongue

The expression goes back at least as far as 1535 where it can be found in the Coverdale Bible, the first translation of the full Bible into modern English. In the book of Matthew, Chapter 26, the translation says 'Jesus held his tongue'.

Holland or The Netherlands

The Netherlands is the country's official name; the passports of its nationals say 'the Kingdom of the Netherlands'. In earlier historical times the nation was called Holland, but the name officially changed in 1815.

Only two provinces of the present nation actually carry the name Holland (North and South). But although 1815 seems a very long time ago, there are still people who think the whole country is called Holland. At least one major international manufacturer there, based in the province of North Brabant, labels all its goods 'Made in Holland', which is not actually true, but presumably that name is more recognisable throughout the world than North Brabant or even The Netherlands.

Holus–bolus

Holus-bolus usually means the total, the whole lot, and it's thought to be derived from an original Greek phrase *holos bolos*, which means all at once, the entire lump. English people gradually rounded that Greek phrase into holus-bolus, which has a slightly jocular air to it.

Home and hosed

It means secure, certain to succeed, sure to win. It's seldom used in the present tense, but usually in the past or the future. If something particular will happen to someone to their advantage, they'll be 'home and hosed'. Or because something successful did happen, they were home and hosed.

The connotation of being sure and certain to win is something of a reversal from the expression's original meaning, which was absolutely literal, and occurred only after all effort had been expended. After hard physical labour, being put under a hose is a certain way of being refreshed and cleaned. So once you're safely home, and hosed, you're in the world of the clean and respectable.

In its most literal form, the expression appears to have originated in horse racing, where the term has been widely used for many years. After training sessions and after races, horses are literally taken home and hosed.

There are two more theories. One holds that, because beer sometimes comes via a hose into a glass, when a job is finished and the feeling is good (because the beer has been poured), the deserving worker is home and hosed. The other rests on the fact that, in sailing terms, an anchor when lifted back home is hosed down. Neither of these theories is as strongly supported as the racehorse image.

'Home sweet home'

It was the title of a song which was the big hit of a London musical written in 1823, music by Sir Henry Rowley Bishop, words by American writer John Howard Payne. The show, which was called *Clari*, hasn't lasted, but the song is still a favourite and the phrase is often used without the music.

Honeymoon

Honey has always meant sweetness. But there is also a cynical belief that the initial thrill in a marriage would last only until the phase of the moon repeated itself after a month. The two ideas joined: so the period after a marriage would be as sweet as honey, but only for the duration of one moon.

That concept has been around at least since the seventeenth century. A piece published in 1656 advised: 'Those married persons that love well at first and decline in affection afterwards – it is honey now, but it will change with the moon.' In Gilbert and Sullivan's *The Mikado*, when the person being married is sentenced to execution a month later, he is told, 'You'll live at least a honeymoon,' meaning one month.

The association with marriage and honey was reinforced in some cultures by presenting the bride and groom with sufficient honey and mead to last them for a month; it was believed that honey and fermented honey wines after a marriage were an aphrodisiac, and would bring pleasure – and fertility.

The custom also developed that after their wedding, people who could afford it went for a holiday, which was known as a honeymoon trip. This became so common that the word trip was eventually dropped and honeymoon meant just the holiday after the wedding.

The old concept still survives, however, and can also be used about, say, a business going into a decline, or a political party. You hear people say that the good times are coming to an end, the honeymoon is over: the moon has changed and the sweetness has run out!

Hoon

The word is generally believed to be a combination of hooligan and goon. One etymologist saw a connection with Jonathan Swift's houyhnhnms – the horses in *Gulliver's Travels*, but the connection is less than clear.

There are also several meanings. A century ago it was a term referring to a man who lived off the earnings of organised prostitution ('hoon' was used as a rhyme for 'silver spoon'). Prior to the Second World War, anyone called a hoon was being identified as loutish, but during the war a change occurred. Conscientious objectors on other than religious grounds were known to the military as hoons – and they were not loutish at all, but thoughtful people, firm in their philosophical conviction that war was wrong. After the war the word remained, but reverted to its earlier sense of 'lout'.

Some grammatical extensions arose: hoonish, hoonism, hooning, hoondom, hoon around, street hoons, hoon it up, a bit of a hoon, hoon-chaser (traffic police) and hoon-bin (place where drunken football louts are put to cool off).

Horseradish

The *Stobart Cook's Encyclopaedia* explains that the word 'horse', when applied to any foodstuff, indicates that the product is big, strong or coarse.

For example, there's horse mackerel (which is an inferior type of fish), horse mushrooms (which are large and tough), presumably horse chestnuts as well, and also horseradish which, compared with ordinary salad radishes, is large, tough and more pungent.

Horseshoe (and good luck)

The symbolism of horseshoes is ancient and varied. Some have seen the shape as related to ancient pagan moon goddesses such as Artemis and Diana, and many believed that a crescent-shaped symbol of those deities (namely a horseshoe) over your door protected the house from evil.

On the other hand, for many centuries horses have carried an image of strength and nobility; as far back as the last Ice Age they were depicted in cave art, even before they became tamed and domesticated. So for a very long time the horse has been perceived as a good thing – and the horseshoe represents the noble qualities of its wearer.

And there is also the significance of iron. There was an ancient belief that iron warded off evil. Houses often had heavy iron nails studding the doors, because these helped to divert bad luck and disease. And a horseshoe is made from iron.

Witches, too, figure in the horseshoe mythology. Belief in these women of occult power goes a very long way back, and one of the beliefs about witches was that they were scared of horses. Witches travelled on broomsticks because they wouldn't ride on horses, and any symbol related to horses was enough to frighten a witch away from your house. Hence, a horseshoe.

H A horseshoe is roughly the shape of a crescent moon, which for centuries has been regarded as a symbol of positive things like fertility, good fortune and hope. It still is: in Muslim countries the Red Cross is replaced by the Red Crescent and has the new moon shape as its symbol.

So, bit by bit, in some complex way and for various ancient reasons, there is a gentle acceptance that the horseshoe had some affiliated powers because it was associated with horses, it was made of the powerful substance iron and, by coincidence, it was in the magic shape of a crescent moon.

Another good story exists to back up the horseshoe's perceived qualities. Ten centuries ago in Britain, a legend grew around a man called Dunstan who was working as a blacksmith. One day an odd-looking creature came to his forge and asked for shoes to be put on his hooves. Recognising that the hooves were cloven, Dunstan realised this was the Devil himself, so told him that to do the job properly he had to tie him to the wall; the customer agreed. Dunstan then shod the hooves, but deliberately made such a painful job of it that the Devil was shrieking with pain and begging to be released. Dunstan then told the Devil he would release him from the ropes, only if he promised never again to enter a house with a horseshoe above the door – and the Devil agreed.

Dunstan eventually became Archbishop of Canterbury and a saint, and although the blacksmith story is somewhat fanciful, it did a great deal to encourage the belief that a horseshoe was not a bad thing to have around.

Into this already complex mix of legend, myth, and belief came Lord Nelson; his relationship with horseshoes was very influential from 1805. Lord Horatio Nelson was a firm believer in the power of horseshoes, and everyone knew that a genuine horseshoe was nailed to the mast of his ship *Victory* when Britain triumphed at the Battle of Trafalgar, thus ending Napoleon's hopes of invading England. So these various ingredients have combined into a centuries-old belief that horseshoes are good.

There is, alas, variation in opinion as to whether the magic depends on their pointing up, or pointing down. Some cultures insist that a horseshoe must be placed upwards, so the luck within cannot run out. Other cultures insist it be pointed downwards so its luck will drip into your dwelling (there is also the interesting side issue that witches will not pass underneath a downward-pointing horseshoe).

So, complex though the matter is, it seems there can be no harm in putting a horseshoe above a doorway, or giving one to a bride; to do so would be following many centuries of belief – and there may just be something in it.

Hotbed

A hotbed is a glass-covered bed of soil, usually heated by fermenting material, used for propagating plants or forcing early vegetables. The word has widened to mean a situation offering ideal conditions for the growth of an idea or activity, especially one considered bad.

Hot cross buns

Celebration buns with a cross shape on them existed for many centuries before Jesus was born. In ancient civilisations, the oxen and the bullocks were important beasts, and in some places an ox was sacrificed once a year during the Northern Hemisphere's spring equinox. There were celebrations and little cakes would be baked with an image of ox horns on them, usually two pairs of ox or bullock horns, one pair upside down on top of the other.

Similarly, there were ancient festivals that celebrated gods and goddesses like Apollo and Diana, and the festival in honour of the moon had little round cakes with a cross dividing the top into four, representing the four phases.

So from those two sources, the custom of baking celebration buns divided on their tops into four was very widely established in many countries before Christianity began to assert itself. People who had become Christian tended to regard practices like these – worshipping the moon and making sacrifices to oxen – as evil, supernatural and unwelcome.

But some customs were so deeply ingrained that trying to eradicate them would have caused trouble. Therefore early Christians adopted these even earlier customs and placed a Christian interpretation on them. Thus people were told that the buns with the bullock horns on them or the four phases of the moon could, by happy chance, also represent the cross on which Jesus died – and gradually they became known as hot cross buns.

See also **Rabbits and Easter**.

Hull (strawberries)

Hull comes from the Old High German *helawa*, meaning 'to hide' and filtered into Old English first as *helan* and then *hulu*, taking on the meaning of the outer casing of something. The main body of a ship is the hull (you can't see what's going on inside), and the same name is sometimes given to the outer casing of a rocket or missile.

The calyx which protects and initially hides the bud of a strawberry flower remains in position after the flower has opened, and long after the fruit has outgrown it. But this persistent little calyx is still called the hull, even though it's no longer hiding anything. So there developed the verb 'to hull'. To hull a ship means to pierce the outer covering, and to hull strawberries means to remove the still-present remnant of the calyx, which had formerly hidden the bud and the young fruit.

Humbug

This very old word, meaning trickery and deceit, has been in use since the 1700s and scholars estimate that it grew out of the words 'hum' and 'haw' (meaning uncertainty or delay) plus 'bug' (taken from 'bugbear', something causing fear or anxiety).

Humbug used to mean a joke, but has developed a connotation of useless pretension –'what a lot of humbug' – concerning unnecessary paperwork or an explanation that sounds unlikely. And in Britain the word is used to describe a type of hard, striped, boiled sweet, although there seems to be no clear connection between that and the other meanings.

Humdinger

The term appears to have grown from within the armed services, initially in the United States, then moved to Britain about 1940.

It means 'spectacularly effective', and since it was originally applied to crafts of war, the derivation is thought to come from combining the two words 'hum', meaning the hum of speed, with 'dinger', a slang word for something good and/or forceful. Together, they indicate a humming, speedy motor that does a dinger of a good job.

Once the word had settled into use, it was applied to many other concepts besides an impressive motor – even an attractive young woman.

Humdrum

The word has been in use since the mid-1500s. The only explanation of its origin is that it's another of those words which has a repetitive bit added to amplify the effect: hum, meaning a steady, even sound without variety, has the echo word drum joined on to double the suggestion of boredom.

Hung/hanged

The preferred usage is that pictures and clothes get hung, but people get hanged.

In English some verbs are classified as strong – meaning that the internal vowel changes from the present tense to the past. A weak verb like 'to walk' just goes: 'Today I walk, yesterday I walked.' But a strong verb such as 'to run' goes: 'Today I run, yesterday I ran,' and sometimes in a strong verb, the past participle changes as well: 'I sing, I sang, I have sung.'

The verb 'to hang' is a strong verb, so its vowel changes in the past tense – I hang, yesterday I hung. But a practice arose whereby the word 'hang' developed two past tenses –'hung' and 'hanged'. It became customary to use 'hung' for all inanimate objects, whereas 'hanged' was used only when describing an execution, a death.

It's believed that the dual usage developed as a way of emphasising the mundane nature of one situation in contrast to the seriousness of the other. Apparently this word usage was encouraged by the judiciary, who also wished to emphasise the seriousness of the situation. When passing sentence the judicial use of the word 'hanged' became a powerful statement, because you never heard it in any other context. They wanted to distance the situation from that of overcoats in a wardrobe, pictures on a wall or laundry on a line.

The past tense also moves into future reference – 'he will be hanged tomorrow' – and it is also used as a participial adjective: 'the hanged man was buried the following day'.

But it is only a matter of usage; Jane Austen and Shelley and Samuel Pepys occasionally wrote of someone hung, not hanged, and it didn't slow down their careers. You can say hung if you want to – it's not a hanging offence.

Hunker down

This term sounds very American but it's more closely connected with Scotland. The basis of the expression is *hunker*, an old north British Isles dialect word for haunches, and related to a word from nearby Scandinavia, *huka*, with the same meaning.

To hunker basically means to lower yourself onto your haunches. Although the word does owe allegiance to Scotland, extending it to 'hunker down' seems to have developed in America in the 1700s, where it meant to lower yourself, either through tiredness, to escape the rain, or to settle in for a long wait.

After the phrase was established in America, it developed a secondary meaning of getting oneself into the mood for hard work: 'It's Monday morning; we're back to work so better hunker down and get the project finished before Friday.'

Hurly–burly

Hurly-burly, meaning uproar and confusion, has been in use since the 1600s, and in those days 'hurling' meant making a lot of noise. Usage modified this to 'hurly' and people added a rhyming word to give the expression emphasis; hurly meant noisy, but hurly-burly meant very noisy.

Hurray/hooray

This is a variation on 'hurrah'. There was fanciful belief that this was a Slavonic word *hu-raj*, meaning paradise, but scholars now discount that and believe that hurrah is a variant of 'huzza', believed to be a seventeenth-century sailors' cheer, possibly from German *hurra*, which means much the same thing.

Huskies

In English, husky has two main meanings: deep and slightly abrasive, as in a voice; or strong and well-built, as in a whole person.

But the Arctic dogs known as huskies have a different history. They are certainly strong and well-built, but with no connection to either meaning of husky. When referring to these particular dogs, in time gone by they were called 'Eskimo dogs'. Through careless usage, the word Eskimo became corrupted to husky, and eventually the 'dog' was dropped altogether. So husky, which used to be an adjective, became a noun – not describing the dogs, but actually naming them.

Hustings

Some believe that the word hustings is modern and American, but it's neither of those things; it's very English and very old. The word came into English as versions of two Scandinavian words meaning 'house' plus 'assembly', and the original meaning referred to a large group gathered around a chief, a lord or a king. One ancient use of the word was the title of the oldest and highest legal court in the City of London, the Husting Court, which survives to this day, presided over by the Lord Mayor.

But the ancient meaning also widened to refer to political gatherings held in the open air. Over the centuries the word has lost one shade of meaning and gained another. The hustings took on the connotation of the actual platform or series of platforms from which political candidates presented themselves. You'll find the word used in that sense in Dickens' *The Pickwick Papers*.

But it lost another connotation. Originally, the people assembled around the chief or king would have been loyal to him; in other words, they were all of one mind. In modern times the hustings are not necessarily outdoors any more, and they certainly don't necessarily involve people who are supporting the cause and the central figure. A modern husting can be indoors and it can be noisy and argumentative. In general, the modern use of hustings can indicate that the process of campaigning and electioneering has begun, usually involving touring and often standing on platforms, either indoors or out.

Huswif/housewife

Shakespeare uses the word *huswif* in *Othello*, 1604, right in the middle of a period when the word was undergoing a change. At that time it did mean a woman who managed a house, but could also mean a bold and shameless woman. Shakespeare uses the word about Cassio's mistress Bianca. She lived in Cyprus and she wasn't a camp follower; therefore she was a housewife. But she is also traditionally played as something of a bold and tempestuous young woman. So in *Othello* the word, with that spelling, appears to mean both things.

In later years huswif diverged, giving birth to two other words: housewife and hussy, often perceived as fairly opposed in meaning, but with a common ancestor (like Miss, Mrs and Ms, they are actually the same word, but their shades of meaning have changed slightly).

The word huswif still survives in the military as the name of a little sewing kit, with essentials tucked into a cloth that is usually rolled up, and is called not a hussy, but a 'hussif' – the old Shakespearean pronunciation.

Iceberg

At first sight this appears to be an unusual combination, because one word looks English and the other isn't. But actually neither of the words is English. 'Ice' meaning frozen water, and 'berg' meaning mountain, have come into English through Dutch and German. The English word ice and the German *Eis* remained sounding exactly the same, but the German word *Berg* and the English mountain, while they mean the same, look and sound quite different.

However, if you ask a German for the German word to describe a big floating mountain of frozen water, he will say *Eisberg*. So, when we say iceberg in English, we are actually using a word whose origin is totally German.

Icon

The word 'icon' comes from the Greek *eikon*, meaning image, and was originally used in English to describe a representation of Jesus or his mother, or a saint, painted in oil in the Byzantine style, often on a wooden panel. So the word has a connotation of veneration and worship, although in its strictly original sense it can simply mean an image, a representation or even a symbol.

Since the early 1900s the word has widened its application to refer to famous people, especially those who are regarded as cult figures. Major achievers in their field can be referred to as icons, for example Sir Edmund Hillary and Sir Donald Bradman; they were the focal point of something admired.

Ideally the word should be used only in connection with someone who represents an ideal and demonstrates supremacy. If the word is used too much, it will lose its power.

Interestingly, the original meaning, and the oldest, has the newest usage. The little picture on a computer screen which guides you towards a particular program is just an image representing an available computer function. It is quite rightly called an icon.

There's no clear rule that a person can be referred to as an icon only after their death. Dame Joan Sutherland and Princess Diana were regarded with (differing but special) respect as icons during their lifetimes.

Iconoclast

Leo III became Byzantine Emperor in Constantinople (Istanbul) in 717 AD. A few years into his reign, he reportedly became concerned that people were venerating icons (especially those depicting revered personages) rather than worshipping the actual religious figures they represented. To this end, he began removing or replacing icons, beginning by taking the relief image of Jesus from the gates to his palace, and replacing it with a simple cross.

Monks who disagreed with this policy described him, in Greek, as an iconoclast – a destroyer of images. This is thought to be the first use of the word in that context. The word has survived in English for centuries, with the slightly adjusted meaning of a person who attacks a cherished belief or institution and tries to display its weaknesses.

(Of that) ilk

Ilk is the modern spelling of the Old English word *ilca* meaning 'of the same family'. It is related to the modern 'like'. But when used as an adjective the old word means 'each', as in 'ilka lassie has her laddie'.

Illegitimate

A major change in social attitudes towards formalised marriage, or lack of it, has caused the word 'illegitimate' and its allied term 'born out of wedlock' to have an antique sound – because whether some people like it or not, the fact of being born to parents not legally married has become a mainstream actuality and its circumstances freely acknowledged.

Give or take some remaining legal barriers (an 'illegitimate' person cannot inherit the throne, or a title, and may have some difficulty in contesting a will) the acceptance of 'partners' and the belated recognition that use of the male partner's surname is a matter of choice, not law, has moved the word firmly onto the sidelines.

To a generation brought up in strict observance of inherited attitudes, which have now become somewhat elastic, the word still has an unpleasant and unwelcome sound but there is no specific ban on using it. On the other hand, younger generations don't even know what it means.

In flagrante delicto
It is Latin for 'with the crime still blazing'. So it means caught red-handed, in the act.

In one ear and out the other
This expression about hearing something that makes little impression and is quickly forgotten was in use in the fourteenth century, and possibly earlier. Chaucer may not have invented the expression, but he certainly uses it in *Troilus and Criseyde* (1374): 'Oon ere it heard, at tothir out it went'.

Over a century later, it can be seen in *The Proverbs of John Heywood*, his 1546 collection.

In the offing
Normally anything with 'off' in it suggests that something is going away rather than drawing nearer. But this 'offing' is a nautical term and, as usual with a nautical term, it's used in slightly different ways by different people. In general, the offing is that part of the sea which can be seen either from the shore or from where you are anchored.

Originally 'in the offing' meant a long way away, the distant horizon. But over time, for no known reason, the term has come to mean something relatively close which is likely to appear or happen in the near future.

(The) invisible man
The idea of invisibility has intrigued people for centuries, way back to the legends of the Arabian Nights and beyond. Hindus and Rosicrucians and adherents of various other philosophies have spoken and written about it, and magicians have devised ways of making things seem invisible.

But in the English-speaking world the first significant presentation of a (fictional) 'scientific theory' and its outcome – human invisibility – was H.G. Wells' 1897 novel, *The Invisible Man*, which made the concept and the phrase famous. Since the advent of movies and television the fascination with invisibility has been explored many times, including items like Harry Potter's invisibility cloak and James Bond's 'invisible' car.

Iota

See **Jot**.

Iron Curtain

This used to be a description of the fireproof panel which sealed off the stage in traditional theatres. The term was used by Lord Munster in 1819 (in neither theatrical nor political context) and can also be seen in H.G. Wells' 1904 novel *The Food of the Gods*, referring to the way a person is held isolated when in police custody.

Since then the term has cropped up many times, with slightly different applications. The first known use as a political image was in 1914 when Queen Elisabeth of the Belgians referred to 'a bloody iron curtain' which had descended between her in Belgium and her family in Germany (she was a princess from Bavaria).

The term appeared in Ethel Snowden's *Through Bolshevik Russia* in 1920 and the Hungarian writer Ferenc Molnar used it in a 1927 play. Nazi propaganda minister Joseph Goebbels used it several times; one occasion was reported in newspapers in February 1945.

But sometimes an existing term is used in a circumstance which catches particular attention, and that person is afterwards credited with having invented the line. Sir Winston Churchill used the term 'Iron Curtain' in a famous speech given to an American college in March 1946, referring to the barrier of secrecy created by those Communist countries which had cut themselves off from the rest of Europe after the Second World War.

Subsequently, Churchill was occasionally credited with having originated the term. He didn't originate it at all, but he did make it famous.

I should cocoa

This comes from Cockney rhyming slang. The phrase when used in full is, 'I should coffee and cocoa', meaning 'I should say so', and indicating that the speaker agrees with and affirms what is being said.

It's the pits

This raises an immediate mental image of a very deep hole, a nadir. But in fact the saying has a much more unsavoury history. Language experts Eric Partridge, R. Hendrikson and Robert Chapman all agree that the term originated among those drug addicts whose pocked and pierced bodies leave only one unused site as a last (and most painful) resort for injection – the armpits.

Ivory tower

The term ivory tower does occur in the Bible, but not in the sense in which it's used today. In the Song of Solomon it refers to someone's beautiful neck, and there is an ivory house in the Book of Kings.

But the more commonly used reference to the phrase comes from a poem called 'Thoughts in August' written in France by Charles Augustin Saint-Beuve in 1837. There is reference to a retreat where a poet could retire from the world into a 'tower of ivory'.

Over the next century and a half, the poet's phrase came to refer to people of high station who are aloof from common life, but are able to observe it without being affected by it.

J

(The house that) Jack built

There may never have been a 'real' Jack at all. The name simply refers to an 'everyman'. The rhyme is very old indeed; one clue to its age is the mention of the priest being shaven and shorn.

But nursery rhymes are often political. 'The House that Jack Built' first appeared in print in the 1750s, and there is a theory that Jack in the poem is actually meant to be the mythical character John Bull, the symbolic representation of an Englishman, and that the rat is William the Conqueror. The symbol of John Bull has been around for several hundred years, so it's possible that Jack is John Bull, but we don't really know.

Officially 'The House that Jack Built' is described as poetry based on the principle of accumulation, because it builds up and up and everything is connected to something else. For this reason, some scholars think it is based on an ancient Hebrew chant about a young goat, a kid, which a man bought his son for two coins, then along came a cat and ate the kid, then along came a dog and bit the cat . . . and so on.

Jack Robinson

Fanny Burney's novel *Evelina* used this expression in 1778 ('I'd do it as soon as say Jack Robinson'); and in 1780 there was a British Secretary of the Treasury called John Robinson who is said to have had the expression uttered in Parliament in front of him, as a kind of joke, so the phrase was well established by the eighteenth century.

One scholar believes it stems from a very old play where a comedy character called Jack Robinson used to visit people and would rush out soon after he arrived. But there is no evidence that the Jack Robinson referred to in the saying was a real person.

Jankers

This is a military slang term meaning punishment for defaulting. Sometimes presented as 'jenkers' or 'jangles', it is believed to be an 'echoic' word, somehow representing the sound of either the noisy bugle call which woke those who were being punished and had to get up early, or dating way back to square-rig sailing days when prisoners and those punished were confined in jangling chains.

The term was used by both the navy and the army. It was heard in the army context during the TV comedy series *It Ain't Half Hot, Mum*, when the pianist committed some misdemeanour and was put 'on jankers'.

Janus

This gentleman was an ancient Roman deity whose main job was believed to be opening up the sky to sunlight each day, then closing it at sunset. Gradually he became perceived as the master of entrances and exits and was thus 'the protector of doors'.

In 153 BC, the days following cold December were declared sacred to the god Janus because they were the precursor to spring, opening of a new seasonal door. Hence, eventually, came the name January for the first month of the New Year. Because Janus's appearance could only be guessed at, depictions of him tried to incorporate the belief that he saw into both the past and the future. Thus he was shown with a characteristic that is definitely not admired in modern times: two-faced.

Jargon

The word has been in English with various spellings since the 1400s. It is believed to have originated in a very Old French word *jargoun*, which describes the sound birds make when twittering. So in English it came to mean something similar – vocal sound but without any meaning. From there the word grew to indicate people's chatter. Gradually the word became a description of words and phrases that only some people could understand and other people couldn't – the 'in-house' vocabulary belonging to a restricted craft or a specialised subject. Such language tends to confuse everyone else with its use of in-words, which only others in the group understand.

There is also thought to be an influence from the old French word *gargon*, which is related to gargle – again, sound without meaning. One quaint development is a fairly new word to describe someone who loves speaking jargon and does so all the time: a jargonaut.

Jay–walking

In the United States there is a rather silly-looking bird called a jay that wig-wags when it walks and has a cheeky face. It is found mainly in country areas. In the late 1880s, the word 'jay' began being used by city folk to describe visitors from the rural community who were unsophisticated and somewhat socially awkward in a city context. They became known as 'jays' – a synonym for 'yokel'.

When cars started to appear on city streets, visitors from the country – less experienced with street traffic – were seen to cross in a careless way, not acknowledging rules, danger or pedestrian crossings. Again, they were walking all over the place like a jay bird. So jay-walking has come to mean crossing through traffic in a wandering, disorganised manner.

Jerseys/jumpers

A jersey is a knitted outer garment which does not have a front closure (as a cardigan does). Although the process of knitting was not invented on the island of Jersey the garment is named after the island, which did originate a fine worsted fabric that resembled knitting.

Another common term for a knitted top garment is jumper. The name was initially used by seamen to describe a loose-fitting all-purpose tunic they could put on over other garments. It wasn't necessarily knitted; sometimes it was canvas. The reason why that garment was called a jumper is lost in antiquity but it is believed it was because there were no fastenings, so it could be jumped into quickly. The name jumper gradually narrowed to be applied only to knitted garments which could be put on in a hurry.

Athletes wearing clothes in order to warm up their bodies before taking part in vigorous sport called these sweat clothes, giving rise to the term sweater, often applied not only to a jumper but also to any knitted top garment.

And pullover is often heard to describe a knitted top that is not buttoned or zipped or laced or domed. The garment is complete and enclosed, and is pulled over the head.

Jerusalem artichokes

This vegetable has nothing to do with Israel and is not an artichoke. The 'Jerusalem artichoke' is an underground tuber native to North America and was taken to Europe by explorers who thought it had a similar flavour to an artichoke. It is actually part of the sunflower family, and its leaves and flowers somewhat resemble those of the sunflower. Hence the Italians called it *girasola*, meaning sunflower, and English speakers mangled *girasola* into Jerusalem – plus artichoke, which they still believed it to be.

The vegetable had troubled times during its early days in Europe. An old wives' tale convinced people that eating it could cause leprosy, because of the ugly, gnarled shape of the tubers.

Job/work

An action or project which involves physical or mental effort is a job. The word is believed to have arisen from horse-and-cart days. A load of produce or goods that was as much as one horse and cart could deliver was called a 'jobbe', which somehow meant a chunk or a lump. Thus eventually a 'job' came to mean anything which represented a finite amount of work.

Tasks undertaken with effort and exertion, either mental or physical, are 'work'. That word originates in the Greek *ergon*, meaning a deed, an effort or an action. The word has gone through several changes to finish up in English as 'work', but the original Greek crops up occasionally in words like ergonomic (still to do with effort).

It is difficult to pinpoint a difference between the two meanings, but in general job refers to some specific effort – either one defined task or daily regular employment – whereas work tends to mean effort in general, even the effort expended in doing a defined job ('He works hard at his job.')

Joe Bloggs

The expression (of unknown origin) is a British way of referring to an ordinary bloke – also sometimes known as Fred Nerks, John Smith or those well-known three, Tom, Dick and Harry. Joe Bloggs

J

sometimes morphs into Fred Bloggs, supposedly because 'Fred' is easier on a keyboard – the letters being fairly close together.

See also **John Doe** and **Tommy Atkins**.

John Doe

This fictitious man originated in England where in certain legal situations a person may not have been specifically named, but was referred to as John Doo or Doe (or sometimes Richard Roe). This system was in use for several centuries but became less common in Britain in the mid-1800s.

A more recent use was in an interim order obtained by lawyers for J.K. Rowling in 2003 when a person not named in court was attempting to sell stolen information about unpublished Harry Potter material. The judgment issued by the Honourable Justice Laddie referred to the situation as 'effectively a John Doe order'.

In America, the name is used in similar circumstances – when a legal case involves a person whose identity is unknown, or is being withheld for some other reason; he or she is referred to as John or Jane Doe (sometimes Roe). Similarly, a corpse, or a patient in hospital whose name is unknown may be referred to as John or Jane Doe.

The term is also used in America a much wider sense as the fictitious name of a 'typical American male', along with John Q. Public, Joe Blow, Joe Sixpack or John Smith. Sometimes the name John Doe with a made-up address and other details is printed onto sample forms to demonstrate how a form is to be filled in.

See also **Joe Bloggs** and **Tommy Atkins**.

John Thomas

Prior to the nineteenth century, the expression John Thomas meant just an ordinary man, and was sometimes interchangeable with John Willie, which meant the same thing. During the nineteenth century, however, John Thomas became a euphemism for the male member, and John Willie went in a similar direction. Both expressions appear to have undergone, shall we say, a narrowing down of focus.

John Thomas received its greatest exposure, as it were, in the famous novel by D.H. Lawrence, *Lady Chatterley's Lover*, which was published in a limited edition in 1928 but completely banned in the United States until 1959 and in Britain until 1960.

Since then, John Thomas has been . . . the full monty.

Joker

Joker, by dictionary definition, means a jolly fellow, but for many years it was in British use to mean an ordinary sort of bloke – not necessarily witty or making funny jokes so, strictly speaking, not a 'joker' at all. Samuel Pepys used it exactly that way in 1669, writing that he had lunch with some old jokers – probably not distinguished gentlemen, just blokes, maybe somewhat lively over their food and drink but certainly not comedians.

In the nineteenth century the word was taken up in Australia and New Zealand, and is used in those countries more than most other places, with exactly the same connotation: an ordinary bloke.

Joker is a versatile word though, and may not always mean a pleasant ordinary fellow, as in 'a good joker'. The adjective before it can change the aspect: a bad joker, a mean joker, a wily joker. And sometimes it's anthropomorphised, so you'll occasionally hear something like 'the puppy was a friendly little joker'.

Jot

This is an unusual case of one word in English being derived from another language, and the original word still existing in English side by side with the slightly altered one. The Greek word *iota*, meaning a very small amount, has been modified into the English word jot, with the same meaning.

But it is not uncommon also to hear the parent word *iota* used in English, virtually interchangeably with jot. Both are used, and they mean the same thing ('jot' can be seen in the King James version of Matthew 5:18).

A secondary meaning has developed for jot: something written down quickly and briefly. It's the 'briefly' that is the clue; a jotting is a smaller version of something bigger.

See also **Tittle**.

Jubilee

If you abide by the meaning given in the Bible, the word jubilee actually means 50 years. So if you say 50th jubilee you're using a tautology (saying the same thing twice), and if you say 75th jubilee you're using an oxymoron (two statements of opposing meaning juxtaposed).

The word jubilee is Hebrew, *yobhel*, referring to the ancient practice of liberating slaves, restoring stolen property and planting certain crops, each seven-times-seven-years-plus-one (50). But not everyone abides by what the Bible says, and words do tend to change their meanings over a period of several thousand years, and are influenced by other similar words. For all those reasons, jubilee has become modified.

Part of the modification came from the more recent Christian church, which gradually watered down the original 50 years to 25, and established various 25-year rituals called jubilees. At the time this was happening, the Latin word *jubilare*, meaning shouting out loud, became amalgamated with the old Hebrew word *yobhel* so that, in English, 'jubilee' developed the double meaning of being a landmark number of years, plus a lot of noise and celebrating. Modern jubilees generally aren't quiet.

Growing out of the Christian modification, there have been other uses of the word jubilee, with other numbers of years, and from very respectable sources. Queen Victoria held a 60th jubilee. So jubilee has undergone a change of meaning, and is now freely used to mark any number of years (over 19) that could be an excuse for a celebration.

Jumbo

Long before jumbo shrimps, jumbo mushrooms and jumbo jets, London welcomed a huge elephant bought from the Paris zoo. He had been born in Africa in 1861, then taken to France. The London zoo bought him in 1865 and he became enormously popular – and enormous. He was known as Jumbo.

Amid great controversy, Jumbo was sold to American showman

P.T. Barnum in 1882, and the big elephant became an A-list celebrity in the US. Advertisers rushed to feature him on posters and packages helping to sell everything from baking powder to laxatives (one advertisement showed Jumbo feeding the Castoria laxative to a baby elephant).

His name caused discussion. Swahili is the national language of Tanganyika (now Tanzania) and all European police officers there were compulsorily required to speak Swahili. Former Tanzanian police officer Ron Callander identifies that Jumbo does not quite match the Swahili word for 'chief' (which is *jumbe*, pronounced joom-bay) but is much closer to the word *jambo* (pronounced jumm-bo), which in Swahili is roughly equivalent to 'Hello' as a greeting and its reply.

In America, P.T. Barnum had little interest in word origins; he just made energetically sure that in English the word jumbo came to mean 'large'. By the time Jumbo died in a train accident three years after he arrived in America, his name was in the English language to stay.

Jumbuck

Australia hadn't seen a sheep until 1788, but the first bale of Australian wool was sent to England in 1807 and sheep numbers continued to increase. By 1879, there were 1 million sheep in Western Australia alone.

Aboriginals had no concept or prior knowledge of sheep, and by 1845 a word being used by natives to describe sheep was being heard (by Europeans) as jumbuck. Various origins of the word have been offered. Etymologist Edward Morris in his *Austral English* (1897) quotes the *Sydney Bulletin* of 1896:

> The word jumbuck for sheep appears originally as jimba; jombock; dombock; or dumbog. In each case it means the white mist preceding a shower , to which a flock of sheep bore a strong resemblance. It seemed the only thing the aboriginal mind could compare it to.

Banjo Paterson's use of the word eased it gradually into international recognition after 'Waltzing Matilda' was first published in 1903.

Junket

The dessert called junket (flavoured milk set with rennet) has been known since at least the 1500s (Shakespeare refers to it in *The Taming of the Shrew*), and it was customarily served in a basket.

The word junket comes from the Old French *jonc*, meaning a reed, so the English name of the dessert actually refers to the basket made of reeds or rushes in which the sweet was presented. Because of the dessert's association with feasts and revelry, the word junket gradually gathered associations of merrymaking. By 1820, junket was being used quite separately from the dessert itself to describe a pleasure trip, and by the 1880s it gathered a pejorative sense of travel undertaken by officials, at public expense and serving little useful purpose.

Although the term has some history of being used to describe genuinely hedonistic travel for pleasure, it is frequently used unkindly to refer to any kind of travel by a public official, even attending a serious overseas conference.

Keep the wolf from the door

It's fairly obvious imagery, as hungry wolves would be very aggressive visitors coming to your door. There were wolves in Britain until the 1700s and an early version of the expression was first noted in English in 1470 (Hardyng's *Chronicon*: 'He maye the wolf werre frome the gayte'), and in 1600 English playwright John Webster wrote: 'keep the wolf far thence that's foe to man'.

A very public representation of a wolf as dangerous hunger is also linked with the *Three Little Pigs*, first published in 1843 as an English folk tale, though it might have roots in an earlier Continental folk tale about three goats (a clue to that being the line about the hair on the 'chinny-chin-chin'; goats have hair on their chins, but pigs don't).

American sources tend to think that the phrase 'keep the wolf from the door' became widely used internationally after the 1933 release of Disney's *Three Little Pigs*. But although the Disney people certainly invented the song 'Who's afraid of the big bad wolf?' they cannot be credited with inventing the expression. It pre-dates the movie by 463 years.

Ketchup

This started out as a sauce made from fish and spices – in the Amoy dialect of China it was called *ketsiap* and had been known since the 1600s. Dutch traders took it from the Orient to other parts of the world, where both the sauce and the name underwent various changes. English people left out the fish, retained the spices and recreated the sauce entirely, using mushrooms, walnuts, cucumbers or oysters. The word first appeared in English in 1690 as 'catchup'.

But the biggest boost came when the Americans, too, left out the fish and added tomatoes. So was born tomato ketchup. It is variously known as either ketchup or catsup.

KFC

In 1929 Harland Sanders began the Servistation Café in Kentucky, which served nicely cooked poultry. Over the next 15 years plans for a franchise grew, and in 1945 a chain of Kentucky Fried Chicken fast-food outlets was founded in Illinois.

The chain has stretched across a large part of the world and in everyday speech the firm's product became shortened to just 'Kentucky Fried'. Over time, a growing consciousness of healthy eating and avoiding eating fat made the word 'fried' somewhat suspect. So in 1992 Kentucky Fried Chicken sidestepped the issue by changing its name to KFC – thus avoiding the dreaded word 'fried'.

All signs, advertising, paper bags and store decoration around the world became just KFC. The recipes haven't changed and the chicken is still cooked in fat, but because the word 'fried' was removed, customers could put on weight without feeling guilty about it.

Khaki

The word is derived from the Persian word *kak* meaning dust or earth. That word travelled into the Urdu language in India as *kaki*, meaning dust-coloured. British military saw the advantages of wearing khaki-coloured garments in battle (instead of red or maroon) and the word has been used in English since 1830.

Kibosh

The word kibosh has been in use in English for nearly two centuries; it is found in print in 1834, then Charles Dickens uses it in 1836, and a few years later you can find it in *Punch*.

It's generally agreed that the word is not of English origin, but there have been several theories about which language it originally comes from. Some scholars say it comes from Turkish, meaning nonsense, a nothing (similar to the Turkish word which became Bosh in English), or a Hebrew word *kabash* meaning 'suppressed' is another possibility. There is an old German word meaning dead body or carrion that has also been cited as an origin. An Italian word meaning tin lid is also claimed – putting the tin lid on something

being an indication that it is closed down, finished for the day. A
Yiddish term meaning 'something inconsequential' has been put
forward, and Irish scholars say it comes from an ancient Irish-Gaelic
term meaning the death-hat, a slang term for a military torture where
a person was tied and a large dribbly candle was placed on their
head, lit, and left.

So there are plenty of claimants. But standing firm among them
is the analysis from the late Scots-born Professor Ian Gordon, who
believed it to be from French.

In French, *caboche* is one of the words for 'head' and in ancient
times hunters used it as a verb: when a deer was killed, it was
caboched – its head was cut off. This terminology crept into English
and drifted into use by painters, especially the people who painted
heraldic coats-of-arms and English pub signs. These signs often
featured a stag, or a bear or a horse, and if the sign showed only the
head, then the painters would say it was a 'horse caboched'.

Now obviously when something is left with only its head, it's not
going to enjoy a great quality of life; by the end of the eighteenth
century, the term caboched had drifted into more common use,
meaning: given the chop, finished, no longer operative.

By the early nineteenth century it was commonly used in English,
and a hundred years later, in 1915, the term became very famous
because of the song 'Belgium Put the Kibosh on the Kaiser'.

The word has had as many different spellings as it's had claims
to its origin; the two favourites are 'kibosh' or 'kybosh'. And you
can choose its origin from Turkish, German, Yiddish, Italian, Irish,
Hebrew or French.

Kick the bucket

Two stories can be found to explain this, but the credibility of one is
overwhelmed by the evidence of the other.

The first version is fairly obvious. If a potential suicide stands
on an upside-down bucket, ties a rope around his or her neck to
something solid overhead, then kicks away the bucket – he or she
will in all likelihood die. That version though overlooks the problem
of how, when the noose won't allow you to bend down, you can

get one leg below the level of your feet in order to actually kick the bucket.

But some historical dialect offers a better substantiated, albeit strange, explanation.

'Bucket' in English has one formal meaning, and one dialect meaning. The formal meaning is an open-topped container with handle, for carrying liquids or other substances. For the other use of the word we have to look into the messy business of slaughtering pigs.

Pigs are slaughtered at ground level, then have to be hung. In many English slaughterhouses the back feet of the pigs, in their death throes, were tied together, the feet often still twitching and kicking, and the carcass was hauled upwards on the remaining part of the rope, and suspended from a beam.

Now the crucial thing is that the strong beam from which the bodies were suspended was, and in some cases still is, called a 'bucket beam'. It has been called that for so many centuries that the precise reason for doing so is long lost, but etymologists connect it to the Old French word *buquet* (not to be confused with *bouquet*), which meant 'balance'.

Kilometre

Kilo means 1000 and metre is a specified distance, so the law of logic suggests that kilometre (1000 metres) would be pronounced killometre, with the same emphasis as killogram or killowatt or killoherz.

But there appears to be some confusion between metre and another Greek word *ometer*, which is an instrument to measure something, as in thermometer, barometer, speedometer, odometer, and those words usually emphasise the central om. Hence kilometre often finds itself mistakenly pronounced as if it were kilometer.

Kindergarten

In general English use, it means organisations where children are taught before they are old enough to go to a 'real' school. But the situation didn't start out that way. Kindergarten was a term associated with the German educator Friedrich Froebel (Fröbel), who in the nineteenth century devised a 'children's garden' (*Kindergarten* in German) wherein a particular education process was practised, geared to the very young. Their faculties of reasoning and intelligence were developed by various objects, toys, games and exercises.

This was very specific, but the word itself gradually moved into being used about any general organisation which cared for very young children. Often these had very similar activities to those promoted by Froebel, but not exactly the same. The word kindergarten became familiar in the English language during the nineteenth century, and it somehow survived the anti-German feeling of the First and Second World Wars.

King Canute

He gets a quite unjustified bad press. Canute (Knut Sveinsson) was a real person from Denmark, who became King of England in 1016 and later was king of Denmark and Norway as well. Legend tells us he was surrounded by sycophants who constantly affirmed that he was the most powerful person in the world and that he was even able to command nature: 'So great, he could command the tides of the sea to go back'.

Canute was a clever politician who knew his limitations, even if his courtiers did not, so he decided to demonstrate that they were overestimating him, and that he did not have the power to drive the tide back.

Canute had his throne carried to the seashore and sat on it as the tide came in. He commanded the waves to advance no further. When the waves didn't stop, but started to lap against his feet and his throne, he is reputed to have said words to this effect: 'Let all men know that even if the deeds of kings may appear great, there is none worthy of the word power but God, whom heaven, earth and sea obey.'

For some strange reason Canute's relationship with reality has undergone a complete reversal in popular belief. People who've misunderstood the story want to say that Canute really believed he could command the waves to stay back, but discovered he couldn't.

This is the opposite of what legend tells: he knew he could not command the waves, and decided it was time other people realised this too.

Kip

The ancestry of 'kip' covers quite a few bases. In early centuries the Danish word *kippe*, meaning 'a little hut' drifted into English and retained the Danish meaning for some time. The English use of the word gradually expanded to mean a roughly built house or shack, and then retained the connotation of 'rough' when it became a slang term for a brothel.

The brothel meaning lasted for a long time, but calmed down a little bit so that a kip became just any kind of boarding house. Then the meaning started to narrow, and from a whole boarding house, kip focused onto meaning just a bed, and then narrowed again to mean a sleep (not necessarily even on a bed).

Kiss (X)

This relates to a custom dating back to medieval times when not everybody could write their name. People were allowed to sign a legal document with the letter 'X', and indeed even those who could write put an 'X' adjacent to their name, either to represent the cross of St Andrew, or as the 'X' which customarily symbolised Jesus (and still does in the word Xmas …). Either way, it was an affirmation of good faith, assuring the document would be adhered to.

But after signing a document, a signatory often kissed it – again to confirm the promise to uphold whatever had been signed. Over the centuries, as more people became literate, the practice of affirming documents with a kiss filtered away (surviving only in some religious ceremonies where the priest kisses a holy book to confirm his accordance with the words therein).

But after all other aspects of the legal ritual had faded away, the association between the letter 'X' and the kiss remained, and still does.

Knocked into a cocked hat

It means to win by a very wide margin. A gun's firing pin readied for trigger release and a cocked hat both refer to something being turned upwards. The hat brim can be pinned together to make points: a bicorn is two points, a tricorn is three.

The expression 'knocked into a cocked hat' originates with the game of ninepins, where all the pins were set up with three of them in the shape of a triangle. When all the pins had been knocked down except those three, they were said roughly to resemble a cocked tricorn hat. Thus the ninepins were said to have been knocked into (the shape of) a cocked hat.

(At a rate of) knots

It's a fairly common way of saying that something is happening at top speed, but this piece of maritime terminology is sometimes misused by landlubbers. The vast dictionary of nautical terms edited by Admiral Smyth says simply that 'if a ship was going 8 knots, then it was going 8 nautical miles per hour'.

So 'knots' isn't an expression of speed: it describes a combination of both speed and distance. One knot equals one nautical mile per hour (a nautical mile is 1.852 kilometres and a land mile is 1.609 kilometres). But saying that someone or something is going at a rate of knots doesn't make much sense for two reasons. The word 'knots' itself indicates a rate – one nautical mile per hour – so you're actually saying 'at a rate of rates'. And, second, there doesn't seem much point in mentioning 'knots' at all unless you say how many: how many nautical miles per hour is this person or this car travelling?

However, logic was never a vital ingredient in the English language, and this expression, like many others, has developed a life of its own and is easily understood, even if it doesn't make much sense. The nautical term knots, meaning distance travelled in a certain time when used by landlubbers in 'at a rate of knots', simply means 'going fast'.

(Note that the word 'knot' arose because in olden days a rope was thrown overboard towing a wooden board of quarter-circle shape behind the ship, and knots in the rope marked divisions in the line by which the speed of the ship could be measured.)

Kowtowing

In historic China, the all-powerful mandarins demanded that people of lower rank performed *k'o-t'ou*: they were obliged to knock their heads on the ground. Travellers took reports to other parts of the world, and although the actual practice of kneeling and knocking the head on the floor never really took off elsewhere, the word, as kowtow, moved into English, indicating obsequious behaviour.

Latter

The formal definition of latter is 'the second item when only two items are mentioned'. Or it is possible to refer to a complete section of something that occurs long after the beginning, such as the 'latter part' of the film.

L

If more than two individual items are mentioned, or a whole string of possibilities is offered, and you want to designate the one at the end, the correct expression is 'the last named'. So: 'Out of cornflakes or muesli for breakfast, he preferred the latter.' But: 'Offered tea, coffee, cocoa, milk or orange juice, he chose the last named.'

(Going down like a) lead balloon

This describes something that was a disaster: a joke that didn't get a laugh; a play to which no audiences came; a proposed plan of action with which nobody else agreed. They all 'went down like a lead balloon'.

The imagery of the expression is obvious. A balloon, to be successful, has to be as light as possible. Anything made of lead is going to sink. The first known mention of a lead balloon to describe something that fails appeared in an American newspaper cartoon in 1924.

Leap year

A leap year is 366 days and it occurs with any year whose date is exactly divisible by 4, except for those divisible by 100 but not by 400. The year 1900 was divisible by 4 and by 100, but not by 400, so it wasn't a leap year. But 2000 was divisible by 4, and by 100, and also by 400 – so it was a leap year.

Apparently the name is because of its having a 'leap day'. This doesn't mean the leap year leaps a day; it doesn't, it adds a day. The somewhat convoluted reason given for the title is: during the non-leap years, the day of the month which falls on Monday this year, will fall on Tuesday next year and Wednesday the year after; but in the fourth year it will fall on a Friday because it will 'leap over' a day.

A more folksy explanation also exists: the reason for the name is that the extra day – 29 February – is hidden for three years, then 'leaps into place' every fourth year.

Less or fewer

Everyday speech is not noted for strict adherence to the rules. One rule that is consistently ignored is the old rule about 'less' being a description of 'quantity' (less sugar), and 'fewer' being a description of numbers (fewer people). The two are often misplaced.

Supermarket express checkouts are a case in point. Some have a sign that decrees '12 items or less', which is grammatically ridiculous. Others abide by good grammar and correctly announce '12 items or fewer'.

Letting one's hair down

It is usually said in a metaphoric sense, meaning the relaxing of standards, or behaving in a way that is somewhat uncharacteristic. The explanation for this expression is quite straightforward because, unlike some metaphors, this one means exactly what it says.

For a very long time, it was a mark of a woman's grooming, breeding and social status, always to have her hair dressed up around her head. It also gave a hint at her wealth, because elaborate hairstyles usually need to be done by another person. Hair was only ever allowed to flow loose in circumstances of the greatest privacy or intimacy.

That image, of hair being up indicating formality and control, lasted a long time. An elderly woman recalls writing a letter to her mother in the early 1930s telling that she had spent the afternoon playing tennis with friends, and remembering that her mother would be pleased her hair never came down once.

So initially, when someone said they were letting their hair down, they actually were doing just that and probably also entering a situation of considerable relaxation. Eventually the expression came to be used just when someone acted in a lively or unexpected way, whether their hair was actually up or down.

Licked them hollow

In early English, 'lick' meant thrash or beat, and some of that meaning still survives. A sixteenth-century expression was to 'lick whole', meaning 'completely' and a seventeenth-century variation was to 'beat hollow'.

Gradually 'whole' and the 'hollow' merged, retaining the 'lick'.

Lick someone's boots

The concept dates back at least to the 1600s, and it can be found in Shakespeare's *Tempest* with slightly different wording. Caliban says, 'How does thy honour? Let me lick thy shoe ...'

Lieutenant

The word is from French and has been in English for several hundred years. In absolutely literal translation it means 'holding the place', which used to mean a deputy, a substitute. But other shades of meaning have adhered to the word over the centuries and now the rank 'lieutenant' carries different levels of accountability in the military, the navy, the police and government (as in 'Lord Lieutenant').

When the word slid over from French into English during the 1300s not everybody could write, and that's how the confusion arose about its pronunciation. Some people couldn't distinguish between the letter 'u' and the letter 'v', so writing the French lieu, l-i-e-u sometimes went astray, and it looked like l-i-e-v. Hence the earlier conviction that the word was said as 'lev-tenant', which gradually became 'lef-tenant' (at least in England).

In America they leaned towards the 'loo' sound, which in fact is closer to the original French *lieu* than the English lef ... but ours not to reason why – just to explain.

Limner

This word came to many people's attention when it was announced that the Queen had appointed a new one. Limner comes from the Latin *illuminare*, to add brightness or light, derivations to be found in English words like luminous and illuminate.

A 'limner' is a person who 'illuminates' manuscripts, putting glorious coloured initial letters and decorations around the words and adding bits of gold leaf.

Universities, churches, city councils and royalty make use of these people to decorate special awards or diplomas. A calligraphist writes the person's name beautifully, and the document will carry a great deal more visual authority if a limner then brings light and colour to its appearance, on and around the lettering.

(Sure as God made) little green apples

It's a very old American expression meaning that something is certain and definite. The saying might transgress Christian-Judaic beliefs, in that Christians and Jews would surely believe that God must be credited with making considerably more than just apples. But this, of course, is exactly what the expression does reinforce – that God made everything, including sour things like little green apples!

Recently there has been some confusion about this expression because of a popular song that said 'God didn't make little green apples' but you have to listen to the lyrics carefully to realise that the negative is deliberate: 'If that's not loving you, then all I have to say is God didn't make the little green apples, and it don't rain in Indianapolis in the summertime . . .'

Little tacker

It is used to mean a young creature, usually a young person (as in a girl or boy), though it can also apply to an animal such as a puppy. 'Little tacker' occupies much the same position as little nipper, or little blighter – when said affectionately. The word comes from the dialects of South-West England, specifically Cornwall and Devon.

Livid

The word 'livid' comes from the Latin *lividus* and means black and blue. It has gathered a somewhat separate side meaning of being angry and, probably because of that, the word is sometimes heard being used to indicate the colour red. While people in anger may sometimes show heightened red colour, they would be most unlikely to turn black and blue, though that is (literally) what livid means.

By stretching the original meaning a little, 'black and blue' could mean a purple-ish plum shade (perhaps like a bruise), which begins to seem more logical.

Living daylights

This emphasises the severity or thoroughness of an action. The image is based on a word not used in common speech any more: 'lights', an old-fashioned word for lungs. In times past butchers kept their ordinary meat slightly separated from their offal, and the latter had a sign over it saying: 'Liver and lights'. This developed into a phrase emphasising violence, in that it would be announced that someone would have their liver and lights beaten out of them, which is fairly self-explanatory.

And over time that became corrupted into the phrase 'scare the living daylights' or 'beat the living daylights', which doesn't make sense but everyone knew what it meant. There was also a side issue: boxing ring slang, where a boxer's eyes were referred to as his 'daylights', and a boxer's wish to beat the daylights out of his opponent also seemed quite valid.

So the phrase 'beat the living daylights' gained a further dimension, and in analysis it means your liver, lungs and eyeballs will be beaten out of you.

Living from hand to mouth

Referring specifically to poverty or tight budgeting, the expression was first found in a treatise by Bishop Reynolds of Norwich in 1640. From then on it was in general use, especially during periods of economic difficulty, such as the Great Depression of the early 1930s.

Living the life of Reilly

Who was Reilly, and what sort of life did he live? According to the expression, he lived luxuriously and comfortably. This particular Reilly is believed to be an example of just how powerful and memorable a character from a popular song can be – like the man who broke the bank at Monte Carlo, or Mrs Worthington, who was advised not to put her daughter on the stage.

The song believed to have inspired this expression is about a fictional man called O'Reilly (sometimes Riley). There was a popular vaudeville artist called Pat Rooney who sang the song 'Are You the O'Reilly?' to enormous effect during the latter half of the nineteenth century. The song was so well known that the audience used to join in each chorus, which went:

Are you the O'Reilly who keeps this hotel?
Are you the O'Reilly they speak of so well?
Are you the O'Reilly they speak of so highly?
Gor blimey O'Reilly . . . you're looking well.

From this song it is believed the expression 'life of Reilly' went into popular parlance.

By 1919 the concept of this fictional O'Reilly had taken hold, and was referred to in another vaudeville song:

Faith and my name is Kelly, Michael Kelly
But I'm living the life of Reilly just the same.

Lodestone and/or touchstone

These are both actual stones. A touchstone is a flint-like stone, either basalt or jasper, which is used to test the purity of gold or silver. The touchstone is rubbed against the so-called gold and then immediately rubbed against another metal whose contents are known and proven. Both rubbings leave a coloured streak on each metal, and by comparing the two streaks, an expert can interpret the purity or impurity of the gold against which the touchstone was rubbed.

But the word has gathered a meaning of being a criterion and a paragon. To say something is a touchstone means you're naming a standard against which other standards are to be judged.

A lodestone (sometimes spelt loadstone) is also a real stone, an oxide of iron known as magnetite. It is the only substance in nature which has magnetic qualities. This has been known for centuries, and lodestones were in use for ships' compasses hundreds of years ago. The word 'lode' has an old meaning – to guide, or a course to follow. It is also found in the word lodestar, which is a star used as a source of reference for navigation. The word lodestone has also gathered a meaning outside its strict definition, in that a person or thing can be called a lodestar or a lodestone by becoming a natural focus of attention.

Sometimes people confuse lodestone and touchstone. It is possible for a person who is a celebrity or leader to be both things. The person could be a natural focus of attention (a lodestone), and also a fine example of how we would like people to be (a touchstone).

But the two things don't automatically go together. One could say of a pop star that the way she dresses and behaves makes her a lodestone – she attracts attention and even admiration, especially from young people. But many parents would not say she's a touch-stone, because they don't regard the standard she sets as very high. They don't mind their children focusing attention on her, but they don't want them actually to copy her and her standards!

Loft should be high

The word 'loft' is derived from the German *Luft*, meaning air, and is applied to places that are high: the gallery where a choir or organ can be placed in a church; the storage room for hay above a stable; the raised structure that houses pigeons; the space directly underneath a roof where a loft apartment is situated.

For unknown reasons, American usage has deliberately moved the word loft downwards, to describe apartments even at ground level. Although a building would normally have its loft up above the ceilings, American apartment complexes may present a whole row of lofts opening straight off the street!

Lord and lady

As a term of rank in the secular sense (rather than the biblical sense, where 'Lord' can mean something rather different), these two words have been around for centuries. Lord can mean a man of high hereditary rank, or a man with bestowed power (such as Lord Bishop, Lord Mayor).

The word comes from the ancient English word *hlaford*, meaning keeper of the bread. His wife would be called Lady (in the British system men always share the title with their wives, but if women have a title of their own, it is never shared with their husbands), which comes from the Old English *hlaefdige*, meaning the kneader of the bread (the *dige* bit at the end of the word still survives as 'dough').

Lost his marbles

In the decades at the end of the nineteenth century and the beginning of the twentieth, playing with marbles was hugely popular among children. Quite complex terminology described many different games and kinds of marbles, which could become treasured possessions. The loss of a special marble – either in competition or by any other means – could cause major distress to a young owner.

A well-known story in the early twentieth century told of a boy whose marbles were stolen by a monkey, and the phrase that someone's marbles had gone with the monkey became an indication that the person was in distress. The equating of going crazy with losing a precious marble had appeared in print by 1902. The concept took hold in Canada where, by the 1920s, losing one's marbles had become indicative of being not quite sane. During the 1930s the saying drifted to the United States.

It was also heard in the positive: to have all one's marbles, meaning to be smart and savvy. English novelist P.G. Wodehouse refers to it this way: 'Do men who have got all their marbles go swimming in lakes with their clothes on?'

By 1950, both versions had become fairly universal.

Lost their rag

Many kinds of shirt are designed to be tucked into the trousers. If the ones that are meant to be tucked in leave their moorings, some people see this as evidence of loss of self-control. 'Get my rag out' is a variation of 'get my shirt out' – to lose control and become angry. 'Lost my rag' is another version of the same idea.

Alongside these are 'lose my cool' (meaning composure), 'lose the plot' (forget the sequence of events), 'lose my marbles' (become irrational and forgetful), 'lose my cookies' (lose physical control, and vomit), and, the ultimate, 'lose it' (lose control of everything).

Lotto

Obviously the word 'lotto' is connected with 'lottery', but it has a slightly different origin. The word lottery is believed to come from Dutch, referring to people holding numbered cards from which random winners are drawn. With a meaning something like this, lottery has been used in English since the sixteenth century.

The shorter word lotto is a close relative but it appears not to be just an abbreviation of lottery. It is an Italian word – or at least an Italian version of the lottery word. The Italian language likes words that are short and sharp with a double consonant in the middle and a vowel at the end.

So the French have been saying their version, *loto*, and the Italians have been saying *lotto*. The Italian version crept into English use in the eighteenth century.

Lounge lizards

When the expression first appeared in print in the United States in 1923 it meant 'sleek adventurous men who frequented places where elegant women gather in expectation of their money and their caresses'. So the concept was that such 'lizards' were always male.

A female version, lounge lizzies, meaning writers of gossip columns or social chit-chat, does exist but has less traction. The original perception prevails – that lounge lizards are men.

Lukewarm

We're actually saying the same thing twice: as the ancestor of 'luke', language scholars point to the fourteenth-century English word *hleow*, which means warm. So if a thing is luke, it's already been described as warm.

Luna rossa

Luna rossa means 'red moon', perhaps properly described as a weather phenomenon rather than an astronomical one. There needs to be considerable heat in the sun during the day, and sometimes during an Italian summer, the moon at night has a reddish tint – it is a *luna rossa*. The locals know this signifies that the summer heat is not going to go away just yet.

Unlike the phrase 'blue moon', which has an idiomatic significance in English, the phrase 'red moon' doesn't seem to have any comparative significance in Italian, though Italian people will sometimes say *Luna rossa stasera, domani sera bella*: 'There is a red moon tonight, so tomorrow will be wonderful.' It has a faint similarity to the English expression, 'Red sky at night, shepherd's delight.'

The song 'Luna Rossa' is very well known, and it also has an air of romance, warmth, happiness, hope and good weather.

Lupin Pooter

This is a character in a once well-known English book, *The Diary of a Nobody*, by George and Weedon Grossmith, published in 1892. It is about a terribly ordinary man in an ordinary suburb with an ordinary job, and yet somehow the book is very funny. The main character is Mr Charles Pooter, who has a son called Lupin.

So Lupin Pooter is 'Mr Nobody's' child!

(Left in the) lurch

The word dates back to an Old French game called *Lourche* which was popular during the 1600s, and is similar to cribbage, played with a little board and pegs. The structure of the game is such that if one player has pegged a score of 51 before the other player has pegged 31, then it is clear that this player cannot beat his opponent – so he is in *lourche*, and when the same game was played in England, that became 'in the lurch'.

It gradually moved beyond just that game, and came to mean being in a helpless plight.

Lurgy

A lurgy is an unspecified illness or germ. It has many applications, covers all kinds of distress caused by illness and is sometimes referred to as 'the dreaded lurgy'.

In 1897 a German firm named Metallurgische Gesellschaft was founded, specialising in metal and chemical processing. This firm used five letters of its name, lurgi, as its cable address, and when it separated into various companies in 1919, one firm, which concentrated on gaseous products, was actually named Lurgi. The name Lurgi was well known to industrial chemists and because the company was involved in metal manufacture, that word was printed on the containers it made, including those containing poisonous gases. So among the Allied military in both wars, there arose an association between the words lurgi and poison gas.

When *The Goon Show* first startled Britain and the Commonwealth in 1951, radio audiences encountered what came to be called 'alternative humour'. The Goons, specialising in creative lateral thinking, wrote and broadcast such icons of appealing nonsense as the 'Legend of the Phantom Head Shaver', the 'Affair of the Lone Banana' and the 'Dreaded Batter Pudding Hurler of Bexhill-on-Sea'.

In November 1954 they broadcast a story called 'The Lurgi Strikes Britain', which was about a mysterious and somewhat ridiculous disease. The word lurgy went into the language almost immediately. Because initially it was only heard spoken on radio, it emerged in print with various spellings. It has been used ever since to mean a slight illness – or worse, a dreaded lurgy.

(The real) McCoy

There are two very similar expressions with a mysterious relationship one to the other: 'the real McKay' and 'the real McCoy'. 'The real McKay' originated in Scotland as early as the 1850s and meant that something was of notable quality and not a poor imitation. It was associated with a whisky and McKay was a shortened version of the name of the producers of this fine whisky – the Mackay family. The pronunciation shifted slightly to McCoy when the expression was taken up in Ireland, and then America.

Although unsubstantiated, many explanations remain current about how McKay became McCoy:

- An American boxer called himself Kid McCoy and was imitated by others, so he came to call himself the Real McCoy.

- A feud between the families of Hatfield and McCoy became so well known that it altered the perception of the original pronunciation of 'the real McKay'.

- A prominent cattle dealer called Joseph McCoy gained a reputation for honest dealing, and among people dealing in livestock was known as the real McCoy because he was reliable.

- During America's years of Prohibition, William McCoy was a dealer in illegal rum and was known not to water the product, but to deliver good-quality 'real' rum.

- Elijah McCoy invented a superior lubrication system for trains and the system was much imitated; engineers not wanting the less effective copies would ask if a system was 'the real McCoy'.

There are more, including the belief that a man named McCoy was admired by criminals for providing them with a reliable form of nitroglycerine for cracking safes.

So with no reliable pedigree of how it happened, the phrase 'the real McCoy' became wedged into American usage, but the original Scottish version is still regarded as the real McKay.

McDonald's hamburgers

In 1940 two brothers called McDonald opened a small but efficient fast-food outlet in San Bernadino, California. They had a distinctive red-and-white colour scheme, and their hamburgers and milkshakes were so successful that they had a sign up saying, '1 million sold.' They introduced sauce dispensers and created a system of assembly-line food workers, one to each task, so hamburgers were ready all the time and customers didn't have to wait. The McDonald brothers opened their first branch store or franchise in 1952 and eventually had more than 10 other fast-food outlets bearing their name.

In 1961 the McDonalds' businesses were bought by a businessman called Ray Kroc, who within a year had franchised over 200 more McDonald's 'restaurants', and then went on and on.

According to American writer Bill Bryson, Kroc ordained that McDonald's hamburgers were all to be 3.875 inches wide, weigh 1.6 ounces and contain just 19 per cent fat. The buns with seeds must average 178 seeds (in 2003 the *London Observer* reported that the number of seeds had gone up to 198).

By 1994 the McDonald's organisation bought more potatoes and beef than any other organisation in the United States and was serving 25 million customers a day in 68 countries, causing it to be decreed the world's largest owner of real estate.

McDonald's arrived in Australia in 1971 and New Zealand in 1976. Forty years later Australia had over 700 outlets, New Zealand had 150, and the world in total had 31,000.

Magdalen College, Oxford

There is a character in the New Testament called Mary who came from the village of Magdala on the shores of Lake Tiberius. In the custom of the time, she was referred to as Mary of Magdala, or Mary the Magdalena. When the New Testament went into English, her name retained the Latin form, Magdalene.

But in parallel, Mary Magdalene had become a very big deal in France: there is an unsubstantiated belief that she actually died there. But certainly her name was used in many religious places in France, in the form of an ancient French variation written as Madeleine. The figure of Mary Magdalene was also popular in England, where 200 ancient churches were dedicated to her.

Various versions of the name Magdalene drifted into English and, possibly influenced by the French vernacular, in English the 'g' sound rather glossed over into an 'aa-oo' sound, and eventually into an 'aw' sound. This was a time in history when not everybody could write, and spelling was far from standardised. So various versions of many words floated around, often in quite respectable circumstances; Shakespeare's spelling was often wayward, even when he wrote his own name. When Chaucer used the name Mary Magdalene three times, he spelt it three different ways – and two of those echoed the vernacular French pronunciation 'Mawdelayne.'

Chaucer died in 1400 and Magdalen College at Oxford University was established just 58 years later when there were at least four different ways of spelling Mary Magdalene in English, though the pronunciation was fairly standard as Mary 'Mawdlen'.

The clerk who drafted the original charter for the college in English read the official name as Maria Magdalene – the full, formal Latin name is *Collegium Beatae Mariae Magdalene* – but he wrote Maudelayne which, with its ancient French origins, was the way ordinary English people said the word. The college has a letter from King Henry VII himself, which uses the Latin spelling, and letters from the reign of King Henry VIII using various spellings: Magdalene, and also Mawdlin. But it was the ancient pronunciation that survived, side by side with the equally ancient Latin spelling.

There is a total lack of consistency in the situation, in that other places in England named after Mary Magdalene are written, and pronounced, Magdalene.

Consonants are sometimes dropped in the pronunciation of an English word, as for example in 'knitting' and 'psalm'. It's quite common, so in some circumstances the 'g' was dropped from the pronunciation of poor old Mary Magdalene, first in French where she became Madeleine, and then in English where she became Mawdlin.

Oxford University, with its Magdalen College, and Cambridge

with its Magdalene College (founded later in 1542) both prefer to stick to the pronunciation which was the norm in medieval times.

Mary of Magdala, as a woman who was believed to have renounced her colourful past and sought purity, was eventually made a Catholic saint. She is the patron saint of repentant sinners and those who follow a contemplative life. Her feast day is 22 July.

But why does the word maudlin mean tearful and sad?

Although nothing much is known for certain about Mary Magdalene, that didn't stop people deciding things about her, and the legend grew that she had been a woman of easy virtue before repenting, and she spent time reflecting on the sadness in her life and wept a lot. Therefore painters often depicted her as a tearful woman, and this was at the time when the 'g' was dropped in pronouncing her name – so the word mawdlin came to be a description of someone who was always sad and weeping. It still does mean that, but the spelling has followed the pronunciation, unlike the University College, which was spoken of cheerfully in the vernacular accent with the dropped 'g', but stuck to the Latin spelling.

Another feature of the Mary Magdalene legend developed when 'fallen' women were referred to as mawdelens, and some institutions that took them in, and sometimes their babies as well, were known as Mawdlens.

Mail

Chain mail and postal mail: the words seem to be identical twins, but in fact they have different fathers.

In a suit of armour, the sections that move are generally made of linked mesh or small overlapping plates called mail. That word is derived from the Latin *macula*, meaning a spot, a circle, a mesh. It can be found in the modern word immaculate, meaning tidy and without spots or blemishes.

But letters in the post get their name from Old German, where the word *malha* meant a bag or wallet, and the word was used to describe the bags in which messages and letters were carried from place to place. The name of the bag became transferred to mean the contents of the bag, which in English finished up as mail.

Man of Kent or Kentish Man

Kent is believed to be the oldest county name in England, dating back to 55 BC. The county of Kent has a river called the Medway passing through it, and for many centuries that has divided the male population; a male born on the west of the Medway River is called a Kentish man, and a man born on the east side of the river is called a Man of Kent. The distinction is quite firm, and there are cases of fathers and sons, or brothers, having been born in different hospitals so that there is one of each within the same family.

Being born east or west of the river makes no difference to women born in Kent – they are all called Kentish Maids.

Man of straw

There is a belief that in centuries past, some men would hang about courtrooms and make themselves available as witnesses who, if paid, would say anything required and swear it was true. To signify this, they had a sort of code that lawyers would recognise: they wore sprigs of straw in their shoes. This kind of witness was of course a fake, not to be believed, hence the connection with a man of straw – weak, unreliable or untrustworthy. Note, however, that there is not a great deal of evidence for this story.

More generally, the term man of straw is taken to be self-explanatory, referring to a person as if they were an actual dummy, someone whose external qualities, no matter how impressive, don't match up with a weak interior. It represents a sham, an argument that can easily be defeated, with no more substance than a straw doll.

Marbles in their mouth

Sometimes the people who say this are confusing two different expressions. 'Marbles in the mouth' goes back to the legendary Greek figure Demosthenes in 300 BC, who was reputed to have overcome a speech defect by standing beside the sea, putting pebbles into his mouth and forcing himself to speak over the noise of the waves. In time he became a great orator. That appears to be the origin of the idea that putting pebbles or marbles in your mouth and forcing yourself to speak in spite of them improves your pronunciation and articulation.

Many people saw Rex Harrison, playing Henry Higgins, put marbles into Audrey Hepburn's (Eliza Doolittle's) mouth in the movie *My Fair Lady*, though it must be pointed out that George Bernard Shaw did not write that piece in his play *Pygmalion*; it was invented by Lerner and Lowe, who wrote the 1956 musical based on Shaw's play.

We must also remember that Demosthenes and Eliza Doolittle both took the marbles out once they'd mastered the knack of rounding their vowels. They never actually spoke to people with their marbles still in their mouth; they merely practised speaking with them there.

Confusion sometimes arises with a quite different expression, plum in the mouth, which generally indicates that a high-class pronunciation is being used.

Nowadays, saying that someone is speaking with marbles in their mouth often seems to mean that someone is speaking indistinctly, which is quite feasible – they probably would. But the original intention of the exercise was to have marbles in the mouth to practise articulation, and then take them out.

There is an old joke about how to be a good public speaker: fill your mouth with marbles and make a speech. Every day, take out one marble and make a speech again. When you have lost all your marbles, then you'll be an effective public speaker.

Mark of Cain

The origin is in Genesis, but there are actually two different expressions derived from the same Bible story.

The Bible says that the mark of Cain protected him from being killed. But, besides that mark, Cain also carried a curse which meant that he had to wander all his life.

People in contemporary times sometimes confuse the two and say one when they mean the other. An actor said in an interview that after he left a long-term role in a television serial, nobody would employ him: it was as if he had the mark of Cain upon him.

That situation is not in fact either the mark of Cain or the curse of Cain, according to the biblical derivation. But both terms are used carelessly nowadays to mean carrying some sort of stigma which everyone knows about.

Marmite and Vegemite

Marmite originated in England in 1902. An illusion arose that it was an extract of meat, but actually it is made only from extracts of yeast and vegetables. The name is the French word for a stockpot or cooking pot, a picture of which is on many of the Marmite containers.

Vegemite, invented in Melbourne in 1923, is basically the same as Marmite – made from extracts of yeast and vegetables. Originally it was going to be called Parwill, but this didn't catch on so a public competition was held and the name Vegemite won.

Maven

This word grew to prominence in the United States in the twentieth century, referring to a person whose opinion is noteworthy and whose advice is followed. It is from an old Hebrew word *mebin*, meaning knowledge or wisdom. From Hebrew it migrated into the Yiddish *mevin*, meaning 'to be understanding'. After a slight spelling change it is now frequently used in American English, where it has come to mean an expert and connoisseur.

Mayday

It is the French word *aidez* meaning help, with 'm' in front (*m'aidez*), meaning 'help me'. In 1927 the International Radio Telegraph Convention adopted this as the international signal for distress, and in English-speaking countries the spelling has become phonetic: mayday.

'May the road rise with you'

A popular blessing made famous by its use in Ireland. There are several verses and occasional variations in the words, but the most famous version usually says:

May the road rise with you,
May the wind always be at your back,
May the sun shine warm upon your face,
May the rain fall softly on your fields.
Until we meet again,
May God hold you in the palm of His hand.

This 'Irish' version is widely known, but the concepts behind the blessing are Jewish. Early Christian clerics in Ireland frequently took inspiration from Hebrew sources and with that wonderful Irish gift for language were able to restate and transform those which inspired them into what one could call a fluid Irish style.

Close study of 'May the road rise' indicates that much of its inspiration appears to come from the Book of Isaiah in the Bible. The line about the road rising with you can be seen to connect with Chapter 40, the famous opening of Handel's Messiah: 'Every valley shall be exalted, and every mountain and hill shall be made low: and the crooked shall be made straight and the rough places plain.' And Chapter 49 says, 'I will make my mountains a way, and my highways shall be exalted.'

Chapter 49 of Isaiah also says, 'Neither shall the heat nor sun smite them, for he that hath mercy on them shall lead them, even by the springs of water shall he guide them'. And in Chapter 55, the words 'For as the rain . . . watereth the earth, and maketh it bring forth and bud . . .' can be seen to mean that the sun will shine warmly and the rain fall in the fields.

Chapter 49 also says, 'I have graven thee upon the palms of my hands,' in which can be seen the image of God holding you in the palm of his hand.

All this is legend, supposition, interpretation and research, rather than absolute fact, but careful examination does seem to support the belief that the Irish prayer comes from Jewish base material, lovingly re-crafted into a mellifluous blessing, as only the Irish can do.

One version of the prayer on an Irish cathedral wall demonstrates the Celtic and clerical sense of humour. The final line reads: 'May God hold you in the palm of His hand – and not squeeze too tight.'

Mess

The original is in the Latin word *missus*, meaning 'to place out', later influenced by the French word *mettre*, 'to place' (food). The short version 'mess' came to mean a group of people who sat together and were served from the same dishes. It usually referred to a group of four; Shakespeare uses it in *Love's Labour's Lost*: 'You three fools lack'd me fool to make up the mess.'

The meaning of four people being served as a separate group evolved into seatings of people of some privilege, hence military officers. But the reference expanded and is now heard in more general use to mean a kind of eating room for everyone.

Micky Doolans

The term may not refer to a specific Micky Doolan, but the frequent occurrence of the names 'Michael' and 'Doolan' in Ireland – where the Catholic church predominated – caused the made-up name to become a slang term referring to all Catholic men. Various forms have evolved: sometimes just Doolan by itself, and sometimes just Micky by itself, or shortened to 'a Mick'.

Middle Earth

J.R.R. Tolkien invented the setting and the language and the characters and stories, but he didn't invent the name. The term Middle Earth is a very old expression, dating back to ancient Scandinavian mythology and drifting into Anglo-Saxon English as *middangeard*. It was perceived as a mystic place, somewhere between heaven and hell.

Middle Earth is actually mentioned in *Beowulf*, one of the oldest surviving pieces of English writing, dating from the late tenth century. As a professor of Anglo-Saxon studies, Tolkien was very familiar with this work. The term can also be found in Shakespeare's *Merry Wives of Windsor* (Act 5, scene V) when someone speaking about Falstaff says, 'I smell a man of middle earth', indicating that it is not a very desirable place.

So Tolkien took a known name, then developed a huge and quite different imagery around it.

Midwife

Because 'mid' sounds a bit like middle, there is a vague perception of a midwife being someone who is placed somewhere in the middle of the birth process. But no, in this context the word 'mid' comes to us as a derivative of the German word *mit* (with), plus 'wife' in its sense of woman or mother. So the actual meaning of midwife is simply – the woman who stays with and helps the mother.

Milk before or after?

Tea came to England at the same time as Chinese porcelain, which was very strong. But the new drink required teapots and teacups, which were shapes not seen in England before, so English ceramicists had to learn to copy these shapes, and those early English pots and cups did crack if they came into contact with something too hot.

Hence the English developed the custom of swirling heated water around in the pot to warm it before pouring in the boiling water, and of putting milk into the cup before the hot tea went in. This was a well-established practice by the end of the eighteenth century. There was less need in the nineteenth century since English ceramics had improved.

Interestingly, people who have milk or cream in coffee almost always put it in after the hot liquid.

Milliner

The word is derived from 'Milaner', meaning someone from Milan. In earlier centuries the city was famous for its manufacture of fancy goods, which travelling salesmen took all over Europe. Eventually the designation settled onto just hats, and in time transferred to the people who made them, whether they were from Milan or not.

Minutes

A meeting may take several hours and a written record of what happened is called 'the minutes', but there is a relationship with the minutes on a clock. Both words descend from the Latin *minutus* meaning small. The minutes on a clock are a small part of an hour, and 'minute' in its French form can describe anything else small.

Describing the record of a meeting as 'minutes' is the same word, but used as an abbreviation of the Latin phrase, *minuta scriptura*, which means 'writing of the small details'. Eventually the expression was reduced to one word – minutes – and the meaning enlarged slightly to its present use, that is: 'an exact record of all transactions'.

Menzies pronounced Mingis

The correct pronunciation of Menzies is 'Mingis'. In very old Scotland there used to be a written symbol rather like a squiggly figure 3, which was used to write down a sound called a palatal, an 'ny' sound.

When people tried to write these words into English there was no equivalent to this squiggly 3 (which was rather like a Greek *sigma*), and so they wrote a 'z' because the old symbol looked a bit like that letter. When English-speaking people saw the 'z', they pronounced it accordingly, which was incorrect.

Thus, the correctly pronounced Scottish Mingis came to be written in English as Menzies. But a true Scot will still prefer the Mingis pronunciation.

Similarly Dalziel: the 'z' shouldn't really be there, and this name can be pronounced as either 'De-ell' or 'Dalyeel'.

Misocapnist

There are three ingredients in the word: *miso*, *kapos* and 'ist'. The Greek for dislike, even hatred, is *miso* or *mis* (found in such English words as misogynist). The Greek word for smoke is *kapos*. And -ist usually indicates a person with the qualities mentioned earlier in the word.

Therefore, a misocapnist is a person who hates smoking and smoke.

Moggy

This usually affectionate word for cat can sometimes carry a vague feeling that the cat(s) referred to is of fairly obscure pedigree. Perhaps companionable, but not very sleek and glamorous. The word itself has carried that sort of shadow around it for many years. Moggy is a variation on maggie, which for many years was a rather derisive term for a dishevelled old woman.

The term maggie gradually shifted from old crones to cows, presumably because cows tend not to be glamorous; they're a bit knobbly in the hips and they don't have an elegant walk. Over time maggie slowly changed into moggy, but still meaning a lumbering cow or a shabby old woman.

But early in the 1900s, when the streets of London abounded with deprived alley cats, the word moggy began to be used to describe these unfortunate street creatures. Eventually the word moved onto cats in general, and it really stuck. But it did develop in meaning, because once it distinctly meant a frowsy cat of not very distinguished parentage, but now it can quite affectionately be used to describe any cat, either alley cats or their more elegant cousins.

Mollycoddle

Generally meaning to indulge, mollycoddle is a combination of two words. Coddle exists as an independent word – to treat gently. Coddled eggs are cooked just below boiling point. A coddled invalid is not allowed to do anything strenuous. Jane Austen writes in *Emma* (1815) about a person being coddled.

The woman's name Molly is usually an informal version of Mary. At times in history it has had unfortunate associations with low life: for some time, a molly or a moll meant a prostitute (for instance a gangster's moll).

But Molly also has a soft and cuddly sound, and from the eighteenth century onwards it was used to identify a person who was overgentle and overprotected – a milksop, a wimp.

Over time, the two words drifted together, with molly becoming an intensifier for the existing term coddle, and by 1849 you'll find Thackeray using the compound word, mollycoddle.

Molotov cocktail

The Russian statesman Vyacheslav Mikhailovich Skryabin adopted the name Molotov in 1906 in order to escape from the Imperial Police. (Molotov is Russian for a kind of hammer.) He was the Prime

Minister of the Soviet Union from 1930 to 1941, and was Minister of Foreign Affairs during and after the Second World War.

Molotov didn't invent the so-called Molotov cocktail, nor was it a Russian invention. In 1940 the Russians were fighting the Finns, and it was the Finns who developed a home-made anti-tank bomb: a bottle filled with inflammable fluid and sealed, with a wick poking out the top. The wick was lit, then the bottle thrown at a tank. When it broke the liquid ignited and spread all over the tank plating.

This was widely adapted for use by the British Home Guard, and Mr Skryabin, aka Molotov, was intrigued with the device and organised the manufacture of similar devices in Russia. Thus the 'bomb' became known by the Russian foreign affairs minister's alias, Molotov.

Momentarily

Momentarily means for a very brief space of time; for a moment. It is sometimes used erroneously as if it meant 'soon'. One of the more ludicrous examples of this is the announcement heard on some planes: 'The aircraft will take off momentarily,' which actually means the plane will take off, zoom into the sky for just a moment and then come down again.

Moniker

The meaning of the word is fairly clear: an informal or slang term (spelt various ways) for a personal name. The term has been in use since the mid-1800s and most scholars agree that it developed out of hobo or tramp talk. Some researchers believe it was a jokey tramp version of the word 'monk', since tramps sometimes joked about their solitary all-male existence and said they lived like monks.

There is also a perceived similarity to the Latin word *monogramma*, which is also a sign of identity, though this seems an unlikely link to hobos and tramps. Even the *Oxford Dictionary* admits that nobody knows for sure where the word came from.

Monkey island on a ship

This is the small deck above the wheelhouse. If a compass is surrounded with steel its function is affected, so on a steel ship the compass is mounted above the wheelhouse (and sometimes magnets are needed as compass adjusters because the steel is still fairly close).

Iron started being used in ships late in the nineteenth century and then steel in the twentieth century, so the need to place the compass out of range is, in naval terms, fairly recent, as is the term 'monkey island'.

You might have to climb as many as three ladders to get to the wheelhouse, and the monkey island was one more ladder up, so there could be a total of four ladders to climb. Among seamen, the word monkey was sometimes used to describe places that were awkward to get to, so although there is no formal derivation to be found, the name (as with 'crow's nest') has a fairly obvious origin – reaching the monkey island required some agility and when you got there it was very high.

Monkey on your back

This usually refers to some kind of persistent problem that clings and won't go away, like having an 'albatross around your neck' (as in Coleridge's *The Rime of the Ancient Mariner*). The use of 'monkey' to describe such a problem is attributed to American underground criminals who used the word to describe a drug habit: a persistent gnawing feeling that you must have a fix. The symbolism relates to a monkey's agility to cling to what it sees as a base, and its ability to remain there.

The usage also appears in Nelson Algren's famous 1950 book *The Man with the Golden Arm*. Algren also uses the term 'the monkey's dead', meaning the drug habit has been kicked.

Over time, the image of a monkey clinging to someone's unwilling back widened beyond drug use, and is now heard in a more everyday context such as someone speaking about having a long-term mortgage.

Monkfish

This ugly-looking, deep-dwelling fish has been known as monk fish for a long time. Argument persists about how the name came about:

- Its misshapen head does have a fanciful resemblance to a monk wearing a cowl.

- Because of the way its head is made, it can appear to be gazing upwards – star-gazing – which contributed to the image of a monk in prayer.

- When you see the fish in the water, it is brown and flaps about a bit, looking somewhat like the robes of a monk.

- It is believed that back in medieval times monks, who didn't eat meat on certain days, liked this better than other fish so it came to be called monk's fish.

Monkfish is eaten quite a lot. One food expert says it has very firm flesh that cooks to a pleasant sweet taste, which is why the monkfish is sometimes called 'poor man's lobster' and in many places the monkfish's liver is regarded as very desirable.

It's called many other things too: angler fish, bulldog fish, toadfish, goosefish or stargazer. It is sometimes sold under the semi-attractive name deep sea cod.

The fish looks so bad that in parts of Scandinavia and Iceland it is considered a joke to feed tourists a delicious dish of monkfish, and then, after they've finished, show them a picture of what they've just eaten. It is so ugly that for many years people who hadn't seen it believed it was only a fantasy like unicorns, and that monkfish didn't really exist.

Moot point/mute point

The two words are entirely different. Moot is often used as a legal term, and means 'open to debate or argument'. It comes from a very old German word *muoze*, meaning a meeting.

Mute comes from the Latin *mutus*, meaning silent, so its meaning is really the opposite of moot, because debate and argument invariably involve talking, while to be mute is to make no sound at all.

Mortar

The English word mortar arises from the Latin word *mortarium*, meaning a bowl in which things are mixed. Hence, putting together two Latin words *pinsere*, to crush, and *mortarium*, a bowl, we get pestle and mortar.

Various substances have been mixed in a mortar, including mixtures that are used in putting up buildings, and over time the word was transferred to the contents of the vessel. Therefore mixtures of cement, sand, lime and so on are referred to as mortar, because they were mixed in a *mortarium*. (This transfer of meaning, where the name of the container is used to describe whatever is in the container, happens quite often in English; see also **Mail**.)

Then an interesting second transfer took place. Once the mortar has been mixed, the tradesman will place a lump of it onto a square board with a handle underneath, from which he trowels it into place. Thus we get the name mortarboard for the academic hat with the flat, square top which resembles the stonemason or bricklayer's tray.

In the sixteenth century there was a firearm known as a mortar piece, which appears to have been called that because it was short and wide-bored, somewhat like a bowl.

Mother's Day

The actual term dates only from 1910, but it grew out of a rather convoluted history going back to both ancient Greece and ancient Rome. People were keen to celebrate the gods they worshipped and, presumably on the principle that everyone has a mother, once a year they would celebrate the mother-figure of all the gods. In Greece she was Rhea, and in Rome she was Cybele.

As was often the case with these ardent religious observances, the seasons and the weather were deciding factors in fixing the date on which they were held. The honouring of the mother goddesses was deemed to be best celebrated in spring – always a good time for a festival.

And as Christian beliefs began to establish themselves, they quietly took on board earlier existing concepts and subtly changed them to suit the new Christian religion; some scholars will tell you that, in this case, the image of mother of the gods slowly became referred to as the 'mother' church, an image strengthened by the emphasis on Mary, the mother of Jesus.

Eventually, Christian churches evolved a yearly celebration called Mothering Sunday, which satisfied the image of the Christian church as a mother to its flock, as well as paying a little attention to real live mothers (which none of the earlier celebrations ever had).

So, on Mothering Sunday, people went to church and then home to their mothers; sometimes, if they lived far from home, they were given a holiday in order to visit their mother, with a simple gift of cake or flowers.

The scene now shifts to 1905, when Mrs Reese Jarvis died in America. She was the daughter of a minister, had herself been a long-time teacher in Sunday school, and was the mother of two daughters. For two years after she died, her daughter Anne Jarvis had been worrying that she hadn't paid sufficient attention to her mother while she was still alive. So, she picked up on an idea another American woman, Julia Ward Howe, had back in 1872; Anne Jarvis started campaigning and letter-writing to urge people to develop an official observance, whereby living mothers were honoured by their progeny and families.

In 1910 this came to pass in the state of Virginia when the Governor proclaimed a Mother's Day for that state. It was a big success, the idea spread, and in 1914 the United States House of Representatives issued a formal proclamation from President Woodrow Wilson that the second Sunday in May each year be designated as Mother's Day all over the US.

Besides America, many other nations now have a version of Mother's Day on varying dates and with significances tailored to their own culture.

Motor/engine

There is no clear and definite distinction. Every engineer and mechanic who reads this is going to have a different opinion, because usage varies from one circumstance to another.

In general (very general), a motor is a machine that converts a form of energy into mechanical energy to produce motion, and an engine is a machine that converts a form of energy into mechanical work. But neither of those definitions works properly and many variations and contradictions arise from them.

There is an impression that a motor is connected with movement, although one commonly hears the driving force of a car referred to as either an engine or a motor, maybe because it produces a form of work which eventually, but not directly, makes the wheels go round. In other words, it's associated with both work and motion. A train is customarily said to be driven by an engine rather than a motor, though it performs the same transformation – undergoing work that later results in movement.

But a refrigerator is normally referred to as having a motor, and a refrigerator doesn't move anywhere.

All of them convert one form of energy into another. In general (again, very general) it is possible to say that a motor is involved in actually moving something somewhere, even as a fan or a washing machine does. And an engine causes work to be done which may sometimes eventually result in motion, but in its direct form is static.

Mountebank

The word is Italian, from *montimbanco*, which in turn comes from *monter banco*, to climb onto a bench. So it means a person who climbs up on a stage to sell something or attract crowds by tricks or oratory – a seller of fake medicines.

The word means much the same thing in English – a charlatan – and has developed the spelling and pronunciation: mountebank.

Movers and shakers

The term dates from 'Ode', a poem by nineteenth-century British poet Arthur William Edgar O'Shaughnessy. He was referring not to activists but to artists:

> We are the music makers,
> We are the dreamers of dreams,
> Wandering by lone sea-breakers,
> And sitting by desolate streams; –
> World-losers and world-forsakers,
> On whom the pale moon gleams:
> We are the movers and shakers
> Of the world for ever, it seems.

In an era of corporate lions, electronic wizards and political fire-brands, the meaning of the term has moved. It is still used to describe those who take the even tenor of our lives and disturb it – people who challenge established laws and morals – but nowadays the movers and shakers tend to be political or corporate people, not artists.

Movie dates

Movies were being made from the 1890s onwards, but in the early decades of the industry, the movies appeared not to have copyright dates on them.

From 1915 onwards, bigger 'classic' movies were being made. In the 1920s the United States government passed a law decreeing that all movies issued had to have their date of production included in the credits. This didn't please the movie industry, which, for various reasons, didn't always want people to know when a film had been made. Sometimes a movie was held back and released a year or more later, under the pretence that it was new. Or a film studio may not have wanted to advertise the actual age of a film released for the second time. So the movie people obeyed the law and included the date of production, but deliberately put it in Roman numerals to make it difficult to work out.

Comparatively few people can read Roman numerals, particularly long ones, and only those with a classical inclination can read them at speed. So the studios obeyed the law, but escaped easy date identification.

Ms

The English word 'mistress' used to be used when addressing all women. It evolved into several other forms which designated the marital status of the woman being addressed: Mrs – a married woman; Miss – an unmarried woman; and Miz – a rustic American honorific that seems mainly to have been Mrs, but was sometimes equivocal: e.g. 'Miz Lillian' (Carter, married, real person and mother of a President) and 'Miz Scarlett' (O'Hara, fictional, unmarried).

By the late 1940s some women were beginning to agitate for a prefix that didn't identify their marital status. Ms started to be promoted in the early 1950s as a possible non-discriminatory courtesy prefix for all women. It was believed to be a modern version of the old-fashioned American Miz. This was a minor puzzle of semantics versus usage, since Mrs, Miss, Miz and Ms are all variations on exactly the same word: mistress.

Ms did not have a smooth passage into the language and was not generally accepted until the 1970s. Some women didn't want to be connected with it at all. The *New York Times* refused until 1986 to publish the word.

In the meantime, 'mistress' had slipped sideways to indicate a woman in a sexual relationship with a man to whom she was not legally married.

Mud in your eye

Although the two images of 'mud' and 'eye' are brought together in the New Testament, when Jesus cures a man of blindness with a mixture of saliva and dust (John, 9: 6–7), this would be an unlikely source for a jocular toast.

More credibly, the horse-racing fraternity has long been aware that fast-moving steeds throw up mud behind them, often into the eyes of the following rider. That rider, now unable to see well, has less hope of winning the race. Hence British huntsmen and jockeys – before the advent of goggles – developed a cheerful reverse-toast: 'Here's mud in your eye,' with the amiable unspoken sub-text, 'So I can win the race.'

In a less amiable environment, among soldiers on the battlefields of the First World War, the expression also had traction; mud in your eye was considered more desirable than blood.

Mufti

The word is Arabic and means a legal ruling within the Muslim faith, or a religious official who has the right to rule on a point of Muslim law.

There are two versions of how it came into English. During the nineteenth century there was a fashion for British military officers, when off duty, to wear an elaborate dressing gown with a smoking cap, a combination which somehow resembled the appearance of the Muslim mufti.

The elaborately named *Glossary of Colloquial Anglo-Indian Words and Phrases, and of Kindred Terms, Etymological, Historical, Geographical and Discursive* (1886) explains that the word 'mufti' may originally have come into use applied to the resemblance to religious leaders when the officers were in their off-duty clothes. From there grew the practice of referring to the officers as being 'in mufti'. The word passed into English and took on a wider meaning of anyone's off-duty clothes.

But there is an alternative version: British officers supervised the issuing of one free set of civilian clothes to each Indian soldier. One officer reported that those soldiers referred to the civilian issue in their own Urdu language as *mufti kapra*, meaning 'garments free of charge'. This, he believes, is how the word slid into English, meaning non-official clothing.

Mug

Mug meaning 'face' was first heard in English in the 1700s. The word came into English from Scandinavia, where the originating word meant 'a drinking vessel'; still, of course what mug actually means in English. But from that base, several other applications have arisen; for instance, someone slow on the uptake can be called a mug (or muggins), meaning that any kind of silly information can be poured into him or her.

The connection with faces came about because there was a popular practice in the 1600s and the 1700s of decorating drinking mugs with caricatures, so the word mug became associated with faces. And from that came 'mugging', meaning the pulling of exaggerated faces.

There have been other, unhappier, developments: a violent robbery facilitated by striking the victim on the head or face began to be referred to as 'a mugging', and the perpetrator, if caught, was taken to the police station where a police photographer took a 'mug shot'.

Mumbo-jumbo

This originated from a report by travel writer Mungo Park in 1759. In Africa he had seen the Mandingo people undergo a strange ritual whereby a quarrelsome woman is brought back to 'order'. A man disguised as a grotesque 'idol' makes hideous noises at night, and causes a crowd to gather, upon which the woman is stripped naked in front of them and whipped by the grotesque while the assembled crowd admonishes her with shouts and scolding. Park recorded that the grotesque was known as Mumbo Jumbo (thought to be a slight modification of Mandingo words *mama dyumbo*).

Over the years, the term has come to describe words that seem meaningless or complicated.

Mum's the word

This version of 'mum' has meant 'remaining silent' from at least 1500 onwards. The word is believed to be simply an imitation of keeping the lips closed. Extending the word mum into the expression 'mum's the word' didn't really take off until about 1850, and because mum is a word meaning silence, the saying 'mum's the word' could be categorised as an 'anti-phonogramic paradox'.

There is another expression in English which seems to be related to 'mum's the word', and actually means the same thing. 'My lips are sealed' is much more recent: it first appeared in a P.G. Wodehouse story (*Leave it to Psmith*) in 1909.

Later the term sprang into prominence when a remark made by British Prime Minister Stanley Baldwin was misreported in 1935. He was asked a trick question and replied, 'My lips are not yet unsealed.' This was a postponed double negative, so in the interests of economy of printing space, most reporters wrote that he had said, 'My lips are sealed.' This abbreviated version became the norm and has been widely used since.

Mum also developed another meaning rather by accident: a shortened form of 'Mummy', a child's affectionate way of addressing their mother. This also didn't come into use until probably the late nineteenth century. Mum has taken off in a big way, and now has various shades or connotations of affection.

Munted

It is used to mean something is wrecked or mutilated, damaged, broken, not in good shape. In the early stages of its popularity, munted was current only among drug users, to mean absolutely overdosed; completely and hopelessly out of control. From there it seems to have widened to mean just drunk (which is a little less dangerous), and then again to refer to anything that is out of order or abnormal.

The origin of the term is very vague. There is a possibility that it is connected to the derogatory and insulting South African term *munt* or *munta*, meaning a black person. There is also a possibility that munted could have arisen out of *The Munsters*, a long-ago TV series.

Having grown as an expression within youth culture, munted is now in general currency, meaning 'out of order', or 'absolutely beyond repair'.

Murphy's Law

There are several different stages to the story. In ancient Yorkshire a concept with which most people are familiar was crystallised into the phrase 'sod's law', which described the frequency with which things can go wrong in ordinary life. Sod's law is considered to be a corruption of God's law: in God's law everything goes well, whereas in sod's law everything goes wrong.

But there was a modern development. There has been dispute for some years about the origin of Murphy's Law, but the commonly believed version is that, in 1949 on an American air force base, Captain Edward Murphy was supervising a technician preparing a test of human tolerance to speed and was installing some essential sensors. Captain Murphy discovered that the technician had put each one of them in upside down. At that point, reports vary about what Captain Murphy actually said. It was either: 'If there is any way to do it wrong, he'll find it,' or, 'If there are two or more ways to do something and one of those results in catastrophe, then someone will do it that way.'

The air base projects manager came to hear of the incident and when he was describing it to a news conference a short time afterwards, he referred to the captain's remark as 'Murphy's law'. The name rapidly went around all the other aerospace engineering personnel and found its way into *Webster's Dictionary* in 1958.

Captain Murphy's statement actually allowed for some optimism. After the original incident, he realised that the sensors looked the same both ways and therefore could be inserted upside down, so he redesigned them. This eliminated the possibility that they could be put in the wrong way. Potential disaster had been avoided.

The final stage in the story seems to lie with the science fiction author Larry Niven, who from 1964 wrote a very popular series of books in which something called Finagle's law occurred, which was a very much simplified version of Captain Murphy's statement. Niven wrote: 'Anything that can go wrong, will'. That's the version now almost universally known as Murphy's law, having developed from sod's law through Murphy's law to Finagle's law, but still credited to Murphy.

A maverick, largely unsubstantiated, version assigns the origin to a Professor Murphy at Long Island University, who asked all his students to throw a pie up at the ceiling and see how many stuck and how many fell face-down on the floor.

Muzak

In 1911 a former US military major, George Squier, patented a system whereby several signals could travel over a single wire from a radio station. The business which broadcast these early transmissions was called Wired Radio.

In 1934 Squier became intrigued with the word Kodak, an invented word that means absolutely nothing but nevertheless became a very successful brand name. So in 1934 the company's name was changed to an equally novel word: Muzak. It has been around to haunt us ever since. Like vaseline and nugget and biro, muzak is a trade mark that has eventually been accepted as a 'real' word. No restaurant, lift, shopping centre or call-waiting is complete without it.

Myth/legend

Quite often the two seem interchangeable. Strictly speaking, a legend is an account of something notable that happened in history, and has become a traditional tale. Sometimes it is not an authentic story, but is popularly regarded as true; sometimes it is an authentic story.

A legend can also describe a person whose exploits, either good or bad, are widely known, and that person can sometimes be regarded as real, like Robin Hood (whose existence is very doubtful) or unreal, like Hercules. On this basis of good and bad exploits, Caligula and Hitler can be described as legendary, but so can Scott of the Antarctic and Mother Teresa.

On the other hand, a myth is a traditional story or character, usually fictitious, with the supernatural often an important ingredient, and frequently providing an explanation for a religious belief, or a natural or social phenomenon. A line in Oscar Wilde's *The Importance of Being Earnest* makes a neat distinction regarding Lady Bracknell: 'She is a monster without being a myth, which is rather unfair.'

A good way of remembering the two definitions is to think of Santa Claus. Santa Claus is a myth based on a legend, because Saint Nicholas was a real Turkish person. He was much admired in Turkey, widely respected there and after his death his good qualities were admired for centuries and he became a legend. But he had never

244

been to the North Pole and he didn't ride reindeer through the sky at night. All that extra detail is mythical.

In general myths are easier to scorn than legends, which is probably why, in modern times, the word myth has taken on a shade of meaning: something that is widely believed but is not true.

N

Nauseated/nauseous

The condition of nausea is named after the feeling of being seasick (from the Greek *naus*, meaning 'ship'). Nauseated used to be part of a verb, requiring an auxiliary in front of it: 'I became nauseated' or 'I feel nauseated'. But over time, influenced mainly by American use, it has shortened to a kind of adjectival adverb: 'I am nauseous', which means the same as 'I am nauseated' but is marginally easier to say. Thus nauseous has become the norm.

Nautical/naughty

The two words aren't connected. The Greek *nautikos*, based on *naus*, a ship, gives us the English nautical. But 'naughty' is quite different. It is a genuine Old English word, made of up two parts: *na* and *wiht*, meaning 'no thing'. The spelling of that changed slowly to 'naught' and the meaning varied slightly to signify 'of poor quality', 'worthless rubbish'.

There was a slow development into two slightly different directions. The spelling and meaning of naught remained exactly where it was, meaning 'nothing', 'a trifle' (its Lancashire form is 'nowt').

But a subsidiary meaning developed: 'naughty', where the earlier meaning of 'poor quality' gained an extra dimension signifying bad behaviour and wickedness. This was the meaning Shakespeare intended when he wrote, in *The Merchant of Venice*, 'So shines a good deed in a naughty world.' Over time, 'naughty' paled in meaning, and refers simply to misbehaviour.

Neanderthal

In the late 1600s, a German theologian and hymn composer called Joachim Neumann enjoyed wandering around the rivers and valleys near his home in Dusseldorf. He decided that some of his works would be published under a different version of his own name – which meant 'new man' – and settled on a Greek word with the same meaning: *Neander*.

After Neumann's death, the citizens of Dusseldorf decided to honour his memory by naming a valley after him, and they used the name he had chosen. Near Dusseldorf, there was now Neander Valley (in German, *Neander-Tal*).

In 1856, a discovery of human remains occurred in that valley, and became known as Neandertal man, meaning 'the man from the Neander valley'.

(In the) necessary

This phrase is an abbreviation of 'the necessary house', one of the many euphemisms for lavatory (toilet, throne room, cloakroom, loo, bathroom, the john, rest room, etc). Lord Chesterfield in 1747 wrote of a man who read all the Latin poets during his visits to 'the necessary house'. The term faded from use during the nineteenth century.

Neck of the woods

The word 'neck' can be used to mean a narrow stretch of land. During the nineteenth century the phrase 'neck of the woods' came into use in the US to mean a place where there was a gap in a forest and a settlement had grown up. But in time, neck of the woods came to mean any settlement or area, whether it was among trees or not.

Neenish tarts

These small tarts filled with a sweet creamy mixture, and iced half with vanilla and half with chocolate, are apparently completely unknown outside Australasia. Angus & Robertson's text on patisserie says they are believed to have been invented in the outback of Australia. Considering what they're made of, the outback connection seems feasible because they can possibly be baked from long-storage ingredients.

The word arose in Australia and the name seems to have come from a corruption of a German word, though it isn't clear which one. An Australian researcher discovered a letter written in the early 1920s which referred to 'Neinisch cakes, made of mother's German pastry'. The word Neinisch also appears in *Miss Drake's Home Cookery*, published in Australia in 1929, in a recipe for Neinisch cake.

But the word Neinisch means nothing in German; it is not a real German word. By the late 1930s the word was still being used in Australia to describe cakes that were sometimes pink and white; they settled into brown and white later.

There seem to have been two changeovers in spelling. After the 1920s the 'I' and 'e' started to reverse, and they were referred to as Nienisch tarts, but this isn't a German word either. By 1955 the spelling Neenish had crept in.

So the sad answer is that, pleasant though the tarts are, scholars can't find sufficient evidence about the origin of the name, which has never satisfactorily been nailed down.

Ne'er cast a clout 'ere May be out

This is an old British proverb, usually said as a kind of rule that people (and especially children) should be careful not to abandon winter clothes too soon, until the warmer spring weather is reliably established.

Clout is an old word meaning cloth or garment. The word May in the proverb has caused confusion, since some people believe the admonition to mean 'don't abandon winter clothes until the beginning of June', when May has finished. But according to the BBC Nature Research Unit, the word refers to the may tree, a type of hawthorn. This gives the saying a slightly more flexible application: winter clothes can be shed when the may tree comes into bloom. Nature knows better than any calendar when the warm weather has become stable.

News

There is a popular belief that the word arose from a picture of a weathervane, showing N-E-W-S on its points, and that the initials gradually amalgamated. But scholars deny this absolutely, and say that 'news' is simply derived from the Old English word *niwes*, meaning that which is new.

Nicked/in good nick

A large number of words and expressions have developed from the very basic activity of cutting a notch in wood – a V-shaped notch called a nick.

Though superseded now, those V-shaped nicks were crucial in such activities as archery, point-scoring in sports, and counting. A nick could be done very accurately, or it could be messy. Cutting a neat, accurate V-shaped notch was admired, so the phrase 'in the nick' gradually became a complimentary description applied to inanimate things, such as machinery which performed well, and then it spread to include humans in fine health, or indeed anything at all that was efficient and neatly done.

Until the end of the 1500s, 'in the nick' was sufficient. Gradually two extra words were added so it became 'in the nick of time', meaning that something effective happened briefly and quickly.

The notch in wood, if it were cut quickly and firmly, also carried an image of chips flying away rapidly, so eventually we have swift movement or speedy departure becoming 'nicking off'.

Some expressions are connected with crime and punishment: nicking something; being arrested or being nicked; being placed in custody or in the nick. The origin of those terms is not 100 per cent certain, but they do seem also to be related the V-shaped notch.

When a notch is made in an innocent piece of wood, it can hardly be to the advantage of the wood. Hence something has been taken away from the wood; it is no longer complete. It has been reduced in value – it has been 'nicked'. Thus is engendered a rather convoluted network of words connected with thieving and being caught. From there it's a short hop to the place of incarceration, the 'nick'.

Describing the lock-up itself as the nick appears to have begun with the military round about the turn of the nineteenth century, when the term was used for the guard room or detention cell. In time it moved to the general justice system and is now widely used to mean the prisons administered by the law of the land.

The V-shaped notch of wood has a lot to answer for. But there are many other nick words that have nothing to do with the wood:

a kind of marble, being in the nude, a noise made by a horse, and the Devil.

See also **Nickname**.

Nickname

This comes from the old word eke, which in simple terms meant 'also'. When the word was used to mean that a person had an additional name, it was called an 'eke name'. So for instance a queen called Elizabeth might also be known as Gloriana, or a queen called Mary might be commonly called Bloody Mary. That second name was in addition to their basic name.

Over time, *an* eke name gradually became a *n*eke name, and then eventually a nickname. A nickname now means an informal name, commonly used about a person instead of the name they might have on their passport or their bank account.

Nicknames

There are a number of traditional nicknames with interesting histories:

○ Someone with the name Clark was often known as Nobby. To the historical working classes, the profession of clerk was thought to be learned and literate, and since the nobility were also thought to be learned and literate, the nickname Nobby became attached to anyone who worked as a clerk, because they were perceived as a 'nob'. Later the term was applied to anyone called Clark.

○ People called Martin were often called Pincher Martin; he was a real person in the nineteenth century – Admiral Sir William Martin – and a strict disciplinarian who was constantly having naval ratings pinched for minor offences. Hence the name – later shared by others with the same surname – Pincher Martin.

○ Men called Miller were usually known as Dusty Miller. This one is self-evident.

○ A man named Wilson was often called Tug. In Britain, young men who weren't rich or well-connected had to work hard to get into a good college; they had to sit term exams and apply themselves. They were called collegers, but they were also known as 'tugs', which is believed to be short for toga, probably indicating a devotion to classical study instead of pleasure. Sometime in the nineteenth century the word 'tug' became attached to a man called Wilson, and it stuck.

○ Men called Palmer were often nicknamed Peddler Palmer. The word peddler is related to the old word 'palmer', meaning a pilgrim who carried a palm leaf as a sign that he or she had been to the Holy Land. But it was also used to describe a trickster who could put money down on the counter of a shop, take the goods and somehow sneak back some of the money – in his palm.

Men called Robert have often been known as Bob, Richard became Dick, Henry was known as Harry and Edward was usually called Ted. These short versions may appear rather arbitrary, but there is no rational answer to this.

Robert is a French name originating in Germany and has several diminutives: Rob, Robbie, Bob, Bobby. The short form, Rob, used to be Hob or Dob, which has now vanished. Richard is also an Old French name from German, and became Rick and Dick. Edward, an old English name acquired later by other languages, became Ed, Eddie, Ned or Ted.

Henry is the other way around; it's a Germanic name, and the formal version used to be Harry. Round about the seventeenth century, Harry somehow became informal and Henry slipped into being the formal version.

Such diminutives still occur in modern times: Barry becomes Baz and Garry becomes Gazza.

Nigger in the woodpile

Originating in the United States, this expression came to mean a concealed but important fact or a catch in a proposal – a hold-up that prevents smooth sailing. The expression first became generally known in 1860 and one suggested derivation was 'nigger on the fence', which implies suspicion, caution and watchfulness.

But a more likely source of the expression is that it arose through black slaves escaping from the Southern States by hiding on freight trains under piles of wood and supplies on railway wagons heading north. So sometimes there really was a black man in the woodpile, which came as something of a surprise at the other end.

Nineteen to the dozen

The expression means to talk 'very fast or for a long time with no indication of stopping', and has been in use for a long time. Richard Sheridan's *Journals* used exactly these words in 1785.

Obviously the image is of a person saying 19 words in the time anyone else would only manage 12, but there's no known reason why it should be 19 rather than 18 or 20. Perhaps it's only that 19 just sounds right.

Noggin

The word noggin, meaning a cup or glass to drink from, has been in use since the 1630s. Gradually the meaning has undergone a transference, so that sometimes it means the container, but it can also mean that which it contains. 'Going out to have a few noggins' usually means you're going to drink the contents of a few noggins. In the eighteenth century, the word also became a British slang term for the head, a usage first printed in Stratford-upon-Avon in 1769. Why noggin became associated with the head is not clear, but etymologist Robert Chapman suggests that a noggin (container) for drinking is similar to a mug, and mug became a slang term for face, so noggin might have then moved on to mean head.

Nonplussed

The word is made from two Latin words *non* and *plus*, which together mean 'no more', 'no further'. So saying you are 'nonplussed' indicates that nothing further can be said or done; you are at a loss, confused, there will be a pause in any action.

252

Norks

Some claim that a similar North-East English dialect word for breasts is the ancestor. But even so, the development of the term in Australia arose from the 1950s advertising by the Norco Dairy company's butter wrapper, which showed a cow with a generous udder.

Sometimes 'norgs', but more commonly 'norks', this became slang for large or perfectly formed female breasts. The rather gormless character Barry McKenzie, created by Barry Humphries, brought the term into wide recognition.

Nothing venture, nothing win

The origin of the expression dates back a very long way. It existed in Latin 100 years before Jesus, and Chaucer used it in 1390 as 'Who that nought dare undertake, By right he shall no profit make'.

By 1523, the phrase had modified into 'He that nothing adventureth, nothing getteth'. During the early seventeenth century it underwent a few more changes, sometimes 'Nothing dare, nothing achieve', 'Nothing venture, nothing have' or 'Nought venture, nought have'.

Shakespeare used a version of it, and in the hands of Sir Charles Sedley in 1668 it became 'Nothing venture, nothing win', which seems to have stuck.

It can't be said that 'Nothing ventured, nothing won' is wrong – the saying has been through other changes, so another version doesn't break any law and they all subscribe to the same basic wisdom. All the versions are examples of a grammatical device called ellipsis or omission: leaving out a few bits because everyone understands that they should be there and there's no need to say them. It is a very common practice.

In most of its forms, this motto is really saying: 'If you have ventured nothing, then you can only win nothing.' In the interests of brevity it has been reduced to 'Nothing venture, nothing win', 'Nothing ventured, nothing won', or 'Nothing venture, nothing gain', and so on.

Not on your Nellie

The phrase expresses disbelief and means 'no way', 'certainly not' or 'that is not going to happen'. The origin is Cockney rhyming slang and, typically, the sense of it is rather convoluted. It isn't referring to a real person, but the full expression is 'Not on your Nellie Duff', the trick being that Duff rhymes with 'puff', which in this context means the air in your lungs; in other words, your 'breath', and breath means life.

So 'Not on your Nellie Duff' really means 'Not on your life' but, as with most rhyming slang, the word that rhymes is dropped, and you're left with the word that doesn't rhyme.

Nous

Not to be confused with the French *nous* ('we'), this one is pronounced 'nows'. It's a term widely used to describe someone who has acumen, brains or ability.

Although regarded as a slang term (similar to having 'smarts'), in fact the word has an impeccable classic pedigree. It is used today in exactly the same way as it was in ancient Greece, whence it comes. *Nous* was Greek for mind and intellect. Plato used it to mean complex matters such as 'the system of divinity springing from blind nature'. It moved into the English language denoting intelligence and understanding, but with the added connotation of someone's having 'horse sense'.

(To the) nth degree

It means to the ultimate. The expression comes from mathematics, where the letter 'n' is used as a symbol denoting an indefinite number. For instance, saying: 'The catering at the wedding was meticulous to the nth degree,' means that it wasn't just good, or excellent, but absolutely beyond expectation to an indefinite level – like the mathematical symbol 'n'.

Nuts

Since the mid-1800s the real nut from a tree has also been used as an informal word referring to the head. Apart from that (for example

'I got banged on the nut'), various side expressions developed, for instance, to 'nut out' a problem, to be 'nuts about' (or 'on') something, or to 'use your nut'. And if something is a 'hard nut to crack' then it is a problem or attitude that requires a lot of mental effort on the part of your 'nut'.

But there are also situations concerning someone who is having trouble with whatever is going on inside their head. Thus we have 'off one's nut', a 'nutter', a 'nut case', a 'nutburger', and an organisation with which you don't agree is 'nutsville'. Then there's a person who is 'nutty as a fruitcake'. And this flaky activity inside the head can transfer to an attitude, or a proposition, which is dismissed as 'nuts'.

A very effective use of this was in 1944 in mid-war. General Anthony McAuliffe was commanding the US Army's 101st Airborne Division during the Battle of the Bulge when he received a message from the Germans demanding his surrender. General McAuliffe replied with one word: 'Nuts,' indicating disbelief and contempt. The Germans had great difficulty translating it.

O

Zero, or nought, and/or the letter 'O' often occurs in phone numbers and code numbers such as the code for James Bond: double-O seven – 007. The zero and the 'O' look the same, and the one-syllable 'O' is easier to say than two-syllable 'zero'.

In the days when all long-distance phone calls had to be made through operators, it was sometimes recommended that the caller said 'O' rather than nought when giving the operator the required number. This was supposed to reduce the possibility of mistake because nought can sound like eight.

But in the computer age more caution has become necessary because a computer keyboard has three 'O'-like characters. There is numeric zero, and also an upper-case 'O' and a lower-case 'o'. It is absolutely essential to hit exactly the right key. In one incident of urban legend a computer operator was having a code read out aloud to her, and the person said 'O' when they meant zero. The woman typed in an alphabetical capital 'O', which was not an intended part of the code, and the computer system crashed.

So 'O' can be dangerous, and nought can be misheard. Only zero reliably means what it says.

Odds and sods

Items additional to the main supply are 'odds' – things that are slightly in excess of a given number, or a surplus. The mysterious word 'sods' usually means lumps of turf or soil, but it has a side meaning of something useless and possibly unpleasant.

There are several combinations with odds: odds and bobs, odds and ends, odds and sods. All of these mean things that are miscellaneous and not in a proper order. In general, the odds and sods version is used when you wish to describe something of little value and even faintly undesirable.

Off the wall

When something is new, completely different from the usual and possibly even a little outrageous, it is said to be 'off the wall'. The imagery is said to be from a game of squash, where the ball moves so quickly that sometimes it hits the wall and comes off at a completely unexpected angle, catching a player unawares.

Oggie Oggie Oggie

This is a famous call from Cornwall. There are several British naval bases in Cornwall and nearby Devon: navy training schools, dock-yards and Royal Marine Barracks. It is believed that men of the sea originated this old word 'oggie' as a slang term for what we call a Cornish pasty, which has been made in Cornwall for centuries and well known to countless thousands of British seamen. The Cornish will tell you that their pasties gave British seamen the strength to sink the Spanish Armada in 1588.

Miners ate oggies down the Cornish mines, and one of Henry VIII's wives wrote a letter mentioning Cornish pasties, so perhaps they gave the King strength too.

The Cornish pasty, or oggie, needed to be nourishing and durable since it was carried down into the mine, and later heated in a tin bucket over a candle. The pasty was and is intended to be eaten held in the hand. Its fold-over shape provides a firm crust as a holding edge, and because the miners' hands were unlikely to be clean, the crust could be thrown away after eating the main portion. Often there was a meat filling at one end, and apple or some similar dessert-style filling at the other.

The threefold call 'Oggie Oggie Oggie' is believed to have begun either from Cornish housewives calling down the mine shaft that the pasties were ready, or as an enthusiastic chant by naval men invoking the strength they believed pasties gave them. The famous Welsh entertainer Max Boyce was intrigued with the call and started to use it in his concerts all over Britain. He was also a sports enthusiast and he helped the cry spread to sports matches and develop a return call of 'Oi oi oi'. Other places have made adaptations of the old Cornish cry, but it all dates back to the humble yet nourishing Cornish pasty.

OK

Ask a 'profundity of professors' and you will get a different answer from each as to where the expression comes from, and each will pour scorn on the explanations of the others. Researchers have come up with 16 different versions, including suggested derivations from expressions that sound roughly similar in languages ranging from Gaelic, Norwegian, Burmese and German to American Indian, Finnish, French and Greek. But the truth is no one knows for sure. Nearly everyone at some time has heard one or other of the 'explanations', and the usual situation is that each person accepts the explanation they heard first.

Old hat

Virtually everything is affected by fashion and everything goes out of date. Some, of course, set themselves against trends and are determined not to observe them, but find that, almost against their will, fashion influences the vegetables available at their local shop, the size of their newspapers, what's in the headlines, the shape of their new house and the plants on sale at the garden centre.

But fashion can dictate change which is wasteful and ridiculous, and especially in clothes. There have been times when the hat, male or female, was of extreme importance. Unspoken forces dictated that the shapes and decoration and fabrics be changed from time to time, and abiding by these changes was of great importance to many people. Pioneer settler women, far from their original home and struggling with a new and difficult life, would still eagerly await ships carrying fashion news from London about what kind of hats should be worn.

The wedding of Prince William proved that consciousness of hats and their fashions is far from dead. There was discussion worldwide about the various manifestations of hats in Westminster Abbey, some being wider than the shoulders of the wearer, and others a minuscule knot of fabric and feathers apparently glued either to the front or the side of the head. Some citizens expressed outrage that the British PM's wife appeared not to wear a hat at all (though those expressing outrage were totally unable to explain why they firmly believed she should be hatted).

So the consciousness of fashion in hats still applies. Fashion decrees that baseball caps are worn back to front, and now encourages knitted beanies that mothers begged their children to wear when they were seven. But many hats are made of very durable materials – wool felt, Leghorn straw, or stitched fabric – and it is not at all uncommon for the hat to outlast the fashion. Well-made headgear is often in good condition when its moment in fashion has passed, so although it is perfectly serviceable, it has become an 'old hat'.

The expression makes an appearance in print in 1911; Sir Arthur Thomas Quiller-Couch in his novel *Brother Copas* writes of religion: 'Men have grown decent and put it, with like doctrines, silently aside in disgust. So it has happened with Satan and his fork: they have become "old hat".'

In time, the saying came to mean anything that was too familiar – boring, because you'd seen it all before.

On the wagon

This dates back to the United States in the 1890s; city dust was kept under control by carts carrying water, which was sprinkled on the streets. People who wanted to slake their thirst on a hot day would climb aboard and have a drink, but of course it was only water.

This gave rise to the expression 'climbing aboard the water cart', which gathered the connotation of deliberately avoiding strong liquor and drinking water instead. By 1901, the expression was in print.

Over the following century the expression has settled into slightly different wording, and become 'on the wagon', but it still means the same.

(Know your) onions

An early editor of *The Oxford English Dictionary* was Charles Onions, and people acknowledged his expertise by complimenting other people for knowing as much as Onions.

But there is also a belief that the expression derives from Cockney rhyming slang, where instead of saying a person knew a lot about things, they'd say he knew a lot about onion rings. And in the usual way of rhyming slang, the describing word has gone into the language and the actual rhyming word hasn't.

Orange

Oranges have been around for a very long time. They are thought to have originated in the tropical regions of Asia and eventually reached Europe and the rest of the world.

The fruit's name goes way back to the languages of South and Central India. It appears in Sanskrit as *naranga*; versions of that word came via the Persian language into Arabic and then into Old French before reaching English and eventually settling into 'orange'.

At the time, the word *geoluhread* identified a certain yellow-red colour in England. The association between the yellow-red fruit and the yellow-red colour was clarified in 1612 at the court of King Henry VIII when the colour was referred to by the name of the fruit: 'orange'. So the colour is named after the fruit.

Ostracise

In ancient Athens, a ceremony took place from time to time aimed at removing an undesirable citizen from circulation. Voters held a piece of pottery or shell called an *ostrakon* (plural *ostraka*), and on this they wrote the name of whomever they wanted to get rid of. All the *ostraka* were put into urns, which were later tipped out and the contents analysed. The name scratched the most times was then given ten days to leave the district, from which he was banished for the next ten years: he was ostracised.

In modern times the essence of the action remains, but without its former formality or severity. Generally, ostracism can now mean exclusion from some kind of group context, achieved by belief and informal judgement, rather than with urns and *ostraka*.

(Besides ostracism, the Greek *ostrakon* also survives in English as 'oyster', probably because the irregular shells and firm texture somewhat resemble broken bits of crockery.)

Outage

Clearly it's a variation of 'out'. Use of the word outage began in America referring to goods lost or mysteriously missing in shipping or storage, or supplies that had passed through a few hands and their quantity didn't seem to have remained intact.

The word moved into that area of softening terms to make difficult situations more acceptable, and at the same time somehow suggesting that nobody was responsible.

An electric power breakdown indicates immediately that there has been a mechanical or human failure. But utility authorities began to prefer describing the situation as an 'outage' because it carried a neutral connotation: the lights have gone out all by themselves, nothing broke down, nobody did it. There was an 'outage'.

Over a barrel

In general, scholars agree that it dates back to a method of assisting someone who has nearly drowned. The poor unfortunate was stretched out over a barrel with their head pointing downwards, so that the water would drain out of their lungs.

Naturally the person in this position was very vulnerable and helpless, and completely under the control of those giving the treatment. Therefore, over time, the expression widened its application to refer to anyone in a position where they couldn't do anything.

There is also a slight possibility of influence from the fact that when people in the old days were being flogged they were tied over a barrel to keep them still, but the drowning one is the origin most widely accepted.

Over the brush

The full expression is 'living over the brush': in other words, living together as husband and wife but not married. It's a very old saying, usually found in the northern part of England, and it may have been derived from an even older English saying: to 'leap over the broomstick', or 'leap over the brush', which meant to go through a mock ceremony and pretend that you are married.

Possibly the couple would quite literally hold hands and jump

261

together over an old broom with a bushy end and declare 'we are married'.

Over the hill

This expression is thought to have originated among soldiers. When someone deserted from the army and walked away from their responsibilities, the other soldiers said he had 'gone over the hill'. But then non-military people began to use it and the word 'hill' began to mean the effective part of your life, starting when you're a child and going upwards until you become an adult and then travelling even higher as you become good at what you do.

But everyone eventually becomes old, so when you start to move a bit more slowly, and you can't work as well, then it's as if you've reached the top of the hill and are now going down – over the other side.

Although there is suggestion that the term was used within the military as far back as the First World War, it didn't appear in print until 1950. An amusing addition arose when it was remarked of someone that he was 'not exactly over the hill – but, shall we say, has a good view of the valley'.

Oxymoron

The word is used to describe a juxtaposition of two ideas which don't comfortably sit together: a 'weak tyrant', or a 'poor millionaire'.

It is a strange word because *oxy* means sharp, keen and acute and *moron* means stupid. Thus, the word itself appears to be an example of internal contradiction: stupidity that is at the same time sharp and keen. This certainly can apply to some oxymorons, where a vivid image is evoked by deliberate contradiction, for example, a 'living death'.

Strictly speaking, an oxymoron and a 'contradiction in terms' could, by splitting hairs, be described as two different things. But in general the two terms are interchangeable.

Pain in the neck

We came to it through politeness, because 'pain in the neck' is a polite substitute for 'pain in the bum' – a metaphorical assessment of an unwelcome task, speech, person, requirement, or anything which causes the speaker displeasure.

The polite version has been in fairly common use since 1910. There are various versions of the original: pain in the bum, pain in the butt, pain in the arse. And a socially acceptable version: pain in the elbow.

Adding the word 'royal' makes it even more impressively painful.

Palindrome

It is a word or phrase which spells the same backwards as it does forwards: 'Madam I'm Adam'; or 'Able was I 'ere I saw Elba'.

The word comes from ancient Greek, *dromos* meaning 'a course', like a race-track, and *palin* meaning 'again', so it actually means 'running back again along the same track'.

The term palindrome is used only of words, not about numbers, but it can be used adjectivally (palindromic). So when you come across a group of digits which reads the same backwards and forwards – the date 27.9.1972, for instance – you can call it a palindromic number.

Pall-bearers

In this usage, the word 'pall' is a shortened form of *pallium*, which is Latin for cloak. At some periods of history a person's cloak was draped over their coffin, and this developed into there sometimes being a flag or, when appropriate, a royal standard.

In other cases, the covering can be of a completely different kind; the coffin of film star Rudolph Valentino was covered in a blanket made of gardenias.

The term pall-bearer is an example of a figure of speech called metonymy, where you name something associated with a concept and, by doing so, intend to include the whole concept. For example, in this phrase: 'This is a law laid down by the Crown', the word

Crown is shorthand for legislation and the government as a whole. Similarly, a pall-bearer is carrying the pall, the cloak, but is also carrying the coffin under the pall.

Often, there is no actual cloak or cloth over the coffin, but the term pall-bearer remains in use. There may be a euphemistic reason for this: pall-bearer sounds less harsh than coffin carrier.

Pan pan

This signal isn't nearly as well known to landlubbers as the distress signal Mayday, but it also denotes a level of urgency, asking that the airwaves be kept clear in case a distress signal is imminent. For instance, if a small fire was discovered on a ship the crew would maybe signal 'pan pan' because there could be a problem that might or might not get worse. If the fire did become serious, the signal would then be changed to 'mayday'.

These spoken verbal signals date back to the 1920s when actual words started to be used in communications instead of Morse code. French was adopted as the universal language for such signals, hence mayday (from *m'aidez*) for distress, *securité* for safety messages such as storm warnings, and pan pan for urgency.

Pan pan is derived from the French word *panne-panne*, which is used to mean a breakdown of the norm: something is wrong but the situation is not yet desperate. If a lift in a big building in France is out of order or being repaired, there'll be a sign up saying *En panne*.

Pant/pants

They are the same word: both abbreviations for pantaloons, which take their name from Pantalone, a popular and eccentric character in sixteenth-century Italian theatre who wore funny, elaborate clothes and trousers often trimmed with ribbons.

There is no real need to keep the final 's' on pants; it is just a custom. 'Pant' has been used in the singular in the United States for many years (since 1893): a pant, or sometimes a pants. No strict rule applies.

But you're not likely to hear of 'a slack'. Slacks were originally trousers of a loose kind from the Old English *slaec*, meaning loose, which goes way back to Latin *laxus*; in English, both slack and lax still mean something loose. Nor will you encounter 'a trouser' (from 'trews', itself from Scottish *triubhas*).

Most things with two leg-holes are referred to in the plural: togs, daks, grunds, undies, knickers, drawers. Sometimes the fly opening on trousers is singular, but in other places it is plural: flies. Fly is short for fly front, where one piece of material overlaps the other (as in part of a tent).

It's worth pointing out, too, that trouser legs used to be separate, and when evolution joined them together, the plural was an obvious carry-over. But then again there is a whole list of single things with two components which are generally mentioned in plural: scissors, glasses, pliers and tights.

Pantihose

Obviously this is a combination of two existing words, 'panty' and 'hose'. Those garments and those two words had existed for many decades before someone had the bright idea of joining them together.

The word panty is a version of pants, which arose from the Italian comedy character Pantalone. Hose is an old-fashioned word. It comes from the word *hosa*, which originally meant male leg covering of a fairly loose kind, often criss-crossed with ropes or leather to keep out draughts and protect from thorns and twigs.

What we call stockings actually have a different history: they originated in ancient Rome. Made out of beautifully soft goat hair, they originally reached only to the shin, like a sort of long sock, but over the decades they grew longer and longer. They were only for men, of course; women were expected to be covered up with skirts.

When William the Conqueror arrived in England in 1066 his troops introduced tube-like leg-covering garments to English men. They were fitting a bit better by then, and the men called them skin-tights. William's son Prince Rufus was known to wear skin-tights which came right to the waist and had knickers built in. These were called stocking-pants, so the garment we call pantihose has actually been in existence since the year 1100.

Tight stockings for men became commonplace, and wearing them in outrageous colours and designs became one way for youthful rebels to upset the rest of society. Chaucer comments on this. We also know from Chaucer that by then women did wear stockings – the Wife of Bath wore red ones. Scholars agree that women had been wearing them for quite a while, but nobody knew – unless they saw them in the boudoir. Elizabeth I received her first silk stockings in 1561 and would wear nothing but silk from then on.

Machines to knit stockings were invented during Elizabeth's reign: the leg-cover industry started in 1589 is still going strong today. In general stockings were called hosiery, and for centuries the industry made separate leg-covering tubes – one for each leg – and generally in two lengths: mid-thigh for women's daily wear, called stockings or hosiery, and long, long ones for ballet dancers, who had access to specially manufactured garments that joined at the top and kept on going right up to the waist. The dancers reverted to William the Conqueror's word and called them tights.

Around the sixth decade of the twentieth century, women's skirts became shorter and shorter, and there was a need for long stockings which came right up to the crotch. So, probably without even realising it, manufacturers came up with a new version of what Prince William Rufus wore in the year 1100.

And then came the word pantihose (or pantyhose). Sometimes they were (and still are) referred to as tights, but the word pantihose has been in common use since the early 1960s, when they were occasionally described as 'the death of the stocking'.

Paparazzi

It is the plural form of paparazzo, which means a particular breed of freelance photographer who makes a living by taking photos of celebrities (often in private situations and against their will) and selling them to newspapers and magazines.

The word sprang to prominence in the 1960 Fellini movie *La Dolce Vita*, in which there was a character called Mr Paparazzo, a photographer who specialised in society and show-biz pics. This character, supposedly fictional, was based on a real person, a photographer called Tazio Secchiaroli who used to hang around Rome photographing film stars and royalty. But the name of the movie character Paparazzo went into the English language very quickly, and within a year people started to refer to nuisance photographers in the plural – paparazzi, a term that has been with us ever since.

The actual word paparazzo is believed to have been borrowed from a book by George Gissing – *By the Ionian Sea* – published in 1901. He told of staying at a small hotel, run by a man called Coriolano Paparazzo, whose name was apparently Greek. Over fifty years later, Fellini and his scriptwriter, possibly influenced by the fact that to Italians the word sounds somewhat similar to the name for a particular insect which is a buzzing nuisance, borrowed the name from that book.

Pardon my French

The expression is usually shorthand for 'I've just said something indelicate but I hope you'll overlook it'. The term was first observed in use in Britain in 1916. It seems to be connected with the British troops who fought in France during the First World War. The theory is that because many British soldiers couldn't speak French, they joked that when French people spoke to them vehemently, they could well be uttering swear words for all anyone knew.

Somehow that became twisted into French words equating with swear words. Hence when one of those was said in the wrong context, the phrase 'Pardon my French' followed. In the United States the term was modified to 'Excuse my French'.

Parka

Although the word Eskimo is used to describe the native inhabitants of Northern Canada, Greenland, Alaska and Eastern Siberia, the term is not quite accurate and doesn't describe all the inhabitants of the area. Within that territory are the Aleutian Islands, whose inhabitants are related to the Eskimos but are a different group.

A common garment in the general area has for a long time been a thigh-length coat with a hood usually made of caribou skin and seal fur. Eskimos and Aleutians and Alaskans protected themselves from the cold with this garment, and coats for women had an extra hood used for wrapping round a baby.

Round about 1930, the design of this jacket moved into the rest of the world, for skiing and general outdoor use, and was known by its Aleutian name *parka*, which in their language is the word meaning what a real one is made from – 'animal hide, skin.'

Parkinson's Law

Cyril Northcote Parkinson was a British writer with more than 60 books to his credit. He had worked in the British Civil Service in the 1920s and 1930s and wrote works on politics and economics as well as a large number of very successful novels, including stories which continued the adventures of C.S. Forrester's fictional character Horatio Hornblower.

In 1957 Parkinson wrote a book called *Parkinson's Law*, the main premise of which was his observation that 'Work expands to fill the time allocated for its completion'. In other words, if you allocate half an hour to clean the oven, you'll get it done in half an hour. If you allocate four hours to do the same thing, it will take four hours. Parkinson was also responsible for the similar observation that 'Expenditure rises to meet income'.

Parky

It's a very old word meaning cold, so old that its origin is lost in the mists of time. But some etymologists believe it is a variation on 'perky', because the cold weather makes you alert, spirited and jaunty, as opposed to the sleepy, soporific effect of warm weather.

Pâté/pesto

The old Greek word *pastos* for sprinkled barley has several modern relations, including pastry, pasta, pasty (white-faced), paste, pastel (pale) and pastiche (bits and pieces mixed up) – and pâté, a meat paste, usually made from ground livers.

The delicacy we know as pesto originated in Genoa, so has an Italian name. In antique times, before there were food processors, pesto was made of nuts and basil leaves and oil, vigorously pounded together into a paste, inside a bowl called a mortar, with a bashing implement called a pestle. The Italian word *pestare* means to pound, as in hit heavily, and the mixture being bashed in the bowl was described by the verb's past participle, *pestato*, meaning that which has been thumped and pounded. Because pounding with the thumping implement was vital, the mixture took on the name of the process, and it became known as pesto.

Patsy

The word has been commonly used in the United States since the nineteenth century to mean someone who is easily deceived, a sucker. The word is believed to be derived from an Italian word *pazzo*, meaning a fool.

Paying through the nose

It means paying out too much money for something – more than it is worth. There is only one explanation for where the expression comes from, and it is very unpleasant.

In ninth-century Ireland a general tax known as a poll tax was imposed on every person within the population, regardless of income. If you failed to pay the tax, you were punished by having your nose slit. Thus the belief arose that if you didn't pay the tax, when you were found out, you'd be punished (1) by having to pay it anyway, and (2) by having your nose mutilated by slitting.

So the cost was very high, and you were paying with, by, or through, your nose.

Penultimate

English has borrowed bits and pieces from many other languages, and the proportion of Latin terminology in English is large. Penultimate uses two Latin words: *paene* meaning almost, and *ultimus*, meaning final. Thus penultimate means almost the end and is generally used to indicate that which comes second to last.

Peppercorn rent

Peppercorn rents originated during the Middle Ages in Britain. Sometimes when a landowner's employee had given especially good service, a piece of property was deeded over to his use as a reward, and a nominal rent was charged as a reminder that the person using the land was still a tenant. He didn't own the land outright, but what he was being charged was very small.

In early times exotic spices like pepper were not all that common, so giving up one peppercorn had a certain mild significance to it. A similar practice sometimes occurred, called a 'rose rent', where the tenant had ceremoniously to hand over a single rose as rent. And other cases existed where a tenant marked his debt to the landlord by cooking a roast dinner once a year, or donating a petticoat to a poor woman.

In the early days of American colonisation there was a similar system known as Quit Rent, where settlers were allowed to occupy land but to do so had to pay a small fee to the King. This system lasted up until the Revolution. But in terms of language, it is the expression 'peppercorn rental' that has survived, meaning a payment for the use of a property, but a payment so small that it does not reflect the actual value of habitation, yet acknowledges that there is an obligation to the owner.

Pernickety

This is a very old Scottish dialect word, with a meaning which simply sounds right: fastidious, punctilious, particular about details and trifles. Americans use a slightly different version, adding an 's' and saying 'persnickety'.

Persons/people

Euphemisms are words or expressions used in an endeavour to describe something hurtful or unpleasant in gentler terms. This has always been the case in politics and commercial advertising, but has also become very fashionable with the rise of so-called political correctness, in business and employment situations, and in the reporting of war.

Instead of losing your job, you may be subjected to 'downsizing' and/or 'redundancy'; genocide is likely to be called 'ethnic cleansing'; the victims of bombing and shelling are 'taken out' or simply become 'collateral damage'; exams are 'assessment events'.

And for some reason, those who make speeches and occasional journalists consider that 'persons' sounds more gentle and polite than 'people'.

(The) Peter Principle

This first appeared in 1969 in a book entitled *The Peter Principle*, written by Canadian educationists Dr Laurence Peter and Raymond Hull. A study of business, the book contained a line that has sometimes since been misquoted. The original line said: 'Work is accomplished by those employees who have not yet reached their level of incompetence.'

Phar Lap

The name of the New Zealand horse Phar Lap comes from the Zhuang language shared between Thailand and parts of China. The phrase literally means 'moving quickly through the sky' and is generally accepted as being long-hand for 'lightning'.

Phar Lap proved to exemplify his name after moving to Australia where he became an A-list winner of the Melbourne Cup, the Cox Plates, and 19 weight-for-age races. When he died under mysterious circumstances in the United States, Phar Lap was acknowledged to be the third highest stakes-winner worldwide at that time (1932).

Picnic

The word comes from Old French, where one of the meanings of *piquer* is to pick things up or get things. And *nique*, in Old French, meant something of little value.

As early as 1694 the expression *pique-nique* in French was used to describe an informal meal of small dishes at which one nibbled, or sometimes a meal to which every guest brought some food. Hence, eventually, we get 'picnic' which, in English, has somehow evolved a connotation of being outdoors, but is still sometimes used for casual

P

eating indoors ('everything was packed ready to move, so we just sat on the floor and picnicked').

Pidgin English

Pidgin English has nothing to do with pigeons. It's a term which arose because of the English insistence that everyone should speak to them in English, and this included conducting commerce with Chinese and Indians. Quite often these groups had learned the appropriate words but had difficulty in pronouncing them. For instance, the Chinese had difficulty with the letter 'b' and an interior 's', so instead of saying 'business' they said 'pidginess'.

In time pidginess became just pidgin, and then the word was used to describe a whole dialect that evolved around the Pacific area and in some cases actually became the language of a community.

The term has spread throughout the world and is used to refer to communication in which the basic language is rendered in a lumpy sort of way but manages to be understood, as in pidgin French, pidgin English, pidgin German. There is another word with a very similar meaning, creole, which refers to a language created from a combination of two other languages.

Piece of cake

The famous etymologist Eric Partridge thinks that it derives from the dance known as the cakewalk, which is cheerful and flowing and jaunty, and engenders a feeling of ease in those who are watching. The people judged the best dancers were traditionally awarded a fancy cake as a prize. Hence, saying something was a cakewalk meant that it was happy and free of stress, and this became condensed over the years into just a piece of cake.

There is an alternative. One of the first times the saying is known to have appeared in print was in the American poet Ogden Nash's 1936 poem 'Primrose Path'. He wrote: 'Her picture's in the paper now. And life's a piece of cake' – which seemed to indicate that 'piece of cake' was a pleasant thing.

Both explanations have two things in common: they acknowledge that cake is pleasant, and they come from the United States.

Pie in the sky

The phrase is American and dates back to 1911. It is associated with a somewhat anarchistic Labour organisation called Industrial Workers of the World, which started a few years earlier and was known jocularly as The Wobblies (because of its initials). The organisation paid a lot of attention to migrant and casual workers, and one of its unifying forces was song. Everyone who joined the IWW was given a little songbook that contained rousing parodies of popular songs, such as 'Hallelujah, I'm a Bum' and 'Nearer My Job To Thee'.

In 1911 they put out a song parody directly aimed at the Salvation Army hymn, 'In the Sweet Bye and Bye'. The IWW workers took offence at its implication that there would be joy in the afterlife so long as one remained meek and compliant in this life.

So out came the parody which, instead of the 'sweet bye and bye' said, 'Work and pray, live on hay, you'll get pie in the sky when you die.' Although somewhat unfair to the Salvation Army, the phrase went into the language very quickly. In time it almost completely lost its sense of religious parody, and instead became a depiction of a dream scenario or an unrealistic hope.

Pig in a poke

Poke is the old word for bag or basket, derived from the French word *poche*. In modern English we don't use the word poke with that meaning, but two versions of the word survive in modern English as pocket and pouch.

'A pig in a poke' has been in use in English for 400 years. It's believed to have originated in country markets where someone would have for sale a small animal squirming around inside a bag, or poke. Telling his customers it was a piglet, the marketer would sometimes succeed in selling it without the customer actually opening the bag to check that it was a pig. So if you bought a pig in a poke, without examining it thoroughly, you could end up with something unexpected, such as an unwanted cat. Hence the meaning: to buy something significant without having thoroughly researched it.

Pilgarlic

A very old term of contempt, 'pilgarlic' refers to a clove of garlic with its skin peeled off, which resembles in miniature the head of a bald man. An underlying factor was the (ancient) belief that a man who had gone bald may have suffered from the pox. So saying he had a head like a peeled garlic clove was an expression of pity – and some contempt.

A 'pilgarlic' came to mean someone you despised but also felt faintly sorry for.

Pillock

This is a contemptuous expression usually applied to a man, or to a piece of information which is regarded as nonsense. The word is an anglicised version of the Scandinavian word *pillicock*, classified as a vulgar name for the male member.

(A similar put-down using a male quality is bollocks, originally spelt 'ballocks', meaning testicles, and like pillock now used to dismiss information with which the speaker does not agree.)

Pineapple

Pineapples are native to Brazil and adjacent parts of South America. They had drifted to the Caribbean islands by the fifteenth century and become quite familiar there. The Caribbean islanders used pineapples as a symbol of hospitality and prosperity, frequently placing one above their door or on their roof.

Christopher Columbus was in the Caribbean in 1493 and he became the first known European to see a pineapple, one of which he took back to the King of Spain. At that time the fruit could not be grown in Europe, and as pineapples slowly began to be imported there, their reputation preceded them – the Caribbean symbol of hospitality, but now including a new dimension: extreme rarity and desirability.

A gift of a pineapple was considered to be extremely special; a portrait was painted of King Charles II of England being given one as a gift in about 1670.

During the 1700s and 1800s, images of pineapples began to

appear with great frequency in European art and architecture. They symbolised hospitality, and people were intrigued by their exotic appearance. Architects and builders frequently included pineapples sculpted from stone, cast from plaster or carved in wood, on gate-posts, door frames and occasionally roof trimmings; the fruit carried a connotation of richness and prosperity.

During the same period, artists and craftsmen created hundreds of different kinds of smaller pineapples as ornaments: in china, enamel, jewels and in embroidery and fabric design.

In a few cases the use of pineapple ornamentation had some logic – pineapples eventually migrated to Hawaii where the climate suited them perfectly, and the Queen of Hawaii slept in a four-poster bed, the wooden pillars of which were carved in shapes of pineapples atop each other.

But in general the inclusion of the pineapple into building design (and particularly the approach – gateways, doors and entrance arches) was based on its early reputation as a symbol of hospitality.

Its use as a decorative ornament was based on the novelty of its appearance and its connotation of being 'special'. The name pineapple came about in English because the fruit had a rough, spiky exterior like a pine cone, and a succulent juicy interior like an apple.

One fascinating piece of social trivia about pineapples concerns American hostesses who wanted to keep up with the Joneses. In earlier centuries the fruit was costly and difficult to obtain. Ships were hot and slow, and fruit often rotted. Ripe, wholesome pineapples were a rarity for the society hostesses of cities such as Boston. If a woman could be seen to have a pineapple in her house she was immediately noted as a person of some substance and influence. So sometimes pineapples were actually rented out by the day when a society woman was having a lunch or afternoon tea party. The pineapple was settled into a 'casual' arrangement of fruit in a bowl, not to be eaten – just noticed. Later, the same pineapple would be sold to another, richer client whose evening guests would actually eat it.

Ping-pong

To begin with, ping-pong is not a Chinese term. The game is believed to have begun with nineteenth-century British army officers using the lids of cigar boxes to bat little balls across a row of books on a table. Later, more efficient little bats were made of vellum and the balls were cut from cork.

By 1891 the game had been made into a marketed item in Britain, and sets were sold under the names Gossima, Whiff Whaff and Flim Flam. Then an Englishman called James Gibb refined the equipment and in 1900 the brand name Ping-Pong was invented and registered as a British patent. This new name for the game was described as being two 'echoic' words: 'ping' for when the bat hits the ball, and 'pong' for when the ball hits the table. In 1901 the term also became a registered patent in the United States. The game and the name took off.

For a couple of decades ping-pong was very big indeed worldwide and it still commands a large following, though now it is generally called table tennis. In 1971 an American table tennis team went to China and that gave rise to the term 'ping-pong diplomacy'. It also became clear that many Chinese and Japanese people were particularly good at table tennis, so a vague legend arose that the game and the name originated in China. In Puccini's opera *Turandot*, first staged in 1926, the three senior courtiers at the Emperor of China's court are called Ping, Pang and Pong. The names just sound Oriental.

But the term ping-pong was well established before radar began using the term 'ping' for a radar signal, and before computers started using the word 'ping' to indicate that a message needs a reply, and then 'pong' when the return message has been activated.

Pin money

Pins were not common in early Britain, and when they were available, were expensive. Husbands who could afford to, allocated an allowance to their wives especially for buying pins. Sometimes a special bequest was left in wills, just to provide a beneficiary with money specifically to buy pins. The first known reference to this can be seen in *The Testamenta Eboracensia* – a will in York dated 1542: 'I give my said doughter Margarett my lease of the parsonadge of Kirkdall Churche to by her pynnes withal.'

Therefore the term 'pin money' was a self-explanatory factual statement, and this usage lasted until at least the seventeenth century. In a Thomas Vanbrugh play of 1696 a character is described as having £200 a year to buy pins. But technology and manufacture gradually advanced, so pins became cheaper, and women with pin money had enough left over, after buying pins, to spend on other things. So the term came to mean small amounts, nothing financially consequential.

Pissed as a newt

Some people who use this expression have no clear idea of what a newt actually is. It is a lizard-like creature, some of which are aquatic, and some not. The reasons for describing anyone as being pissed as a newt are mysterious, though it is conjectured that because some newts live in water, this gave someone the fanciful notion of their being totally immersed in 'drink'.

Another theory suggests that because a newt's skin fits neatly over a rather complex body shape, it could have engendered the expression 'tight as a newt'. This later evolved, when the word 'tight' gained a sub-meaning of being drunk, and was later joined by the colloquial 'pissed'; the poor old newt and its sleek-fitting skin had been designated through tight, to drunk, then pissed.

Any way you look at it, it's an odd expression – real newts never get drunk.

Playing gooseberry

Some scholars think this expression dates back to a time when many more people lived rurally than do now, and sexual freedom was often rather more restricted. So if two people wanted to get closer together than the social rules allowed, they might have to go out into the fields to work, taking a trusted third person with them. Often, so it seems, they would be picking gooseberries.

The group of three looked more discreet than just two, and the third person would tactfully go on picking gooseberries, ignoring whatever antics the other two were up to – hence, playing gooseberry.

The odd thing is that, like some other expressions, this one has reversed its original meaning. Nowadays when you hear about someone playing gooseberry, it usually means that their presence is preventing the other two people from having fun.

Poach

Poaching eggs and illegal poaching are from two different words that have finished up looking and sounding the same. Poach, as in eggs, relates back to Old French word *pochier*, meaning to enclose in a bag. It is the ancestor of things like a 'pig in a poke' (a bag), and the more common words 'pocket' and 'pouch' and 'pucker' (to make a little bag with your lips) and 'pox' (the skin forms a tiny hole like a bag). And when you break an egg into boiling water, the white ideally remains around the yolk as a little bag – not broken up as in scrambled eggs.

Meanwhile, the poacher goes to trespass on another person's land for the purpose of acquiring something unlawfully. According to the ancient German word *poken*, he is thrusting himself into someone else's territory (from the same source we get the fireside poker). In a joint use of the two words, the poacher may very likely be carrying away his poached fish or birds in a pouch or pocket.

Po-faced

There are two elements here. The origin of the expression seems to be 'poker-faced', meaning to assume an expression that gives nothing away – either as stiff and unyielding as a poker standing by the fire, or as unmoving and undemonstrative as a person playing poker and not wanting to reveal what they have in their hand.

But although po-faced is descended from poker-faced, it doesn't mean quite the same thing. It can mean either expressionless, or showing stern disapproval and distaste (possibly influenced by the word 'po' once being a common term for a chamber pot).

Poinsettia

The flowers are named after the first American ambassador to Mexico, Joel Poinsett. Besides carrying out his diplomatic duties, Poinsett was an ardent amateur botanist who looked for unusual plants. In 1825 he noticed something growing wild in a Mexican ditch, took it back to his glasshouse in South Carolina, and fostered the plant. Now, in the United States, at least 60 million poinsettias are sold each year during December alone.

Poisoned chalice

A chalice is an elaborate drinking cup, usually on a stem, often with two handles, and customarily very decorative and precious. The concept of poisoning the drink in a chalice really emerges in the legends of ancient Greece, when the accepted mode of execution for those condemned to death was poison, and those who were ordained to die were given hemlock to drink. A famous example was the teacher and philosopher Socrates, who eventually was tried for impiety and corruption, was sentenced to death, and was given hemlock in a beautiful engraved silver chalice.

Over several hundred years, the act of taking a poisoned chalice developed two strong images. Because a chalice itself is rather grand, the expression encapsulated a situation whereby something seemingly attractive and advantageous could in fact have a distinctly bad side. In modern terms, a husband is given a wonderful and lucrative job, but it requires him to be away from his wife and family for two weeks out of every three; the chalice (of his desirable new job) has a touch of poison (he misses his family).

By the time of the legends of King Arthur, and much later Shakespeare, the word chalice had taken on a connotation of being a distant vision that man cannot attain, and the 'poisoned chalice' came to mean inevitable punishment for wrongdoers.

There is a version of the poisoned chalice situation in *Hamlet*, when the King prepares a poisoned chalice for Hamlet, which is later drunk by Gertrude. And in *Macbeth*, Macbeth is hesitant before he kills Duncan, and is aware that while Duncan's death is to his advantage, there will doubtless be retribution. Macbeth says:

... this even-handed justice,
Commends the ingredients of our poison'd chalice
To our own lips.

Through the Bible, the chalice had also gained a connotation of being sacred because of its association with the Last Supper. Much later the image of a chalice became associated with the Christian service of Communion, and there is a hint in the book of Corinthians that if you drink the wine without having repented, then you are damning yourself – the chalice is more or less poisoned.

So there's a whole host of images to warn that a chalice – no matter how beautiful – can sometimes bring danger with it.

Poker

Poker with cards has nothing to do with the rod pushing coals into a fire – that is named from the German word *poken*, meaning to thrust. The name of the card game is also from German but from a different word altogether: *Poch-spiel*, which means a game involving bragging or boasting.

(North and South) Pole

Children at school sometimes say they develop a mental image of the South Pole having a great big post sticking up into the sky like the school flagpole, with a flag on it saying 'South Pole'.

But like many words, 'pole' has several meanings.

It is of course the big post sticking up, from which a flag flies; that came from the Latin *palus*, meaning a stake (as in fence palings). But the Greek word *polus* is quite different – it meant a 'pivot' or an 'axis'. Both those words filtered into English and finished up with the same sound and spelling – pole – but totally different meanings. When you put the flag up a pole, you're using the Latin word *palus*, but when you revolve a sphere on its axis, you're using the Greek word *polus*, and the northern and southern tips of the planet we live on are called poles because they are the extremities of a sphere.

Sometimes you'll hear the word poles used outside its earthly connotation, but in a similar area of meaning, indicating opposites and contrasted tendencies: 'My sister and I are poles apart,' meaning their personalities and interests are like the opposite ends of a sphere.

Politically correct

That phrase as we now know it began to appear in the United States during the 1970s when people started to avoid expressions or actions that could denigrate or offend minorities or people considered to be disadvantaged by gender, race, class, sexual orientation, religious beliefs or disability.

Initially this expression was considered a very good thing and many people could see the sense of modifying what they said so as not to be offensive. In 1991 an American dictionary was published called *The Bias-Free Word Finder*, which was supposed to help you find politically correct terminology to replace the offensive words you might have used before.

But since 1991 the expression has had a more or less complete reversal of intent. Unfortunately the enthusiasm for being correct started to get out of hand. For instance, traditional phrases such as 'the right hand of God' were republished as 'the mighty hand of God' in case the traditional version offended left-handed people. And people started being jokey about political correctness – such as wondering how you would describe a Catholic in a wheelchair wearing a fur coat.

Nowadays many people find it difficult to take political correctness seriously because it seems to have gone too far and it's becoming hard to sort out which are the genuine politically correct words now present in the language (such as 'disabled') and which are the made-up jokey ones: crippled (otherly abled), janitor (maintenance engineer), or short (vertically challenged).

Polka/polka dots

The polka dance originates from Bohemia (now the Czech Republic), where the word *pul* means half and *pul-ka* means a half-step – that little bounce a dancer does in a polka. Polka dots are regularly spaced spots of the same size that appear on fabric.

Any connection between the polka dance and polka dots is slight, to say the least. One feasible theory says that printing a pattern on fabric involves plates carrying a design, which is then repeated over and over. But the dots we know as 'polka' were so large that each printing plate contained only one-and-a-half dots, which when repeated over and over, produced an overall pattern of big dots. The supposed similarity between the plate containing half a dot, and the dance containing half-a-step is believed by some to be the reason for naming them 'polka dots'.

Strangely, dancing the polka doesn't necessitate wearing spotted fabric, but Spanish flamenco dancers very often do wear dresses covered with matching spots. But they're never called flamenco dots; the Spanish call them *lunares*.

Poloney

In some places this sausage is called polony. In the US and Canada they tend to call it bolony or baloney. Although the name clarifies its city of origin, Bologna, it isn't so called in that city. There it is known as *mortadella*. Mortadella has been made in Bologna for at least five centuries, and legend has it that it used to be made of donkey meat, but some time ago the ingredients shifted to mainly pork.

A real bologna sausage is made of 60 per cent minced pork meat from the animal's body, plus meat from the minced cheeks. The mix is then flavoured with black pepper, peeled pistachios, cinnamon, anise, cardamom, coriander, nutmeg, cloves and mace.

Strips of lard are added, plus 3 per cent salt, and the whole mix is then put into its casing and simmered for somewhere between 12 and 20 hours, depending on the size of the sausage. They can vary from 2 kg up to 50 kg in weight.

That is a true bologna/mortadella sausage. There are variations in the ingredients when it's made in other places, including cubes of red peppers and fat.

(Note that the sausage is not necessarily connected with 'baloney' meaning nonsense; that is believed to have arisen from a gypsy word *pelone*, meaning testicles, used to mean that something is a nonsense.)

Pontificate

The Concise Oxford Dictionary says that 'pontificate' refers only to the duties of the Pope, whereas 'pontify' means acting authoritatively, as if one were the Pope (and especially if one is being a bit pompous and claiming infallibility).

The dictionary is academically correct, but it can be a losing battle when you're up against a huge tide of general usage that has moved the word pontify into near-oblivion. In the twenty-first century, the word pontificate has come to mean acting in pontiff-like manner. Nowadays pontify and pontificate are interchangeable.

So you don't have to be the Pope to pontificate. The word describes a person acting as if they were Pope, and expecting everyone to believe that everything they say is infallible.

Pontoon

Some words with pont in them are somehow connected with bridges – such as pontiff for the Pope (who is perceived by some Christians as the bridge between themselves and God) and pontoon, a floating vessel used for support or for acting as a temporary bridge.

The card game is no relation to this. The game aims to acquire cards with a face value of 21 and was properly called *vingt-et-un*. This French term became abbreviated by English speakers into just *vingt-un*, which eventually was corrupted into pontoon.

Poodle-faker

A poodle-faker is a man who specialises in being friendly with women who might be useful for his promotion, either socially or professionally. He becomes over-polite and attentive, rather like a lapdog, and is rewarded with friendly affection and either invitations or recommendations.

The expression has been used quite often in the military, about young officers who cultivate the goodwill of senior officers' wives. It's a derogatory term, of course: military men do not commonly have a high opinion of poodles, or of those who fake their behaviour.

Poop deck

This shipboard term comes from the Latin word *puppis*, meaning the stern or aftermost part of the vessel. In modern times the actual aftermost part of a ship is generally called the stern, but the word poop survives as the aftermost and highest deck, often forming a roof for the cabin directly underneath it.

There's no connection with a couple of other poo words in English. The childish words 'poop', or its reduced version 'poo', meaning excrement, come from an old Dutch expression meaning a sudden blast through a pipe. And the American expression pooped, meaning tired and worn out, is thought to be simply a made-up nonsense word.

Poppycock

It's an expression which developed in the United States, based on the Dutch word *pappekak*, which means faeces that are not firm. The actual origin of the word is Latin *carcare*, but it was the Dutch version which became known in the States.

This Dutch word gives rise to two other English words: pap, meaning soft food, especially for babies and invalids; and cack, a childish word for excrement. Poppycock, which is a combination of them both, means worthless material or nonsense.

Posh

For many years it was believed that 'posh' was an abbreviation for 'port out, starboard home', referring to bookings on steamships travelling to and from India, when rich people paid extra to ensure the cabins on the cooler side of the ship both ways. This explanation is now discredited as a fiction: researchers can find no evidence whatever that port out, starboard home was an expression or a practice ever used.

But lurking in the background had been a word 'poosh' with two 'o's, or sometimes spelled 'push', which meant smart and dandified. P.G. Wodehouse uses the word in *Tales of St. Austin's* (1903) when a character describes a bright waistcoat as 'quite the most push thing at Cambridge'. The modern word posh is widely believed to be a variation on push/poosh.

Potato/spud

This is another example of a word's meaning shifting between the container and whatever it contains (see **Mail**, **Mortar** and **Ratbag**). This one refers to a small, sharp implement used for digging up vegetables. In very old Britain this digging implement was called a *spudde*.

By the mid-1800s the name of the implement had transferred to refer to the root vegetables it was used to dig up. And that's where it has stayed. The word doesn't seem to be related to the more common word spade, which comes ultimately from the Greek *spathe*, a blade, from which in English we get spade, spatula and spoon – but not *spudde*, which was distinctly dialect.

Prang

The word prang was certainly in use in Britain by 1940, mainly as RAF slang for a crash landing or an incident which damaged an aircraft. It's thought to be more or less onomatopoeic, being a made-up word that echoes the sound of metal being violently impacted.

Prat

For some 400 years 'prat' carried a connotation of referring to one's rear nether regions – buttocks or bum. A 'pratfall' developed among theatrical comedy performers as part of their routine, literally falling spectacularly on their rear end. That word is still heard occasionally, referring to an unexpected fall, either literal or figurative, which causes someone else amusement. The name for this comedy action narrowed down and came to be applied to a person whose behaviour or intellect was considered to be inferior: a prat. And, through a curious anatomical reversal, in low-life slang the word developed a further meaning, applicable only to women, and not meaning their buttocks.

Precinct

There are many words signifying an area, whether a political area, a geographic area or an area of interest: province, ward, electorate, riding, catchment, borough. Precinct is simply another one of those.

It comes from the Latin *praecinctum*, *cinctum* meaning girdled or encircled, and that's the clue, because, like some of the words already mentioned, precinct usually means a defined area, with a line around it – but not always. It's a bit different from electorate or province because precinct can mean either a very firmly defined place, such as part of a cathedral or a section of a city, or it can quite rightly be used in a rather more vague sense, such as saying that 'a murder took place within the precincts of the dance hall', meaning just somewhere nearby.

In the United States the word is used widely to name election districts with a distinct line around them, and also areas of police authority.

Presidential-style campaign

Within the various systems categorised under the heading Western democracy, there are two main divisions, parliamentary and presidential. In the parliamentary system, the nation's power is in collective representation. Voters are asked to vote for a party, whose policies are outlined by its various candidates. So the party elected represents the faith of a majority of voters in what that party represents. Those people elected then choose a Cabinet and proceed to govern the country by collective Cabinet responses, not just the dictates of one person.

The presidential system places considerably more emphasis on the elected president, who although he may be actually appointed by a formal 'electoral college' after the votes have been counted, still more or less single-handedly represents the image of his party.

In terms of campaigning before an election, a presidential campaign concentrates its energies on the person who seeks to be a political leader. The parliamentary system, in theory, puts forth candidates who present the policies of their party, with less emphasis on the representing personalities.

Each system has its critics. Political scientists will tell you that the parliamentary campaign can result, and has resulted, in a national leader who is actually unpopular, though the party is not. A presidential campaign, heavily built around image, can be criticised as resembling a beauty contest or a talent quest.

One has to point out that the term 'presidential-style campaign' is often allocated by the media rather than necessarily being the conscious decision of the people involved.

(A) pretty pass

There are 43 meanings of the word 'pass' in English and they nearly all have something to do with allowing things to move from one place to another. But there is one use in which 'pass' means a state of affairs or a condition.

It appears as an example of alliterative irony: it is ironic to use the word 'pretty' about something deplorable, and combined with pass it makes an amusing alliteration.

In modern vernacular, when something goes wrong people often say, 'That's great,' which carries the same sort of irony, but without the alliteration.

Prevaricate/procrastinate

Prevaricate comes from the Latin *praevaricari*, meaning to walk crookedly. Retaining connection with its Latin meaning, English has developed the word 'prevaricate' to mean speaking falsely with the deliberate intention of deceiving: to tell a lie.

Procrastinate also come from Latin: *pro*, meaning in favour of, and *cras*, referring to tomorrow. In English it means to defer, to put off.

Propaganda

The word has quite a simple history and the verb from it is used frequently: propagate. The two Latin words for 'cut' and 'fasten' come together to make the word propagate; that is, to reproduce.

In 1622, when Pope Gregory XV was the pontiff, there was a big committee dedicated to creating ways of enlarging the numbers adhering to the church, and it was called the Sacre Congregatio de

Propaganda Fide: the sacred congregation for propagating the faith, or spreading the word. But of course the idea was very much to promote the faith as desirable, and to influence people to become believers.

So in reality, the word propaganda should mean simply propagating or spreading information about, but since the time of that committee the word has gradually gone into popular usage, meaning information whose dissemination is controlled and very organised to achieve a specific purpose. Propaganda has lost its relationship to straightforward information, and now commonly refers to information that has been structured so as to influence those who hear it.

(A collection of) prostitutes

A group of cats can be called a clowder of cats, and many skylarks together are known as an exultation of larks. Legend has it that a group of university men once coined a series of terms that could describe a gathering of ladies of the night. They were: an essay of trollops; an anthology of pros; a jam of tarts; a fanfare of strumpets; a peal of belles; or a company of solicitors.

Proven/proved

Formerly the word 'proven' was used only by the Scottish judiciary, as in 'proven' or 'not proven' at the end of a court case. Now it seems to have become an advertising adjective, as in 'of proven quality'. The word does exist, but strictly speaking 'proven' is the past participle and should have an auxiliary (it is proven, or the matter has not been proven).

'Proved' is the past tense.

Pull your finger out

It means to get going, work efficiently. One version of the origin is that it began as 'take' your finger out, and occurred as part of the activity around cannon fire. For ignition, gunpowder was poured into a small hole which was then blocked with a wooden rod. In the heat of battle, and in a hurry, the poured-in powder was sometimes held in simply by blocking the aperture with a finger. When ready to fire, someone would call 'take the finger out'.

The saying appears to have moved into use later by the RAF, where cannons weren't used, but minus the cannons the expression was perceived as advice regarding intimate foreplay. Servicemen are reputed to have said it to their fellows whose relationships with women had not yet reached full intimacy; they were advised to cease preliminaries and start concentrating on more satisfying activities.

Originally, the phrase was never said in polite company, though occasionally a Latinate version was used when someone would say, 'De-digitate!' as an admonition.

But the blunter version was wrenched into public fame in October 1961 when Prince Philip made a widely reported speech to a large gathering of businessmen. Advising them that Britain must not become complacent, HRH said: 'Gentlemen, it is about time that we pulled our fingers out.' A startled world realised that the expression had moved from the locker room to the front pages.

Punch

In spite of its name, punch the drink has no connection with being hit with a fist; the two words look and sound the same but have different ancestry. The punch you drink is named from an ancient Sanskrit Indian word *panca*, meaning five, which somehow came to refer to the traditional five ingredients in a punch: alcohol, water or milk, sugar, spice and lemon juice.

To punch – as in striking forcibly with a fist, and usually suddenly – is a variation on 'pounce'.

Put his foot in his mouth

The generally accepted origin of this expression relates (somewhat surprisingly) to bishops. There was a time in history when bishops were less than popular, because they were seen as too controlling.

During the 1500s a very common phrase arose in households, especially the kitchen, so that when some mixture burnt on the stove or was spilled on the floor, people would say, 'The bishop's put his foot in it,' thus blaming some invisible bossy figure for having caused a mess or caused distress.

In time, putting your foot in it moved away from bishops and became an indication of any foolish or unlucky statement or movement that upset the even tenor of life. By the eighteenth century, around 1770, 'putting one's foot in it' had extended to the mouth and focused the foot's clumsiness on things said, rather than soup spilled or meat burned.

Puttee

A puttee is the long strip of fabric which was wound round the leg from ankle to knee and was frequently a part of military uniforms. Apparently the belief was that scorpions and snakes would be able to bite through trousers but not through the puttees. The word comes from India. *Patta* is the Sanskrit word for cloth, and that developed into the Hindi word *patti,* from which comes the English word puttee.

(Puttee has nothing to do with putty, the sealant for window panes, which derives from the French word *potée,* meaning a full pot.)

Putty medal

Old soldiers used this expression when someone did something they considered silly. Obviously a good medal would be made of gold or silver, or at least would look like gold or silver. Because they represent ritual significance and long-term prestige, medals usually last a lifetime as a symbol of something done well.

The saying 'putty medal' began as a sarcastic comment on something incompetent, which deserved only a medal made of something transient like putty that wouldn't last and wouldn't look good – just as the job that earned it wasn't well done.

Over the years the phrase changed its significance and became a joking way of encouraging someone, maybe a child, more or less commending then for some minor achievement but gently letting them know that there is still some way to go: 'That's worth a putty medal.'

There may be other aspects to the term. In heraldic or blazonry terms the shape of the German medal called the Iron Cross is known as a cross patee. During the First World War there was a proliferation of various classes of the Iron Cross, so it is possible that the term patee cross or patee medal came to mean something fairly ordinary; there were so many of them that they no longer had great significance.

Put your best foot forward

Humans have only two feet, and grammatically speaking to have the best of anything there must be three: the positive, the comparative, and then the superlative – good, better, best (see also **Better and best**). So, speaking literally, we can really only put our better foot forward.

But ungrammatical or not, 'best foot forward' has settled into use meaning to do your utmost, to extend yourself and try your hardest. It has long ago lost any connection with the fact that we have only two feet.

Qantas

Qantas is an acronym, for Queensland And Northern Territory Aerial Services, first registered in 1920. It is in such frequent use now that it is perceived as a 'real' word – and is thus the only word in English where 'q' is not followed by 'u'.

Quarantine

The word began in Latin and comes to English directly from the Italian version, *quaranta*, meaning 40. A quarantine is a period of isolation for humans or animals to inhibit the spread of existing or possible health problems. In early times a quarantine period was 40 days, hence the name. In contemporary times the period of quarantine is adjusted to be the maximum known incubation period of suspected diseases.

Queen's Birthday in June

Queen Elizabeth II's grandfather George V's actual birthday was on 3 June, and this was about the time the annual British summer Trooping the Colour ceremony was held. So over a period of 25 years the public became accustomed to the two things being simultaneous – the monarch's birthday and Trooping the Colour.

The real birthday of Elizabeth II's father, George VI, was quite close to Christmas, which was thought to be a bad time for a public holiday, plus it was in the middle of the British winter. His father's birthday was a more convenient date, so George VI's birthday was celebrated on his father's birthday as a 'commemoration', and George VI's daughter Elizabeth II (who was born in April) retained the same structure.

The 'commemoration' of her birthday is combined with Trooping the Colour, an ancient ceremony to familiarise soldiers with the flag they are supposed to follow in battle.

Queer my pitch

This expression means to spoil the action in someone's field of activity, and was first seen in *The Swells' Night Guide* in 1846. It has nothing to do with a cricket pitch. There are 36 different meanings for the word 'pitch', and this one refers to an old-time fairground or market where the man selling his wares or promoting a show by calling out loud was referred to as having a pitch. The pitch was both the area declared to be his when he was in action, and the sales patter he constantly used.

If something happened to upset the natural flow of his salesmanship – a heckler, a dog-fight, a shower of rain – it was said to have 'queered his pitch', or damaged the effectiveness of his salesmanship.

Sideshow salesmen or barkers are not as common now, but the expression remains.

Quintessence

This used to mean 'five' of something. Medieval philosophy believed that everything in the universe was composed of four elements – fire, water, earth and air. But there was a mysterious fifth element within the composition of the celestial bodies, which was also latent in all things: the quality that could be described as life, or love, or spirituality. This was the quint essence – the fifth element, the invisible force that everything possessed, but which couldn't be seen.

Over time, this term quint essence came to be applied to the essential part of any substance, or an extract that carried the quality which characterised it. The two words joined together and became one – quintessence.

The Quomps

Sometimes thought of as a fictional place – but no, it is real. The place known as the Quomps is near the town of Christchurch in Dorset.

The River Stour flows there, and Quomps is a very old nickname for an area of its banks (a combination of 'quagmire' with 'swamps'). The word can still be heard there to describe that part of the bank, and sometimes in summer a rock festival is held on that very place, and it is called Stomping on the Quomps.

Quorum

A quorum is the minimum number of people who must be present at a formal meeting, society, committee or board of directors, before any valid business can be transacted or an authoritative decision made. The number varies from one organisation to another, and has usually been ordained when the organisation is established.

Rabbits and Easter

Easter is seen as commemoration of a death and celebration of a resurrection. Rabbits have very little to do with either, but at a pinch they are more significant in terms of resurrection than of death.

When Christianity spread through Europe, there were already a number of centuries-old celebration systems in place that couldn't easily be dislodged, and so were absorbed and re-branded. Among these were beliefs about the rabbit or, to be strictly accurate, the hare. In ancient Mexico, ancient China and ancient Egypt, various aspects of the hare or rabbit's characteristics were very highly regarded – their speed, their shyness and of course their fertility.

In Europe, the hare and rabbit were widely associated with the coming of spring because they represented fertility and life. There was an old belief that infertile women could become fertile if they ate hare or rabbit, and these creatures were widely believed to have a link with the moon, since the dark patches visible on its surface somewhat resembled leaping rabbits or hares.

The rabbit's fairly obvious liveliness in the fertility department could be seen as representing new life, so it came to be incorporated into Christian celebrations of Easter. The image of a rabbit became even more firmly established when retailers discovered that they could sell thousands of toy and chocolate rabbits around Easter time – even if most people had forgotten why rabbits were there at all.

Raining cats and dogs

This expression has accrued many 'explanations', some of which are quite bizarre and not really credible. A recognisable form of it first appeared in 1653 in a work called *City Wit* by the English playwright Richard Brome, in which he wrote 'it shall rain dogs and polecats', so it's been around a long time.

A more 'modern' version appeared in Jonathan Swift's *A Complete Collection of Polite and Ingenious Conversation* in 1738: 'I know Sir John will go, though he was sure it would rain cats and dogs.' But Swift had hinted at it earlier than that, as we shall hear in a moment.

Besides cats and dogs, rainstorms have given rise to several other idioms: raining like pitchforks, or hammer handles, or chicken coops. But the image of cats and dogs has been the most durable, even if mysterious. Of its four 'explanations', three of them stretch credulity:

- Cats and dogs sleeping on or under the roofs of thatched houses sometimes fell through when it rained.

- There are those who put their faith in the fact that a Greek word for waterfall or torrent, which when heard by non-Greek-speaking Englishmen, sounded a bit like 'cats and dogs'. Since it was only mentioned during downpours of rain, some confusion arose.

- It has also been seriously suggested that because in medieval times the drainage in British towns was messy and inadequate, during a storm drowned cats and dogs would be seen floating down the open drains, and people would think they had fallen from the sky.

There is actual evidence that Jonathan Swift might have been an early proponent of this last theory, as seen in his poem 'Description of a City Shower' (1710), which says:

> Now, from all parts the swelling kennels flow
> And bear their trophies with them as they go,
> Drown'd puppies, stinking sprats, all drench'd in mud
> Dead cats and turnip tops, come tumbling down the flood.

But what does have serious credibility is that the concept comes from ancient Northern European mythology, and there is so much of that already entrenched in language and custom that this could quite conceivably be another example.

Odin was the Scandinavian god of war, wisdom and poetry; in English he was called Woden (Wednesday is named after him) and he was often depicted surrounded by wolves and dogs. Within the mythology surrounding him was the belief that his dogs controlled the wind – in fact, they were the wind. Alongside this, the image of witches included the belief that their cats could transform themselves into other natural forces. During severe wind and tumultuous rain, Nordic mythology perceived this as Odin's dogs of winds chasing the magic cats – and the cats transformed themselves into rain in order to escape the dogs.

Considering that most world cultures and their languages contain ample contributions from mythical and legendary persons and happenings (including our names for the days of the week), that version rests on a firmer basis than cats and dogs living in thatched ceilings, or city folk being dumb enough to think that dead animals in the gutter had fallen from the sky.

Raisins/sultanas

Sultanas are small and usually made from white seedless grapes. Raisins are larger, normally made from red grapes and often have seeds. There is a difference in the origin of the names. What we call sultanas were originally made from a type of grape itself known as the 'sultana', basically an Arabic word meaning the wife of a sultan (which itself means 'strong leader').

In English, dried red grapes are called raisins, from the French word *raisin*, which simply means grape. Usually, French people say *raisin* when they mean grapes, and *raisin sec*, dried grapes, when they mean what we call raisins.

Ram stam

This expression, found in Scottish dialect, means thoughtless, pre-cipitate and reckless. It is also a slang name for a kind of home-brewed beer, possibly because drinking it is inclined to make people giddy and foolish.

There is a relationship with 'ram jam', meaning stuffed with some-thing, usually food. Stam sometimes occurs as a shortened form of stamp. When the two are put together, the idea arises of something being done forcibly and hastily, such as hastily packing a suitcase rather than carefully and slowly, folding everything up neatly.

Rant

In English, 'rant' means to rave foolishly. Its ancestor is a Dutch word which came originally from a German word meaning to jump about, to frolic and gambol. The word has been in English a long time, used both by Shakespeare (*The Merry Wives of Windsor* : 'I'll rant as well as thou') and Robbie Burns ('they ranted and sang').

With those two writers the word may have been in transition between its meaning of dancing and gambolling, and its more recent meaning of loud, impassioned talk.

Rapscallion/scallion

There is no connection between the two words. Scallions are a kind of spring onion characterised by not having a fully-developed bulb (*Allium fistulosum*, closely related to *Allium ascalonicum*, which is also known as a shallot).

Both those words – scallions and shallots – are derived from the Greek word *askolonion*, which itself is derived from the name of the ancient Israeli town Ashkelon where, centuries ago, an abundance of onions was grown and exported to Europe. So the word scallion is derived from Hebrew. But the word rapscallion is derived from an Old French word *rascaille* – originally meaning 'rabble' – which in English gives us rapscallion and rascal.

Rapt

It means totally engrossed, and comes from the Latin *rapere*, to seize. The word was out of fashion for many decades because of its rather poetic image, but in recent times has been taken up as a synonym for stoked or chuffed.

Ratbag

The expression ratbag is believed to have originated in Australia, first noticed by etymologists in 1910.

The meaning isn't difficult to grasp – an ill-disposed or worthless person, possibly with near-criminal tendencies – but like most pejorative terms it has come to be used by people who are angry simply because they don't like someone.

Semantically it comes into the same category as mortar, in that the qualities of the rat have been transferred to the innocent bag in which the rats are being carried. When you call someone a ratbag, it's not really the bag you're talking about.

The term was in fairly common use in Australia in 1937 (William Hatfield), and the comedian Roy Rene used it in 1945 (*Mo's Memoirs*) and R.D. Fitzgerald in 1962 (*Southmost Twelve*).

So the term was not unfamiliar by 1965, when William Dick's Australian novel *A Bunch of Ratbags* was published. This may have encouraged the expression into wider use, though its use internationally was tentative. At a conference in Toronto where on-the-spot translations were being provided, an Australian's reference to some politicians as a 'pack of ratbags' caused total bewilderment among the translators, who told their various delegates that the politicians were 'a lot of bags in which rats were being carried'.

Raveled/unraveled

Strangely, they mean the same and are both correct. This is a bizarre case of a word and its own negative both meaning the same thing. 'Ravel' can mean 'to tangle or tease out and fray', but it can also mean 'to separate strands', or untangle – which is essentially the same as unravel. If you look up 'ravel' in some dictionaries, it gives the meaning: unravel.

There are other, similar contradictions: 'flammable' means the same as 'inflammable'; 'cleave' means both 'to stick to', and also 'to tear apart'; 'chuffed' can mean 'pleased' or 'displeased'.

Real estate

The word real comes ultimately from the Latin *res*, meaning 'thing'. Thus the various modern meanings of 'real' are to do with truth, and things that exist or occur in the physical world. Real estate generally means property that is immovable – it is land, it exists; it can't be carried away.

There's another shade of meaning in legal documents, such as a will, where you could have a substantial estate, with thousands of dollars in shares and trusts and annuities, but in legal terms those parts of your estate will normally be described separately from anything solid that can't be carried or transported, such as land and properties. Those are the only things described as 'real'.

Rector

The word 'rector' comes from the Latin *regere*, to rule. Its relatives can be found in English words like director or regime (a ruling system). A rector is sometimes described as a cleric in charge of a congregation, a religious house or a college. Gradually the term came to be used sometimes to refer to a person, qualified cleric or not, who was the head of a school.

Red carpet

Red doesn't signify the only kind of VIP. People often associate purple with royalty, saffron yellow with some Eastern religions, and white with a high-ranking Catholic such as the Pope. Various political parties use blue or green. But there is a fairly strong tradition that red indicates importance. And there's no doubt that the use of a red carpet and the phrase 'roll out the red carpet' imply treatment that's either luxurious or respectful, or both.

The concept of using a red carpet for important people is very old indeed – it is mentioned by the Greek dramatist Aeschylus in the fifth century BC. And red has consistently cropped up in many contexts where something important is indicated. Extending the term to 'red carpet treatment' went into general use after the promotional efforts of an American train service.

Starting in 1902, a luxury train called The Twentieth Century Limited ran between New York and Chicago. The train had only first-class carriages and was famed for its elegant appointments and its high-class dining. Obviously only rich or important people travelled on it. Starting in 1938, and for the next 30 years, passengers boarding the train in New York would find the entire length of the departure platform covered with a red carpet on which they walked to enter their carriage.

Redneck

The term first arose in the 1600s, when the English used the term 'red necks' to disparage the Scottish Covenantors who disagreed with bishops. They identified themselves by wearing a red cloth around their neck, and sometimes signed their petitions in blood.

During the 1880s, the term re-surfaced in South Africa, as the Afrikaans word *rooinek* (red-necked), a disparaging term used by South Africans of Dutch descent (the Boers) during the wars in South Africa, to describe British soldiers whose fair skin was not accustomed to the hot African sun.

The term was found in the United States soon after, in 1893, now describing men who worked in the fields, exposed to sun and dust. From being somewhat patronising it became a put-down description for poor uneducated rural folk, or those who favoured segregation of blacks, and was in common use by 1900. Over the following century its application widened and, not necessarily describing just rural communities and manual workers, it was heard as a derogatory term for those perceived as not supporting modern developments.

Red sky at night, shepherd's delight

The most famous conveyor of this well-known weather report was Jesus of Nazareth. He is quoted as referring to it in the Book of Matthew, 16: 2–3. The usual translation of his words is: 'When it is evening, ye say, "It will be fair weather, for the sky is red." And in the morning, "It will be foul weather today: for the sky is red and lowring." '

There is a strong likelihood that Jesus was quoting a much older Jewish observation or Israeli proverb widely known to all rural folk and men at sea. He would originally have spoken in Aramaic, so whatever he said went through a minimum of four translations before it reached English.

Red tape

Since at least the seventeenth century, British government offices and British lawyers have used a pinky-reddish tape to tie documents into bundles. The phrase 'red tape', symbolising bureaucracy and official stalling, was commonly known during the 1800s and was referred to by Charles Dickens in *Hard Times* and also by Thomas Carlyle. Both wrote rather bitterly of the slowness of establishment procedures bogged down in paperwork and delayed decision-making. The shorthand for these processes, according to Dickens and Carlyle, became red tape.

Refugee

This word operates on two levels. The finite legal definition of a refugee comes from the 1951 United Nations Convention and the 1967 Protocol on Refugees: 'A refugee is a person who owing to a well-founded fear of being persecuted for reasons of: (1) race, (2) religion, (3) nationality, (4) membership of a particular social group, or (5) political opinion, is outside the country of his nationality and is unable or, owing to such fear, is unwilling to avail himself of the protection of the country of his nationality.'

Even though a person might fit into any one of the five categories mentioned, that person is not automatically classified as a legal refugee. On arrival in a new country he or she must make an application to the immigration officials there for recognition as a refugee. Then the applicant goes through a review process, which is entirely a matter for the laws of the country concerned. The United Nations High Commissioner for Refugees recognises that granting asylum is the unfettered right of a sovereign nation.

After going through a legal review successfully, the applicant may be classified officially as a refugee and granted political asylum and given the status of a resident alien. A further stage, some time later, would be the granting of full legal residency and then, even later, comes the possibility of citizenship and a passport.

Outside the strict requirement listed for being a Government-recognised refugee, a less formal use is sometimes heard – when someone simply seeks an alternative place for social or domestic reasons, like an unhappy marriage, a household that watches rugby, relatives with noisy children, and so on.

Reiterate/iterate

In English, using the prefix 're' usually indicates doing something again, as in 'restore', or 'reinstate'. And 'iterate' means to do something or say something a second time – to repeat it, from the Latin *iterum*, meaning simply 'again'.

The curious thing is that 'reiterate' literally means 'again' twice. This just shows that the structure of English is sometimes illogical. And the placing of a prefix, which usually alters the meaning of the word in front of which it is placed, in this case doesn't change it. Active and pro-active belong in this group: they mean the same thing and the prefix is an affectation. The same applies to flammable and inflammable – both mean likely to burn and the prefix is unnecessary.

With iterate and reiterate, it might just be a matter of vocal flow; it's actually easier to say reiterate.

Relict

A 'relic' is something that has survived from the past, and 'relict' is an archaic way of spelling it. The word comes from the Latin *reliquiae*, meaning remains.

Both 'relic' and 'remains' are still in use, but in modern times we generally think of a relic as something that was always inanimate, and the word remains is still occasionally heard to describe a dead human body. But for quite a long time in the history of English, the word relic (or relict) was used for both, particularly in parts of the Christian church, where a relic specifically meant a 'preserved' part of the body of a long-dead saint, or something used by or associated with a saint, and therefore venerated as having become holy itself.

Over the history of Christianity, some extraordinary things have been acclaimed as official relics, including the tip of the Devil's tail, a candle lit by Jesus' angel, some hay from the manger in which he was born, some nails used in the crucifixion, the finger of Thomas that had touched Jesus' wounds, and a tiny bottle of milk from the Virgin Mary's breast.

Apart from that specialised use of the word relic, it also went into common usage in the more general sense of something being left over from someone or something – and this included a man's widow, who was sometimes referred to as a relict of her husband; some widows are described like that on gravestones.

Around about the time when people stopped referring to widows as relicts, the 't' slowly edged out of the spelling and the word became relic – and that word slipped out of use as a reference to people.

Restaurant/restaurateur

The origin of both words is the root of the French verb *restaurer*, to restore. The present participle of that verb, restoring, in French, is restaurant. When the word travelled into English, they kept the participle ending but used it as a noun; technically, it became a gerund (a noun ending in –ing and created from a verb). It still made sense: a place you went to for a restoring.

The description of the person who runs the place also follows a French pattern: the root verb *restaur*, plus the affix *ateur*, gives us 'restaurateur' (with no 'n').

So in English we are using two French words for two different things, and they have stayed exactly the same in English as they are in French.

Rhubarb

When a crowd onstage is expected to make a general sound but there are no actual written words, it is a very old theatre tradition (thought to date back as far as Shakespeare's actors) that they all say 'rhubarb' to one other. From this the audience gets a sort of vocal confusion – exactly as a large group of people would sound. Nobody really knows why – perhaps it's because the word rhubarb contains the sounds 'oo' and 'ah', moves the face and is easy to remember.

Over several hundred years this practice has filtered into the language in general so that, besides the plant, the word rhubarb has taken on an extra area of meaning: noisy nonsense, spoken rubbish, or a noisy argument.

(Rhubarb is a strange-sounding word of somewhat convoluted origin, believed to have filtered through into English via a tangled route from the Latin *rheubarbarum*, meaning 'the barbaric root from the Volga', rhubarb having originated in China and arrived in Europe by way of Russia.)

Right as rain

There have been many versions of the 'right as—' expression, dating as far back as 1546, and from there on declaring that something was as right as – a trivet, a leg, a line, a lodestone, a bank, a book, nails, or ninepence. None of them makes any actual sense, but they somehow emphasise that everything is correct and as it should be.

'Right as rain' didn't appear until the early 1900s, and it doesn't make any sense either. The only supposed reason for 'right as rain' replacing all its predecessors is that it is easy to say, and has a pleasing alliteration (like 'fit as a fiddle' or 'good as gold'). And there are some circumstances where rain is perceived as a good thing, so the phrase has a certain biological logic.

Right down to the wire

The term began to be used in America in the 1940s, taken from American horse-racing where the finish line of a race is called 'the wire', where stewards observing the finish end could see and be certain which horse's nose was first over the line. A race described as going right down to the wire was when several participants appeared to finish closely together, and the winner was uncertain (until announced as a result of the stewards' observation).

Rigmarole

In the London Public Records Office there is still a document, dating from 1296, which is a register of pledges of loyalty to King Edward I. It was known as the Statute of Rageman – 'rageman' being a very old name for an official who administered and supervised taxes.

The document is prodigiously long, with many alterations and changes of address, and its name gradually developed into the Ragman Roll. This phrase began to carry a general sense of some kind of catalogue, especially a very long and convoluted catalogue or list, then eventually it changed slightly to rigmarole, which means a lengthy and unwelcome discourse that is probably boring.

(Between a) rock and a hard place

The concept goes back at least to 350 BC when Homer wrote of Scylla and Charybdis, the two evil monsters guarding the Straits of Messina, between which one sailed with great caution and fear. 'Between Scylla and Charybdis' came to mean being between two equal difficulties.

That progressed into 'between the devil and the deep blue sea'.

In 1917 disputes erupted in America between mining companies and miners. A new American version of the old expression emerged in 1921, when the dispute was described as being 'between a rock and a hard place'.

Roger (and out)

Enterprises and occupations that make use of a set of initials for some purpose, to ensure accuracy when giving out those initials will often use a full word to represent each one. Examples include flight reservations and police instructions. There was even a TV series called *Juliet Bravo*.

The system dates from early radio telephony when 'Roger' used to be the confirming word for the letter 'r'. At the end of a radio-telephone message, the protocol was to say Roger, meaning the letter 'r', which meant 'received'. 'Roger and out' meant that the message had been received and there was no further reply. In later years the alphabet code was changed slightly and nowadays they use Romeo for 'r'.

In its time, 'Roger' was simply a convenient name. When used as a present tense verb – 'to roger' – the meaning is quite different, as anyone who's read Robbie Burns will know.

Rookie

Often said about a young sportsman or policeman, or anyone new to a position. It has been used in the United States since the 1890s to refer to a beginner or a newcomer. The only known origin is that 'rookie' arose as an early mispronunciation of recruit.

Rort

The word can mean boisterous, noisy and rowdy (derived from the Old English word *rorty*, meaning fine, splendid). But a separate meaning is that someone has set up a system which advantages them at the expense of an existing organisation, or other people.

It has been suggested that the word might be a combination of racket and tort, but some scholars don't agree. The formal definition of rort is 'an incident or series of incidents involving reprehensible or suspect behaviour, especially by officials and politicians', but its derivation is firmly classified as 'uncertain'.

Rotten Row

The famous Rotten Row is an equestrian area of Hyde Park in London. During the 1600s it was known as a dangerous area where highwaymen were prone to attack. King William III ordered that 300 lanterns were to be hung, and lit every night to provide more safety, thus making it the first road in England to have night lighting.

Legend would have it that the Plantagenet kings in the 1300s used this road to ride to the royal forests; thus it was referred to as *route du roi* (the king's road), which over time in English became 'rotten row'. There are scholars, however, who dismiss this story as mere folklore. They can only offer instead the notion that the ground underneath was not too firm – it was a rotten road.

Round robin

It's believed to be yet another term which has drifted ashore after originating at sea. Sailors, and more particularly French sailors, sometimes wanted to convey necessary information to their superiors, but did not want just one identified person to be the messenger. So the missive would be signed by everybody, signing their names in a circle. It was impossible to know who was the first person to sign.

The name is believed to have come from *ruban rond*, a ribbon tied around in a circle, but in English it was corrupted into a 'robin'. The original meaning of the phrase has also had two developments: 'round robin' is sometimes used to describe a sports fixture with a group of teams in which each team plays every other team. And the term is now sometimes heard to describe those multi-address newsletters, Christmas greetings and e-mails that one person sends out to 25 friends.

Rouseabout

The term originates from an Old English word – roustabout or rouseabout – meaning a restless person or a handyman-worker with no clear task.

From the 1880s on it was applied to farm helpers, deck hands, oil riggers, wharf workers, circus and carnival labourers (as in Elvis Presley's 1964 movie *Roustabout*). By 1861 New Zealand was using rouseabout to describe a shearing shed worker who attended to the fleeces, and in the following two decades the term appeared in Australia, originally meaning a 'general handyman' but eventually taking on the shearing shed connection, usually shortened to 'rousie'. Etymologist Eric Partridge attributes its later spread into wider use after members of the Australian Air Force used the word when referring to ground staff.

Royal

The word 'royal' comes from the Latin *regalis*, meaning 'derived from a king or a monarch'. The idea that royals are people exalted socially and politically through superior heritage is deeply built into everyday consciousness. But if there is no royalty, clearly the word royal loses its meaning altogether. And if all nations became republics, then 'royal' words would have to be eliminated.

Perhaps card players would have to think up a new name for a royal flush, and beekeepers and cosmetics people would be obliged to drop the first word from royal jelly, which might become just 'jelly', causing confusion in supermarkets.

Royal Navy/the Andrew

In Britain, from the thirteenth century on, thousands of men were 'impressed', which meant that they were seized out of pubs and off the streets and simply forced into military and marine service. This

enforcement was carried out by groups officially called Impress
Service, but known as 'press-gangs'. The Royal Navy is said to have
relied on 'press gangs' as a method of providing men for the service
up to 1830.

During the 1780s and early 1800s and the Napoleonic wars, there
was a man in Portsmouth called Andrew Miller who was widely
recognised as a very efficient and successful press-gang organiser. His
reputation was such that when a raid resulted in men in Portsmouth
being forced into naval service, people began to say they had been
'snatched into the Andrew'; the name spread, and stuck, and became
a slang term for the Royal Navy itself.

Rudolph the Red-Nosed Reindeer

In 1939 Robert May, who lived in a little Chicago flat with his wife
and three children, wrote some Christmas advertising material for a
big American store called Montgomery Ward. Clement Moore's 1822
poem, 'A Visit from Saint Nicholas' had invented the image of Santa
Claus – and although St Nicholas/Santa Claus was from Turkey and
would never have seen a reindeer, Clement Moore's invention of
eight flying reindeer was now firmly ensconced in the public mind
as the creatures who drew Santa Claus' sleigh.

Robert May wrote a fanciful poem about a ninth reindeer who
didn't fit the sleek mould of Dasher and Dancer and all the others.
He was an unglamorous reindeer with a red nose, and his name was
Rudolph.

Montgomery Ward printed the poem as a giveaway pamphlet and
it was tucked into the parcels of anyone who bought a Christmas
gift from one of its many branches; over the following ten years they
actually gave away 10 million copies of the poem, which became
sufficiently well known to be the subject of a little movie cartoon.

But it still didn't make Mr May rich, until his brother-in-law
Johnny Marks took the poem and set it to music. Then, in 1949, a
miracle happened – the cowboy star Gene Autry decided to record
the song and that record changed the history of mythology.

The public loves an underdog and Rudolph was exactly that. He
was somewhere between the Ugly Duckling and Cinderella and,

red-nosed though he was, he did get to go to the ball. The original recording sold 50 million copies, subsequent recordings by other people sold 50 million more, and Rudolph has been with us ever since. The writer, Robert May, died in 1976. By then he had six children and lived in a lovely house.

So Rudolph the Red-Nosed Reindeer has no real role in the genuine Christian heritage of the Christmas season, but he does have his place in the folklore created by American advertising.

Rugby

The game could have grown up with a different name. Rugby has nothing to do with rugs; it is the name of an English town and its school. Whether or not William Webb Ellis was the boy who picked up the ball and ran with it at that school (there is considerable doubt about when he did it – or if he did it at all), the town's name lives on in countless clubs, stadiums, changing sheds and millions of television screens.

But the town wasn't always called Rugby. That name developed over the centuries from the town's original name; the *Domesday Book* in 1086 identified it by the name Rocheberie. Gradually the town's slightly cumbersome name smoothed out from Rocheberie to Rokebi, later Rokeby and finally Rugby.

Its famous school began in 1567, generously endowed with estates and a mansion from the bequests of a rich local who had made a fortune selling imported ginger, cinnamon and cloves to the court of Queen Elizabeth I. Perhaps it's just as well the town's name changed. It's hard to imagine teams of blokes going out to play a game of Rocheberie.

Rule Britannia

'Rule Britannia' was the hit song from a popular London musical in 1740: *Alfred: a Masque*, music by Thomas Arne, words by James Thomson. James Thomson was a famous Scottish poet who contributed the words of 'Rule Britannia' to the English language (plus a great deal else . . . including the phrase 'elegant sufficiency', which is in his poem 'The Seasons').

People are inclined to sing 'Britannia rules the waves', but that isn't correct. Britannia rules the waves would be a simple statement of naval supremacy. But the song actually says 'Britannia rule the waves'. This subtle use of the subjunctive structure expresses a wish: Britannia (we wish that you will) rule the waves (a similar subjunctive construction can be found in 'God save our gracious Queen.')

Rumpus

The word has been known in Britain since the mid-1700s. In fact there are three similar words – rumpus, ruction and ruckus – and all three have mysterious origins.

'Ruction' is believed to be a shortened form of insurrection, the term entering English speech from the so-called Irish Insurrection in 1798. Insurrection still means the defying of authority, but the shortened version ruction simply means a noisy disturbance or interruption.

'Rumpus' appears to have originated among eighteenth-century students in Switzerland speaking Swiss German, and meant then (as now) a lot of noise and activity.

Then there is 'ruckus', which American scholars say is a combination of rumpus and ruction.

Runcible spoon

Nobody knows what this is. Its most famous appearance is in Edward Lear's 'The Owl and the Pussycat'. Some people believe it means a kind of spoon that is divided into three curved prongs, but there's little or no evidence that Lear meant that. The general belief is that it's a cute word he simply made up.

S

(Get the) sack

It's a very old concept and a very old expression, thought to have originated in seventeenth-century France among artisans, who customarily worked with their own tools though the bag in which they kept tools was handed over to the employer for the time that they worked there. If their work proved unsatisfactory, the employer simply left their bag out next to their workplace. That was a signal that their tenure was terminated – they had been given the sack and must put their tools into it and look elsewhere.

There are occasional reports of a modern version of this ancient practice in contemporary business situations, where a person whose employment has been summarily terminated is given a box to contain such of their desk papers and accessories as are personal, before they and the box are escorted from the premises.

Salmonella

This is a bacterium which has nothing to do with fish. In 1900 it was named after an American veterinary surgeon whose work was significant in identifying it: Daniel Elmer Salmon.

St Fiacre

Fiacre was a monk in Kilkenny in Ireland, but he moved to France, where the bishop said he could have as much land as he could till in one day. Fiacre cleared enough land to set up a monastery where travellers often stayed. Legend says that he was a marvellous gardener, and admiration abounded for the wonderful vegetables he grew to feed guests who ate at the monastery. That is why he has become the patron saint of gardeners and florists.

But Fiacre was very much against women, who were not allowed into his enclosure, and anyone who sneaked a woman in suffered severe punishments. The belief that he inflicted great discomfort on women may be the curious reason for his being listed (*Wordsworth Dictionary of Saints*) as the patron saint of people suffering from venereal diseases.

When Fiacre died, in approximately AD 670, many miracles and medical cures were attributed to him and pilgrims travelled to his shrine. Some of the pilgrims who had haemorrhoids believed they would be cured if they sat on the stone where Fiacre customarily sat.

To visit his shrine, pilgrims left from Paris at the spot where a famous hotel, Hôtel St Fiacre, was built. In 1620 this is believed to have been the first place in the world to offer horse-drawn carriages for hire, thus giving the French language the word fiacre, and the concept of transport for hire developed into what we call taxis. St Fiacre is also the patron saint of taxi drivers.

San Fairy Anne

There never was such a person. During the First World War, the English heard French people saying *Ça ne fait rien*, which means 'it's nothing – it doesn't matter'. Although they understood what it meant, English people couldn't pronounce it, so created a Franglais version – San Fairy Anne – and used it in the same way.

Santa Claus

It's an extraordinary example of how literature and commerce can combine almost to obliterate the actual facts, because Santa Claus didn't come from anywhere near the North Pole; he was born and bred in Turkey, and known as Nicholas. He became a bishop in the town of Demre (which used to be called Myra), and died there, about AD 399. Some of his bones can still be visited in the Antalya museum in Turkey, and there is a bronze statue of him nearby, showing him surrounded by children and with a sack on his back.

A church of St Nicholas has stood in Demre since the sixth century AD, but has been reconstructed more than once over the centuries; there have also been a lot of additions to the image of St Nicholas. Not much is known about him anyway, but a legend developed that he was very kind to poor children, and that he once saved a family of poor girls from being sold into slavery by secretly dropping gold coins down their chimney.

He died on 6 December, a date that, in his honour, came to be

313

Scommemorated in some places around Europe as a time for giving gifts and being unselfish. This practice continued for several hundred years, with Nicholas dressed as a bishop, riding a white horse.

When early Dutch settlers went to live in New Amsterdam (now called New York) they took the St Nicholas celebrations with them, and paraded in the streets with someone dressed as a bishop. They called him by his Dutch name *Sinterklaas*, and English-speaking American journalists, reporting the festivities, spelt this wrongly, so there came one of those wonderful examples of a name being born through a printing mistake: they wrote instead 'Santa Claus'.

This was the beginning of the huge change that took place in people's perception of dear old Turkish St Nicholas. New York in December was cold, and the men portraying Nicholas were Dutch, so a vague idea of furs and ruddy faces began to be associated with the name.

The master stroke of transformation took place in 1822 when a poet called Clement Moore wrote a poem about St Nicholas, and from his imagination he created the jolly personality, the bundle of toys, the white beard, the generous girth and the eight reindeer. This poem was titled 'A Visit from Saint Nicholas', but almost everyone in the English-speaking world knows it by the opening line: ''Twas the night before Christmas'. Notice also that it moved the celebration date from 6 December to 24 December.

This poem crystallised the image of Santa Claus as he is known today. In the public's mind, St Nicholas in the poem somehow became transposed to the name they'd heard: Santa Claus.

There were further major developments. Clement Moore's poem depicted Saint Nicholas as a cheerful little elf, but when people started to dress up as him, he had to be of normal human height. And of course the first drawings of this new legend, in 1863, were published only in black and white so the colour of what he wore wasn't too important.

By 1870, the invented figure of Santa Claus was firmly entrenched in the American notion of marketing. The belief was encouraged that everyone must receive gifts at Christmas, so of course everyone had to buy them. Santa became big business.

And then came the final stroke: the invention of colour printing. The colour red is very striking, so the red bishop's robes the early Dutchmen had worn when celebrating St Nicholas were brought back; those early illustrations of Santa Claus in black and white furs erupted into advertising, now bright red because it caught people's attention and sold things better. American advertising firmly advanced the image of Santa Claus, and almost wiped out his true origins – except in Turkey, of course.

The new Santa Claus also practically obliterated the much earlier image of a figure called Father Christmas, who'd been busy since the fifteenth century. He was connected to the European legend of Woden, the gift-giving god figure, and was usually big and brawny with a hairy chest.

So now it's almost as if we're talking about two entirely different people: the Turkish St Nicholas, who didn't even know the North Pole existed, and the American-invented Santa Claus who dates back to the 1820s and has become a marketing triumph.

Santayana

George Santayana was born in Spain in 1863 but went to study at Harvard University where he eventually became a lecturer in philosophy. He was a respected philosopher, a poet and novelist, a critic and social commentator.

One of his famous books was *The Life of Reason*, published in 1905, and that contained one of his most often-quoted statements: 'Those who cannot remember the past are condemned to repeat it.' He died in 1952.

Sashay

The French word *chassé* means – literally – a chasing, a driving away. It became the name of a dance step where the dancer's feet appear to 'glide away' from normal walking. This ballet terminology crept into common usage describing someone who moved as if they were dancing. In English the French word was corrupted to become 'sashay' and is used to describe walking elaborately, making a self-confident display out of just moving from one place to another.

Sausage

In England, a dialect term from Lancashire is *snackies*, meaning a small morsel of food, and possibly derived from a Dutch word *snakken* meaning 'a bite'. Lancashire *snackies* are believed to be the origin of 'snack' and also 'snags', referring to the casual and informal eating of small amounts. In Australia and New Zealand, snacks are still small amounts of food eaten in an informal manner, but snags has attached itself only to sausages.

'Snarler' first appeared in print in 1941 as Australasian military slang during the Second World War, when servicemen said rather uncharitably that the sausages they were served were probably made from cats and dogs. And they had so much fat that, when cooked, they hissed and spat, or snarled; really unpleasant ones were also called growlers or barkers, although the last two terms have not gone into common usage.

The British military equivalent of the Australasian snarlers was the word bangers, again because of the noise sausages often make when they're frying. British servicemen described this as a bang, and Australasians called it a snarl. Hence, bangers and snarlers.

Saved our bacon

In the same way that 'saved our skin' doesn't mean just skin, but the whole body, there was a time when 'bacon' was shorthand for the whole pig – and also a metaphor for a person's own body.

Among thieves, 'saving the bacon' meant to escape capture or a problem – saving one's body from harm. The term occurs in a poem from 1654 in the Irish collection *Momus Elenticus*: 'Some fellowes there were ... To save their bacon penn'd many a smooth song.'

The expression remains with much the same meaning as it always had; if your bacon has been saved, you have somehow been rescued and advantaged.

Saveloy

Saveloys are a kind of sausage, highly seasoned, smoked and containing saltpetre, which carries a bright red colour. The name saveloy in English is a corruption of the sausage's French name, which comes from the original Italian name *cervellato*. That in turn comes from *cervello*, derived from the Latin *cerebellum* – and all of those are words meaning 'brain'. When saveloys were first invented they were made of minced pigs' brains, and their name meant 'little brains'. They might not be made of minced brains nowadays, but that's what the name means.

School

This word has a fairly rich ancestry. It began with the Greek word *skhole*, which migrated into the Latin word *schola*. In those ancient times there was a great love of learning, conversation and debate, and generally people's time was roughly divided into two activities: work, which was what you had to do to keep everything going; and *schola*, which meant non-working time when people got together to talk, discuss and learn. The modern concept of non-working time as 'leisure' didn't quite apply: the *schola* time was used for learning.

Eventually the word developed the meaning of people gathered together in order to be instructed and to learn. The word went into many other languages, like Dutch, German and French, and is still there in various forms. The Yiddish version *shul* is commonly used to describe the synagogue because that's where people go to learn about the scriptures, the psalms and the laws for living a good life.

Since the development of mass media and labour-saving devices, the connotations of the word school have more or less reversed. In recent centuries children have had to go to school, whether they wanted to or not, and the joys of learning, which used to be a desired activity, face strong competition from the joys of leisure activities and entertainments, which often require less effort.

Scotch a rumour

The words connected with Scot, Scots, Scottish and Scotch all relate back to the Latin *Scottus*.

However, there is a similar-sounding but different word altogether: the verb 'to scotch'. This is thought to be derived from the Old French word *escocher*, meaning 'to cut', and has been in use in English with that meaning for at least 400 years. You'll find it in *Macbeth* (c.1611) and in Izaak Walton's *Compleat Angler* (1653). Walton uses the verb to scotch meaning 'to cut' or 'to cut a notch', and from that there slowly developed a supplementary connotation of 'cutting out', meaning hindering, blocking, putting an end to. Hence to scotch a rumour means to get rid of it, to cut it out and away from the body of truth.

There are two other surviving uses of scotch meaning 'to cut' in common English terms: hopscotch, in which the ground is cut into squares with lines and you hop from one square to another; and butterscotch, a toffee-like confection made from sweetened butter, which after being boiled is extremely hard, so has to have squares cut into it, or 'scotched', before it is cooked, so it can be cut or broken into pieces.

Scot free

The term has nothing to do with Scotland. In earlier centuries there was an English word *sceot*, which was originally a Scandinavian word meaning 'payment'. The word was used in English as the name for a kind of British municipal tax, which was levied on people and businesses proportionate to the value of their property. One way of describing the *sceot* tax (slightly inaccurately) would be 'means test'. In parts of Britain the tax was in force up to the 1830s.

Some people who should have paid the *sceot* were able to wriggle their way out of it and yet not break the law – what is now called tax avoidance. These people were *sceot*-free, and gradually two things happened: the pronunciation changed to 'scot'; and the term came to mean someone getting away with doubtful behaviour and yet not being in any way held responsible.

Scotland Yard

As almost everyone is aware, Scotland Yard isn't in Scotland. Before the death of Elizabeth I in 1603, Scotland and England had separate monarchies. But after Elizabeth died King James VI of Scotland took over both thrones and while remaining King of Scotland, became also King James I of England. The position of monarch of both countries was resolved into one person and has remained so ever since.

But when there were kings and queens of Scotland, there were ambassadors from Scotland to England, and sometimes the Scottish king or queen would come to visit London. On such occasions all these dignitaries stayed in a sort of palace in one part of the city. The town square where this palace stood became known as Great Scotland Yard.

Over 200 years later in 1829, when the headquarters of the Metropolitan Police were established in Whitehall, the entrance to the police establishment opened into Great Scotland Yard. Gradually the name of the city square was shortened to Scotland Yard, and that became a shorthand way of referring to the police. Even the term Scotland Yard became shortened as well: often it was just the Yard.

In 1890 the police administration shifted to another address, christened New Scotland Yard. Another shift came in 1967, but the name Scotland Yard had by then become fixed in people's minds.

Screaming abdabs

These started out as the 'habdabs', which was a slang term for the bits at the end of a meal. Things like dessert and maybe cheese or nuts – those were the habdabs. During the Second World War the military took up the word and it lost its 'h' to become the abdabs, which gradually moved from food to drink, and was used about people who'd drunk too much. The term moved into more serious vein when it came to mean delirium tremens.

Later 'screaming' was added and the expression came to mean any period of intense frustration or confused exhaustion.

Second to none

Some people see a curious discrepancy in this expression that makes it a nonsense. 'Second' is not as good as 'first', but 'none' means there is nothing there; so if something is less than nothing, can 'second to none' be used to mean something is excellent?

Yes, none does mean nothing or no one. But in this case another logic applies. You are indicating that the object or person you are talking about actually is number one – the top, the best. There is nobody to whom that person is second; they are second to no one.

Seedy

This is a verbal contraction of the expression 'going to seed'. It is generally perceived that garden plants look their best when they are in flower, but if they move onwards to the state of producing seeds they tend to look a bit straggly and not quite so glamorous. Hence, if a person is looking untidy and not as fit as they used to be, you'll hear someone say they're going to seed. From that has evolved the expression seedy, meaning not quite crisp and flourishing.

The difference is that, when said about a person, going to seed is quite often a long and even permanent process, but when someone says it about themselves, that they are feeling seedy, the straggly state is usually temporary.

See-saw Marjory Daw

The nursery rhyme is connected with sawing wood. Two-man cross-cut saws and pit saws were manufactured at least as early as 1622 and possibly before. At more or less the same time a little ditty came to light, which usually goes:

> See-saw Marjory Daw,
> Jacky shall have a new master,
> Jacky shall have but a penny a day,
> Because he can't work any faster.

In those days the song was not a children's song, but was chanted by builders, specifically two men using one saw, to help them maintain their to-and-fro rhythm and thus work efficiently.

There was also a slightly ribald undertone to the words, because during the seventeenth century Marjory Daw was a slang term for a woman of easy virtue, so the to-and-fro rhythm had another significance for the men who were singing it and doubtless kept them cheerful.

The song gradually spread and eventually became adopted by children, who weren't using a cross-cut saw but were playing on a see-saw. The song (and the word see-saw) moved from working sawyers into children's playgrounds.

Segue

The word is Italian: *segue* means 'now follows'. It is written on one section of a piece of music which is intended to follow on immediately after the previous section finishes. About the middle of the twentieth century the term began to be used in a slightly different context, but still about music, when two separate records were coming up on radio and announcers would say that they would 'segue' – meaning that the records would follow each other, without any talk in between. According to traditional usage, this was not 100 per cent accurate because the two records were different pieces of music.

But it did make sense, and by the 1970s use of the expression had extended from radio people announcing records into general usage: to move from one topic or event to another seamlessly and smoothly.

Sent to Coventry

Coventry is a real city in Britain and in centuries past the citizens thereof had a deep-rooted distrust of the military. In fact they hated them. And there was a very powerful social custom: if a woman in Coventry was seen talking to a soldier, that woman was completely ostracised and nobody would talk to her. This custom was not unknown to soldiers themselves, and they knew that if they received a transfer to Coventry, they would have no social life; women would be too nervous even to talk to them.

So the expression is actually what the soldiers would say; if a soldier was 'sent to Coventry' literally, he knew that nobody would talk to him. Hence the expression – being sent to Coventry means you will get the silent treatment.

September, October, November, December

The names of these months mean seven, eight, nine, ten – but the months to which they are attached are the ninth, tenth, eleventh and twelfth. Our calendar has an immensely complex history. We now enjoy a fairly stable 365 days divided into 12 months with seven-day weeks and a leap year every four years. But it wasn't always that tidy.

S The calendar as we know it now has had three major overhauls: first the Roman Republican calendar, followed by the Julian calendar, then the Gregorian calendar.

In ancient Roman times, what we call a year used to begin in March. This was partly because before that time it was too cold for armies to set out to war but the weather started easing up a bit then, and so the month was named after Mars the god of war. The armies were able to march and the year's activities began.

In those days there were ten months in a year. After March came April, named for Aphrodite, goddess of love and beauty. Then May honoured Maia, goddess of spring. June was believed to be named in honour of the influential Junius family, and by happy coincidence the first day of that month was already dedicated to Juno, goddess of marriage and women's well-being. Quintillus and Sextilus were the fifth and sixth months, followed by September (the seventh), October (eighth), November (ninth) and December (tenth).

But various upheavals occurred. Ancient Romans were very keen on commemorating celebrities, so Mark Antony renamed the month of Quintillus (fifth) and called it July, to commemorate Julius Caesar. Similarly the month of Sextilus (sixth) was renamed August to commemorate the emperor Augustus.

In 1582 Pope Gregory made a stern effort to tidy up the calendar, which was beginning to wander all over the place. And somewhere during the calendar revisions, the beginning of the year was changed to honour the god Janus who faces two ways and guards entrances and exits; he gave his name to January.

There was also an ancient sacrificial event when maidens lined up and were slapped with a piece of goatskin called a februa in the belief that this would keep them virginal and make them fertile – later on. This festival gave its name to another month, February.

But in shifting the year's official starting point back two months, it somehow got overlooked that there were now 12 months in the year, and that the last four of them were named with words that meant seven, eight, nine and ten.

Serpent and the elephant

This phrase is used by Charles Dickens in *Hard Times* and refers to the visible signs of the Industrial Revolution. The serpent is the smoke spiralling from big industrial chimneys, and the elephant is the steam engine. On other occasions Dickens, with heavy irony, described the enormous factories that grew around the English countryside as fairy palaces, because when their windows were lit at night they looked like real palaces. But in daylight the illusion was destroyed.

Setting their cap

In centuries past, people wore hats a great deal more than now. There were special hats men put on when they were smoking, distinct hats women wore if they were widows, elaborate bonnets for going visiting in, caps for wearing around the house, even long floppy hats people wore to bed.

Young women often wore lightweight hats or caps made of muslin, especially if there were visitors coming to the house. The expression grew out of the belief that if the household was expecting a visit from an eligible young man, the daughters of the family would take particular care over their muslin headgear, making sure it was fresh and clean and crisp. Less reverent members of the family, probably their brothers, would say the girls were 'setting their cap' at the visitor.

Gradually, when people stopped wearing hats all the time, the expression drifted away from actual hats or caps and began to mean the way a person was behaving – organising him- or herself to attract the attention of someone desirable.

Setting the world on fire

The expression's ancestor comes from ancient Latin: *Tiberum accendere nequaquam potest* – 'In no way can he set the Tiber on fire'. This fathered versions in French referring to the Seine, in German referring to the Rhine, and other areas referring to their own rivers (e.g. Liffey, Volga, Danube).

In English some variations appeared over later centuries; Chaucer has 'Set the world at six and seven' (in 1374), and Shakespeare has 'Then may I set the world on wheels' (in 1594). But in line with the original Latin, the English expression 'He/they will never set the Thames on fire' settled in to describe someone lacking drive and initiative.

Then in 1940 American writers Eddie Seiler and Sol Marcus with composer Bennie Benjamin wrote a song called 'I Don't Want to Set the World on Fire'. It was first recorded by a group called The Rockets, and didn't make much of an impact. But in 1941, the Mills Brothers and the Ink Spots took the song up, sang it much more slowly, and it became not only a hit but a standard.

That song became so recognisable that it put the phrase about setting the world (rather than the Thames) on fire into wide circulation.

Seventh heaven

The background to this expression is complex, based on the imagery attached to the two words 'seven' and 'heaven'.

Versions of the word heaven have been in the English language for centuries, dating back to the Old English *heofan*, and there are similar versions in Dutch (*hemel*) and in German (*Himmel*). The word has developed various other connotations since its use in biblical texts, for the Bible doesn't paint any clear picture of heaven (although hints can be found that there could be divisions in heaven).

There are poetic references to an afterlife but no complete description of heaven, and the Jewish concept in the Bible is that the exact nature of the immortality of the soul is known only to God. Another interpretation of the Jewish concept is not that people are in heaven, but that heaven is in people. As Christianity developed, it generated different connotations based on interpretations of translations of the Jewish concept of heaven as mentioned by Jesus, who was Jewish.

Nowadays, according to *The Oxford Dictionary of Christianity*, the usual definition of the word heaven is based on the distinctive hope of followers of Christianity that the faithful will rise after death and join Jesus there.

But there are other meanings of heaven. Centuries ago astronomers were aware that there must be something beyond the visible sky, and although they didn't use the words outer space, that is essentially what they meant. Quite unbowed by the fact that they had never been beyond the sky and probably thought nobody ever would, those ancient scientists divided their concept of space into plural 'heavens'.

That wording still remains with us, in expressions like 'the heavens', meaning the vast areas of space.

Now: 'seven'.

It seems quite an ordinary word. But for many centuries the figure seven has had a mystical resonance. The Pythagoreans noted that it comprised four plus three, both lucky numbers, so seven was treated as mystic. Ancient peoples in Babylon and Egypt revered seven sacred planets. The Jewish concept of the seven-day week is now more or less universal, and from that developed the concept of sabbatical leave after seven years' work, and also the Jewish concept of jubilee – seven times seven years plus one (50 years).

We are aware of the seven virtues and the seven deadly sins, and a belief that the seventh child of a seventh child is of special interest. Ancient alchemists worked with seven metals; the Japanese have seven gods of luck.

Some Christians have divided the life of the Virgin Mary into seven joys and seven sorrows, and their church services may contain seven sacraments. The ancients spoke of the seven wonders of the world.

Even natural features like the Seven Hills of Rome and the Seven Seas of the world add to the special qualities that surround seven. Jesuits believed that the first seven years of a child's life fashioned its character forever. Pillars of wisdom come in sevens, the most famous samurais were a magnificent seven and the ancient German folktale gives Snow White seven companions.

A legend tells that in approximately 4500 BC the Babylonian goddess Ishtar rescued the soul of her dead husband by travelling to the underworld, which had seven gates, and at each gate the price of admission was that she shed one of her seven cloaks or veils. (This

325

shedding of seven veils was added by Oscar Wilde to the biblical story of Herodias's daughter, and the name Salome was added by someone else. Neither her name nor her dance are mentioned in the Bible.)

Shakespeare divided man's life into seven ages and a type of rugby game has seven people in each team. There is even a perceived 'natural phenomenon' called the seven-year itch.

Clearly, then, placing the word 'seven' alongside the word 'heaven' is combining two words that both carry a lot of baggage.

The term seventh heaven as we use it comes from the Muslim religion. Among some Muslims, there is a belief that heaven is the place of the afterlife. But unlike the Jewish heaven, which is inside people, or the Christian heaven, a mystical place you go to after death, the Muslim heaven can be described in great detail, and is subject to distinctions of rank, class and depth of earthly faith.

Here is one interpretation of the seven 'levels' of heaven:

○ The lowest level is made of silver, and is inhabited by angels who hang glowing lamps on chains – hence we have stars.

○ The second level is made of gold.

○ The third is made of pearl and has huge books that contain the names of the newly born, while the names of the newly dead are diligently blotted out.

○ Next is the fourth level, made of white gold, and the angel of tears lives there, weeping endlessly for the sins of mankind.

○ The fifth is made of both silver and fire, where the avenging angel presides.

○ Number six is made of rubies and garnets, and that's where the guardian angel of heaven and hell lives, made half of fire and half of snow.

○ And the seventh level, made of divine light, is beyond the power of the tongue to describe. Those who live there are each larger than the whole planet, each inhabitant has 70,000 heads, each head with 70,000 mouths, each mouth speaking

70,000 languages. All the inhabitants and their tongues are forever employed chanting the praises of the Most High.

Clearly, heaven number seven is spectacular. And the inhabitants must also be very happy, because that's what the expression means. If you're faithful enough and lucky enough to have passed through the gold and the silver, the snow and the fire, the garnets and the rubies, and reached the final level, then it is a kind of ecstasy. You are in the seventh heaven.

Shambolic

This is derived from 'shambles', which is a modern version of an old Latin word for a bench or table. In English it came to mean the table used by butchers for chopping beasts into portions. Shambles therefore became the word for a slaughterhouse or a place where meat was prepared.

An historic part of York is still called The Shambles, from the time when butchers' shops were located there. And because meat preparation is always messy, the word shambles came to mean disorder, and a floppy, disorganised way of walking was called 'a shamble' because the legs were all over the place (like an animal's legs on a butcher's table).

But shamble(s) remained a noun some bright spark turned it into an adjective and said, 'This is a shambolic state of affairs.' A new word was born.

Shampoo

The word comes from India and originally had nothing to do with hair. A Hindustani word, *champo*, means to knead or press, and originally a shampoo meant a massage. Somehow it moved upwards to apply to the head alone – and then became a cleansing substance for the hair.

Many words that came into English from India retained much of their original meaning – curry, jodhpurs, calico, bungalow, pyjamas, chutney, dungarees, verandah. But shampoo took a more restricted route and instead of applying to the whole body, narrowed itself down to just the head.

Shanty town/sea shanty

The two words sound the same but they have different ancestry. The French word *chanson* (a song, from *chanter*, to sing) became the ancestor of the term 'sea shanty'.

But the shanty in 'shanty town' is a different word altogether. It comes via Canada, from a different French word *chantier*, which means a supporting framework. *Chantier* eventually gave rise to two English words: gantry, which is a supporting framework in building and engineering projects, and shanty, which is a rather rough living structure. Neither a gantry nor a shanty is known for its fine detail.

She

Why do classic phrases like 'she'll be right' and terms like 'she's a great little car' or 'she's really turning out to be a great day' use the female gender?

The concept isn't new. For a long time things without gender have nevertheless been assigned one, and often without any logic. For centuries the moon has frequently been referred to as she, and the ocean and rivers too at times. Various sections of the Christian church are customarily referred to as 'she' or 'mother', though the ruling hierarchy may be entirely male.

Ships have been 'she' since ancient times, when seagoing vessels were always dedicated to a goddess under whose protection they were thought to be, and whose effigy was affixed to the prow. Belief in goddesses diminished, but the female figure in front was retained as a decoration, and the habit had grown of referring to the ship and the goddess as one and the same.

So, though there's no logical reason in many cases, there's ample precedent for assigning a female gender where no gender exists. This practice is referred to in *The Oxford Dictionary*, which also explains that 'she' has developed a meaning of being 'an impersonal reference to the state of affairs … as in "she's OK" '.

(The whole) shebang

We know where and when it came into use, but not exactly how or why. Shebang is an American slang term for a temporary dwelling, a shack, a hut (sometimes spelt 'chebang').The earliest recorded use of shebang in print is by Walt Whitman in *Specimen Days* (1862).

One theory about the word's origin is that it comes as a version of the Anglo-Irish 'shebeen', an illegal drinking establishment. In America, shebang began by meaning a hut, and sometimes also a building in which people got drunk, and then it occasionally meant a horse and cart. But gradually it came to mean just 'everything'.

Several expressions have incorporated the word 'whole' as an intensifier: a whole box of dice; the whole kit and caboodle; the whole enchilada; the whole ball of wax; the whole hog. None of these is actually referring to the things they name; they are just a novel and pleasing way of saying 'anything' or 'everything'.

This happened to shebang during the 1800s; 'whole' became attached to shebang. Mark Twain didn't invent the complete term, but his use in print (in an 1869 letter to his publisher) was an early example of the transition from shebang (a little hut) to whole shebang (whatever matter or subject is under discussion – everything).

Sheila

Sheila is a term of disapprobation that has been taken over and used by its subjects, who now use it with some pride and humour. This sometimes happens. The BBC explains the term Desert Rats as an equivalent development; Mussolini said it about the troops as an insult, but the troops took it up themselves as a gesture of defiance, and eventually as a matter of great pride.

Sheila is an Irish name derived from Celtic (as *Sheela*) and was frequently used as a generic name for any Irish girl (just as any man was 'Paddy'), gradually becoming a slang term in the British Isles from about 1832 onwards.

It surfaced in the Southern Hemisphere towards the end of the nineteenth century. Originally it was a shade disrespectful – a young woman to whom the speaker was not married – but eventually love took over and Sheila was no longer appropriate usage – until after the wedding, when she became 'the old Sheila'.

Some women seemed to realise, very sensibly, that if you can't beat them, join them, and in some circumstances 'sheila' has moved in to become the opposite of bloke – simply a user-friendly gender description. So the word is now not necessarily a put-down, but a cheerful and self-confident acknowledgement that women can do their own thing.

Forthright author Sandra Coney called her book about 'women of dash and daring' *Stroppy Sheilas and Gutsy Girls* – and she meant it as a compliment.

She'll be right

This is Australasian. The Australasian vernacular often uses 'she' to mean 'it', for example, 'She'll be Jake'. Adding '—will be right' is thought to have arisen in New Zealand, about 1920, but the phrase is now used in both countries.

Shepherd

Cows tend to be in a herd, and sheep in a flock, but sheep are looked after by a shepherd: a sheep herder. The word 'herd' comes from an old Greek word meaning a group, and in English it has come to refer to a large group of animals, usually mammals.

One of the archaic uses of the word 'herder' was to describe a person who looked after any form of livestock at all. This has remained with us, in 'shepherd' and 'goatherd', which seem fitting with cows and goats, but in earlier times sheep were also assigned to a 'herd'.

Now, of course, multiple sheep are commonly called a flock, which comes from the Latin for downy, fluffy things. We still use that word for mattress fillings and wallpaper that has been made fuzzy. So the word for a group of sheep changed, but the word for the person looking after them didn't.

Shepherd's pie/cottage pie

Shepherd's pie as we know it originated in Scotland and the north of England. The pie was traditionally made with sheep meat, layered with carrots and onions, and with mashed potatoes on top. The original traditional version was always mutton, associated with the households of shepherds because they had access to sheep.

If the pie was made with minced beef, the name became cottage pie.

Nowadays, there are so many variations that both names tend to be used in a rather muddled way: some recipes have spices in the mix or Worcestershire sauce; some are with or without cheese on top of the potatoes; sometimes there are mushrooms, or turnips or swedes; there is a version made with beef brains; and another version made with chicken. And strangely enough, Americans have a shepherd's pie made with ham and sweet corn, and there can also be a vegetarian shepherd's pie.

But the place of origin is Scotland for a real shepherd's pie, made of sheep meat. In olden times it would not necessarily have been minced, because mincing machines as we know them weren't developed until the 1870s, and the concept of shepherd's pie is much older than that; the meat was probably chopped rather than minced. At some unknown time in history, it apparently occurred to someone that leftover roast meat could be used economically and imaginatively by chopping it (or later mincing it) and making a pie with a potato topping.

Shickered

There is one school of thought that the word (which has various spellings, and means drunk) is from an Arabic source, and was brought into English by soldiers.

But there is a Hebrew word *shikor*, very old indeed, which was adapted into the Yiddish language spoken by Jewish people in Europe. When many Yiddish-speaking Jews went to live in New York about 1900, the word shikker meaning drunk was introduced to English-speaking people. And you still occasionally hear the word in the United States. It became particularly popular in Australia and New Zealand.

Shimmy

Chemise is a French word, and 'shimmy' is the Anglicised way of saying that. They both come from an old Latin word *camisia*, which itself was borrowed by the Romans from an Arabic word *qamis*. In general all those words described a loose garment falling from the shoulders.

When the Latin version entered Old French it still meant that, but usually a garment worn underneath other clothing. From France, the chemise drifted into English and it's been spelt several different ways over nine centuries, but the meaning has remained similar.

Along with the popularity of the term shimmy came a new dance that was characterised by a lot of shaking and sliding, rather like a garment not fitted to the body, and hence it too was called the shimmy.

Ship-shape and Bristol fashion

The word 'shipshape' has long carried an image of everything being in order and methodically arranged, as things are (ideally) aboard ship. During the era of sailing ships and particularly in the eighteenth century, Bristol was a very important commercial port in the United Kingdom. The port has a high range of tides, and a large difference in the water level between ebb and flood – something like 10 metres.

At low tide, ships in the harbour could be left high and dry, and if not properly constructed and laden, would either break their backs or their cargoes would shift. So ships that regularly visited Bristol had to be of specially stout construction, and carefully loaded. Thus, vessels coming in and out of Bristol had a reputation for being especially efficient – they were 'ship-shape and Bristol fashion'.

Shoes

Queen Victoria's diary tells that when she and Prince Albert first went to live at Balmoral Castle, an old shoe was thrown after them for luck as they entered the house.

Social researcher Rudolph Brasch explains that through the ages shoes have carried a great deal of symbolism: they have been seen as aids to fertility, and as the home of the soul. When people were beginning a journey it was a customary to throw an old shoe at them; it was believed to convey to the travellers all the good luck and experience of the shoe's former owner.

Old shoes carried more use and wisdom than new, and of course new shoes have always been expensive, so using old shoes had an economic influence as well. Shoes also carry a connotation of ownership, dating as far back as the Bible – in Psalm 60: 'Over Edom itself I cast my shoe' – and signifying rulership and domination.

At weddings, old shoes symbolise future fertility, they convey good luck to the married couple and they signify the bride's family transferring ownership of or control over her to her new married state.

In 1855, when that diary entry of Queen Victoria's was written, she and Albert had been married for nearly 15 years but the throwing of shoes still carried powerful signals of good luck, wisdom and, of course, their dominion over the new Balmoral Castle.

The cultural significance of feet and shoes remains strong. We talk about being under the boot of tyranny; royal personages may not be depicted on a mat; and some religions and cultures prefer shoes to be left outside places of worship and outside houses.

Shonky

Shonky is designated by *The Oxford Dictionary* as being an Australian word, which came into common use late in the twentieth century, meaning imperfect, unreliable.

It has an unfortunate similarity to the word 'schonk' – an offensive slang word for someone Jewish. But the use of shonky in Australasia is unrelated to any sort of racist reference; most Australians and New Zealanders wouldn't be familiar with the (British and American) put-down version. The Australian version is believed to be related to the ancient British word *wonky*, and derives from an English dialect word *wancol*, meaning unstable and liable to break – which is more or less what shonky now means.

Shortnin' Bread

It doesn't mean what we would call shortbread, or even bread. The song is believed to be a genuine slave song that originated among the plantation slaves in America, and was used as a lullaby. It was first published in 1915 but is much older than that.

The word 'short' is often used as an abbreviated version of 'short-crust' and describes a kind of dough or pastry that crumbles easily when it's been cooked. And shortening can mean any kind of cooking fat. There is a vague rule that 'short' dough has half the quantity of fat to flour.

In plantation times 'shortnin' bread' was made after a pig-kill, with half the quantity of fat to cornmeal (not wheat flour) and containing bits and scraps of bacon, and served with bacon gravy.

And African American slave talk also had its own double meanings: 'shortnin' bread' was also another phrase for intimate activity.

Shot his bolt

It means to do everything to the limit of your power and even slightly beyond, to exhaust your current possibilities.

The expression comes from archery. The crossbow was the heavy artillery of ancient warfare, and the crossbow shot a very heavy arrow called a 'bolt'. The tension needed to do this was such that the crossbow had to be 'wound up' with a windlass. Sometimes in the heat of battle, when time was of the essence and the crossbow archer had discharged his weapon, re-tensioning of the bow took so long he could take no further part in the action. He had 'shot his bolt'.

The expression has been in use since at least the year 1200.

Shuffle off this mortal coil

It means to die, and it's a direct quote from Shakespeare's *Hamlet*, the famous 'To be, or not to be' speech, in which Hamlet says:

> For in that sleep of death what dreams may come
> When we have shuffled off this mortal coil ...

He was using the word coil in its sixteenth-century meaning: the trouble and activities of the world.

S

Silver beet

Silver beet is known by other names – Swiss chard, mangol, spinach beet, and sometimes just spinach (though this last is inaccurate because spinach is a different plant altogether).

The name silver beet came into popular use in the early part of the twentieth century mainly because it isn't all green. The leaves have very wide prominent stems of silvery-white (quite different from the stems of spinach). There are variants of the same plant with coloured stems, rather than silvery-white, these being known as 'silverbeet colours'; rainbow chard; rainbow silverbeet; or fanciful names like 'bright lights'.

Silverfish

An annoying wingless household insect fond of warm dry places, formally called *Lepisma saccharina* because it likes eating carbo-hydrates: books, flour, photos, carpet and any kind of starch.

Silver fox

A North American animal, known as 'red fox' but which can manifest itself in several colours – grey, reddish-brown, black, and 'silver' (basically black hairs with silver tips), which became very desirable in fashion wear.

(The term is also sometimes used as a complimentary term to describe a man whose hair has turned grey but who has retained smooth grooming, and a silver tongue.)

A silver fox is not to be confused with a silverback, which is a male mountain gorilla whose rear area develops a silvery-black colouration.

Silvertail

The word is used in several different ways: it's a kind of cat, a kind of plant, and the name of a sports team; but it also independently developed a slang meaning referring to a rich person, a swell, a toff.

In 1897 it was described as an Australian bush term for a 'swell' – 'a man who goes to the manager's house not the bushman's hut'

(Edward Morris). And from there it's developed a side connotation of social climbing, and being affected.

Singlet

For several hundred years, men wore a fairly tight top, with sleeves and a little skirt. These varied a great deal, with padding and decoration, but they were firm in construction, and it seems that because they always had an outer layer of fabric and an inner layer, a lining, they were called doublets.

The lining was important. It not only kept the garment firm, but for decorative purposes the outer layer often had slashes cut in it so that the brightly coloured lining showed. Sometimes the lining was pulled through the slash and puffed out a bit. Rich people, including Henry VIII, had slashed doublets with jewels and embroidery on the bits of lining that poked through.

But during the eighteenth century, fabrics and lifestyles changed, and some garments for men's torsos were made with only one layer of fabric. These floppier tops came to be worn underneath rather than on top, and usually had no sleeves, and – the important bit – no lining. So, because the traditional top had two layers of fabric and was called a doublet, the undergarment with only one layer of cloth was called a singlet.

Ordinary singlets have no sleeves, but there are singlets with sleeves – and if the sleeves are long to the wrist, they were originally contrived by an ancestor of the late Princess Diana when he was feeling the cold. To this day, long-sleeved singlets are named after her family – spencers.

(There are variations in use among cultures. In some places the word singlet is not used, the same garment being referred to as an undershirt or vest; the latter usage is confusing, since in other places a 'vest' is a waistcoat.)

(At) sixes and sevens

This means things are in confusion, or people are in disagreement, and the expression could well be several thousand years old. An early reference to sixes and sevens can be found in the Book of Job in the Bible. Translated into English, the phrase says 'God shall deliver thee in six troubles, yea in seven.' It is difficult to associate that with the modern use of 'at sixes and sevens', so the Book of Job might not be the source at all. Chaucer uses a similar term in 1375 but, again, the meaning isn't 100 per cent clear.

The explanation of the term's history which has the most credence is that it refers to throwing dice – in particular to gambling in a risky and impetuous way, throwing dice with little regard for the consequences even when considerable stakes are involved. Thus the connection with confusion and an unpredictable outcome.

Sixty-four thousand dollar question

The ancestor of the phrase was born in 1940 in an American radio game show called *Take it or Leave it*. It had a series of quiz-like questions, and if one got through all the preliminaries, the climax of the show, the big prize – in those pre-inflationary times – was $64.

That part of the show became very famous and the phrase '$64 dollar question' rapidly entered the American vernacular. In 1950 the show changed its title and became *The $64 Show*. Five years later, it shifted to television and the prize was raised to $64,000.

But in 1958 there was a major scandal in America over quiz-type game shows. It transpired that sometimes contestants were told the answers and sometimes they were advised not to answer correctly and they would be 'well treated' the following week. This scandal reverberated for years.

The show we're talking about – *Take it or Leave it*, which became the *$64 Question* and then the *$64,000 Question* on TV – actually weathered the storm and went back onto American television in 1976 with the prize raised to $128,000, but it was short-lived. However, unlike most television game shows, this one had a legacy; it put the phrase '$64,000 question' into the language, meaning a crucial point, a key issue, which must be answered.

Skew-whiff

The 'skew' bit relates to being crooked. That word came into English from an Old Norman French source word meaning 'to take an oblique course', recorded as early as 1470. A century later the word 'askew' turns up, meaning 'obliquely, to one side'.

The second part of the expression – 'whiff' – sometimes has the 'wh' and sometimes not (as in 'skewiff'). But it seems that it began as 'skew' plus 'whiff'. When used by itself, the word whiff means 'a puff of wind' – the operative word being puff, because a whiff is a gentle or slight wind. Thus, if it's attached to skew, giving skew-whiff, then the implication is that something is off-line, out of kilter, not in balance – but just slightly, only a little bit, as if blown off-centre by a gentle breeze. And the combination of those two words has been together since the 1700s.

Skite

This is an abbreviation of an old British word – *blatherskite*. 'Blather' comes from an Old Norse word *blathra*, meaning nonsense, and *skite* seems to be interchangeable with *skate* in some dialects of northern England and Scotland to mean a silly, talkative person.

So a *blatherskite* was a noisy person who talked a lot of nonsense. Shortened to just skite, its application has changed slightly so that it means an irritating way of boasting unnecessarily.

Skulduggery

The word is used today to mean something underhand, deceptive, or clandestine. Its origin lies in an old Scottish term spelt *skulduddery* or *sculdudrie* (note the 'd's), which meant 'unpermitted sex' or 'obscenities and indecencies'.

Slappers

The word has been used in Northern English dialect since the late 1700s, where it referred to a big person, usually clumsy and usually female. The word drifted into more common usage during later centuries and, possibly influenced by the term 'slap-and-tickle', gradually gained a connotation that a 'slapper' was likely to be quite forthcoming in allowing some slap and tickle. Gradually the term had moved from depicting someone clumsy, to a woman of a flirtatious nature, and then to a woman renowned for her generosity of shared experiences.

There are doubts about the origin of the word; in Ireland they see in it an echo of the Irish word *sliobaire*, meaning 'dirty'. Yiddish speakers claim it as a variation of *schlepper*, a clumsy or stupid person, and pragmatic English speakers claim it as onomatopoeic – simply the sound made by two bodies when in intimate conjunction, which some people were believed to hear more frequently than others.

(Open) slather

Slather is heard used in three different ways:

1. Sometimes in Britain nowadays it is used to mean a scolding or even a beating-up: 'The boy received a severe slathering.'

2. The same word is used in the United States and although it probably has the same ancestry, its meaning there is different. Slather means a large amount, or to spread thickly: 'He slathered butter on his bread.'

3. The form 'open slather' has only been around since the nineteenth century, and is believed to be Australasian, meaning a free-for-all, anything goes.

'Slather' has a slim connection with the old Irish word *slighe*, which means an access. So open slather means access from a wide variety of vantage points – anything goes.

Sleaze

Sleaze is a wonderful word, almost onomatopoeic; it sounds like slime and slippery and ooze, and that's more or less what it means – squalid. *Chambers Dictionary* and the *Oxford* both tell us that the word was being used 300 years ago to describe thin, cheap, insubstantial fabric. This use appears to have developed into a wider application: not just fabric of low quality, but anything else perceived as squalid and distasteful, particularly behaviour or a lifestyle.

(Doing a) slinter

The expression comes originally from Dutch, then Afrikaans – *schlenter*, then *slenter* – and moved out from South African slang into wider usage, with the same meaning: an underhand trick, a sham, a fast one.

Smithereens

This comes from an Irish word, *smiodar*, meaning 'pieces'. An *–een* ending indicates a diminutive, so *smiodar-een* means small pieces. In English this took a while to settle down; 'smiddereens' and 'shivereens' showed up in the 1800s, before smithereens took over.

Snake oil

The manufacture of what are usually called 'patent medicines' began in England and they were being licensed by the early 1700s. Considerable quantities were shipped to America, but this export trade stopped when the Revolutionary War began.

Entrepreneurial Americans moved very quickly to fill the gap, and during the 1800s so-called medicines to cure all manner of complaints abounded. There was Enriched Vegetable Compound, Swamp Root Kidney and Liver Medicine, Kikapoo Indian Cures, Seminole Cough Balm, Celery Compounds, Great Sulphur Nostrum and a bottled cure for cholera that was widely used by missionaries to deal with anything among the heathen from corns to toothache. Also available was an ointment to cure baldness and another to develop the bust. A man called Sutherland had seven daughters with long hair – a total of nearly 11 metres of hair. He made a mixture called Seven Sutherland Sisters Hair Growth Tonic.

Amid all this, there was a definite belief that extract of snake could help some medical problems. There actually were people who killed snakes and extracted their secretions, and it was widely believed that the Native Americans used grease from rattlesnakes to alleviate the pain of rheumatism. Some very brave travelling medicine men actually stood on public platforms while they killed the snakes and squeezed their juice into the medicine. So naturally a whole host of medicines began to appear which purported to contain genuine snake oil.

However, as science advanced and gullibility retreated, it was gradually revealed that many of the bottles supposedly containing snake-oil cures actually had only a mixture of turpentine, camphor, beef fat and some ground chili pepper, which imparted a slight warm sting to the skin.

So the term 'snake-oil salesman' began to gain disrepute, and when the American Federal Pure Food and Drug Act came into effect in 1907 the phony remedies were curtailed. But the reference to snake oil remained, indicating 'medicine' of very doubtful value.

There are genuine medicinal qualities to be found in some snakes: the Chinese water snake is a source of an enzyme that helps decrease blood pressure and the Malayan viper produces heparin, which is a blood anti-coagulant. But these treatments are not available off the backs of trucks.

Snob

There was a belief that 'snob' arose as an abbreviation of the Latin phrase *sine nobilitate*, meaning 'of a humble social background, without a title'. But actually the word snob was first recorded in the late eighteenth century as a term for a shoemaker or his apprentice. It was gradually adopted by students at Cambridge University but not to indicate someone's family origins – rather to indicate all dwellers in the same town who were not students.

This gradually widened in use to mean a person with no 'breeding', just an ordinary working man. A further development took place so that 'snob' began to mean not just ordinary people, but social climbers who copied the manners of the upper classes.

Unfortunately, these people who were not noble, having man-oeuvred themselves into a higher level of society, and being in an upper circle by virtue of circumstance, tended to have an exaggerated disapproval of people who were not part of the upper circle (unlike genuine aristocrats who were normally quite relaxed and comfortable anywhere).

S

So the word 'snob' came to describe someone with an exaggerated respect for high social position or wealth, and who looks down on those regarded as socially inferior.

It's quite possible that the phrase *sine nobilitate* may have appeared in one context or another, but the accepted origin of the word 'snob' is that originally it meant – a shoemaker.

Snork

In Australasia it is a casual term for a baby. Etymologist Eric Partridge believes that it is derived from the word stork – part of the old myth adults told children: that babies were brought by a stork.

This ancient story originated in Scandinavia and was popularised by Hans Christian Andersen. In some Scandinavian areas, storks customarily nest on the chimney-tops of houses. The birds are monogamous, and may live for 70 years, returning to the same chimney every year. Thus the families who live below have ample chance to become familiar with the breeding of storks. So an explanation grew that storks could very conveniently drop a new little baby down the chimney.

This explanation is deeply entrenched in popular culture; it even surfaces in countries which have no storks.

Australians and New Zealanders were party to stork legend, but steered the issue towards something less fanciful. Eventually, instead of saying that someone had a visit from the stork, the word 'stork' was corrupted and saying that someone had a snork became an antipodean way of referring to the old myth but putting a vernacular spin on it.

While this word had a rhyming connection with the sound of 'stork', it could well have been influenced by awareness of an old dialect word in England: *snorken*, describing animals grunting, particularly little pigs, which came to be known as *snorks*. Put the two influences together and snork as an affectionate term for a baby came into being.

Soccer

The word football is a generic term – games in which a ball is played with the feet. There are at least five different kinds. The word evokes several different things in Britain, New Zealand, the US and Australia.

The correct and original name for soccer is Association Football, and if you take the three letters 'soc' from the word association, then add another 'c' and 'er' to them, that is the origin of the word soccer. It's a slang abbreviation. The word soccer has been in use since the late nineteenth century, and for a short time it was spelt socker, but the spelling has simplified. And the word soccer isn't welcome in Britain: there, it's just football.

Sold down the river

This American expression dates from the time when slaves were bought and sold. Circumstances on plantations on the lower reaches of the Mississippi River were believed to be much harsher than elsewhere, so to be sold down the river was seen by the slaves as heading into an unpleasant environment.

Soldier/warrior

There is a subtle difference. By dictionary definition, a warrior is a person engaged in, experienced in or devoted to war (it is actually derived from the word for war). A soldier is a person who serves, or has served in an army.

But the usage varies, especially when it comes to memorials for those who were engaged in battles. Belgium, France, the Crimea, the US and Canada definitely opt for the name 'Unknown Soldier', because by using that word they would include all those people in the army who weren't necessarily front-line fighters but nevertheless lost their lives: drivers, nurses, doctors, ambulance people, communications people – they're all in uniform and members of the army, so they are all soldiers.

The word 'warrior' would seem to narrow the field a bit, because its connotation is only those who actually fight, excluding the support personnel. But the phrase 'Unknown Warrior' is also used

– the tomb in Westminster Abbey is that of the Unknown Warrior, whereas the American memorial in Arlington is usually referred to as the Tomb of the Unknown Soldier. But each has sometimes been referred to by the alternative name: 'Warrior' for Arlington, and 'Soldier' for Westminster Abbey.

So although the two words have slightly different meanings, they are sometimes somewhat casually interchanged – and the world doesn't stop turning.

'Solemn jubilee'

There are shades of gloom around the word 'solemn'. But that is a fairly narrow interpretation – it can be serious and sincere, but also entail pomp and ceremony, inspiring awe. The expression solemn jubilee occurs in John Milton's poem 'At a solemn music', written in 1645. At that time, all these shades of meaning were still current with 'jubilee'. It was considered quite appropriate that respect – and joy – can be shown in various ways, and not necessarily with gaiety and fireworks. Milton's words:

> With Saintly shout and solemn Jubilee,
> Where the bright Seraphim in burning row
> Their loud up-lifted Angel trumpets blow.

So as well as 'solemn jubilee', Milton provided the music world with the words for a famous oratorio solo for soprano, with trumpet.

Solomon Grundy (born on Monday)

He never existed. The word comes from an Old French word *salmagundy*, which was cold chopped meat mixed with eggs and onions – a sort of hotch-potch. From there it drifted into English in the eighteenth century, meaning a cook, and later because it sounded like a name, Solomon Grundy, people thought it might have referred to a real person.

(The) Solomon Islands

The Solomon Islands have nothing to do with being solemn and very little to do with King Solomon. The natives who lived there for centuries were disturbed in 1567 by an explorer from Spain, Alvaro de Mendaña de Neyra. In the paternalistic vocabulary of the time, he was credited with having 'discovered' the islands.

The people living there seemed to de Neyra's eyes to be wearing ornaments made from something that looked like gold. And, in a fit of fancy, he imagined he'd found the legendary country mentioned in the Bible's Book of Kings, the land of Ophir from which gold was brought to King Solomon. So, Alvaro de Mendaña de Neyra announced to the rest of the world that he had named the islands the Solomons – and the name stuck.

It is believed to be the only country in the world named after a biblical character – not just mentioned in the Bible, like Israel, but named after a biblical person. Countries named after a person are rare: Saudi Arabia is a rare example of a country named after a family, as is Liechtenstein, and America takes its name from a man's first name.

Sonny

A term used to demean a man. It is considered equally demeaning for a man to address a woman as 'girlie'.

Sook

Sook and sooky are believed to derive from a tenth-century Old English verb *sucan*, which meant to suck. That became a dialect word for a baby, and it might have been influenced by the Welsh word *sweard*, to tame. So sook, or sooky, used to mean just a genuine baby, but has now become derogatory and means either someone who acts like a baby, or is a coward.

Sound bite

The expression, meaning a short, pithy piece extracted from an interview or speech, began to be used in the 1980s. The practice probably arises from the assumption that the modern public will not follow anything for more than a few seconds, and the use of sound bites has now led to people deliberately making short statements for quick use. Reporters for the electronic media are reputed to say to interviewees: 'Give us enough for a sound bite.'

It's called a sound 'bite' because it is a quick, short snatch at something. It's apparently unrelated to computer bytes, but retains the undertone of a high-tech approach. Interestingly, it's now used when speaking about television, which has pictures along with the sound bite.

Southpaw

A very American way of saying left-handed, originating in baseball. In regulation baseball, the batter faces east so that the afternoon sun doesn't shine in his eyes. The pitcher is therefore facing west. In the case of a left-handed pitcher, his throwing arm and hand are on the south side of his body; hence the expression southpaw.

Baseball dates a long way back in Britain. Long before America knew of it, Jane Austen mentions it (in *Northanger Abbey*) as do other English writers in the eighteenth century. It began to interest the Americans in the early nineteenth century, and the first regulations concerning baseball were drawn up there in 1845. Formal rules were established in 1920, and the word southpaw has been used among Americans for that long or even longer.

Sow your wild oats

This is agricultural vernacular. In this context 'wild' doesn't actually mean barbaric or violent, but uncultivated, growing in its original raw state – like wild flowers or wild onions.

Thus, if you plant good cultivated seed, you get reliably good plants; but if you collect seeds in the wild, they may grow into plants that are a bit rough and don't make good produce. A wise farmer will sow good quality cultivated oats; sowing wild oat seed would be foolish, because this would give rise to a bad crop.

So sowing wild oats refers to the fact that youthful excessive behaviour doesn't necessarily lead on to good, solid adulthood. The expression has been in use since the sixteenth century with this meaning. But nowadays it has taken on a distinctly temporary feel: if you sow wild oats when you're young, you probably do get the roughness out of your system, and later on you turn into a good, productive, cultivated oat.

S

Spade

The word spade is used in a very underhand way as a derogatory term for African Americans. It is believed to derive from the fact that the symbol for spades on playing cards is always black.

(Call a) spade a spade

To call a spade a spade is an expression from ancient Greek (*spathe* in Greek was a flat sword or blade) and originally meant much the same as it does now (that an honest person would call a spade simply what it was, and say anything else with equal honesty).

The expression filtered through into English and has been there for over 450 years. It has gradually taken on a connotation of describing a person who uses outspoken language, quite the opposite of spin doctors, political press secretaries and the people who create advertising-speak. Charles Dickens used the expression in 1854 in the way we use it now: in *Hard Times*, a character says, 'There's no imaginative sentimental humbug about me. I call a spade a spade.'

There's a famous and amusing use of the expression in Oscar Wilde's *The Importance of Being Earnest* when one bitchy society woman says to another, 'When I see a spade I call it a spade.' The other replies, 'I am happy to say that I have never seen a spade.'

Spam

In 1937 the Hormel Food Co. launched a competition to find a name for a canned meat product. Apparently the company didn't want to call it pork loaf (though that's what it was) and was not permitted to call it ham because the meat was shoulder, rather than hindquarter. A competition was staged with a prize of $100 for a possible name, and won by New York radio announcer Kenneth Daigneau who suggested 'Spam', a condensed version of 'spiced ham'.

Years later (1970) the Monty Python crew performed a ludicrous television sketch in which a rundown café served only variations of Spam, the customers' indignation climaxing in a ridiculous song called 'Spam'. This contributed greatly to the word becoming widely known, even when the commodity itself wasn't.

Brewer's Dictionary of Modern Phrase and Fable credits the Monty Python sketch with the use of the word spam to mean the unwanted email material which arrives relentlessly.

Spanker/spanking

The name of a fore and aft sail placed in the aftermost part of a sailing ship is a 'spanker' – in full referred to as 'the spanker mast'. Admiral Smyth's *Sailor's Word Book* explains that the word 'spanking' has a maritime meaning of 'strength, spruceness and size as in "spanking breeze"', which indicates a relationship between the name of the spanker sail and the ship's speed.

The other 'spank' was defined in 1727 as to slap with the open hand. The word is thought to be imitative, named for the noise it makes. There appears to be no connection between the sail and the word meaning to slap.

Spare

It comes originally from an Old German word *sparon*; by the time it migrated into English it was 'sparion', and then it slowly narrowed down to just 'spare'. Over the years it has gathered no fewer than 17 slightly different meanings – one of them was once quite commonly used to describe someone who had no excess flesh, and you still occasionally hear it used in that sense.

There is reputed to have been a tricky incident involving the King of Siam (Mongkut), who was described by a British journalist as 'a spare man' because he was thin. The king read this, and was very querulous because he thought it meant he was surplus to requirements, to be used only in emergencies. He didn't know all the 17 meanings.

Spare is one of those irritating words that mean the opposite of itself: a spare person is lean without unnecessary weight, but spare can also mean extra, in excess of what is needed.

Sphinx

The word sphinx is from ancient Greece, where there were legends about creatures known by that name. But there is no connection between the famous Egyptian sphinx near Cairo, and the sphinx of Greek legend. By coincidence, both were half human and half beast, but the similarity ends there. The two similar creatures evolved quite independently in two quite different cultures.

Many cultures have various myths and legends about creatures which are part-human and part-animal. The Greek word arose in the fifth century BC, thought to be derived from *sphingo*, meaning to strangle, to bind tight (a descendant of that word remans in English, to describe the human sphincter). The female sphinx strangled and throttled their victims. That kind of sphinx had a lion's body and the head of a human, a falcon or a sheep. Some had the wings of eagles and some had serpents' tails.

This Greek sphinx was a demon creature of death, devouring and destruction. One of the most famous was she who threatened the life of everyone including Oedipus if he could not answer her riddle; hence the word became closely associated with riddles and enigmas, although its actual origin means strangle and throttle.

The civilisation of Egypt is so old that it seemed ancient even to the Greeks, whom we associate with the cradle of Western civilisation. And the ancient Egyptians also had mythical creatures with factors both human and non-human. Travellers from ancient Greece, when visiting Egypt, saw these figures represented in monumental stone statues, and seeing in them a slight resemblance to their own half-animal myths, referred to them by the same name – sphinx.

However, the Egyptian creature is male, with a beard, representing qualities far from the Greek legend. Instead of demonic strangling, the Egyptian figures represented wisdom, calm assurance, strength and nobility.

But gradually this essentially Greek word came into general European use to describe the essentially Egyptian concept of a creature with only the vaguest resemblance to the evil female monsters of Greek myth.

S

Spic and span

The two words have been used together for over 400 years and are seldom – if ever – heard separately. People like the double use because it makes a double emphasis.

The old meaning of 'spic' is related to the modern word spike. A spic was a shiny new nail. The old meaning of 'span' was a chip, as in a chip of wood. So when people said something was spic and span new, they meant it was as if the nails were gleaming and the wood was freshly shaped.

The expression must have been around during the 1500s – you'll find it in Sir Thomas North's translation of *Plutarch's Lives*, published in 1759: 'gilt armours and purple cassocks, spicke and span new'. In time the expression dropped the word 'new' so that nowadays when you say something is spic and span it doesn't necessarily have to be new, just tidied up and looking good.

('Spick' with a 'k' – also spik, and sometimes spic – is a derogatory term for foreigners, based on the phrase 'No spika-da-English'.)

Spill the beans

It usually refers to divulging information which was meant to be kept quiet, to let out a secret. There are several versions of the origin, and unfortunately two of those versions make good sense, so one has to make a choice:

1. There is a system, still used in some circumstances, where a person is proposed for membership of an organisation, and the other members place either a white or black ball into a container; if everyone puts in a white ball, then the person is accredited with membership, but if one or a prescribed number of the balls is black, then the proposed member has been black-balled and is not permitted to join.

   This dates back to ancient Greece where the elite were very fastidious about who they would admit to membership of secret societies. A common voting method was for members to drop either a white bean or a brownish-black bean into a jar. White meant acceptance and black rejection of the new application. A pre-decided number of black beans meant rejection. But the jar wasn't transparent, so to find out the exact balance of the vote, the beans had to be tipped out and the blacks and whites counted. Hence the outcome of the voting, the truth of the situation, was effected by spilling the beans.

2. But there is another school of thought that the concept originated in Turkey among gypsies who, for a fee, would foretell the future of a client. They didn't use a crystal ball or tarot cards or tea leaves – they put a handful of beans into a cup, shook it about, then spilled it out on the ground. Then they interpreted the patterns the beans made and predicted what was going to happen in the future; hence, the spilling of the beans had revealed what hitherto had been unknown.

There are a couple of other possible explanations – that 'bean' is an Americanism for 'head', so if you reveal what is in your head you are spilling your bean; and there's a very old English saying, 'He knows how many beans make five,' indicating that a person is shrewd and/or knowledgeable, so he could probably spill what he knows.

There is, alas, no way to be certain which explanation is the true origin of this very common expression, but the possibilities make colourful reading.

Spin doctor

This term came to notice during the 1980s. Its first known appearance in print was 1984, when a report on a debate between Ronald Reagan and Walter Mondale mentioned that the statements each was making must have been put together by spin doctors.

Most people can throw a ball. But in high-level sports, some people learn to throw a ball very skilfully and by giving it a clever spin they can fool people about the exact path the ball is going to follow. In ball-throwing sports, the term 'spin doctor' arose to describe such people.

Gradually the term moved away from sports and since the 1980s has been used to describe people who control information. They put a favourable spin on certain announcements by arranging words to give a desired impression, rather than making a simple statement of fact.

Spitting image

The expression dates back at least a century in the English language. The word 'spit' has five different meanings in English, and among these is an old one meaning 'copy'. It is also related to another, better-known meaning – to eject suddenly from the mouth. In earlier centuries, when people said something was a spit-and-image of something else, they meant that the resemblance was so close it looked if the copy had been spat out of the mouth of the original.

By 1895 the phrase had shortened to spit'n image. After that, edging into spitting image didn't take long, but still meaning exactly the same as it always has meant: an exact copy.

There is a belief that use of the term was influenced by an ancient form of receipt, which involved carving notches on a stick, then splitting the stick into halves for each party of the transaction to keep. To prove that one had a genuine receipt, the split wooden bits must tally exactly with the other half; that is, together they made a splitting image. It's not impossible that this use did combine with the ancient image of someone exactly like you being spat from the mouth, to result in the modern usage.

Splice the mainbrace

The term dates back to sailing-ship days, when the heaviest piece of running rigging was called the mainbrace. The job of splicing it was difficult and tiring. When the job was done, the reward for all who took part was an extra ration of rum.

There is still a descendant of that custom, even on non-sailing ships. When a ship's company deserves special congratulations, or on ceremonial occasions such as when a new monarch succeeds to the throne, the order is given to splice the mainbrace – and extra grog is served. In non-nautical life, the term has come to mean simply: let's have a drink.

Spondulicks

The term was first noticed in the mid-1800s in the United States. The origin, however, is unknown. There are many informal words for money – some with a reason behind them, others simply made up: dough, moolah, pony, quid, nickers, smackers, bread, ace, beans, boffo, bones, buck, bullets, clams, fish, scrip, plug, sinkers, wagon wheel, cabbage, coconuts, lettuce, kale, folding green, joey, long green, rhino, mazuma, pap, bob, plaster, lucre, rivets, marigolds, dosh, readies, scratch.

Spondulicks may simply have been one that was made up. But there is a remarkable similarity to the Greek word *spondylikos*, which in ancient times was a special kind of seashell believed to have been used as currency instead of coins. What is hard to explain is how a word from ancient Greece suddenly leapt back into use in nineteenth-century English.

Spoonerism

The Reverend William Spooner (1844–1930) was Warden of New College, Oxford and had an endearing habit of absent-mindedly muddling the initial letters of successive words. This aberration is now named after him as spoonerisms.

Some of the howlers attributed to him include: The Lord is a shoving leopard; the cat popped on its drawers; a half-warmed fish; a blushing crow; and a well-boiled icicle.

Spot on

This concept was originally heard as 'bang on', an air force expression meaning 'alert, ready, and absolutely accurate'. The change to 'spot on' is believed to have been influenced by the placing of coloured billiard balls on their 'spots' after having been sunk. The re-spotting of the coloured balls (other than red, which remained potted) would have to be precisely on the correct spot – 'spot on' – for the game to be played fairly.

S

Spuds

Spud is thought to have descended from a word that was quite common 500 years ago: spudde or spudder. This was a kind of knife, and the word eventually widened its application so that spudder came to mean a spade.

Things dug up with a spudder were called spuds, and because potatoes were among the things most commonly dug up, the meaning narrowed down so that spuds eventually meant just potatoes.

Stairs/steps

There is no rule about this – but although they are virtually the same thing, common usage places stairs inside a house, and steps out in the open air.

One possible reason for this distinction is that inside premises such as a house, the word stairs can be seen as an abbreviation of staircase. A staircase has to be built within a planned framework or 'case' to support it. Abbreviating the word staircase to just stair or stairs still carries that hidden acknowledgement that a clever carpenter defied gravity by getting it all together.

Outside, there are two kinds of step shapes. Sometimes they exist naturally, but more commonly they are man-made, by cutting chunks out of a cliff going down to a beach, or placing stones to create outdoor steps that lead grandly to the entrance of an imposing building. Those are certainly steps, and man-made, but they are supported by Mother Earth – and seldom if ever do they have a carpenter-built 'case' holding them together.

On the outside of some buildings there are exterior staircases, like fire escapes, and those of apartments in big blocks with different floors that might all open from the one stairway. But either inside or out, what we call a staircase, or just stairs, has a framework holding it together. What we frequently call steps are an arrangement we can walk up and down on, but generally speaking it is the planet itself taking the weight, and not a designed wood or concrete case.

But the words can be used in either sense – there's no rule.

Stakhanovite

The term Stakhanovite dates from 1935 when a Russian coal miner called Alexei Stakhanov produced more loads of coal than his fellow workers, by means of rationalisation. He so far exceeded the compulsory daily requirement that he was given a special reward. This began a system called Stakhanovism, which was the Soviet name for 'raising production by offering incentives to efficient and enthusiastic workers'.

The word crept into English to refer to an exceptionally hard-working person, whose dedication and productivity are beyond the norm.

–stan

The suffix –stan is derived from the Farsi word *ustan* or *istan*, meaning 'state' or 'country'. Many centuries ago the Persian Empire stretched over an enormous area, and its official language was Farsi. Established areas within the empire were known as a stan, meaning a state. The sense was roughly similar to that in which the word State is used in the US, where each state is an almost autonomous area, but still under the ultimate control of a federal government.

Eventually some of the Persian Empire's states became completely independent countries, but many of them retained the old Farsi word *stan* in their name, even when the people no longer spoke the language. Since then there has been a slight shift of emphasis in the meaning of the word, and stan has come to mean country, or the land of:

- Turkestan, land of the Turks
- Tadjikistan, the wreathed people's land (they wear turbans)
- Uzbekistan, land where the Uzbek language is spoken
- Afghanistan, land of Afghan, the legendary forefather of the Afghan people
- Baluchistan, the land of the Baluchs – the 'tufted-hair people'
- Kazakhstan, land of the Kazak (the 'free men')

○ Luristan (now part of Iran but still proudly known by its original name – land of the Lurs tribe).

Pakistan resulted from the partition of India. The new name of this country was first proposed in 1931 and established in 1947, although its precise meaning is not clear. The Urdu word *paki* can mean people pure in spirit. But the name is also believed to represent the initial letters of Muslim states – Punjab, Afghanistan, Kashmir, Iran – plus 'stan'.

Stiff cheese, hard cheese

It means you're having bad luck and is self-explanatory because the word 'stiff' is often used to describe working parts that aren't moving freely. And although cheese shouldn't actually move, neither should it be tough and unyielding. So cheese that is either stiff or hard isn't good enough, and you are unlucky to have been served it.

Sometimes the 'cheese' bit is left off, and if you have a misfortune someone might say, 'Gee that's stiff' – shorthand for stiff cheese.

(A) stitch in time saves nine

If a thread is loose, it is better to mend it straight away before the weakness allows other threads to become loose and serious repair is required. Such simple advice was being given in the 1700s and was published in Thomas Fuller's *Gnomologia, Adagies and Proverbs, Wise Sentences and Witty Sayings, Ancient and Modern, Foreign and British* in 1732 as: 'A Stitch in Time May save nine.'

Within just a few years, the application to sewing had extended as a metaphor into general advice about other forms of activity (as it still does) and the tentative 'may' had been edged out (as it still is). The new version was used by astronomer Francis Baily in 1797 about retaining a boat in the middle of a river:

> ... watching the moment she began to vary, and thereby verifying the vulgar proverb, 'A stitch in time saves nine.'

Why he called it vulgar is not quite clear, but it's lasted in that form for over two hundred years since. If you see something going wrong that you could fix up right now, then it's best to do something about it as soon as you notice it.

Stoned

The term is believed to have originated among jazz musicians and originally it was 'stoned out', meaning drunk. By the 1940s it had assumed a secondary meaning of being drugged, especially on marijuana which, unlike heavier drugs, leaves a person still able to talk and think and reason, albeit in a euphoric state.

History is silent about exactly why the word 'stoned' was used to describe this state. But it would be more than possible that the person in the drunk or drugged state was behaving as if they'd been hit over the head with a stone.

(The) straw that breaks the camel's back

The concept goes back 2000 years to the Spanish writer Seneca, and is about the last tiny amount of something which reduces a previous situation to ineffectiveness. By 1677 Archbishop Bramhall has adjusted this to 'the last feather which breaks the horse's back', and by the time it got to Dickens in *Dombey and Son*, it was the last straw breaking the camel's back.

Over time there have been variations, sometimes a reference to either a camel or a horse wearing shoes which hold them back. And the expression is often heard in abbreviation, as just 'the last straw'.

Strike

This is not a new phenomenon at all. There is information on record that builders on the tombs of the kings in ancient Egypt stopped work to re-negotiate, and this has been happening ever since.

The name for this kind of stopwork action comes from its use in a maritime context. For centuries the word 'strike' was used on sailing ships referring to the lowering (striking) of a vessel's sails so the ship couldn't move, and refusing to raise them until matters had been discussed. This was usually the first thing rebellious sailors did to assert their control over the ship.

The expression came to prominence on land in 1768, and since then has remained in use – a strike, to strike, going on strike – meaning work will cease until some agreement is reached.

There are substitute terms, 'work stoppage' or 'industrial dispute', but strike still holds its place. (Curiously, in theatre and TV the word retains its ancient use; 'strike the set' means to lower the scenery and/or move it out of the way.)

Stump up

Two expressions come from tree stumps, both of them American. In pioneer times people used to stand on the stump of a tree to speak at rural meetings and that custom is now applied to politicians making speeches while touring different areas and campaigning – they are 'on the stump' or 'stumping'. Now that their speeches have the advantages of PA systems, PowerPoint presentations, spotlighting and television coverage, standing on a tree stump no longer applies – but it's still called being 'on the stump' or 'stumping.'

To stump up has a slightly different meaning. It involves someone needing money, or being required to pay money owing, so a person is either paying a debt, or backing something financially. Either way, money has to change hands. And 'to stump up' recalls an earlier pioneer era when money might be slapped down onto a flat surface, like a tree stump.

Subfusc

This is heard in university life. *Fuscus* is Latin for dark and *sub* means below. Thus the English word subfusc means very dark indeed.

In some universities, 'subfusc' means academic dress, usually a capacious black gown. The word is quite common in those circles and even appears on invitations to indicate that academic gowns are to be worn.

Suffer fools gladly

The originating phrase that undoubtedly inspired this comes from the Bible, Corinthians II, Chapter 11, where you'll find the line 'For ye suffer fools gladly, seeing ye yourselves are wise.' It's fairly likely that over the years some assertive souls have pointed out that they do not wish to be included in that, and therefore have said, 'I do not suffer fools gladly.' They have dared to turn the Bible back to front.

Suffragettes

The words suffragette and suffragist have nothing to do with suffering. They come from the ancient Latin *suffragia* meaning broken pieces, usually crockery and pottery. Paper wasn't common in those times, so people voted by laying down a piece of broken pottery, *suffragium*, onto one named pile or another. Hence suffrage – the right to vote.

During the nineteenth century, some women had a parliamentary vote in the Isle of Man, and all women could vote on Pitcairn. New Zealand suffragists won their case in 1893 for parliamentary votes for all women, and Australian suffragists won Federal Parliament voting for all women in 1902.

The word 'suffragettes' was coined by London's *Daily Mail* to describe women campaigning for the vote in England, and the word attached itself to the history of female suffrage in some nations where it had not previously been used. The British suffragettes succeeded in 1928, gaining voting rights for all women on the same basis as men. American suffragists won full voting rights for all women in 1920.

Sugar daddy

This term was in use in the United States during the 1930s, and meant then what it means now: an older man who spends lavishly on a younger woman, in return for sexual favours. It may or may not be derived from an ancient usage of 'sugar' in Scotland to describe a dear old man. But wherever it came from, it seems to fit the situation.

One development is the term 'saccharin daddy', meaning a sugar daddy without the sex.

Sun over the yard arm

This goes back to the times of sailing ships. The yard is a long spar that supports and spreads the sails and the yard arm is one of those, tapered at the ends. An old naval expression had it that when the sun could be seen over the yard arm it was time for a drink.

Nowadays when people say this it has a connotation that the day is slowing down and evening is coming, but the reference can be somewhat elastic; by some people's reckoning, the sun would get 'over the yard arm' round about noon.

Sure as eggs

This popular phrase is both an abbreviation – and a mistake. It's a shortened form of 'sure as eggs is eggs'. The term has been in use since at least the mid-1800s: you'll find it in the operetta *Cox and Box* (1867) and later in Agatha Christie's *The Mysterious Affair at Styles* (1920).

But the expression actually comes from quite a different source which has nothing to do with eggs. It traces back to a mathematical statement that sounds similar: 'X is X', which means that X exists and is a certainty. Over time the saying X is X became corrupted to 'sure as eggs is eggs' (meaning the same thing – a certainty) and eventually to just sure as eggs.

Suss

It's a trendy abbreviation of 'suspect' or 'suspicion', and is very recent – mid-twentieth century. Over the last few years suss has broadened its meaning a little. Besides meaning to suspect, to sniff out or discover the truth, it now includes the meaning to surmise, to imagine what is likely.

And indeed it is very similar to another trendy modern word, 'recce', which is an abbreviation of reconnoitre, to have a good look at the territory.

Swansong

The swan figures in many legendary images. The Greek god Apollo was believed to have been changed into a swan and this gave rise to a long-held belief that, after death, the souls of all fine poets passed into the body of a swan, even Shakespeare – the Sweet Swan of Avon.

In Greek mythology the beautiful woman Leda was seduced by a male swan, who was actually Jupiter in disguise, and she laid eggs which resulted in four children, one of whom was the beautiful Helen of Troy. (Strangely, stories and movies about Helen of Troy never mention that she began life by breaking out of a swan's egg!)

Amidst this many-faceted fascination with the swan, intrigue developed because, unlike most other birds, the swan does not sing. (Though one kind, the whistling swan, does make a marginally musical sound.)

So someone came up with the weird belief that swans do sing, but only once in their lives, and most beautifully, just before they're about to die. Whoever that someone was, it was a long time ago because Plato was talking about it 300 years before the birth of Jesus. And a lot of other very eminent people talked about it too: Cicero, Seneca, Euripides and Aristotle among them. Some denied that it was true, but the legend continued to take hold.

Poet Edmund Spenser referred to it in the sixteenth century, and Shakespeare referred to it in *Othello* early in the seventeenth. The line between myth and legend was well and truly crossed – many people believed then, and somehow believe now, that a swan will sing only once, just before it dies.

In more recent times, the term has taken on a slightly different meaning, namely that someone is doing something for the last time – even if they have been quite good at it for years. We now use swansong not about someone whose life is coming to an end, but about someone whose effective working days are numbered, and their swansong could be their last great effort.

Let's leave the last word on this matter to poet Samuel Taylor Coleridge, who wrote in 1809:

Swans sing before they die – 'twere no bad thing
Did certain persons die before they sing.

Swear like a trooper

The expression arose in the eighteenth century when soldiers lived quite differently from their twenty-first century counterparts. Most eighteenth-century soldiers were not educated, their social position was more clearly defined (and was bound to be fairly low on the scale), and they were not the focus of vibrant television recruiting commercials and media interviews. The non-fighting behaviour of the eighteenth-century solider was less exposed to public scrutiny, and such soldiers swore a lot in their tough all-male environment.

In current times when the expression is used, it is usually said about someone who isn't a soldier, which carries a subtle connotation that though it's okay for soldiers to swear (and in all probability they still do), hearing it from someone else is unexpected – they are the ones earning disapproval, not the soldiers.

But the origin of the expression is easy to see: to swear like a trooper means to break into profanity as frequently and pungently as an eighteenth-century soldier.

Sweet Fanny Adams

Sweet Fanny Adams was a real person, but her connection with the expression is gruesome. Fanny Adams was a little girl in Hampshire, in England. In 1867 when she was eight years old, she was found brutally murdered in a hop field, with her body hideously dismembered and spread all over the place. The case was widely publicised (just as such cases are today), and everyone knew who sweet Fanny Adams was.

Round about the same time, the navy introduced a new kind of food on ships: tinned mutton. Rather callously, the sailors referred to this messy food as Sweet Fanny Adams because of its similarity to unidentifiable body parts. The use of the term became quite common and eventually came to mean something worthless or, later, nothing at all.

Then, during the twentieth century, military personnel further corrupted the image because the initials coincided with those of another vernacular phrase, sweet f*** all. There was no connection between the two expressions; they just happened to have the same initials.

This expression gradually became reduced to initials, sweet FA, or just SFA, which at least had the advantage of removing poor little Fanny Adams from the image.

Swells

There is sometimes confusion between swells and just big waves. Mariners don't always agree about what properly constitutes a swell, but do agree it is not to be confused with waves, which are a different matter altogether.

In general, a 'swell' is recognised to be a state caused by wind which generates heaving of the sea within a defined area, resulting in a group of waves that break only when they reach shallower water (hence surf). But until that point, the swell is mainly under the surface of the sea and may or may not be visible. One swell (singular) can be the cause of waves (plural).

A particular swell is formally designated by its height and the direction of the wind that produces it. It would be rare to find two different swells in one fairly small place (e.g. when a radio reporter says 'there are big swells in the harbour' he probably means there are big waves in the harbour, but caused by just one swell).

A basic rule for landlubbers could be: normally, waves (plural) are caused by just one swell (singular); so if you see waves, no matter how big, call them waves, not swells.

Sydney or the bush

The use in Australia is fairly straightforward, if you accept that the bush means anywhere distant from the mainstream, the 'mainstream' in this case being Sydney. It is sometimes used in a context where 'Sydney' means being a success and becoming financially comfortable, or finishing up in the 'bush', where a livelihood is in more straitened circumstances.

The expression has been used since the late nineteenth century, indicating that you have to make a choice about something: will you

S choose Sydney, or the bush? *An Economic History of Australia* uses the expression, explaining that it is something most Australians say when they're gambling with a decision.

Tack – as part of land

The word 'tack' has a very old meaning in Scotland and parts of north England. It comes from an even older word related to 'take.' The three main uses of this form of 'tack' are to do with land which is leased or rented:

1. The money paid for the leasing of land can be called 'the tack.'

2. The land being leased is sometimes called 'tack land.'

3. The time period of the lease can be referred to as 'a tack of . . .'

Tacky

For reasons so old that nobody can remember why, the word 'tacky' had long been used in a rural context to describe a broken-down horse. By the mid-1800s the description had widened its field to refer to anything else (besides horses) that was inferior, even shabby, including as well a connotation of the vulgar.

The term gradually came into wide use, its basic 'worthless horse' meaning believed to be influenced by the image of a common tack (as in tacked up, thumb-tack, carpet-tacks, tin-tacks) being at the very lowest order of fastening, and often implying an afterthought, that something isn't completely substantial (as in 'tacked on'). Add to that the mental image of glue that wasn't yet cured, and the combination of factors made 'tacky' into a useful wide-ranging description of something not worthy of respect – just like its siblings, tatty and/ or tawdry.

Tad

The word originated in the United States, first seen in 1915. It means something very small, and is believed to be derived from 'tadpole'. Over time, tadpole became shortened to tad, and no longer referred just to a small creature, but to a small amount of anything. 'Do you have milk in your tea?' 'Yes, but just a tad.'

Taking the piss

To make fun of and reduce pomposity by deflating a person's self-importance. The term arises from a very basic physical situation: when a person badly needs to go to the toilet, and then does so, they feel deflated – albeit willingly and pleasantly. But if fun is being made of someone considered to be pompous, then figuratively they are being dealt a similar feeling of being deflated – but unwillingly and less pleasantly.

'Taps'

Bugles or wind instruments have been used for military signals over many centuries. Horn calls were used during biblical times, during the Roman Empire and in practically every battle since. These various calls and signals customarily include one that marks the end of the day – either the day's fighting, or the end of recreation after the fighting.

The British military has signalled the end of the day with a bugle tune called 'The Last Post' since the nineteenth century and still does (and it is often played at funerals).

American military had a slightly different set of calls, and up until 1862 they customarily used a French tune to end the day. It was called, in rough translation, 'Put out the fires'. Americans referred to this tune by the word 'Taps', actually a shortened version of the Dutch word *taptoe*, which signalled the closing off of barrels of beer because the soldiers had to stop relaxing and return to the garrison.

(That Dutch word *taptoe* eventually became what we call a 'tattoo' – a ceremonial return to barracks. See **Tattoo**.)

In 1862 General Daniel Butterfield decided that the usual tattoo or Taps bugle call was too formal. Calling in a bugler named Oliver Norton, he hummed bits and pieces of bugle calls he knew and between them they cobbled together an entirely new tune. Butterfield could neither read nor write music, but he was an experienced military man; he knew all the signals well and he was able to dictate what he wanted. The tune they devised was used that night. It never had a name – it was simply called Taps, and it was so effective that it quickly spread throughout the Civil War and was officially adopted by the United States Army in 1874. Because of the way the tune goes, the soldiers began to call it the Go-to-sleep call, or the Put-out-lights call. Six different versions of words have been written to the tune.

The British concept of Scouting became very strong in the United States and the American Taps song gravitated towards the American Scout movement.

A word of caution: people sometimes think the British Last Post bugle call and the American Taps are the same thing. Not so. There is a similarity in the tune, but they are entirely different pieces of music with different histories.

(Edinburgh) Tattoo

This has nothing to do with the word 'tattoo' meaning a design engraved on the body; that is a Tahitian word which Captain Cook came across in the eighteenth century and took back to England, where it has become the accepted word for a design put into the skin with indelible dyes.

The military word tattoo entered the English language a century before Captain Cook sailed the Pacific, and although it is pronounced and written the same way, it has an entirely different meaning and ancestry. A military tattoo is the signal that it is time for soldiers to return to their barracks – the music of drums and fifes tells them their leave is up. This ritual and its music eventually evolved into a large military ceremony called a tattoo.

During the seventeenth century, the drums and fifes players went out into the villages to play the music recalling the soldiers, and the men would leave their socialising and their village friends, to fall in and march behind the musicians. Naturally the villagers gathered to watch.

When this happened in Holland, the innkeepers would call *taptoe*, which roughly means 'Close down the barrels', so the beer stopped flowing and no grog was sold while the troops marched out of town. In time, the ancient Dutch phrase filtered across to England (not many kilometres away) where it gradually became 'tattoo', and the instruction to stop selling grog became the name of the military ceremony itself.

Tatty

This one-word description of something being worn out, shabby, unkempt, and of poor quality is close relative of the word 'tattered.' Dating from the ancient German word *zæter*, meaning 'rag', English and Scottish versions can be found from the 1400s onwards, generally referring to 'something matted, or torn loose and hanging'. During the 1930s this developed into the modern put-down 'tatty', which means something either does not please the sensitivities of the observer, or is noticeably past its use-by date.

Tawdry

In the year 640 there was a British princess named Ethel-dreda who married Prince Tonbert when she was still young. It was not a happy union, and Ethel-dreda retained her virginity throughout the marriage. When Prince Tonbert died, Ethel-dreda, popularly known as Audrey, was pressured for political reasons into a second marriage to the King of Northumbria. But again, she declined conjugal rights and the marriage was dissolved. Audrey became a nun and founded a monastery, which formed the basis of the magnificent Ely Cathedral.

Audrey had lived a life of penance, austerity and prayer, and became a saint – she is the patron saint of Cambridge University. For centuries, the people of Ely held a fair on St Audrey's day (23 June), and because Audrey in her youth had liked necklaces and fancy things, many stalls sold lace and homemade jewellery, and travelling peddlers sold little gimmicks, often of shoddy workmanship.

Hence, things which were not well crafted became referred to as 'St Audrey', as if they had come from that fair. And over time, the name St Audrey became shortened to 'tawdry'.

Teach your grandmother to suck eggs

The ancestor of the expression is found in the works of the Dutch scholar Erasmus, writing in the 1500s. The expression was translated into English but over the centuries it has gone through various forms: 'teach an old dame to spin', 'teach your grandmother to grope ducks', or the version that probably led to the eggs: 'teach your grandmother to sup sour milk'. It had certainly become eggs by 1749 when it appeared in Henry Fielding's famous novel *Tom Jones*.

The expression is intended to mean: Don't tell someone how to do something they already know how to do.

Teenager

The basis of 'teenager' is the much older word teen, which is not an abbreviation; it is in fact the origin. Arising in Britain from a variation of 'ten', the word teen was being used to refer to English adolescents in the sixteenth century and can be found in Wycherley's *Gentleman Dancing Master* in 1673: 'Poor young things, when they are once in the teens, think they shall never be married.'

And gospel minster Isaac Taylor in London published *Advice to the Teens* in 1818.

The word later moved to America, and in 1919 Carl Ed began his comic strip about adolescence, 'Teen', which was twice made into a movie – in 1928 and 1934. So the word teen was around very early, and then started to go through further stages.

In 1921 the Canadian *Daily Colonist* mentioned 'teen age girls' – two words, but soon the two words became hyphenated; in 1937 *Time* wrote about 'the concern of German parents for keeping their teen-age son or daughter out of one of the Hitler camps for young people'. The hyphen remained through the 1940s and teen-ager became a universally known term. But over the next couple of decades the hyphen was gradually dropped.

By 1960 British writer Kingsley Amis (in *Take a Girl Like You*) wrote of Jenny: 'Instead of having been a teenager all she had managed to do was spend a certain amount of time getting from the age of twelve to the age of twenty.' Teenager – minus the hyphen – became the norm.

By a strange reversal of history, America then reverted to the ancient British word teen – before marketing came up with 'sub-teen', 'tweenies' and various other eye-catching variations.

Tell the truth and shame the devil

It has long been believed that the devil enjoys deceit and lies. Therefore, if there is a temptation to tell a lie – choose instead to tell the truth, for the devil doesn't like truths and will be displeased and shamed.

In 1548 the saying appeared in W. Patten's *Expedition into Scotland* in a context which suggests it was already well known then. Later, in Shakespeare's *Henry IV* Part 1 (1597), Hotspur says: 'And I can teach thee coz, to shame the devil by telling truth.' Ben Jonson and John Fletcher both used the term later that century. In over 400 years the expression seems to have changed little.

(Lead us not into) temptation

It worries some people that this implies the Lord intends to lead us into temptation, and is being asked not to. It is the problem of translation. The Lord's Prayer has its basis in ancient Jewish prayers, and scholars believe Jesus would have been familiar with the Hebrew versions. Jesus is reported to have taught his version to his disciples, and the text which later became familiar to English speakers came through biblical Aramaic and Greek before it came into English.

There have been difficulties with the translations all along; for instance, with the word 'bread'. The word originally used was one that might not have meant what we call bread at all. A number of scholars have studied the texts and made various alterations over several hundred years.

In the mid-1970s an interdenominational Christian group called the International Consultation on English Texts proposed some preferred reassignments in the English text of the Lord's Prayer that had been in use for some time. One of the lines they had concerns about was 'Lead us not into temptation', which is 'an inverted negative with ellipsis in the second person imperative case' – in other words, it's saying 'Do not lead us into temptation', thus clearly suggesting that the Lord might do so.

The Anglican church accepted the proposal of a slightly different translation in 1977 and the Catholic church has also made a slight variation along the suggested lines, so nowadays it seems to be generally agreed among the major Christian groups that it is acceptable to say: 'Do not bring us to the time of trial,' or 'Save us from the time of trial.'

And that, it is to be hoped, negates the impression given by the former English version of the Greek version of Jesus' Aramaic version of the ancient Hebrew prayer – that the Lord would deliberately tempt people.

Terrorist

The word is originally French and has been in use since the late 1700s. During the French Revolution in 1789 there were people who believed that violence and bloodshed were necessary methods for propagating their own principles of political supremacy. They were referred to as *terroristes*.

Over 200 years later, the meaning hasn't changed much, but the weapons of warfare have advanced considerably. The word means the same as it did in the eighteenth century, but terrorism in the twenty-first century brings much greater violence to far more people in a much shorter time.

Terrorism is perceived by some as using and favouring violent and intimidating methods in order to coerce a government or community. The reason for saying that is how 'some' perceive it, is that a definition of terrorism depends which side you're on – an event interpreted by the people it affects as severe coercion and terrorism, could probably be described by its instigators as a liberating blow for freedom.

Testimony, testify, testicle

They all mean the same thing: some form of witness. *Testis* is the Latin word for witness, meaning making a statement, and various grammatical forms of the word mean various related things: *testificari* survives as testimony, the giving of information sworn to be true, and *testicularis* survives in English as testicle, which was seen by the ancient Romans as being witness to, or a statement of, virility and masculinity.

There is reason to believe that in some ancient civilisations, when young men applied to graduate into full citizenship, they were obliged to give testimony to the city council that they were adult, which actually meant showing their testicles in order to prove that they were fully grown and were not eunuchs or women in disguise. So in the original Latin, giving testimony actually means showing the testicles and allowing them to be examined.

Third World

There was, and still is, only one world (as far as we know). But in April 1952 French historian Alfred Sauvy started the expression Third World, setting it on a comparable basis to the expression Third Estate at the time of the French Revolution: 'At the end, this ignored, exploited, scorned Third World, like the Third Estate, wants to become something too.'

Three years later, in 1955, there was a conference in Indonesia involving 1000 representatives of 50 states. During that conference, the French diplomat Georges Balandier referred specifically to the 29 African and Asian nations as the Third World. The term was reported, it quickly took on and has since broadened in meaning to include any underdeveloped nations. At that time the 'numbered worlds' were understood to be:

- First World   the 'Western bloc' of democratic fully developed countries
- Second World   the Communist bloc
- Third World   the 'developing' countries
- Fourth World   countries capable of development but which have not yet begun to develop
- Fifth World   countries for which there is little hope.

The term 'developing countries' is seen as a more polite way of saying undeveloped countries. These are perceived as: countries with insufficient agricultural and industrial productive capacity to generate the savings required to sustain investment and economic growth. Common features include dependence on the export of primary products, widespread poverty and disease, and illiteracy.

(Give) three cheers and one cheer more

Many people know the line only from the Gilbert and Sullivan opera *HMS Pinafore*: 'Give three cheers and one cheer more, for the well-bred captain of the *Pinafore*.' But W.S. Gilbert did not invent it.

It's somewhat deceiving. Because a naval captain in that opera is cheered, we think it's a naval custom. But in fact the research library of the Royal Navy says that although the practice did exist, there is no record of it being a specifically naval custom; it crops up in various places to indicate a very special occasion, sometimes involving the navy, sometimes not.

The custom of giving three cheers plus one cheer more goes much further back than Gilbert and Sullivan; there are records of its being a yacht club ritual well over 100 years before when, say, an admiral and a captain were at the same ceremony and three cheers would be given for the admiral, who acknowledged this, and then one cheer more for the captain. And the pattern is sometimes followed when ships pass each other at sea – each ship gives three long toots on the whistle, followed by one short toot.

You'll find it in Chapter 13 of Dickens' *The Pickwick Papers* where it occurs as a special amplification of a joyous occasion – and that was 41 years before *HMS Pinafore*. Dickens, like Gilbert, uses it in a rather comic, non-military way.

Three wise monkeys

The concept of three wise creatures who see no evil, hear no evil and speak no evil may have existed in China as far back as the fifth century BC, long before it became popular in Japan. So the basic idea could have been around for over 2000 years, reminding us that evil is a matter of choice.

But the actual image we have in modern times, of three monkeys shielding their eyes, lips and ears from evil, definitely originates from seventeenth-century Japan. The earliest known depiction of the celebrated trio is to be found on the walls of the magnificent Toshogu shrine in the little town of Nikko, and it's still there – on the walls of the stable, which houses the temple's sacred horses. Why on the stable walls? Japanese people believe that monkeys are always friends to horses, keeping them free from illness and providing them with amiable company.

The Toshogu shrine was finished in 1636, and the popularity of the picture of three wise monkeys gradually spread around the world. By the end of the nineteenth century they had become an established image in Western decor.

But since monkeys are more famous for being mischievous and full of devilry, why then does the old legend describe these three as wise? The Japanese say that it is a trick of the language. The motto 'See no evil, hear no evil, speak no evil' has existed in Japan for hundreds of years. But the Japanese language has a certain way of making a verb negative: they add the word *zaru*, and when this is added to a word like, say, 'run' you end up with the equivalent of 'run-not'. So in the motto it is, see-not evil, hear-not evil, speak-not evil.

The Japanese word for monkey is *saru*, so some scholars believe that, over the centuries of saying the motto, the word *saru* became associated in people's minds with the word *zaru* in the motto. Hence, in time, the instruction 'See-not evil' took on the added meaning that monkeys exemplified the saying. And that had happened by the time the famous carving was done in 1636.

By now, literally hundreds of thousands of versions of the three wise monkeys exist, in every conceivable substance: miniatures made in gold and set with jewels, shelf-size in brass right up to life-size wise monkeys of concrete for garden decoration. They can be found made of porcelain, alabaster, plaster of paris, wood, bronze, nickel and pewter. They adorn door knockers, cigarette boxes, bookends, paperweights, wine bottles and toasting forks. The three wise monkeys are everywhere.

Thrilled to bits

It's an old expression in English, sometimes heard in such variations as 'to fall to bits', where 'to bits' means 'completely apart'.

This word 'bit' comes from the Old English word *bite*, meaning a piece small enough to be torn off with the teeth. So, to be completely pedantic, the expression once meant to be so thrilled that one had fallen apart into little bites.

Throw the book at

It originated around the court of law – not in the court. The expression isn't very old; it was seen in print in 1932 and in those days it still had connotations of actual law. The 'book' was the register of all acts deemed to be criminal and the punishments for them, so to say 'throw the book at' someone meant to file all criminal charges that were possible in a particular circumstance.

Nowadays it has broadened a bit: it still means that a set of regulations will be invoked, but not necessarily criminal charges.

Throw your hat in the ring

It means a willingness to do something probably daunting. In the days when boxing matches were rather less organised than they are now, pre-Mike Tyson and global telecasts, a freelance boxer would stand in the ring and issue a challenge. Then whoever was inclined to accept the challenge threw their hat into the ring.

The phrase came into the language about 1820, meaning to put yourself forward for a job or a responsibility. When he was running for President in 1912, Theodore Roosevelt used the expression publicly: 'My hat's in the ring, the fight is on and I'm stripped to the buff.'

Tiger for punishment

The expression's ancestor was 'a tiger for work', originally from Britain; Clement Scott's *Dramas of Yesterday and Today* mentions it being used in London during the 1840s. By 1896 the expression was in use in Australia, where there are no actual tigers but the beast is a legendary image of power and energy and fitness.

Over time the tiger comparison came to be applied to other matters besides work (a 'tiger for his food') and slowly moved to 'a tiger for punishment'. This had a two-edged meaning: either that the person was energetic and willing, like the original 'tiger for work'; or that they were unable to learn from an earlier mistake and went back again to a situation where they knew they'd come off second best. 'Tiger' is sometimes replaced by 'glutton' as in 'glutton for punishment'.

Tigris River

Iraq and its surrounding territories were once known as Mesopotamia, reputedly the home of the biblical Garden of Eden.

The languages of the area are thousands of years old, and the original name of the Tigris had nothing to do with tigers. The early name of the river *Idiglat* (meaning 'a swift flowing river') is believed to come from the ancient language of Akkadian, 3000 years BC.

In ancient Hebrew it was referred to as *Hiddekel*, but the Greeks referred to it with a name from their own language – *Tigris*. In this context, the word meant 'swift', retaining at least in part the river's ancient original name.

The river is nowadays generally known by that Greek name Tigris; the same word passed through later centuries and various language shifts to eventually become attached to the swift creature now known as a tiger.

Time immemorial

People don't usually have an exact date in mind when they say 'time immemorial', but there was once a definite time-span.

It was originally a legal term, defined in British law by a statute of Westminster in the year 1275. The law-makers decided to fix a time limit for the bringing of certain legal actions, and that time limit was to be the reign of King Richard I. Anything which happened before then was said to have happened beyond legal memory – or in 'time immemorial'.

Richard I became king in 1189, so if you wanted to bring a legal action about something, it had to have happened since that date.

Over the centuries, the legal aspect has faded away and the meaning has expanded somewhat so that when people say 'since time immemorial' they mean that something has been in existence for a very long time.

Tin-canning

This was sometimes called tin-kettling, and was a common ritual well into the twentieth century, particularly in rural districts.

The tin-canning happened sometime after a young couple married. If they went to their house to begin married life straight away, friends and neighbours gathered late at night, carrying buckets and baby baths and tins filled with stones and sticks to hit things with. They made a great deal of loud noise, marching in circles around the house if that was possible. Or if the couple went away on a honeymoon, the noisy visit would happen on the first night they came back.

Villagers gathering together and bashing tins is a very old British custom but it originally signified extreme disapproval. If someone in the village had done something unkind but not illegal – if, say, a wife or husband was known to be unfaithful – the neighbours would have no hesitation in gathering round the house at night and making a noise to express their displeasure. It is the origin of the expression ran-tan, which was originally ran-dan and meant everyone gathering together and making a big noise in order to humiliate a person who couldn't be legally charged with a crime.

From Britain to the South Pacific, the mechanics of the tin-canning ritual remained exactly the same as they had been for centuries, but the intent became reversed. In a weird kind of way the tin-canning was intended as a welcoming gesture, an expression of goodwill.

But the ritual was not always popular with everyone – a letter to the *Brisbane Courier* in 1870 was less than enthusiastic, and refers to:

> ... a great nuisance that residents in any but the principal streets of this town are exposed to. I allude to the barbarous practice that is so general, of rattling tin cans before the house where a wedding takes place. This relic of the dark ages should be put a stop to; for not only is the annoyance felt by those for whose especial benefit or otherwise the noise is made, but also by all within a considerable radius of the house. And it is not only the noise of the tin cans that I have

to complain of, but also the fearfully obscene and blackguard language that is used by those who indulge in the 'fun', as they call it. Only last Sunday night a group made the night hideous till past 10 o'clock, and, in spite of the repeated efforts of several men, they persisted in keeping up the annoyance, using foul and blasphemous language ...

See also **Going on the ran-tan**.

Tinker's dam

In this context, 'dam' means a structure to hold something back, possibly from the old-time tinkers' (metalworkers) trick of using a ball of bread dough to plug a hole while they soldered it from the other side, creating a miniature dam. When the soldering was complete, the bread was useless, not worth keeping – so not to 'give a tinker's dam' meant not to care.

It's also possible that confusion over the word 'dam' has led to a drift towards saying 'not worth a tinker's curse', but it really meant dam as in a river dam, and not damn – as in damnation.

Tissue of lies

The word tissue comes from Latin *texere*, meaning 'to weave'. In earlier times it was used to describe thick, luxurious fabrics, though nowadays it has evolved more towards a thin, delicate fabric, or even a thin substance that isn't actually woven at all, like tissue paper.

But the earlier image of weaving survives in the expression 'tissue of lies', in which tissue means a woven fabric intertwining several different threads. The implication is that one falsehood invariably leads to another and a web of deception results.

Tit for tat

A form of this expression, meaning retaliation, has been used in English for centuries. Before the sixteenth century people said 'tip for tap', possibly derived from Dutch *dit voor dat*, meaning 'this for that', which itself derives from Latin *quid pro quo*. After the mid-

1500s the expression subtly changed to 'tit for tat', and became part of Cockney rhyming slang: 'titfer' = 'tit for tat' = 'hat'.

Titles

If Mr John Smith becomes Sir John Smith, his legal wife can quite correctly choose to be called Lady Smith, if she consistently uses her husband's surname. There is no legal requirement for a married woman to use her husband's surname; it is only a social custom. Mr John Smith can quite legally be married to Ms Joan Wilson.

But if John Smith becomes Sir John and his legal wife has always been called Ms Joan Wilson, then she cannot be called Lady Wilson. Nor can she use any title at all if the pair are long-time partners but not actually married. A woman shares her husband's title only if she legally shares his surname (only a duke's or an earl's daughter has the word 'Lady' in front of her first name).

If a titled man and his wife divorce, the divorced wife still retains the title as long as she still carries her ex-husband's surname. If the titled man then marries someone else, the new wife would automatically share her husband's title if she takes his surname. So if Sir John and Lady Smith divorced, and he remarried but the former Lady Smith didn't, then Sir John's new wife would be Lady Smith and his ex-wife would still also be Lady Smith – until she married Mr Brown, when she would immediately cease to be Lady Smith and become just Mrs Brown.

This can happen at quite a high level – there once were two Duchesses of Westminster, and two Duchesses of Marlborough.

Curiously, if a man has a title he always shares it with his legal wife, whereas if a woman has a title of her own (such as Dame, Lady, Princess) she never shares it with her legal husband.

This applies even to the Queen. Her father was a king, and he shared the title with his wife, who was called Queen Elizabeth, and was addressed as Your Majesty. But Prince Philip, although married to a Queen, is not called King and is not addressed as Your Majesty.

A woman with her own title on her first name can change her surname as often as she likes, but she still keeps the title on her first name. For example, Dame Zara Holt remarried and became Dame Zara Bates, and Princess Anne has had two husbands, but she still remains Princess Anne. Diana, on the other hand, was only a princess by marriage: the title was attached to her even in divorce, but only so long as she retained the surname of Windsor. Ditto the Duchess of York who remains a Duchess and a Princess (as still sharing Prince Andrew's surname), but if she remarries, she loses all that and becomes just Ms Sarah Ferguson – or Mrs Newhusband.

Tittle

The term comes from printers, as early as the 1600s, and possibly before. It can be seen in the King James Version of the Book of Matthew, 5:18.

In printing, a tittle refers to a tiny piece of print like the dot over the letter 'I' and the little additions that are made to the tops and bottoms of some letters to influence their pronunciation (as in Spanish). These are also sometimes called diacritics.

'Tittle' was sometimes used by people who wanted to compare a situation with something detailed and exact. There's a line from a Beaumont and Fletcher play: 'I'll quote him to a tittle,' meaning that everything will be exact, every tiny dot in place. In this age of electronic printing, it has come to mean a very small amount.

See also **Jot** and **To a T**.

Toadstools

Quite simply, toadstools have long been regarded as little stools for toads to sit on; mushrooms are unsuitable because toads are sometimes poisonous, and likewise toadstools. So an association grew between toads and the fungus named after them.

There is another theory: that toadstool is a German word, because toadstools are usually perceived as poisonous and the German word is *Todes-stuhl* – 'the chair of death'.

(Drink a) toast

The custom of taking a sip of drink to salute someone originates in ancient Greece, during the sixth century BC when political poisoning was not unknown, especially via decanters of wine. To demonstrate integrity to guests, a host would always sip the first wine poured from the decanter, and the others then knew it was safe to follow suit. This gradually developed into a practice of acknowledging the first drink taken as a sign of friendship or acknowledgement.

The ancient Romans developed a new twist: they added a piece of burnt bread to the glasses of wine. Winemaking wasn't so sophisticated in those days and it was believed that a tiny quantity of charcoal (as in burnt bread) actually reduced the acidity in wines. The Latin for 'parched' or 'roasted' is *tostus*, hence our word 'toast'.

Over hundreds of years, the two customs blended into a single concept: the Greek custom of drinking to salute a person; and the Roman habit of dunking a piece of toast into wine.

To a T

The most widely believed explanation is that the expression comes from the T-square used by architects and draughtsmen. This is used to draw absolutely accurate angles, parallels etc. and so the connotation has carried over to other areas: 'to a T' means 'as if drawn with a T-square', therefore exact.

This explanation has been disputed on the grounds that the expression is in fact older than the term T-square and comes from the expanded saying 'to a tittle'. A tittle is a tiny stroke in printing (see **Tittle**) and saying 'to a tittle' meant that standards of exactness were being applied. Over time the saying became abbreviated: 'to a T'.

Togs

Quite simply, 'togs' is descended directly from the ancient Roman word toga, which itself comes from a Latin word *tegere*, meaning to cover. The word has migrated into English as togs, meaning clothes, and also as a verb, as in 'all togged up' meaning wearing full and elaborate clothing.

But the noun 'togs' survives mainly to describe swimwear; it is simply a modern version of toga.

Tommy Atkins

He was not a real person. The name comes from a document given out to all people who enlisted in the British Army from around 1815. The recruits were given an introductory booklet containing several forms to be filled in.

To clarify how the forms were to be filled in, there was a sample copy already completed. The sample document had the invented name in the space after 'Recruit's name'. The name Tommy Atkins quickly came to apply to all British soldiers, and was often shortened to just 'Tommy'.

This is somewhat reminiscent of a British rock group whose members had had some bad patches on the dole; when they formed a band they named it after the number on the top of the official government unemployment register form – UB40.

See also **Joe Bloggs** and **John Doe**.

Tom Pepper

'He tells more lies than Tom Pepper…' But Tom Pepper never did exist. The expression is an old nautical saying referring to a mythical character that sailors used to say was kicked out of hell because he told so many lies.

This piece of folklore has been around at least since the middle of the nineteenth century, but isn't often heard, so you can assume that anyone who says it probably has a nautical background or had a father or grandfather who did.

The expression doesn't really make sense. One would think that telling lies was a recommendation for staying in hell but, according to legend, Tom Pepper was thrown out.

(Go to the) ton

A real ton used to be a common measure of weight and it became a slang expression meaning 100. The most common use of this expression was in motorcycle racing, where doing a ton meant going at 100 mph, which was considered an ultimate test for both the machine and the rider. This gave rise to a slang description of young

382

people who rode motor bikes too fast in general: they were called 'ton-up kids'.

The term ton is also used in darts and cricket to indicate 100, and in underworld slang it used to mean £100.

Toodle-pip

There have been several variations on this way of saying goodbye: toodle-oo, tooraloo, tottle-oo, tootle-pip and just toodle by itself. There are two explanations, one rather more believable than the other.

Some scholars have a theory that toodle-oo is an English imitation of the French goodbye phrase *à tout à l'heure*, meaning 'see you later'. But there is no solid evidence for that. The other explanation is based around the Old English word toddle. In the eighteenth century, the word meant stroll away, leave. Nowadays we use it mainly to describe a baby learning to walk, but the old meaning of walking away occasionally still survives; you might hear someone say, 'I must toddle now.'

The development from toddle into toodle-oo or tootle-oo was just a sort of comic extension. From there toodle-pip or tootle-pip developed more recently, with the suffix 'pip' borrowed from the radio signal announcing the hour.

'Too late,' she cried, and waved her wooden leg

This is a strange one and its origins are murky. There are numerous variations on the 'Too late, too late' part, and the full expression appears to be a combination of two different phrases which have somehow become joined up.

Among the many versions of 'Too late, too late', one was widely known in the military – a joke about a man who fell into a sea full of sharks. He called for help but before assistance could reach him the sharks attacked and had damaged him below the waterline, so that when help did arrive, he called out, 'Too late, too late' in a very high voice. You sometimes still hear that phrase just on its own, said in a falsetto voice.

Then after the First World War girls started going to public dances uncchaperoned, just turning up at such events in groups. If a fellow was clumsy, or for some other reason not a desirable dance partner, the word would go round very quickly; apparently a catchphrase developed that when a man asked a girl to dance and she didn't want to, instead of saying 'no', she would say, 'I'm sorry, but I've got a wooden leg.'

Somehow, the 'Too late, too late' phrase (either the shark-bite, or one of the many other versions) joined up with the 'wooden leg', and a new expression developed: ' "Too late," she cried, and waved her wooden leg.'

Tot

Little children have been referred to as tots since the early 1700s. There are two separate versions of the word tot: as the verb 'to tot' (meaning to determine a sum, to 'tot up' a bill – short for 'total'); and as a noun, usually meaning something small.

This latter usage came into English from Denmark. In ancient Greek, *tutthos* meant 'very small and young'. This drifted into Old German as *tutta*, meaning a nipple, and that word moved into ancient Scandinavian as *tuttr*, meaning a dwarf or small person. *Tuttr* developed in Swedish into *tutte* – an affectionate term for a little child – and in Danish that became *tommeltot*.

That in turn drifted into English as tot, meaning a small child, or a small amount of something (besides a small child, it can also mean a small measure of spirits, such as a tot of rum).

Touch wood

This goes back to very early times when it was believed that a lot of objects in nature had supernatural powers and were inhabited by spirits. Many trees were believed to have sacred significance and some in particular were thought to possess the power of protection, for example the oak, the ash, the hazel and the willow. So, in order to make sure something good happened, and to avert bad luck, people would appeal to one of these trees and the spirits in them – or better still, hug the tree.

Over centuries, the actual focus on specific trees for specific things has faded away, and the hugging has been reduced; however, its legacy remains very firmly in our culture, because when people want to avert bad luck, they often say 'touch wood' (or 'knock on wood' in the United States). Sometimes, in this age of plastics and formica, you'll see people desperately looking around the room for something made of genuine wood.

There is also a connection with touching a copy of the cross on which Jesus died: touching wood somehow symbolised your connection with this icon, thus showing your own willingness to be a good person, and bringing good things to you. This is another example of Christianity attaching significance to an existing belief. The concept of trees having a benign spirit is much older, so 'touching wood' was firmly established long before the time of Jesus.

Trafalgar

Although strongly identified with a famous part of London, Trafalgar isn't an English word. All the places in London named for it commemorate the battle which took place in 1805 near the south coast of Spain in waters off a headland called Trafalgar Cape.

Its name and the exact Arabic derivation are lost in antiquity. There are two schools of thought about the Arabic origin. In Arabic, *tarf* means sand or earth and *el garb* means the west, so a sandy point to the west could be tarf-el-garb. But it is also believed that particular cape may possibly have been the site of one of the legendary pillars of Hercules, in which case the name might have been *taraf-al-aghar*, the pillar from the cave.

Tragedy

The word tragedy came into English from the Greek *tragos*, meaning he-goat, plus *idia* meaning song: thus, *trago-idia* – the song of the goat. The origin of this somewhat unexpected connection is so many centuries old that there has never been a 100 per cent reliable explanation of the relationship between billy goats, songs and tragedy, though scholars down the ages have tried to find plausible reasons.

Every search dates back to the festivals of Greek plays put on in honour of Dionysus (the Greek god of wine, fruitfulness and vegetation), in which there would also be a prize for the best play. There is a strong association between these festival plays and goats, on several levels. Plays frequently featured the evil doings of satyrs, and to play that part actors would dress in goat skins.

Sometimes the prize for the best play presented was a goat – rather like winning a pig or hen at a country fair. And whatever the prize, or whatever the play was about, a goat was normally sacrificed in the name of Dionysus, the performance coming on the heels of the sacrifice.

Over time these festival plays fell into the pattern of telling unhappy stories, and the sad plays somehow acquired the name *trago-idia*, the song of the goats – a story of pity and fear leading to a catharsis and death, bringing a sense of closure to those watching.

(The goat turns up in another rather unexpected place; antique furniture often has legs which curve outward then narrow down to an ornamental foot. These are called 'cabriole' legs, from the French *cabrioler* – 'to leap like a goat', from the Latin *caper*, meaning goat.)

Tranklements

This is an English dialect word that is quite well known in the area from which it comes – the Black Country, roughly between Birmingham and Wolverhampton. People from that district are well acquainted with tranklements, which simply means small possessions, ornaments and things found at jumble sales.

The British Library has placed tranklements in a 'word bank' of regional dialect words that are seldom heard outside their home locality. In spite of its narrow range, it has been adopted by an Irish band calling itself The Tranklements, possibly just because it's an attractive sounding word.

See also **Bric-a-brac**.

Tripe

This is spoken to express disgust, or to mean useless talk. The connection between actual tripe, and something needing to be described as off-putting, is not difficult to grasp on the part of those who don't like tripe.

The word tripe has been in the English language for over 600 years, meaning the lining of an animal's stomach cavity – and if you see it in its raw state, it is distinctly unattractive. Even after it has been cleaned and dressed it is still not entirely appealing.

The eating of tripe may well have arisen among people at what is called 'the lower socio-economic level' where every part of a beast was used because they couldn't afford to waste anything. Nowadays the world is fairly clearly divided into those who really like tripe, and those who can't stand the thought or sight of it.

But although the eating of tripe has a long history, describing something you don't agree with as tripe is not a very old expression. Cricketers have used the expression since about 1920 to mean easy bowling, and they seem to have borrowed that from the military, which had been using the word for a century to describe anything dirty – probably because tripe in its raw state is very dirty indeed. And they would also say that if someone was in trouble, they were in tripe; being surrounded by tripe would undoubtedly be an unpleasant situation.

Round about the same time, tripe became attached to the word 'hound', and a tripe-hound was a low, disgusting fellow. Fairly early in the twentieth century this expression was transferred to newspaper reporters. Gradually though, the term moved away from journalists to sheepdogs, and then to just any old dog at all.

But there could be significance in the fact that it was a slang term meaning newspaper reporters because, by a slight shift in perception, it didn't necessarily mean that they wrote material that was dirty and filthy, but that a lot of what was written and reported was useless and boring. Hence a badly written book would be sheer tripe, a speech could be all tripe, and so on.

Trollop

The two theories about this word are closely related to each other, and they both relate to words that came into the English language from German over 300 years ago.

The German word *trollen* means to wander, and two common English words are descended from it: stroll (meaning to amble about) and trolley (which rumbles along but has no driving force).

That particular German word may also have become shortened in English to 'troll', which is now a real English word with two separate meanings: to draw a fishing line through the water; or to wander the streets, possibly looking for sexual adventure. There's an obvious similarity between that second meaning of troll and trollop, but they're not necessarily from the same source.

There was also once a very old German dialect word *trull*, which meant a prostitute. That German word also migrated into English in the 1600s, and changed its spelling to become troll. This was often used to describe something hanging loosely, like baggy clothes. So a word used to describe a woman whose clothes were ill-fitting and haphazard may have extended into meaning a woman whose morals were also loose, *trull* becoming troll, and then trollop. Nobody is sure.

The male equivalents of trollop are: rake, roué, libertine, lecher, Don Juan, Romeo, philanderer, ladykiller, seducer, Lothario, bed-hopper and the more recent favourite, stud.

One essential point is that the famous novelist Anthony Trollope (whose name has an e) has nothing to do with trollops. That surname comes from Troughburn, an ancient settlement in Northumberland, which in even older times (1450) had a Norse name *Trolhop*, meaning Troll Valley and referring to the mythical giant cave-dwelling creatures that turned to stone if exposed to sunlight – a convenient name for an area showing stone outcrops.

Trug/truck

The word 'trug' has had two meanings in English: it is the rather pleasant name for a flat gardening basket, but in the seventeenth century it was also the slang word for prostitute, and the terms 'trugging' or 'trug-house' were not used in polite society. Gardeners will be pleased that this meaning has vanished.

According to scholars the English word trug is closely related to the old German word *Trog*, which also gives us the English word

trough. But there is no connection between trug/trough and truck.
Truck comes from old Anglo-Norman, originally Latin *troclea*. The
modern word truck is a shortened version of truckle.

There are many meanings for the words truck and truckle, but
they nearly always have something to do with movement: bits of
boats are called trucks; theatre and TV scenery is built on wheeled
platforms known as trucks; and beds that can be rolled are called
truckle beds.

As a verb, 'to truck' can mean things moving from one ownership
to another, and it can also mean to barter and have business dealings.
You will hear that use in: 'I will have no truck with him' – I won't
have any association or business dealings with him.

But another very old meaning of truck is 'little bits and pieces',
especially garden produce. A nineteenth-century advertisement
referred to gardeners having a truck basket, into which you put bits
and pieces of things you need when gardening, plus the fruits and
vegetables you were picking. That is distinctly an old meaning of
truck, but it is mere coincidence that the basket they described was
also called a trug basket; they are two different words.

Tuck

There is a frail and distant connection between a dressmaking tuck,
and the daily nourishment. The dressmaker's 'tuck' comes into
English from the German *zucken*, the old meaning of which included
'to twist and stretch', and the word was used to describe a place in
fabric which had been pulled and gathered. That eventually became
the English word tuck, meaning to gather fabric into a fold – and in
doing that, a part of the fabric was pushed out of sight behind the
fold or 'tuck' (as in tucking someone into bed).

As far back as the 1400s a tenuous connection appeared to grow
in Britain between dressmaking tucks and the school shop that sold
food. When fabric is made into a tuck, part of it disappears behind
another part (inside the tuck). A joking comparison transpired that
when food was eaten, it also disappeared like the fabric inside the
tuck.

The similarity grew into the language, and by the 1700s food which had been 'tucked away' began being referred to as just 'tuck'. It can be found in *Tom Brown's Schooldays* and other school stories – especially those regarding Billy Bunter. Hence school tuck shops.

The word reached Australia and went into fairly general use there in the mid-1800s (G.A. Wilkes cites 1861). For some unknown reason the Australians added 'er', so tuck became tucker, as in 'tucker box' and 'tucker bag'.

So it seems that it all comes from a common German source, and the English words exist side by side quite comfortably. The dress-maker makes a tuck, and in doing so folds one piece of the fabric behind another and hides it. Taking food then eating it also causes it to be hidden; it's still there, but is tucked inside. So food in general, even before it's eaten, became tuck or tucker (a fairly rare example of Australians making a word slightly longer, instead of shorter).

Tulips

They are called tulips because of the way they are shaped, but it has nothing to do with lips. Tulips originate in Turkey – myriads are grown in Holland and around the world, but the plant definitely comes originally from Turkey – and their name is a Turkish word *tulben* meaning 'turban' because of the way that tulip petals sit: they look a bit like a wrap-around turban.

Turncoat

Turncoat has a fairly simple meaning: a person who deserts one cause in order to support another. They deny what they said they believed in before, and embrace something different, usually the opposition.

There is a widely accepted story that in long-ago Germany the powerful Duke of Saxony owned land on the Franco-German border and, because negotiations of one sort or another often took place there between French and German interests, the duke had a coat or cloak made up that was blue on one side and white on the other.

When he wanted to show that he was acting in the interests of France, he wore the white side of the coat outermost, and when he wanted the Saxon Germans to have faith in him, he wore the blue side out. So the Duke of Saxony is believed to have been the original turncoat, but he was acting in the interests of harmonious politics, rather than betrayal.

The word stayed on, but gradually the meaning evolved into something slightly different: fighting men who deserted one army for another could also change the colours they showed in battle by turning their coat or tabard inside out. So now the word is firmly associated with a person who deliberately deserts his principles and takes on a different colour.

Turn over a new leaf

It means to make a fresh start and mend your ways. There is sometimes confusion about whether the comparison is with spring growth on a tree, or the pages of a book. It's definitely a book: leaf is an alternative way of saying 'page'. Probably the earliest publication of the expression was in *Holinshed's Chronicles of England, Scotland and Ireland*, published in 1577, which says 'he must turn the leaf and take out a new lesson' – and that indicates a book, not a tree.

In Oscar Wilde's *The Importance of Being Earnest*, Miss Prism suggests someone turn over a new leaf, and his reply is that he has already begun a whole volume (because, of course, Miss Prism's admonition concerned the leaf/page of a book).

Twit

'Twit' is now a noun, but is thought to have started life centuries ago as a verb – *atwitan* – meaning 'to reproach or taunt'. *Atwitan* was used in a context of reproving ignorance. Gradually the 'a' was dropped to form *twitan*, and then the two final letters also faded away; during the eighteenth century the shortened word 'twit' came to mean someone who is reproached for not being properly informed. By the mid-twentieth century a twit was someone whose level of intelligence was deemed to be lower than your own.

There are also some side issues. The word 'nitwit' sounds similar but has a different history; a nitwit is someone whose wit (that is, knowledge) is the same size as the egg of a louse. And the sound birds make is often referred to as 'twitter' – to us the sounds are meaningless. The similarity of sound and meanings among twit, nitwit and twitter are coincidences, but have strengthened the basic concept of all three.

Two-fingered salute

This ancient and well-known gesture of sticking two fingers in the air has quite a different origin from the one usually called 'giving the finger, which is just one finger stuck in the air, though both are gestures of derision and insult.

It is generally accepted that the two-fingered salute originated with military bowmen over 500 years ago. Before battles, there was a formal pronouncement by heralds that bowmen captured by the enemy would have the precious first two fingers on their right hand cut off. The opposing side would often belligerently stick up their two fingers, to show that they were still whole and healthy and intended to remain that way – and they shouted insults while they did so.

Gradually, this became a general gesture of defiance, with the backs of the fingers facing outwards.

Many centuries later, Sir Winston Churchill created history by turning his hand round the other way and turning the traditional gesture into a V-for-Victory sign. It is reported that sometimes, when he was with the troops and there were no cameras present, he would deliberately reverse his hand and make the old-fashioned insulting gesture, while looking up at the sky where the Germans were expected. The troops enjoyed that enormously.

The one-finger salute, believed to be of American origin, is much more recent and rather more anatomical. Sometimes described as the check-your-oil gesture, it is always done with the hand facing inwards and the middle finger lifted and facing outwards. It refers to a crude and uncomfortable bodily exploration.

Ulan Bator

Ulan Bator is the capital of Mongolia and the name commemorates the eminent Mongolian Dandimy Sühbaatar, who was responsible for founding the modern republic of Mongolia. He was known as the red warrior. Hence *ulan* meaning red, and *bator* meaning warrior.

Umpire

The word originated in France, but there is a quaint fact about its use as we know it today. The original French word was *noumpere,* applied more to legal situations where an impartial arbitrator was required for a dispute. *Noumpere* meant 'not a peer' – a peer in the sense of an equal. The arbitrator could not be associated in any way with either party in the dispute. The word found its way into English (with the same meaning) during the fourteenth century.

Gradually, two things happened. First, a process called 'juncture loss' took place, in which a letter from one word migrates across a space to a neighbouring word. Hence, a *n*oumpere slowly became a*n* oumpere, and later an umpire.

And second, the word – and its associated practice of arbitration – moved mainly (but not entirely) towards the upholding of rules and decision in sporting situations.

(Another example of juncture loss was a '*n*apron', which became '*an* apron'.)

See also **Nickname**.

Uncle Sam

The original Uncle Sam was a real person. Sam Wilson was born in the United States in 1766. He became experienced in the meat industry and was hired by the US Army to inspect the meat bought by them. Most of his fellow workers addressed him as 'Uncle Sam'.

There was a war in 1812 and Uncle Sam Wilson either supplied meat to the army or inspected meat they had already bought – it's not quite clear but, either way, when he declared the meat to be acceptable he put his initials on the barrels, and because everyone called him Uncle Sam he wrote 'US', instead of his real initials: 'SW'. When people assumed that the initials US stood for the United States, they were told that, no, they stood for Uncle Sam.

By 1852 there were cartoons depicting this benign old man, and gradually the phrase Uncle Sam came to signify the nation or government of America.

Uncle Sam Wilson was known to be a man of great fairness, reliability and honesty, and those who knew him took very kindly to his being associated with the image of all Americans. He died in 1854, and his grave is in Troy, New York, where he lived. There is a statue of him in that town commemorating him as the original Uncle Sam. In 1961 the American Congress declared that Samuel Wilson was the inspiration for the symbolism of the Legend of Uncle Sam.

Undertaker

Almost every form of society has rituals and legal formalities and tribal customs surrounding death. And there are also practical matters: a body, a grave, a venue, a death certificate and so on. Coping with all this can be very traumatic for those who are closely connected with the deceased.

Up to the 1600s, the term 'undertaker' was applied to anyone who was undertaking an organisational task. It was a sort of title that included functionaries in the political and magisterial arena, and also the people who supervised after-death matters. It was based simply on the perception that these people 'undertook' whatever had to be done.

The term gradually slipped away from all the other people, but remained in use in the funeral context – though perhaps the more genteel 'funeral director' is now taking over.

Under way

During the eighteenth century one of the meanings of 'under' was 'in the course of'. That survives in terms like: 'under consideration' (in the course of being considered); 'undertaking' (to take things on a course of action); 'undergo' (in the process of being subjected to something – an exam, a surgical procedure); and 'under way' (in the course of a journey, either literally – the 'ship was under way' or figuratively – a project which has been started and is now being carried out).

Union flag/Union Jack

Flag terminology is immensely complex. There are 19 different meanings for the word 'jack' and one of them is that, in nautical terms, a jack is the small flag that flies at the bow of a ship to show its nationality.

When Britain's official flag settled down in 1801, its exact design and colouring were meticulously written out by Order of Council, which described it as 'the Union Flag'. That order still stands today, so although in everyday speech people tend to say Union Jack, most of the time it isn't correct to say Jack at all, one reason being that it might not be on a ship at the time.

When it's above Buckingham Palace and being referred to by BBC commentators or British journalists, it is called by its correct formal name – the Union flag, or just the Union.

The correct formal wording of the Order of Council, 1801, was:

> The Union Flag shall be azure, the Crosses saltire of Saint Andrew and Saint Patrick quarterly per saltire, counter-changed, argent and gules, the latter fimbriated of the second, surmounted by the Cross of Saint George of the third fimbriated as the saltire.
>
> By Order of Council the broad white band of Saint Andrew's cross should be uppermost at the top left-hand corner, at the hoist.

('Saltire' means diagonal; 'argent' is silver; 'gules' is red; and 'fimbriated' means fringed, seen around the outside.)

Up the chute (shoot)

This is derived from 'up the spout' – an old expression for taking something to the pawnbroker. When something was pawned, the pawnbroker put the pawned item into a little cage – a spout – that took it into a protected area. Being up the spout (later 'up the chute') came to mean short of money, even bankrupt. Then it expanded to include being sick, in hospital or in prison, and now it means flawed in some way.

USA or US

The abbreviation US has been in evidence since at least 1818. The use of this abbreviation links up with the cartoon figure called Uncle Sam to symbolise America in general and the government in particular.

Hiram Ulysses Grant, whose mother's maiden name was Simpson, was accidentally enrolled at military school as Ulysses Simpson Grant, a change of name he retained. He became president, and the initials US gave him a link to the symbolic figure of Uncle Sam.

There was also a period when the dollar sign had two perpendicular lines running through it instead of one. American patriots joined up the two lines at the bottom, to place the 'U' over the top of 'S' – another way of promoting the name of the country. That didn't survive, but shows that abbreviating has been going on for a long time – see also **Dollar ($)**.

Note that the USA isn't the only nation state whose name begins with US: its neighbour Mexico is properly entitled the United States of Mexico. It seems, though, that custom and usage has found a solution, at least among English speakers. When people mean the United States of Mexico they simply say Mexico, and when they mean the United States of America they simply say America – or USA, or just the US.

See also **Uncle Sam**.

(St) Valentine

He has absolutely nothing to do with chocolates and expensive roses. There were two men known as Valentine who eventually became saints, and it's not quite clear which was which, but the feast day of St Valentine was established a very long time ago as 14 February.

Some extraordinarily thin myths and well-cultivated legends have tried to encourage a connection between Valentine and lovers, but there is no guarantee at all regarding the truth of any of the stories, and since both the original gentlemen were Catholic priests they would have had no experience of romance or marriage.

The truth about the connection with lovers, if there is one, seems to be more in the date, mid-February being the time of year in the Northern Hemisphere when birds start to mate. Birds must be fairly public about this, because their mating rituals and the time they performed them are well-documented – see your *Encyclopaedia Britannica*. Even Chaucer mentioned it in his *Parliament of Fowls*, over 600 years ago:

> For this was on Saint Valentine's Day,
> When every bird cometh here to choose his match.

Not only Chaucer but everybody else in the Northern Hemisphere seemed to know that mid-February was mating time, and although most birds are not notable for romancing, the two ideas – awakening love, and St Valentine – gradually came together (if you'll pardon the expression).

This concept has been wildly encouraged by merchants and marketers so nowadays the public is exhorted to buy any number of products that have nothing whatever to do with St Valentine or birds, all through a somewhat tenuous connection with mating. The encouragement of the legend is really all about spending money.

Velcro

In 1948 Swiss mountaineer George de Mestral became annoyed at the prickly burrs of mountain bushes, which clung to his clothes and to his dog. He decided to try turning the plants' pesky characteristic into an advantage for himself, so approached textile experts who might be able to reproduce the hooks found on seeds in a version which would then cling to any fabric with a loopy surface.

Only one weaver in France managed to do it. He made two strips, one with hooks the other with a loopy surface, and he took them to the Swiss mountaineer. They called it 'hooked locking tape.' It took until 1955 for the invention to be patented, by which time George de Mestral had dreamed up a name: *vel* from the first part of *velours* (French for velvet) and *cro* from the first part of *crochet* (French for a little hook). Thus, Velcro. Where would we be without it?

Vent (your spleen)

In ancient times various organs were regarded as the 'seat' of certain emotions (and the heart is still regarded as the source of affection and love, just as people without courage are described as lily-livered).

The humble spleen is a fairly obscure internal organ, seldom mentioned. But it was thought to be the seat of a person's ill humour, bad temper and mirth. Over the centuries the mirth somehow became forgotten, and only outbursts of bad temper were described as exploding from the spleen (being 'vented', from the Latin *ventus*, meaning wind). That use of the word spleen is still occasionally heard; thus it joins the heart and liver as internal organs still perceived as being connected to emotions.

Vested interest

Most of the various meanings of 'vest' originate in the Latin *vestis*, meaning clothing. One meaning of vest (when followed by 'in' or 'with') concerns the conferring of authority, as in 'by the power vested in me by ...' or 'the executive was vested with the authority to ...' Following that track, the word vested became a legal term meaning to have an established right to something (e.g. property). The term is often used informally to describe a situation where it is to someone's definite advantage that a project succeeds – they have a vested interest in its success and may make a personal profit.

Vice (chancellor) and vice (sin)

There is no connection between these two uses of the word 'vice'. In English, the word has three quite separate meanings – and each one is derived from a different Latin word:

1. **vitium: vice**   behaviour lacking in morality; corruption

2. **vitis: vice**   a holding device with jaws and a tightening screw

3. **vix: vice**   in place of, acting as deputy.

Thus from *vix* comes the word vice used to indicate 'next in rank': vice-president, vice-admiral, vice-consul and vice-chancellor.

(Computer) virus

There used to be germs, then scientists discovered the virus, which was much smaller, and quickly became very fashionable. Being 'down with a virus' sounded much more trendy than 'sick with a germ' and the word germ all but faded from consciousness.

In 1972 a science fiction writer dreamed up a story about a weird computer glitch that not only disabled computers but was able to replicate itself. The matter achieved a much higher profile in 1983 when a real American scientist, Fred Cohen, demonstrated a development that was very close to the fictional one. At the time, a colleague named Lane Adelman suggested that if this mishap should ever happen, it would be 'like a virus'.

It did happen. A computer disruption developed which did exactly as fiction had predicted – it could disable an electronic system, replicate itself and infect its surroundings to devastating effect. It was called a computer virus. Within ten years of the expression first being heard, the problem had become so common that it hardly needed the word computer in front of it – just virus would do.

Walkman

The founder of Sony, Masura Ibuka, was a frequent traveller; he wanted to listen to music while travelling but not to bother other people.

At his request, Sony technicians developed a small battery-operated radio and cassette player that used headphones and with which you could walk around. It owed some features to an existing cassette player called Pressman, and with that product's name in mind, plus the popularity of Superman, the Sony team registered the name Walkman. Like many other trade names, Walkman gradually became part of the normal language.

Since 1979 there have been over 200 different models of the device. Later models included the facility to play compact discs. Nobody other than Sony can use the name Walkman, so other firms bringing out other versions had to invent similar (but different) names. And note that the plural is Walkmans.

Walla-walla-cat's-meat-eat-brown-bread

This was a popular vernacular saying in Britain during the 1940s. Every decade has fashionable nonsense phrases – some last and some don't. In ye olden times there was 'O waly waly', and 'Hey nonny no', and some people still say things like 'nanu nanu' (a survivor from the TV show Mork and Mindy) or 'yabba dabba doo', as Fred Flintstone did.

They become sound pictures with a fragile and transient life, and their meaning usually adapts to the context in which they're said. But, as with all pictures, some stay on the wall and some disappear into the cupboard, and walla-walla-cat's-meat-eat-brown-bread has nowadays gone into the cupboard.

The explanation behind this particular strange expression is unfortunate. Shortly after the Second World War, Britain began to have a number of immigrants who were dark-skinned. This didn't go down particularly well with some of the locals, and the phrase originated as a sort of taunt or put-down. 'Walla-walla' imitated the supposed sound of jungle rituals; 'cat's-meat' because many of the immigrants were so poor they subsisted on meat the British would only feed to cats; and 'eat brown bread' was a rhyming substitute for 'dead'. So, broken down like that, the phrase meant: 'Darkies – drop dead!'

Not very praiseworthy.

Wally

Slang for an inept or ineffectual person. It came into fairly general use in the late 1960s, and its origin has been the subject of dispute: scholars of urban vernacular lean towards its having arisen when someone in the crowd was calling out for their lost dog Wally during a rock festival, but can't agree which one – Hendrix in Sweden, January 1969, or Woodstock in August of the same year. But language scholars lean towards a derivation arising from the old Scottish term *wallydrag* – 'a feeble person'.

(Some Scottish people prefer to see the term as referring to Mel Gibson's movie portrayal of the Scottish historical figure William Wallace – the screenplay of which was a very distant relative of the known historical facts.)

War

Military terms change frequently; the methods of fighting battles have altered radically over time, so the language to which people of one era became accustomed doesn't always have time to catch up before the military comes up with new inventions, if not new words.

Added to this is the fact that a huge political spin is often put on words being used to report war, because the authorities have decided that the non-combatant public must be fed a certain impression of the conflict's progress. Hence, people listening to radio reports or reading newspapers find words and terms being used which do not abide by their dictionary definitions. This can result in a certain vagueness.

The word 'war' is subject to constant pressure. In fully formal terms the word means the existence of declared armed conflict between one nation state and another. According to that definition, there never was a war between the United States and North Vietnam, no formal war over the Falkland Islands, and the situation between the United States and Afghanistan in 2001–2 was not actually a war because no formal declaration was made by one nation state to another.

However, the dictionaries have had to admit that the word war has been used so often outside that formal context that nowadays you'll find it means open armed conflict between two or more parties, nations or states.

See also **Asymmetrical warfare**, **Collateral damage**, **Ethnic cleansing**, **Ground Zero**.

Warm fuzzies

Warm fuzzies acknowledges that something has been well done, or encourages people around to feel good. The expression came to notice in 1975 when published by American educationalist author Claude Steiner in a fanciful story called *The Fuzzy Tale*. The story tells of a family that gives out 'warm fuzzies' but is tackled by an evil jealous witch who psychs them into ceasing to do so – and the town starts slowly wilting …

From the same book comes the opposite – 'cold pricklies' – resulting from a put-down, a snide acknowledgement, anything that deflates someone else's enjoyment.

Wash your dirty linen in public

It can't be established that Napoleon actually invented this but in 1815 he certainly said it – or a near-equivalent. Translated, Napoleon's line was, 'It is in the family, not in public, that we wash our dirty linen'.

Watergate

A theatre in London named Watergate must have caught the eye of an American building firm, who used the same name for a big complex of flats and offices in Washington (begun 1963, finished 1971).

Some office suites in the Watergate building were occupied by the headquarters of the Democratic Party. During the 1972 American elections, the Republicans tried (illegally) to bug the Democrats' communications. They were apprehended and the incident was covered up.

The eventual disclosure of the whole story by two Washington journalists resulted in serious charges of corruption and eventually led to the resignation of President Richard Nixon in 1974.

Since then, whenever there's been a seemingly simple incident which actually leads to revelations of corruption or disruption of the status quo, journalists have enjoyed finding the core-word of the situation then adding 'gate' to it, so we've had Dianagate, Closetgate, Nipplegate, Baftagate, Kanyegate – and any number of other scandals considerably more minor than alleged corruption in the American Administration.

(Woman who) wears the pants

Pants have changed their name various times, but awareness that an authoritative woman can rule the house – and is said to 'wear the pants' in doing so – has been around a long time.

One of the earliest known versions of the expression occurs (albeit back-to-front) in the book *Songs and Carols of the 15th Century* with the line: 'The most master of the hows weryth no brych.' Shakespeare refers to it in *King Henry VI, Part 2*, when the Duchess says scornfully, 'In this place most masters wear no breeches.'

So, britches/breeches/pants/trousers – the expression and its sentiment haven't changed much.

Weasel words

These are words that detract from or weaken the effectiveness or force of another expression. The description was coined by Stewart Chaplin and first appeared in print in 1900 in *Century Magazine*. The article – 'The Stained Glass Political Platform' – referred to the words 'duly protected' as weasel words.

But the phrase became much more famous when Theodore Roosevelt used it in a speech in 1916; he said, 'When a weasel sucks eggs

403

the meat is sucked out. If you use a weasel word, there is nothing left of the other.'

There are some wonderful comments about weasel words in Joe Bennett's book of his collected columns, *Sleeping Dogs and Other Lies*. He points out that the phrase 'streamlining their operations in response to market forces', and also 'restructuring', both mean, quite simply, that people are going to be sacked. Similarly he explains that a 'strategic plan to modify core business' means they're going to start doing something different.

Wedding breakfast

The basic meaning of the word breakfast is to break a fast – to eat after you haven't eaten for some time. In modern usage, 'breakfast' has come to mean the first meal of the day when you haven't eaten anything since dinner the night before, but at other times in history the word was used to mean any meal at all after you hadn't eaten for a while; Shakespeare used it in this sense.

It is human nature to have a social gathering after an important ritual event – a university graduation, a homecoming, a burial, a major sports match, a marriage. Within the British heritage, the Christian rituals associated with a marriage have slowly been added to or incorporated into the rituals of pre-Christian times.

When Christianity in Britain was younger, a couple who declared themselves committed to each other only went to the church for a blessing. Gradually, however, the commitment ceremony itself moved towards being held at the church, although not inside it. There was an initial reluctance about a Christian priest announcing inside a church that a man and woman were now officially allowed to sleep together.

So marriage blessings or marriage ceremonies, when presided over by priests, were usually conducted on the steps outside the church, and after this, the gathered guests would all move into the church and take part in a mass. That's the clue, because there was a rule that people did not eat before participating in a mass. Hence, after the wedding ceremony, and the mass that followed it, the bridal couple and the guests would literally break their fast. For many centuries the word 'breakfast' was still applied to this after-ceremony function.

In recent times the word 'breakfast' has been used less frequently. Marriages take place at various times of day and there is awareness of relevant religious versions other than Christian – all with their own traditions. Hindus, Jews, Buddhists, Sikhs and others have different marriage customs, nearly all of which involve an after-ceremony celebration of some kind.

General usage now tends to call this a reception, rather than a breakfast.

Week

The Jewish concept of a constant cycle of seven successive days, as outlined in Genesis, is generally known as a week. In ancient Greece, the word *taxis* had a connotation of speed and things being efficiently organised. This gave rise to the East German/Scandinavian gothic word *wiko*, meaning order, and that was the ancestor of the German word *Woche*, meaning a week. *Wiko* also drifted into Old English to name a succession of seven days, gradually evolving from words such as *wice, wicu* into week.

Alongside this were the two expressions *feowertiene nihte* and *seofan nihte*. One of those vanished in English. *Feowertiene nihte* became fortnight (never used by Americans), and *seofan nihte* was modified into se'en night, meaning a week, but its use simply died out, and the older word 'week' became the standard term in standard English.

(As) well as

Apart from meaning a hole in the ground, the word 'well' has at least ten shades of meaning. Sometimes it functions as an intensifier, simply reinforcing the word it is placed with: 'I knew him well' (underlining that you really did know him); 'He was well informed' (he was wisely and comprehensively informed); 'the house was well protected' (not just lightly protected); or 'the meat was well done' (not pink, but cooked right through).

When 'well' is used as an intensifier, and is combined with 'as,' you get 'as well', meaning 'in addition to'. So you could say the man was famous – and rich as well. The second bit of the description intensifies, or somehow enhances, the first part of the description: 'the day was wet, and a terrible wind was blowing as well'.

Welshed on a debt

Sometimes spelt as 'welch', it means that an agreement to pay something or do something has been broken – the debt wasn't paid or the promised action wasn't effected.

The term is not uncommon, but in essence is quite offensive to Welsh people. Although the precise explanation is uncertain, the *Morris Dictionary of Word and Phrase Origins* points to an ancient nursery rhyme as having laid the groundwork for an unfair perception: 'Taffy was a Welshman, Taffy was a thief ... Taffy came to my house and stole a side of beef.'

The origin of the song is uncertain, but it supposedly arose many centuries ago when the Welsh reputedly raided the border areas between Wales and the Saxons, and Saxon cattle were seen to have disappeared overnight.

This connotation is believed to have become intertwined with a scurrilous practice on English racecourses. During the 1700s and 1800s the race-track culture in England included some unscrupulous bookmakers who would take bets on a race, accept the money but, when the race was over, would have vanished with the funds. These unreliable bookmakers sought refuge by hurrying over the border to Wales, for which reason they became known as 'welshers'. The *Morris Dictionary* points out that there is no objection to the first part of the nursery rhyme ('Taffy' being a version of 'David' and a generic name for all Welshmen), but the spurious image of Welshmen being thieves is undeserved in referring to anyone escaping from a financial obligation, since it was English bookmakers heading into Wales for safety, not Welshmen.

The *Morris Dictionary* is not able to present 100 per cent certainty, but offers this 'reasoned explanation', which is a comfort to the Welsh.

Wendy

J.M. Barrie's character of the boy who wouldn't grow up was first seen in the 1904 play, *Peter Pan*. The book, *Peter and Wendy*, was published in 1911. Barrie can't be credited with inventing the name Wendy, but he certainly popularised it.

A legend has grown that Barrie was inspired to use the name because of his friendship with a little girl who lived nearby, called Margaret Henley, who died when she was only six. Little Margaret used to call Barrie her 'friendy' but couldn't pronounce it properly so it came out 'fwendy,' or 'fwendy-wendy', in some versions of the story.

There were, however, people called Wendy before the Peter Pan story. The name may possibly be derived from Gwendolyn and it can be found in British and US Census statistics throughout the 1800s. In ancient times there were also at least two Emperors of China called Wendi, though one feels that their connection with Peter Pan would have been slight.

What goes round comes round

This seems to mean that even if whatever happened was initially unknown, eventually its details will leak out and must be faced up to.

The first known use of the expression in print was by American writer Eddie Stone, 1974, in *Donald Writes No More*.

While this form of the expression thus appears to date from the 1970s, the concept behind it has appeared throughout many centuries and differing cultures. Language scholars point to the English expressions 'What goes up must come down' and 'You get what you give,' plus mentioning those beliefs which acknowledge that fate or kismet will dictate circumstances, whatever we say or do. The Russian equivalent is 'As the call, so is the echo' and Shakespeare had a version in *King Lear*: 'The wheel is come full circle.'

In current times the expression has developed the connotation that if you start a piece of slander about someone, eventually you will be identified as the bad-mouther; or if you do something underhand or illegal, eventually you'll be found out.

What you don't know won't hurt you

This has been tracked back to 1576 – in a book called *Petite Palace of Pleasure*.

Whipper-snapper

The term is usually used by a person of maturity about someone else who is younger, inexperienced and possibly even impertinent. It has been used in the United States more frequently than in Britain, though it originates in England – as far back as the 1600s – and its history is strange.

In the 1600s 'snipper-snapper' described young people who were fond of cheeky remarks and repartee and crisp patter. This earned such people a reputation of being foolish wasters of time and not very effective. Nowadays we would call them lippy, or smart-mouths. Round about the same time there developed a custom among young men known as ne'er-do-wells (which was the seventeenth-century way of saying hoon) who used to stand on street corners, idly flicking a whip just to pass the time. They were referred to as 'whip snappers'.

Over the years a gentle amalgamation of the terms took place and snipper-snappers and whip-snappers combined to become whipper-snappers.

White rabbits

For many centuries, mankind has been intrigued with the mystery of animals, and people have developed dozens of suspicions and beliefs about such creatures as cats, dogs and rabbits. Almost all of these beliefs have no basis in fact; they stem from some sort of desire to link attractive animals more closely to humans.

Saying 'white rabbits' on the first of the month is linked into beliefs so old that there is no single answer to the question of why people believe it will bring good luck. Over the centuries, dozens of semi-supernatural things have been believed about rabbits and hares. Here is a selection:

○ If a rabbit or hare crosses your path in front of you it is a sign of good luck, though the quality of the luck varies depending on whether the rabbit is going right to left, or left to right.

- If a rabbit crosses your path behind you, that's bad luck (though it isn't clear how you would know that a rabbit had crossed behind you).

- If a rabbit runs through your yard you will have children.

- Hares are actually witches in animal form – keep away from them.

- Alternatively, hares contain the spirits of dead grandmothers, so be nice to them and never eat them.

- It is very bad luck to shoot a black rabbit.

- If you dream about rabbits then misfortune will visit you.

- Many people believe a rabbit's hind feet touch the ground before its front feet do, so power, speed and luck are associated with the hind foot of a rabbit. If you carry one, you will have more power, speed, luck and fertility – like rabbits.

- If you ever lose your rabbit's foot, your luck will turn bad.

- If the rabbit's foot is taken from a rabbit killed during the full moon by a cross-eyed person, it will bring exceptionally good luck.

Most of those things mentioned are associated with British superstition, going right back to a belief that Queen Boadicea used rabbits to help her plan the route her army would take.

But there are many other rabbit stories in other cultures – Mexican, Korean, Aztec, Buddhist. Buddha created a calendar system from the 12 creatures gathered around him, one of which was a rabbit.

Now somewhere in the middle of all this a belief arose that mentioning rabbits on the first day of the month brought good luck for that month. Unfortunately, like many old superstitions, there is no definitive statement about exactly who said so, or exactly what to do. Even the day is in question. One version of the superstition is that you must say this on the first day of the new moon (not necessarily on the first day of the month).

In addition to that confusion, there is more confusion about what you must actually say. A selection:

- You must say 'white rabbits' once.

- You say 'white rabbits' three times.

- You say just 'rabbits' once – or three times (no need for the 'white').

- Contemporary America has produced two variations – 'wabbits' (which is 'white rabbits' condensed) or 'bunny bunny bunny'.

Those who argue for the use of 'white rabbits' rather than just 'rabbits', point out that there is an established association of white with purity, and also that white rabbits are quite rare.

To add to the confusion, there is dispute about exactly when you say it and to whom:

- You must say it out loud first thing on the first of the month before you speak any other word.

- It must be spoken before your feet touch the ground.

- It won't work unless you say it to someone on the first of the month and you must say it before they say it to you. The person who says it first gets the luck, the other one doesn't.

- Here's a killer – saying 'white rabbits' first thing in the morning doesn't work unless you said 'black rabbits' last thing the night before.

When your number is up

This old expression is believed to have originated in the navy. When someone died and his place in the dining room was empty, the other men said he had lost the number of his place in the mess. This resurfaced as an expression in the US Army – a soldier who has been killed is said to have lost his military number.

Hence 'when your number is up' had a connection with death.
It is used rather more widely now, indicating that someone who's
been up to no good is about to be found out, and will be required to
account for it, or that something you dread will happen but, as with
death, advance warning is unlikely.

Whoa to go
'Whoa' is an old English word, used to stop horses – it's a variation
on 'Ho', which is just a yelling-out word to attract attention, as in
'Land Ho!'

'Go to Whoa' has been in use in Australasia since 1950, and is
simply a slightly colourful way of saying 'from start to finish', or
to be moving and come to a stop, or something having run its full
course.

So somewhere within those 50 years, some smart person has
started using it back to front, 'whoa to go', which means that which
was at rest has started to move, something or someone has been
activated. There's no copyright on linguistic evolution.

Wigwam for a goose's bridle
The phrase means nothing; it has no defined origin and it isn't a
cover-up for anything else – even when it turns up as a 'whim wham
for a goose's bridle'. It's just an amusing invented nonsense phrase
that indicates something is foolish, impossible or private – and
people say it when they don't want to explain whatever they're being
asked about (or don't know).

(Give you the) willies
It's a feeling of discomfort and nervousness. This arose in the United
States towards the end of the 1800s but is now fairly universal
throughout the English-speaking world. There are two theories about
the origin. One is that it is related to an old expression 'the woollies',
which refers to the itchy sensation on the skin when wearing wool
(and we're talking nineteenth-century wool here, not fine-weave).

The other theory is more interesting. In 1835 the German writer
Heinrich Heine published a book called *From the German*, which

included reference to folklore belief from the Slavic countries about *wilis*. These are wood-nymphs, the spirits of maidens who have died with a broken heart, usually because they were jilted. The young women are found in the Serbian and Croatian languages as *vila*.

Besides Heinrich Heine's book, the Slavic legend received two other major boosts toward worldwide recognition. One was the ballet *Giselle* in 1841, which has an entire corps de ballet of *wilis*, and then in 1905 came Franz Lehar's operetta, *The Merry Widow*, in which the leading lady, the widow, who is a Slav from Montenegro, sings a song about a *vila* – a witch of the wood (which in the English translation comes out as 'vilia').

The Merry Widow and the ballet *Giselle* took the words *vilia/ wilis* and the concept right round the world and brought increased recognition of the words into the English language. And because they were eerie, ethereal creatures, people feeling creepy about something said they had 'the willies'.

So, two possible explanations: one about woolly underwear and the other about beautiful forest ghost-women.

You choose.

Wimp

Wimp first appeared in print in 1920 in England and came into use among university students, but referring only to girls and young women. The word travelled to the United States where, like 'bimbo', it underwent a sex change and its application was slightly redefined – it came to be said about men who were cowardly, feeble, or ineffectual. Eventually reference to either sex came within its realm.

The most diligent of scholars cannot agree on the word's origin. Some think it is a shortened form of 'whimper'. Others think it arose from 'Mr Wimpy', who was always in trouble in the Popeye cartoons. A third offering is that the term is derived from 'wimple' – a soft, floaty piece of fabric worn by women under the chin, from one side to another (not necessarily the stiff, starched wimple associated with nuns, but the original wimple worn by medieval women – something silky and soft).

(The) wind up

Many believe it to be an expression from First World War pilots. If they could feel the wind coming up around their legs in those early open-structured planes, they must be at stalling speed and were about to crash – and so they felt frightened.

Etymologist Eric Partridge doesn't quite concur. He agrees with the First World War pilot bit – the phrase dates to 1916 – and although he can't be definitive, his research shows that in the early days of flying, when the wind was strong it was dangerous to fly at all, which made everyone a bit nervous. Therefore when pilots said someone had 'the wind up', it meant that they were acting as nervously as if they had to fly a plane in a strong wind.

Woebegone

The word seems to be telling woe to be gone – sadness is being ordered to go away, though the person about whom it is said seems on the contrary to be mired in woe.

But there is a deception in that word 'begone'. Usually it means 'go away', but what we have in this case is a much older word, absolutely archaic – *begon*, meaning 'to be beset with, surrounded by'. Thus came the saying 'me is woe begon', which means 'woe is besetting me, surrounding me, attacking me'.

Over the years the four-word expression contracted to a single word – woebegone.

Wolfenstein/Castle Wolfenstein

These are not real places. They exist only inside a computer game with a manufactured Gothic vocabulary. In spite of not really existing, they have a horde of devotees who do clever things on computers on which they fight imaginary creatures and take unto themselves imaginary glory.

The name is probably based on the lead character in Mary Shelley's famous novel of 1818 about a young doctor called Frankenstein, who created a monster by assembling various human parts. She is believed to have named the doctor after a castle in Germany called Castle Frankenstein, which does exist.

Womb/tomb

Both are enclosed dark spaces, which suggests the possibility of a connection, but they have come into English from different languages and it's just a coincidence that they both mean a cavity of some kind.

The word 'womb' is found in Old English and it came there from the Old High German word *wamba*, meaning a hollow space, a cavity. We have to move from Old German to ancient Greek to find the other word; *tumbos* means a hill or mound, and eventually came into English as 'tomb'.

So in fact the meanings are opposite: two enclosed spaces, but one you come out of for (hopefully) a long time, and the other you go into forever.

Worcestershire sauce

The generally accepted story is that during the 1830s a British nobleman enjoyed a certain sauce in India, and brought the recipe back from India to Worcestershire in 1834. He gave it to the local chemists, Mr Lea and Mr Perrins, asking them to make it.

The resulting mixture had a disastrous flavour, which everyone hated, and it was forgetfully left in the cellar. Three years later someone saw it, and bravely decided to taste the strange three-year-old mixture of salted anchovies, garlic, cloves, onions, tamarind and chilies. Behold! They had accidentally done what the Indian cooks forgot to put on the recipe – left it to mellow.

A marvellous, rich, dark liquid was now available, and was first sold in 1838. Oceans of it have been used since, especially since Americans took to it in 1874 and later used untold quantities in Bloody Marys.

Americans insist on calling the sauce by its full name – 'Wor-cest-er-shire' – while many other people refer to it as 'Wooster' (as in Bertie). And some places call it simply 'black sauce' or by the name of its first makers – 'Lea and Perrins'.

Working like a navvy

Originally the word navvy was short for navigator – not navigating at sea, but navigating the construction of canals. The canals themselves used to be known as navigations and the men who constructed them were called the navigators.

Obviously, in an era long before front-end loaders, there was a great deal of heavy digging and excavating to do, so working like a navigator meant hard physical work. The phrase was eventually shortened to 'working like a navvy', and later the expression was applied to anyone who worked hard, not just at digging canals.

Wowser

There have always been people who declined to drink alcohol. Those who did not drink, strongly disapproved of those who did – gaining a reputation for over-developed morality, driving them to deprive others of their sinful pleasures, especially liquor.

In return, those who did partake often made put-down remarks about those who didn't, and one of the sneer terms was 'wowser' – a person who drank no alcohol and thus, by implication, was a kill-joy, a dullard, determined to impose narrow restrictions on some activities that others thought needed no revision. The word is based on the Old English dialect word *wow*, meaning to complain, and as 'wowser' it gathered a strong pejorative connotation. It first appeared in *Australian Truth* in 1899.

Xerox

The particular copying process described as Xerox was invented by Chester Carlson in 1937 and was originally called electrophotography. In 1952 his company registered a new word as its trade name: Xerox, which is made from the Greek *xero* meaning dry, and *graphos*, meaning writing or drawing.

Xmas

Contrary to comment that sometimes surfaces, it is not at all disrespectful to refer to Christmas as Xmas.

In ancient Greece the letter *chi* was written with a symbol very like a modern 'X'. Thus the word Christ (a title assigned to Jesus by later worshippers, meaning 'the anointed one') was written as *Xristos*. This was frequently abbreviated to just 'X'. So if long precedence brings respectability, then writing 'Christ's Mass' as Xmas has been considered acceptable for over 1000 years.

Xylophone

A real xylophone is made of wood. Small tablets of wood are placed in a row and each makes a different tone when hit with a hammer. It is named from the Greek *xylo*, meaning wood, and *phone*, meaning voice or sound. Hence xylophone – sounds made from wood.

Yacker/yakka

Yacker (also seen as yakker, yakka and yacca) is from an Aboriginal dialect word *yaga*, which simply means 'work'. A slightly anglicised version of it in use was noted by the Rev. W. Ridley in 1856. During the later part of that century, the word filtered into general Australian usage, sometimes as 'hard yacker' signifying hard work, often shortened to just 'yacker', and it has been appearing in print as an acceptable informal term since 1920. Its meaning is easily recognised throughout Australia and New Zealand, though likely not understood elsewhere.

Yankee

This word has been in dispute for years, resulting in 16 different versions of the word's origin. There are two main theories:

○ Native Americans, coming to terms with early European settlers and attempting to say the word 'English', came out with 'Yengeese', which eventually became 'Yankee'.

○ Dutch settlers in New York used a derisive name, Jan Kaas (John Cheese), to refer to English colonists in Connecticut, and that deteriorated into 'Yankees'. (A secondary version of that same story is exactly the opposite: that the derisive name Jan Kaas was not said *by* the Dutch settlers, but *about* them.)

To sum up: nobody knows exactly how the word Yankees evolved.

Yarpie

Yarpie (jarpie) is a slang term for Europeans who come from South Africa – and is not considered polite. Basically, it is a variant on the name Jakobus, which looks like Jacob but can translated as James. The Afrikaans version of the name Jacob is *Jaap* (pronounced 'yahp') and a diminutive or affectionate version is *Japie*. But used carelessly outside its original Afrikaans context, it has become less welcome, with a connotation of being unsophisticated and low-class.

Yeah, right

Does it mean 'Yes'? Only partially. The effect of the phrase depends somewhat on the vocal tone with which it is said (paralanguage – the conveying of information by the sound of the voice, rather than the words). Although the words are supposedly agreeing with whatever statement came before, saying 'Yeah, right' implies that the speaker does not in fact agree at all and is calling the previous statement into question.

There is a legend that a professor lecturing an English class explained that a 'double negative' actually implied a positive. 'For instance, if there is a family wedding and I say, "I can't not go", I am actually saying I must go. The "can't" plus "not" cancel each other out.' A student asked, 'Is there an equivalent – double positive terms having the result of cancelling each other out?'

The professor answered, 'No.'

From the back of the room, a voice said: 'Yeah, right.'

So although superficially the phrase 'Yeah, right' appears to be a confirmation, it has actually become a form of vocal irony.

Your Worship

This traditional way of addressing a mayor goes back a long way in history. It comes from an Old English word used in the twelfth century, *weorth*, which is the ancestor of the word 'worth'. When it was attached to the word *scip* it became *weorth-scip*, meaning a vessel or container that contained or carried something valuable. *Scip* became the modern word ship, and in time *weorth* became abbreviated, so we now have the combination as 'worship'.

Another meaning of the word developed: the verb 'to worship', which is rather different, meaning 'to show profound religious devotion to anything considered divine'. The two words have the same ancestor but slightly varying meanings. 'Your Worship' is used to address somebody of worth, such as, presumably, a mayor. As a verb, to worship means to observe religious devotion. They're not quite the same thing.

You've got another think coming

The original expression was, 'If you think that, you've got another think coming.'

It may have evolved from another expression which went, 'You've another guess coming', but certainly early in the twentieth century people were saying, 'You've got another think coming,' as a folksy piece of advice that was never intended to be grammatical, just an amusing way of saying, 'You're wrong.'

Somehow an alternative version arose: 'You've got another thing coming.' That version sprang to prominence during the 1980s in a hit recording by the British heavy metal band Judas Priest, who made a record called 'You've Got Another Thing Coming'. Segments of the recording went on to be used as the soundtrack for TV commercials about hamburgers. This gave the phrase enormous coverage and now there are people firmly wedded to either 'think' or 'thing'.

Yule log

Many of the customs and activities associated with Christmas have nothing to do with the birth of Jesus, and the yule log is one of them.

Christianity absorbed all kinds of rituals associated with deep, dark winter. For many centuries, countries with terribly cold winters held a midwinter festival in December, which served to establish that the cold months were halfway through, and the warmer months were now on their way. A festival of 12 days evolved, and nobody is sure why. It was possibly because the year had been divided into 12 months, and there could have been a certain appropriate symbolism in 12 days of festivity and goodwill.

In English, the word yule has an ancient and mysterious ancestry. Some believe it to be a Norse word for wheel; others are convinced that yule is a surviving form of one of the 200 names for the powerful Norse god Odin (as in *yölfödr*). Either way, in Scandinavian countries the term yule became the general name for the whole 12-day Christmas festival. A big log was set alight to honour the sun and to symbolise the light and warmth that would come when winter was over.

Y This custom filtered through to England in the eleventh century as a celebration of the turnaround of seasons, but was gradually adapted into Christian festivities because December was chosen as the month in which the birth of Jesus would be celebrated.

Some special customs grew up around the yule log. It must never be bought; to be really effective, the yule log had to be a gift from someone. Little figures made of dough were baked sitting along the log in the fire – and much later grew into a tradition of 'gingerbread men'. The wassail bowl would be drunk, indicating goodwill and good health for everyone – and that survives as what we now call 'Christmas drinks'.

It was believed that good luck would come to the house if the log remained burning for 12 days. Besides which, a holiday for servants continued as long as the log continued burning (hence the legend that in the middle of the night servants would creep down to the log and dab water on it to make it smoulder and burn more slowly).

But after 12 days it had to go. It isn't entirely clear why. The only explanation offered is that having 12 days of festivity represented the hope that 12 happy months would follow. So on the 12th day the yule log went, but a small piece of it was kept to be used as the lighting-up stick for the next year's yule log.

Obviously the custom of burning yule logs, or any sort of logs, was more feasible for rural people. But a feeling of attachment to the custom was so strong that people moving to city areas wanted to keep the tradition alive, so they invented a substitute – a dark brown sponge, formed into a roll and covered in chocolate icing. Thus was born the chocolate log!

Zany

The basis of the word is the Italian word *zanni*, which served two purposes. It was a diminutive for the name Giovanni (John), but also meant a silly fool. The latter use crept into English, but slightly softened in application to mean something or someone pleasantly funny and whimsical.

Zap

This word was invented in 1929 by Philip Nowlan, the creator of the comic strip character Buck Rogers. The word was short, didn't take up much space in a cartoon frame and its unusual aspect lent itself to bold and dramatic borders on the speech balloons. It usually indicated either a quick movement, or a telling strike (from something like a ray gun).

Quite quickly, zap went into the language and developed various other shades of meaning: to bombard with protest; to speed through television commercials; to effect an electric shock; even to kill. It has also become a noun indicating energy and power – 'He shows a lot of zap.'

Zeitgeist

This is a combination of two German words: *Zeit*, meaning time or period of time, and *Geist*, meaning spirit. Together, as Zeitgeist, they mean the prevailing attitude, or general outlook of a specific time period, as reflected in its literature, art, politics, philosophy and customs.

Zero

The familiar word zero came into English from Italian, where it was a development from the medieval Latin *zephirum*, which in turn came from the Arabic word *sifr*, itself derived from the Sanskirit *sunya-m*. That meant 'empty place', the same meaning zero has today.

Zip/zip code

There is very little connection between these two terms. The zip which closes things up was invented in 1893 by American engineer Whitcomb Judson, who referred to it as a clasp-locker, and later a universal fastener. Later it was called a 'hookless fastening' and a 'C-Curity'.

Initially, the device caused problems and it went through several developments before 1921, when the Goodrich company started using an improved version on galoshes. The company named these overshoes 'Zippers', thought to be because of the noise the fastener made as it was closed. The name of the shoes became transferred to the fastening that closed them, and the world gained zippers, which was often shortened to zips – and the abbreviated name remained in use.

Over 40 years later, the US Postal Service began a process of refining people's addresses to include a group of numbers that would speed mail district identification, and thus delivery. Beginning in 1963, the number system was called a Zone Improvement Plan code – zip code for short. It is believed that the postal authorities deliberately planned the name so that it would give the impression of enhanced speed, and zips – having proved quicker to use than buttons – certainly carried that connotation. This is the only connection between the two uses of the word zip.

Zoroastrian

Rock star Freddie Mercury was born of Iranian (Persian) parents and his real name was Farouk Bolsara. The family's religion was Parsee, based on the teachings of the ancient philosopher Zoroastra.

Zoroastra (also known as Zarathustra) dates back to Persia in 1200 BC when he became the centre of and prophet for a religion fostering belief in a single God. The German writer Friedrich Nietzsche examined the ancient teachings in his work *Also Sprach Zarathustra* (1890), which caught the attention of composer Richard Strauss, whose later tone poem of the same name (1896) was known in English as *Thus Spake Zarathustra*.

Before Freddie Mercury's death and his Zoroastrian funeral, the biggest previous publicity Zoroastra had enjoyed in the Western world was the use of Strauss's music in the 1968 movie, *2001 – a space odyssey*.

Zydeco

It is folk music indigenous to south-west Louisiana and west Texas, derived from Old French (Cajun) and African-American (Creole) idioms, and developed from the mid-nineteenth century onwards.

Zydeco music, combining elements of rock, Caribbean rhythms, blues, jazz, funk and hip-hop, is constantly changing form, depending on the band. Most of the music isn't written (or at least published), so the same song played by two different bands will sound different. Instruments usually include piano accordion, saxophone and sometimes fiddle, with washboard percussion and sometimes drums and electric bass.

Appendix:
Around the world

Borrowed words

Many languages borrow – a large proportion of languages nowadays have a complex set of borrowings from other cultures. Sometimes in English the words were borrowed several hundred years ago, and may be versions of Arabic (as in coffee), Scottish (as in whisky), Japanese (tycoon), Dutch (yacht), or Turkish (tulip).

And all those languages themselves frequently borrow words from other languages. For example, the word 'bar' is fairly universal. It has travelled into English through Latin and French, but the English version is widely used, even in places like Japan.

As the centuries have progressed, people have travelled and invented things and been intrigued by other nations' foods or cultures or plants, with the result that words are forever crossing borders, sometimes changing their meaning as they do so. A living language is flexible and moulds itself to what people want to say at any given point. And modern communication techniques have made words of all kinds more accessible than they ever were before.

The medical and legal professions tend to base a great deal of their communication on the Latin language, for the simple reason that it's no longer used in everyday life and is therefore unaffected by changes in meaning or borrowings. So when accuracy is vital in stating a law or specifying a medicine, very often Latin is the safest language to use.

Some people are uncomfortable with regarding a foreign word as 'borrowed', because whatever is borrowed is usually returned – and language crossovers aren't returned, they've come to stay. One could say that a word in English is derived, copied, modified, cloned from, or that it originated with, the other language. But although those terms are accurate, they sound clumsy. Informally, 'borrow' seems to be acceptable.

Italian language on printed music

The reason for this usage is evolved custom. Some forms of classical music – symphonic and concerto music and opera – went through crucial phases of their development in Italy.

It cannot be said that the Italians were solely responsible for the final traditions of those forms; German, Austrian and French composers were also heavily involved in the growth of what we call classical music. But the terms the Italian composers used became very widespread and dominant to the point that they're now almost universal.

Almost universal – because you will sometimes see music with German or French instructions on it. But many people are comfortable with the Italian expressions, and it certainly makes things move more smoothly for international artists performing in different countries. Whatever else they can't understand, they can all follow the conductor when he says *forte* or *piano* or *allegro*.

A similar thing happened with ballet, where the terms used are normally French.

Japanese car names

Honda is named for the company's founder Soichiro Honda and Suzuki is named for its founder Suzuki Michio. Mazda was founded by Jujiro Matsuda, whose name resembled the Zoroastrian God of Reason, Mazda.

Isuzu is named after the Isuzu River, Mitsubishi is Japanese for 'three diamond stones', which is part of the family crest of the company's founding family, and Nissan is Japanese for 'Japanese industry'. Daihatsu, Japan's oldest vehicle manufacturer, has the rather prosaic meaning of 'Generator manufacturers'.

The word Subaru carries double significance in Japanese. In ordinary language it means 'unite', but is also the Japanese name for the constellation of stars known elsewhere as Pleiades (and used as the Subaru company's logo since 1955).

Datsun was originally named with the initials of the three men who first invested – Messrs Den, Aoyama and Takeuchi (encouraged by the fact that *dat* in Japanese roughly translates as 'very fast'). By 1918 the company was producing other models, named Dat-son (as in 'son of Dat'). But a change was made. The Japanese word for 'bankrupt' is *toson*, and because of some unease that this sounded too similar to Datson, a discreet change was made to Datsun.

Sakichi Toyoda made a deliberate alteration in his own name to form the brand name Toyota. The name Toyoda takes ten brush strokes in Japanese writing, and by changing the 'd' to 't' he created the word Toyota, which takes eight brush strokes – and eight is considered a lucky number. The family decided that Toyota also had a cleaner sound and easier pronunciation for the Western market – an important consideration.

When in Fiji

Many languages contain words which are pronounced quite differently from how they look. English is absolutely full of them. The word 'enough' has 'gh' pronounced as 'f'. The plural 'women' has 'o' pronounced as 'i'. 'Position' has 'ti' in the middle as 'sh'. Put those three oddities together and you get 'ghoti' – pronounced 'fish', as George Bernard Shaw pointed out.

Other languages do it too. Look at the Polish name, Lech Walesa: you won't see the letter 'n' in the surname, but it's necessary to say it.

Regarding Fiji, Professor (of Linguistics, University of Hawaii) Dr A.J. Schutz explains that the Fijian alphabet uses some familiar letters in an unfamiliar way. Dr Schutz reports on the effort of the early missionary who wanted to teach Fijians to read English. He first tried to write down the Fijian language as he heard it spoken, placed 'm' before the consonant 'b', and 'n' before the consonant 'd'. This confused the Fijians, since those consonants are always spoken as if an 'm' or 'n' preceded them, but looked wrong when written that way. Placing the 'm' in the written form made the people think they had to say two 'm's – the written one, and the 'invisible' one which always came before.

And since consonants in Fijian are always separated by a vowel, an extra vowel crept into the equation as well. So when the Fijians saw him write the name of the island Lakeba as Lakemba, they explained that this looked (to them) as if it was called La-k-em-emba (with an extra 'm', and therefore an extra vowel before the obligatory 'mb' sound, which was quite normal for 'b'). Removing the unwanted 'm' caused the Fijians to say, 'You have now known the nature of our language.'

So from then on the 'm' before 'b' remained invisible in writing – but was always pronounced when speaking. As with the invisible 'n' before 'd' (Nadi is pronounced 'Nandi') and 'g'. And 'c' remained written as 'c', instead of 'th' which is how it's pronounced (Cakobau = 'Thakombau', and Rabuka = Rambuka).

(Adrian Room's *Placenames of the World* recounts that 'according to story', missionaries in the Pacific area ran out of 'n's when printing news-sheets, so left them out of place names. Professor Schutz would doubtless agree with Mr Room that this is a 'story'.)

Bibliography

The following works of reference were consulted in answering the questions in this book:

A Bee in Your Bonnet, Rudolph Brasch, Angus & Robertson, Sydney, 2001

Alabaster, Bikinis and Calvados, Toponymous Words, Christopher Smith, Century Hutchinson, London, 1985

American Slang, R.L. Chapman, Harper Collins, New York, 1998

American Heritage Dictionary of Idioms, Christine Amner, Houghton Mifflin, Boston, 2003

America's Popular Proverbs and Sayings, Gregory Titelman, Random House, New York, 2000

Austral English, Edward E. Morris, Macmillan, London, 1897

Biographical Dictionary of Scientists, ed. Roy Porter, second edition, Oxford University Press, New York, 1994

Brewer's Dictionary of Modern Phrase and Fable, Adrian Room, Cassell, London, 2000

Brewer's Dictionary of Phrase & Fable, rev. Adrian Room, Cassell, London, 1996

Concise Dictionary of Slang and Unconventional English, Eric Partridge, ed. Beale, Routledge, London, 1989

Collins English Dictionary, ed. J.M. Sinclair, Harper Collins, Glasgow, 1998

Curious Facts, John May, Secker and Warburg, London, 1981

Dictionary of Australian Colloquialisms, G.A. Wilkes, Sydney University Press, 1985

Dictionary of Catch-Phrases, Eric Partridge, Routledge & Kegan Paul, London, 1977

Dictionary of Clichés, Eric Partridge, Routledge and Paul, London, 1978

Dictionary of Curious Phrases, Leslie Dunkling, Harper Collins, London, 2004

Dictionary of Eponyms, Cyril Beeching, Clive Bingley, London, 1983

Dictionary of Symbolism, Biedermann Wordsworth Reference, Hertfordshire, 1996

Encyclopaedia Britannica, 30 vols, Benton, Chicago, 1974

Extraordinary Origins of Everyday Things, Charles Panati, Harper & Row, New York, 1943

Facts on File Encyclopedia of Word and Phrase Origins, Robert Hendrickson, Macmillan, New York, 1997

Heavens to Betsy, Charles Funk, Harper Perennial, New York, 1955

Hog On Ice, C.E. Funk, Harper & Row, New York, 1985

How Did It Begin? Rudolph Brasch, Fontana (William Collins), 1985

In Words and Out Words, Fritz Spiegel, Elm Tree, London, 1987

LINGO Dictionary, John Miller, Exisle, Wollombi, 2009

Lock Stock & Barrel (no author listed), Past Times, Oxford, 1998

Longman Guardian New Words, ed. Simon Mort, Longman Group, Essex, 1986

Loose Cannons, Red Herrings, R. Claiborne, W.W. Norton, New York, 1988

Origins: A Short Etymological Dictionary, Eric Partridge, Routledge & Kegan Paul, London, 1966

Oxford Dictionary, New Shorter, ed. Lesley Brown, Clarendon Press, Oxford, 1993

Placenames of the World, Adrian Room, David & Charles, UK, 1974

Port Out, Starboard Home, Michael Quinion, Penguin, 2004

Red Herrings and White Elephants, Albert Jack, Metro, London, 2004

Sailors' Word Book, Admiral W.H. Smyth, Conway Maritime Press (Brassey), London, 1867

Stone the Crows, Ayto and Simpson, Oxford University Press, 2008

Take My Word for It, Ian Gordon, Wilson & Horton, Auckland, 1997

The Reader's Encyclopaedia, William Rose Benét, A & C Black, London, 1965

The Real McCoy, Georgia Hole, Oxford University Press, 2005

Thereby Hangs a Tale, C.E. Funk, Harper & Row, 1950

There's a Reason for Everything, R. Brasch, Fontana/Collins, 1982

Twentieth Century Words, John Ayton, Oxford University Press, Oxford, 1999

Useful – the origin of everyday things, Joel Levy, New Burlington, London, 2002

Wordsworth Dictionary of Saints, Wordsworth Editions, Hertfordshire, 1992

Also by Max Cryer

Preposterous
Proverbs

We've all grown up with proverbs and we probably repeat them without much thought. Yes, 'a bird in the hand is worth two in the bush' and 'absence makes the heart grow fonder', but such sayings have almost become clichés – and it is the same in every country and culture.

In *Preposterous Proverbs*, language expert Max Cryer looks at a vast array of proverbs from around the world on subjects ranging from birth, food, women and love to money, animals, sin and death. He has chosen some of the most interesting and perplexing, and analyses their meaning and truth with his characteristic wry wit. A great book to dip into, *Preposterous Proverbs* will take you from Greece ('A thousand men cannot undress a naked man') and Japan ('Fools and scissors must be carefully handled') to Russia ('The more you sleep, the less you sin') and India ('A fat spouse is a quilt for the winter').

EXISLE
PUBLISHING

www.exislepublishing.com

 **e-newsletter**

If you love books as much as we do, why not subscribe to our weekly e-newsletter?

As a subscriber, you'll receive special offers and discounts, be the first to hear of our exciting upcoming titles, and be kept up to date with book tours and author events. You will also receive unique opportunities exclusive to subscribers – and much more!

To subscribe in Australia or from any other country except New Zealand, visit www.exislepublishing.com.au/newsletter-sign-up

For New Zealand, visit www.exislepublishing.co.nz/newsletter-subscribe